BRODSKY:
A Personal Memoir

by

Ludmila Shtern

Baskerville Publishers, Inc.
2711 Park Hill Drive
Fort Worth, Texas 76109

This book is a translation by the author of her book in Russian *(Brodsky: Osya, Iosif, Joseph)* much expanded by the addition of new material in English.

Shtern, Ludmila.
  [Brodskii. English]
  Brodsky : a personal memoir / by Ludmila Shtern.
    p. cm.
  Book has been annotated so extensively for the English-speaking reader that brackets have been used to prevent the text being carpeted with footnotes. The new material in this edition includes poetry and photographs that are published for the first time. All poetry that has not been attributed to a translator was translated by the author.
  Exp. and translated ed. of: Brodskiæi. 2001.
  Includes index.
  ISBN 1-880909-70-7 (cloth : alk. paper)
  1. Brodsky, Joseph, 1940—Friends and associates. 2. Shtern, Ludmila—Friends and associates. 3. Poets, Russian—20th century—Biography. I. Brodsky, Joseph, 1940- II. Title.

  PG3479.4.R64Z86713 2004
  811'.54—dc22

                                    2004016882

ISBN 1-880909-70-7

Manufactured in the United States of America
First Printing, 2004

ACKNOWLEDGMENTS

Many people helped me to make this book a reality and I am grateful to all of them.

First, I would like to mention my dear friends and friends of Joseph Brodsky for their invaluable help while I was writing these memoirs: Misha Baryshnikov, Mikhail and Vika Belomlinsky, Yakov Gordin and Tata Rakhmanova, Galina Dozmarova, Igor and Marina Yefimov, Roman and Larisa Kaplan, Lev and Nina Loseff, Mirra Meilakh, Mikhail Petrov, Evgeny and Nadya Rein, Efim Slavinsky, Aleksandr and Galina Sheinin, and Alexander Sumerkin.

My sincere thanks to the Women's Studies Research Center at Brandeis University for helping me translate the book and to its director Shulamit Reinharz for her encouragement and support.

I am indebted to my close friend Boris Shvartsman for sharing with me numerous photographs from his unique collection.

Bengt Jangfeldt, Brodsky's friend and Swedish translator, very kindly supplied the photo used on the cover.

I would like to thank Francine du Plessix Gray for reviewing the chapter "The Libermans and Libermania."

I am most grateful to Professor George L. Kline, Brodsky's friend and translator, for his suggestions regarding certain poems and for his close reading of the entire text, which helped me to improve it.

I also would like to thank deeply my friend Leana Yefimov, my daughter Katerina Simons, and my grandson Daniel Simons (the first real American in our family) for helping to naturalize my immigrant English.

My sincere gratitude goes to Publisher Ron Moore for his interest and support, and to Jeff Putnam, my Editor and friend, for his enthusiasm, his encouragement, and his hard and excellent work.

Above all I am deeply grateful to my husband Victor Shtern for his unconditional love, constant help, and endless patience in spite of my unbearable temper.

EDITOR'S NOTE

Ludmila Shtern has annotated the book so extensively for the English-speaking reader that brackets have been used to prevent the text being carpeted with footnotes. In the same way no attempt has been made to set off the poetry with different-size type, or to frame it extravagantly with space and indentations. The text therefore resembles Brodsky's declamatory style, in that emotional and factual information, along with rhetoric and imagery, flow together. The poetry in the book doesn't embellish the story: it is inextricably part of it.

The new material in this addition includes poetry and photographs that are here reproduced for the first time.

All poetry that has not been attributed to a translator was translated by the author.

To the dear memory of my beloved friends
Genna Smakov, Alex Liberman and Tatiana Liberman

BRODSKY:
A Personal Memoir

Preface

THE LIFE OF JOSEPH BRODSKY was full of high drama created by the clash of his poetic gift with the stark realities of the Soviet State. His gift was recognized early, with many prominent Russian intellectuals predicting a bright future for him even when his work had not yet been commercially published and was available only through *samizdat*, the Russian word for the process whereby uncensored manuscripts are typed by volunteers and secretly passed from friend to friend.

For good reason the great Russian poet of the previous generation, Anna Akhmatova, addressed the following lines to young Brodsky:

I will cry for myself no longer now
But in this World I would not see
The golden brand of the failure
Upon your still untroubled brow.

Anna Akhmatova knew what she was talking about. Her poetry was targeted for political criticism by no less than the Communist Party Central Committee. Her husband, the poet Nikolai Gumilyov, was executed by a secret police firing squad. Her son, historian Lev Gumilyov, spent eighteen years in Soviet concentration camps. Her poetry was banned and circulated in *samizdat* only, even though, under the Russian criminal code, people who shared uncensored manuscripts were subject to criminal prosecution.

As with his poetic gift, Brodsky's talent for independent thinking was also recognized early, and the Soviet State responded with increasingly harsh persecution. His work was repeatedly rejected by government censors. He was arrested and twice tried as a *tuneyadets* (social parasite); he was confined to a psychiatric clinic, spent time in the notorious Leningrad prison, "The Crosses," and was sent into exile in a remote village in the Arkhangelsk region, where he was forced to work as a farm hand. Finally, Brodsky was expelled from his native Russia in 1972, just a few days before U. S. President Richard Nixon came to visit with a list of dissidents to be protected from government persecution.

A few years later, the Soviet government refused to allow his parents to leave the country to visit him. When his parents died one after the other in Leningrad, the government did not let Brodsky come to their funerals...

In the West, Brodsky was received with open arms, and his fortunes improved dramatically. He became one of the most famous literary figures in the world. He was the first foreigner to serve as Poet Laureate of the United States, and he was showered with numerous honors, including a MacArthur Foundation Fellowship, a Nobel Prize and France's Legion of Honor. In the Soviet Union, on the other hand, he remained persona non grata, his name could not even be mentioned in a literary discourse, and his work remained unpublished.

It was only in the 90s, after the collapse of the Soviet Empire, that Brodsky's *oeuvre* came to light and was released in his newly democratic motherland. Russian publishing houses competed with one another for the right to publish him. Those who lost in the competition published his work illegally. Now readers there snatch up every Brodsky book they can lay their hands on. Poets, writers and literary critics of every description feel the need to quote Brodsky in their work and public appearances. His name is everywhere. Brodsky's literary stature in his own time resembles that of Dostoyevsky, Tolstoy or Chekhov in theirs.

To be sure, all his poetry in Russian has been published in that country to critical acclaim and public excitement. In addition, articles, essays, reviews, interviews he has given—everything written about or said of Joseph Brodsky in English has been translated and widely published. Moreover, his persona has become larger than life. He has been proclaimed a living classic, and as such has taken his place in the history of 20th-century Russian literature.

Even so, the story does not have a happy ending. Brodsky never came back to his native country. The Russian government never apologized for anything done to him... He died relatively young, and the impact of his death can be compared to the impact of the early death of another great Russian poet, Alexander Pushkin, 155 years ago: "The sun of Russian poetry has set."

Since Joseph Brodsky passed away eight years ago not a day passes without my thinking about him. Sometimes, doing something as mundane as cleaning my house or cooking dinner, I mumble his poems the way people hum some persistent melody. Or a line of his poetry will flash in my mind, precisely reflecting the mood of the moment.

I am haunted by his poetry as if he were still among us, a poet whose latest poem has just been published in the *New Yorker* in between "The Talk of the Town" and some aggressively fashionable short story. Brodsky's personality also haunts me. I often ask myself in various situations: "What would Joseph have thought about this? What would he have done?"

Russian society is unlike the West in that poetry and poets traditionally played a very important role, rather like prophets. For more than two hundred years, poets were meant to describe what was good and what was bad in our experience, explain what to do in love, teach us social justice and the meaning of life. This public perception of poetry was not very different from the government's position. The Russian government, the Tsarist and the Soviet alike, also wanted poets to teach, describe and explain. Of course there was a big difference: from the government's point of view, serving it gave meaning to personal life.

The popularity of some poets in Russia could be compared to the popularity of the kings of rock 'n roll and pop music in America. Their books were published in millions of copies. In the sixties, readings by such poets as Voznesensky and

Yevtushenko could fill stadiums.

Unfortunately, Brodsky never had such an opportunity in Russia, though he was more than a great poet. His persona was gigantic, his personality very powerful. His manner of speaking—chaining words one to another with a rising and falling intonation, as if he were struggling to overcome a stutter—often charmed me even when I disagreed with him. That's why for those of us who were close friends, his absence was so painful.

Obviously, geniuses and "living classics" have friends just like everyone else. Yet to declare oneself the friend of such a person when writing a memoir seems suspiciously like name-dropping, and can provoke a smirk.

Still, during the eight years since Brodsky's death an avalanche of claims upon Brodsky's friendship has descended on Russian readers. Of course there are among them authentic and honest notes written by people who knew Brodsky in the different periods of his life. But there has also been an abundance of fantastic tales. While reading them one gets the impression that Brodsky drank vodka, stood in lines, asked for advice and shared his most intimate thoughts with a vast rabble of literary aspirants and dilettantes.

Such recollections are presumed to guarantee admission to a certain "intellectual high society"—a literary circle where everybody is somebody. No doubt Brodsky would have been pleased to learn he had such an army of close friends.

Reading these stories one wonders: with such an intense social life, when did Brodsky have time to scribble his rhymes? By the way, the use of the word "rhymes" is not an unceremonious way of speaking on my part. Brodsky himself, while talking about his occupation, carefully avoided words like "poetics" or "lyrics" (and didn't much like "creative") in favor of such words as "rhyme" or "a little verse."

"Iosif Aleksandrovich"—his first name and patronymic—is a formal, respectful Russian way to address an adult, especially someone older. In Leningrad Brodsky was too young to be called "Iosif Aleksandrovich." However, that's how his American students jokingly addressed him, imitating his own amusing habit: while talking about his favorite Russian writers he did not use their last names, but cited them using a first name and patronymic.

4

For example: "I read a story by Fyodor Mikhailovich yesterday..." (Dostoyevsky) Or: "In a few poems of Aleksandr Sergeevich I notice that..." (Pushkin). Or: "Yevgeny Abramovich, in his last poem..." (Baratynsky).

So how are my memoirs going to be different from other reminiscences?

Brodsky and I met when he was nineteen years old. For me, then, he never became Iosif Aleksandrovich, but was Osya, Oska, Osyunia, Osenka. Only in America when he hit forty, did he become Iosif or Joseph.

Though the tone of this book might seem too familiar, I guess thirty-six years of friendship warrant the use of it. Of course, during his lifetime—in Russia as well as in the States—Brodsky was surrounded at times by people who were closer to him than I was. However, when he emigrated from the Soviet Union in 1972, his closest and dearest friends were left behind. They met again sixteen years later, in 1988, when the Soviet government lifted the iron curtain and let its citizens visit other countries. This enormous distance in time and space played an important role in the relationship between Brodsky and the friends who had stayed behind. Although Brodsky kept his love and affection for such friends over the years, changes in his own life, in his professional and social status, had made him unrecognizable. His new obligations, new circles of friends, his influence in the literary world and a wealth of opportunities had turned this red-haired boy into a very important literary figure. The almost unbearable burden of fame had made an impact on his character, his outlook and lifestyle. It seemed as if Brodsky and his Russian friends existed in different galaxies. Unfortunately, some of these friends either did not recognize the fact of Brodsky's evolution, or did not want to take it into consideration. Thus when they met Brodsky sixteen years later there were signs of discord in their relations.

In the U.S., Brodsky met and became close to numerous Western intellectuals and Russian emigrants, none of whom had known the shy—yet arrogant—young poet. In the last ten to fifteen years of his life Brodsky's gradually increasing authority in literary matters had become incontestable. He became "*le maître*" and was treated almost with reverence. In the eyes of his new friends Brodsky's image was as bright as bronze, or marble at sunrise.

My situation was quite different. Where Brodsky was concerned, I was privileged to be born and to live in the right place at the right time. In other words, when the future Sun of Russian literature turned up in the periphery of a few Leningrad galaxies, I was there.

We met in 1959 and in the next thirteen years, right up to his emigration from the Soviet Union in 1972, spent a lot of time together. He loved our home and was often hanging around. We happened to be among the first who heard his poems.

Three years after Brodsky's departure from Leningrad our family also immigrated to the U.S., and we continued to see each other regularly till January 1996. In other words, we witnessed almost his entire adult life, both in the Soviet Union and in the United States.

The continuity of our relationship accounted for certain peculiarities. It seemed to me that Brodsky perceived my husband Victor and me as relatives. Not the closest and most beloved ones, perhaps, but we certainly belonged to the same flock, we were absolutely his people.

Sometimes I upset him by hovering over him like a Jewish mother. He grumbled that I was bossy and didn't mind my own business, that I was giving him unsolicited advice and condemning some of his actions in a tone that already no one could assume while talking to him. On the other hand, he did not have to show off and pretend in front of me. He was always himself.

He could be tactless and uncivil with me, then. He could snap at me and roll his eyes while saying my name. He could ask me to make unpleasant phone calls on his behalf or to do unpleasant errands for him. He also had the luxury of calling us anytime to complain about a toothache or chest pain, or about the hysterical character of a current girlfriend. He could call after midnight to read a new poem, or at seven o'clock in the morning to get some important information. I remember one such phone call: "Hi, how is it called ... a woman's thing that is a combination of a bra and something that holds up stockings? Could it be a corset?" "I don't think so. But why do you need a corset?" "I've got a cool rhyme to it."

6

Brodsky's openness to me, then, is the reason I felt I could write a worthwhile memoir about him. In showing him as he was and as I knew him, I will necessarily reveal the ups and downs of our relationship, and mutual offenses, but these Brodsky understood very well, and I never doubted that he appreciated our friendship in his own way.

After some interesting literary discussion or an exciting conversation or a piquant personal situation he often repeated half-jokingly: "Memorize all this, Ludessa, I want you to be our Pimen." [Pimen was the medieval Russian monk who, according to legend, transcribed current events and was the epitome of the truthful historian.]

This book represents my memoirs about our youth and the friends I had in common with Joseph Brodsky. You will read about the time, the sixties, when the forces that later broke the "The Unbreakable Union of Free Republics" (the first line of the Soviet anthem) first appeared. You will read about the people, the "sixtiers," who lived free under oppression and created the forces that broke the Soviet Union. The reader will encounter a lot of "I" and "we" pronouns—they are unavoidable. Otherwise, how would I have known everything that is written here? However, my book is by no means a documentary biography of Brodsky, and it doesn't pretend to offer chronologically sequential material. Since I am not a literary critic, it is also not a scholarly analysis of his poetry. Rather, this book is a mosaic of true vignettes, stories and miniatures, related to Joseph Brodsky and the people around him.

There is a common American expression: "the guy next door." For Russians it means "one of us." In this book, then, I wanted to tell about the great Russian poet Joseph Brodsky, whom I knew because of the circumstances of my life, and perceived as one of us.

1

When He First Knew Us

To EXPLAIN WHY AND HOW I happened to appear in Joseph Brodsky's orbit, I must first say something about my family and myself.

I had the good fortune to be born to wonderful parents who belonged to St. Petersburg's intellectual elite. Both were very handsome, brilliant and highly educated, witty, with a great sense of humor. They were generous, hospitable to my friends, and unconcerned about their material welfare. I grew up in an atmosphere of unconditional love and trust. They never offended or humiliated me when I was a little girl, and there was very little that was forbidden to me.

My father was a born scholar. He was logical, just, scrupulous, and a bit punctilious. His memory was legendary. By heart he knew hundreds of poems, names, dates of events in world history, as well as the phone numbers and birthdays of all of his friends. He preferred a calm and measured life, but fate was not to favor him in this regard.

My mother was his exact opposite. Strikingly beautiful, she was a classic bohemian flower: artistic, unpredictable, spontaneous and capricious. Multi-talented, Mother was not only an accomplished actress and a movie star—she translated books from German to Russian, wrote plays and other scripts, a memoir and collections of poems. She published her last poetry collection when she was ninety-nine years old.

From the standpoint of conventional psychology, my parents appeared to be totally incompatible. Yet to general amazement they lived together in love and relative harmony for forty years.

My father, Yakov Ivanovich Davidovich, graduated from the Sixth Gymnasium—quite famous before the Revolution because its patron was the young Crown Prince Aleksei, the only son of the last Russian Emperor. My father's classmate and closest friend was Prince Dmitri Shakhovskoi, the future Archbishop Ioann of San Francisco. Both young men loved Russian poetry and loved to discuss politics. After the Revolution, during the Civil War, both served in the White Army. My father was wounded and sent to Kharkov hospital, which was later captured by the victorious Red Army, whereas Prince Shakhovskoi managed to go to the Crimea and subsequently to emigrate to France.

In time my father became a legal scholar—one of the Soviet Union's few experts on labor law and the history of law and the state. Even so, as Russian black humor would have it, he received the Soviet era's *complete gentleman's kit*. The "complete kit" of a "real gentleman" had to include a doctorate, an arrest, a prison sentence, a heart attack, and very often a one-way ticket to the GULAG.

Due to his heart condition, my father was not inducted into the Army when the Second World War began. Instead he was assigned to hide and save the rare books and manuscripts of the Leningrad Public Library when the Germans were threatening to capture the city. He was arrested when one of his colleagues informed on him to the KGB. Father had been overheard saying that the Soviets should have been arming the military instead of hugging and kissing Ribbentrop. As a result Father spent the first winter of the Leningrad siege in the city's investigation prison, the so-called "Big House." During the interrogation an investigator cracked my father's skull with a volume of Karl Marx's *Das Kapital*. Father survived by sheer accident.

Fortunately, his case attracted the attention of the general military prosecutor—who turned out to be one of my father's former students at Leningrad University. One line, *"Set him free,"* scribbled with a red pencil on my father's file, was enough to effect his release. Half dead from starvation, he was freed and made it to the city of Molotov (now it is again Perm) in the Ural

Mountains, where my mother and I awaited him. He was sent to us by the only way out of the besieged city of Leningrad, across the frozen surface of Ladozhskoe Lake, the so-called "Road of Life." Day and night it was under German artillery and air attacks; many of those who were spared by the fire drowned in ice-holes made by shells and bombs.

After the war, my father returned to Leningrad University and defended his doctoral thesis. But he didn't enjoy his professional life for long. In 1947, he was accused of being a "cosmopolite" (a label attached to somebody who appreciates Western culture and hence is not sufficiently patriotic), fired from his job, and suffered a massive heart attack. The combination of this heart attack and a congenital heart defect incapacitated him for twelve years. Father only returned to teaching in 1959. Four years later, he died from yet another heart attack.

While in Leningrad, we lived on the third floor at 32 Dostoyevsky Street. A lawyer named Zoya Nikolaevna Toporova lived with her son Victor and her sister Tatiana on the floor above our apartment. We were not only neighbors, but also good friends. (I am not sure that Zoya ever was my father's student. It is possible that they met later.) Both sisters frequently came down for a cup of tea, and Zoya and Father discussed many complicated legal cases.

The day after Joseph Brodsky's arrest, his father, Aleksandr Ivanovich Brodsky, asked my father to recommend a lawyer for Joseph. Knowing the Leningrad lawyers very well, Father suggested the two best people: Yakov Semenovich Kiselev and Zoya Nikolaevna Toporova. After both lawyers met with my father and Brodsky Senior, it was decided that Kiselev should not be involved in the case. The reason for this decision was political. Although his last name sounded ethnic Russian, Jakov Semenovich Kiselev was a Jew and had an ethnic Jewish appearance. In addition, his patronymic (Semenovich) was suspicious—in other words, it was rather Jewish. This innocent fact could provoke mob fury during the trial.

Zoya Toporova was also Jewish. But her patronymic (Nikolaevna) and her last name sounded Russian, and her face was without a strong indication of Jewish origin. Such a face could belong to a "Russian" person. Zoya Toporova was brilliant, highly professional and courageous. Since we lived in an utterly lawless country (or at least in a country that did not respect its own laws), all concerned—including Kiselev, my father, and Zoya herself—knew in advance that it would be impossible to win this case. All that could be done was to make the sentence as mild as possible.

In 1956, we moved from the hell of a communal apartment on Dostoyevsky Street to a separate apartment on the Moika River. It was in a huge building that looked out on three streets: Fonarny, Moika and Pirogova. The entrance to our apartment was on Pirogova Street. It was narrow and ill-favored, a dead-end street—maybe the only dead-end street in Leningrad. The dead end was a dirty gray wall with a tiny secret door. The door was also gray and dirty, and so indistinguishable from the wall that many of the people who lived on Pirogova Street didn't know it existed. Through this door one could slip into the enclosed garden of the former Yusupov Palace. (Now the beauty of the Palace has been restored.) The garden was isolated and invisible from the street.

On one occasion my father took me, Brodsky and our mutual friends, Sergei Schultz and Genna Smakov, into this garden and told us in great detail how the murder of Grigori Rasputin had been committed there. Father knew from which door Count Felix Yusupov had run out, where Vladimir Purishkevich, a member of the State Duma, was standing and what Yusupov's wife, the beautiful Irina, was doing at that moment.

After that time, Brodsky often squeezed through the secret door into the Yusupov garden. "I love it," he said, "because no one in this world knows where I am. It's quite a cool feeling." And he mentioned the dead end of Pirogova Street in his poem dedicated to my mother's 95th birthday [reproduced in its entirety at the end of this chapter].

Russian history was my father's hobby and the passion of his life. He knew the history of the Russian royal family thoroughly and was a connoisseur of Russian military uniforms. As a result, he served as a consultant on many historical movies, including *War and Peace*.

My father collected pewter soldiers. Twice a month, he organized "military" evenings to which he invited his friends from the military section of "The House of Scholars," all of whom were passionate about Russian military history. In particular, I remember two of them: Roman Sharlevich Sott and Colonel Ilya Lukich Grenkov.

Roman Sharlevich was short and very skinny, with a face that was pale and nervous. His huge bulging eyes made him look like a crawfish. When he laughed his eyes almost jumped out of their sockets. A fabulously beautiful mustache stood out from under his thin hooked nose. From time to time, he combed this mustache with a tiny silver brush. Mother admired his gallant aristocratic manners and called him "my count." My nanny, Nulya, disagreed: "Roman looks like a hungry grasshopper."

Colonel Ilya Lukich was just the opposite: fluffy and cozy. His pink smooth cheeks reminded me of large steaks. When he laughed, they rose and completely covered his eyes.

Both men came with their own pewter dragoons, uhlans and cuirassiers. Father would close the cover of our Becker grand piano and he and his friends would stage one famous battle or another on its black polished surface. Often, some of my friends would come for these events. Brodsky, who very much loved these military performances, tried never to miss them...

"Tonight we are staging the Battle of Borodino," Father begins excitedly. "The piano top is the Borodino Field. We stand 300 meters to the east from Bagration's flèches. The village of Borodino is 700 meters to the west. The French attack first. Two divisions under Generals Dessen and Kompana are advancing from the right. The armies of the vice-king are moving in from the left."

"Wait a minute," Ilya Lukich interrupts coolly. "Now they don't move anywhere. Did you forget, Yakov Ivanovich, that they started attacking us only after they got support from Claporen's division, not a minute earlier?"

At that very moment, Roman Sharlevich, losing his aristocratic manners, screams: "Wrong, absolutely wrong! If you know nothing, don't butt in, my good friend! Napoleon called off Claporen's division, and instead, sent out Friant's division. It was his fatal mistake, by the way! And when our dragoons started the attack..."

"They didn't, they didn't!" Ilya Lukich shouts, stamping his feet. *"Yakov Ivanovich, tell him that the dragoons had been ordered not to move forward until..."*

With his eyes shining and his elbows leaning on the piano, Joseph Brodsky listened with interest to these explanations of our commanders-in-chief. He wanted to know every detail of the military mistakes made by both Napoleon and Kutuzov...

Once, Father invited Brodsky and me to join him on a visit to the Russian Museum. We passed a huge painting by Ilya Repin titled "The Meeting of the State Council." This painting, the most monumental of Repin's works, was commissioned by Tsar Nikolai II. Eighty members of the State Council are depicted on the 12 x 27-foot canvas. Brodsky stood in front of the painting and asked: "How many faces in this crowd can we recognize?" I recognized four politicians; Brodsky, seven.

"Many," said my father. As we sat on a bench in front of the canvas, Father told us about each and every person in the painting, including their lineage, family and social status, and their great service to the motherland—as well as some piquant gossip about their intrigues and extracurricular activities.

After that time, Brodsky viewed my father as an authority in many areas of interest.

Brodsky was also very fond of my mother.

Mother came from a Jewish "capitalist" family. Her grandfather owned a hardware factory in Latvia. As a result of finding a history of the factory in a public library, my father discovered that the factory had an eight-hour day as early as 1881 and all the workers got paid vacations. As an expert on workers' rights, my father heartily approved.

Mother's father, Philip Romanovich, was a well-known mechanical engineer in St. Petersburg. Once, when relaxing in Basel (or some other Swiss resort), he ended up in the same hotel where Lenin was staying. They became friendly over old Russian love songs; Lenin sang and grandfather accompanied on the piano. In the evenings, after drinking their fill of beer, they would go on long walks through the sleepy streets of Basel and Lenin would expound on his ideas about the theory and practice of the

Revolution. When they parted, they exchanged addresses. I don't know which address Lenin gave to my grandfather—the *Shalash*, maybe (the straw hut in the middle of nowhere where Lenin allegedly was hiding from the Provisional Government at the time of the Revolution)—but Philip Romanovich actually received two or three letters from the future leader.

I think Lenin's ideas had a great impact on my grandfather. In the end of 1918, having seen enough to grasp the motion of events, he grabbed his wife, his five-year-old son and his eighteen-year-old daughter (my future mother) and made haste to emigrate. Halfway through the process, my revolution-minded mother escaped from her parents and returned to Petrograd (as St. Petersburg had been renamed). It would be fifty years before she would encounter the remnants of her family.

Mother's life in general, and her career in particular, were remarkably varied. In 1917 she finished the Stoyuneena Gymnasium. Many famous young ladies were schooled there, including the writer Nina Berberova and Elena Sikorski, the youngest sister of Vladimir Nabokov. Afterwards Mother performed in both the theater and in films, with leading roles in some of the famous movies of her time: *Napoleon Gas, Grand Hotel,* and *Minaret of Death.* Nicknamed the "Soviet Gloria Swanson," she was incredible—a real femme fatale.

Mother attended the poetry seminars of the great Russian poet Nikolai Gumilyov (Anna Akhmatova's husband). At one of the lectures, she asked, "Nikolai Stepanovich, is it possible to write poetry like Akhmatova?"

"Like Akhmatova, probably not," he said. "But to write poetry is easy. All you have to do is find two decent rhymes and fill the gap between them with something that isn't too stupid."

Mother met Akhmatova, as well as the poet Mandelshtam and the writer Gorky. She played cards with Mayakovsky. Literary giants such as Victor Shklovsky, Roman Jakobson, Mikhail Zoschenko and other legendary figures were among her friends. When she was ninety years old, Mother wrote a memoir about these people entitled *While We're Remembered.* [Mother died in July 2002 at the age of 102.]

After retiring from the theater, Mother busied herself with translations and other literary pursuits. She translated five

German books about the history and theory of German cinema. She also wrote five plays that were performed in various Soviet cities. When she moved to Boston at age seventy-five she organized a theatrical troupe. With typical ironic self-effacement, she named it "The Émigré Not-So-High-Falutin' Ensemble." For this group she created sketches, wrote songs, and made her own appearances on stage. She wrote more than forty stories that appeared in the Russian press in America, France and Israel. Of course her most remarkable achievement was the last book of verse I mentioned earlier, published three years before she died.

Thanks to my parents, I grew up surrounded by fascinating people. Our home was frequented by the academician Orbeli (director of the Hermitage Museum), Lev Rakov (director of the Leningrad Public Library), the artist Nathan Altman (who created a famous portrait of Akhmatova), Nikolai Akimov (the avant-garde theater director), and Boris Eichenbaum (a famous literary critic and specialist on Tolstoy).

When I was in the ninth grade I had an amusing encounter with Eichenbaum. Assigned to write an essay on Tolstoy, I chose his *Anna Karenina*. That evening we had guests over, Eichenbaum among them. I excused myself from dinner saying that I had to finish writing my essay, which was due the next day. "What are you writing about?" he asked. When he learned that the subject was *Anna Karenina*, he got very excited and said, "Do you mind if I write it for you? I want to know if I would make it in the ninth grade in a Soviet school."

The next day, I submitted his essay. Eichenbaum got a C for his work. With a sour face, my teacher asked me, "Where'd you learn all this crap?" Professor Eichenbaum was quite upset with his C and with the snickers and jokes of his friends.

In the years that followed, the old guard began to die off. The house started to fill with my friends instead. My parents accepted and befriended most of them. Then in 1964, my father passed away. Nevertheless, my mother remained the soul of the place for everyone who came until 1975—the year we emigrated.

In December of 1994, we celebrated my mother's 95th birthday with pomp. Well-wishers came from the States, from Europe. The poet Kushner, who was visiting Boston at the time, came and brought a poem that he had written for my mother. Brodsky was invited, of course. He did not feel well and couldn't come to Boston from New York. Instead of giving a phone call or sending a postcard, he wrote my mother a congratulatory ode:

To Nadezhda Philippovna Kramova on the occasion of her 95th birthday, December 15, 1994.

Nadezhda Philippovna, dear,
To reach ninety-five
Demands stubbornness and strength—and
Allow me to offer a little verse.

Your age—I reach towards you with the thicket
Of ideas, but with simple language—is the age of masterpiece.
With masterpieces
I am somewhat familiar.
Masterpieces are found in museums.
They are hunted by ravenous connoisseurs and safe-cracking gangsters.
But we won't let you be stolen.

To you we are green vegetables
And our tenure is insignificant.
But to us you are our treasure
And we are your living Hermitage.

Thinking of you, I imagine
The achievements of Velasquez
"The Battle" by Uccello
and "Breakfast on the Grass" by Manet.
Thinking of you, I remember
Yusupov Palace, the waters of Moika,
The House of Communications near, its
Antennas like a stork's nest.
Like a rare araucaria,
Keeping Ludmila from the world,
And where rarely my drunken aria
Was heard on the porch.

1: When He First Knew Us

A curly black-haired mob
Was there day and night,
Flashing its talents and slurping
Like a flock of shiny galoshes.

Whenever I remember your living room
To every blabbermouth accessible,
I freeze, sigh, and swallow a tear.

There was drink and nourishment,
Pasik excited my gaze,
There I tested assorted husbands
For the charms of their dames.

Now it is the property of strangers
Under a new lock and key,
We are ghosts to the new tenants,
Almost a biblical scene.

Squeezing someone in the hall
In front of regimental banners
We are there like the Sistine Chapel,
Obscured by a haze of time.

Oh, wherever we are in principle,
Grumbling and heavily sighing,
We are, in essence, modeled by your furniture
And you are our Michelangelo.
Who knows, maybe a grateful nation
In the name of "restoration"
Will one day touch with a paintbrush
Our shadows in that dead end.
Nadezhda Philippovna! Boston
Has many virtues.
Everywhere stars and striped bed sheets
In Vitya's honor.

Everywhere—guests from the prairie
Or a temperamental African prince,

17

Or simply castaways of the former Empire,
That fell face down in the dirt.

And you, like a Bourbon lily
In a crystal frame,
Squint at our efforts
Looking from afar.

Ah, we are all a bit pariahs here
And a little bit aristocrats
But it's good in a foreign hemisphere
To drink to your health!

Mother was so moved by his ode that she answered it in verse. Her audacity seemed like insanity to us—like sending a sonata to Mozart. This is what she wrote:

To J. Brodsky

Not a friend, not an age-mate,
I am 40 years his senior.
But when I heard footsteps on the stairs,
Muttering behind the door,
I ran into the entry hall
As if to a source of light,
To let into the apartment right away
The young poet.
And the poet wandering through the rooms,
Pausing in front of a bookcase
Whispered almost inaudibly,
"I came to read some verses."
And from the window to the door,
Measuring the room in footsteps,
He began calmly and sternly,
But was soon overcome with emotion,
He did not notice when the verses
Suddenly became tolling bells
And the plates with snacks trembled
And disturbed neighbors pounded on the wall.

On the occasion of her 100th birthday in 1999—just before the new millennium—my mother was inundated with letters and flowers and postcards and poetic congratulations. Though bathed in all this love and glory, my mother did not lose her sense of self-deprecating humor. "It appears that antiques are in fashion again," she said with a happy smile.

2

The Panoramic View

JOSEPH BRODSKY ENTERED VARIOUS ORBITS in the Leningrad galaxy during the period 1957 to 1960. Different circles of friends gave me different dates for their first notice of him: Galina Dozmarova—1958, Yefim Slavinsky—1960, Boris Shvartsman—1961.

One of Brodsky's first friends was Yakov Gordin. Today Gordin is the director and coeditor of the best St. Petersburg literary magazine, *Zvezda,* and makes frequent television appearances to comment on literary, political, and economic affairs. He is known as the author of several collections of poems as well as books on Russian literature and history, including a recent one that recounts 170 years of the Russian-Chechen conflict. When he first met Brodsky, Gordin was a 22-year-old aspiring writer, recently discharged from the Soviet Army. This was unusual—very few people in our circle had served in the Army. Gordin had been conscripted because he had lost his student deferment when he temporarily left the university. [All Soviet students, even if they studied art and literature, were obliged to take ten courses of military training while in the university, and graduated with the rank of reserve lieutenant, but that was usually deemed preferable to two years of active duty as a private. Since this is not a book on the Soviet Army, however, I will refrain from describing how a thinking person might feel in an army trained to "bring freedom on the points of their bayonets to all the nations of the world" (the words of a popular song).]

Gordin met 17-year-old Joseph in 1957 at one of the meetings of a literary club run by the Leningrad newspaper for young readers called *Smena* (a play on words because it means both "young generation" and "relief of the guard"). Though five years is a huge difference at that age, Brodsky immediately befriended Gordin. Their relationship is described in a poem Brodsky wrote thirteen years later.

> I saw many signs today
> in the sky, on the water, suggesting
> trouble is on the way, or meaning
> I'll get drunk—you, Yakov, know I may
>
> because this clear chilly day
> is your birthday, that's what the numbers say
> (surely known to your wife, Tata,
> and that toddler of yours, Alexei).
>
> Never! Only a few of us remain
> and always fewer. We'll take a while
> wherever, in jail or underground,
> to celebrate—in our style—
>
> this birthday. As for the other nonsense
> we will assign it to this day forever—
> "Day of Nobility and Kindness,
> And Gordin's Traits"—hooray!

In the essay "The Brodsky Case" (1989) published in another Leningrad literary magazine [*Neva*, for the river], Gordin recalls one literary evening in the winter of 1958 where he presented a research paper about Russian Poetry of the twenties. Unexpectedly, 18-year-old Joseph asked permission to comment and started his speech by quoting from the Trotsky book, *Literature and Revolution*.

In the Soviet Union of the late fifties the very name "Trotsky" was taboo. You could pronounce it publicly only if you followed it with a stream of curses and accusations directed at this man's memory (by this time Trotsky's life had ended in Mexico, where he had been killed by one of Stalin's agents). It goes without saying that very few people had actually read Trotsky's books. Joseph had, though, and quoted from this one because he thought it relevant to the discussion. Gordin writes of his amazement at the level of internal freedom young Brodsky had achieved. Most Russians, especially intellectuals, even if they did not have a slave mentality, felt they had to compromise and modify what they said to protect themselves from the wrath of the system. It came as no surprise that the chairman of the meeting wasted no time publicly condemning Brodsky. The condemnation wasn't loud and clear, however: he was so frightened he pronounced Brodsky as Trotsky and Trotsky as Brodsky. Gordin thinks that the chairman further protected himself by reporting the incident "to the proper authorities" [a euphemism for the KGB].

Dozmarova, Slavinsky, Shvartsman, Gordin—these people represented different intellectual groups in Leningrad. Membership was poorly defined, as members mixed, divided, and got together again in a way that is reminiscent of Brownian motion. Still, some approximate boundaries can be set.

Some of Brodsky's close friends need to be mentioned here because they played an important role in his life. Some are no longer living, others avoid the spotlight… For example, when I asked Slavinsky, my old friend from the mid-fifties, why he hadn't written anything about Brodsky, since he'd known the poet for ages, he said, "You know, I'm not the type to brag about 'myself and Brodsky.'" Was he blaming me for what I was doing? Dozmarova, with whom I had studied in college, later became involved with the Academician Sakharov's circle and compiled a book about his struggle, persecution and defense. She answered the same question thus: "What does it matter what I know about Brodsky?" Was she saying that I should be silent, too? And Boris Shvartsman, who offered Brodsky "political asylum" for a while when Brodsky's parents were angry with their son, said, "Who am I to demonstrate my intimacy with Brodsky?"

Unlike my humble friends, and at the risk of seeming arrogant, I have decided to tell everything I know about Joseph. Not only will I demonstrate my intimacy, I may even sound proud of it.

I'll start with the company that I was a part of. The narrowest and best known circle consisted of three poets: Evgeny Rein, Anatoly Naiman, and Dmitri Bobyshev. All three were studying at The Leningrad Institute of Technology, in the School of Chemistry. The reason for their education in chemistry was exactly the same as for mine in geology: they needed a profession that would insulate them from the dangers of a literary career. Still, because of their free spirit they had clashes with the Institute administration. Rein, Naiman and Bobyshev and later Brodsky were to figure in later literary history as the "magical chorus" or as "Akhmatova's orphans."

Anna Akhmatova had been the target of a special decision of the Central Committee of the Communist Party of the USSR. In 1946, Andrey Zhdanov, then one of the Secretaries of the Central Committee, presented the case against her. The Committee discussed the state of Soviet literature and found that some writers and poets did not sufficiently devote themselves to the praise of the Soviet people, who had selflessly labored to produce the abundance of goods, housing, and river dams that were brightening our future. Also, these writers and poets failed to praise the Communist Party that had unselfishly directed the efforts of the Soviet people who had selflessly labored to produce the abundance of goods, etc. Akhmatova was attacked personally. She was accused of being a relic of the past who was corrupting the moral values of a younger generation.

The proceedings of the Central Committee were published in the newspaper *Pravda* ("Truth"), *Izvestia* ("News") and promptly reprinted in all other Soviet newspapers. Despite her fame as a poet of the "Silver Age" of Russian poetry—one of the best woman poets ever—she immediately disappeared from the Russian literary scene as if she had never lived, while her books disappeared from the shelves of bookstores and public libraries. Akhmatova was expelled from the Union of Soviet Writers. None of her poetry was allowed to be published or reprinted.

The three young, soon-to-be-orphaned poets had developed a great love for Akhmatova's poetry. Rein's aunt was a distant relative of Akhmatova, and he volunteered to help the old poet with chores around the house. She accepted his offer. Rein brought

Naiman and Bobyshev to help him, and Akhmatova became a mentor to them also. For a while, Anatoly Naiman became Akhmatova's secretary and they even worked together on Russian translations of the *Canti di Giacomo Leopardi*.

Brodsky met this trio in 1960 and till 1964 the four poets were inseparable. They were the nucleus of a much larger gang, many of whom became Brodsky's friends for life: writers Genna Smakov, Yakov Gordin and his wife Tata, Igor Yefimov and his wife Marina, physicist Misha Petrov, graphic artist Misha Belomlinsky and his wife Vickie. The gang changed over time. In the beginning of 1964 Bobyshev faded out because of dramatic circumstances to be explained in a later chapter. And at the end of the sixties, Sergei Dovlatov appeared on the horizon—the future star of Russian prose. However, he became close to Brodsky only afterwards, when they both lived in New York City.

Another group, in which Brodsky made his presence felt even sooner, consisted of geologists—mostly alumni of the Leningrad Mining Institute. In 1957-1961, Joseph went on geological expeditions for two to three months at a time. In those days this was the only way to see the world, or rather, the Soviet Union. Also, geology was the "safest" profession. In the Siberian Taiga, in the Yakutsk tundra, in the steppes of Kazakhstan, the political ideologies and world views of geologists concerned no one. If the Leningrad "Gabriela" [slang for KGB] got a hold of them, these geologists would wind up in approximately the same places anyway—without a geologist's pay.

The chance to go to the ends of the earth, far away from the all-seeing eyes of the KGB, was the salvation of many of our friends who didn't want to be sheep and dared to have their own opinions. Even so, the profession wasn't my first choice. Since I was very much the child of literary parents who went into shock at the sight of a mathematical formula, I dreamed of going into diplomacy—a utopia for members of the Jewish ethnic minority. Then my gentle and mild-mannered father put pressure on me for the first time in his life. "I beg of you, go into geology. You'll have to lie less. Granite consists of quartz, feldspar and mica under all political regimes."

I applied to the Leningrad Mining Institute. It turned out to have more poets and writers per square foot than the Writers

Union. I did not regret a single moment of my geological youth.

Brodsky had friends among field geologists his whole life. Even though he did not attend the Mining Institute (he only finished seven years of school, and never got his high school diploma) he was often seen reading at the Institute's literary evenings.

The third group of friends to which Brodsky belonged was defined by their shared love of America and Poland—American jazz and modern literature and Polish magazines and movies and later, Polish poetry. Not that the Polish culture held any special attraction for these young Russians. It just happened that Polish magazines were allowed to circulate in Russia legally, and the Polish language was fairly close to ours. These magazines were our windows on the Western world. One of Brodsky's first translations was of the Polish poet Galchinski. This group of friends nested on Blagodatny Street, in a tiny apartment that was rented by Slavinsky and his young wife.

Afraid that I would get the dates wrong, I called Slavinsky in London (where he has been working for the BBC) to ask when Brodsky had appeared on his horizon. Here is an excerpt from his letter: "We met Brodsky in the summer of 1960 on Blagodatny. Joseph had half a thousand friends of my caliber. We had so many people there, I can't really remember who brought who in. His early poems were met with criticism ('lots of hot air and pomp') and I remember saying that it would be good for him to meet someone from the Institute of Technology trinity. [Rein, Naiman and Bobyshev, mentioned before as those who were about to be called Akhmatova's orphans.] That is exactly what happened. We talked about poetry nonstop and he listened closely to my opinions. Already in 1965 when I was putting together an anthology of Leningrad Samizdat I included about ten of his poems.

"Later in Rome, Brodsky readily agreed that yes, there was a lot of hot air in his poems. That was early in the 80s when we were strolling around Rome and he was reading his poems, each one better than the last. At some point during the night I remember saying, 'You're inching towards a Nobel.' Of course, I wasn't the first one to notice this, and I didn't say it as high praise, but just as an attempt to fully appreciate his class of writing."

The fourth group consisted of the Shvartsmans, the architect Yuri Tzekhnovitzer, the composer Sergei Slonimsky, and their friends.

Boris Shvartsman, a first-class photographer, created many portraits of Brodsky and other literary figures. One of the most popular is of Brodsky wearing a cap and a scarf. Smiling and squinting, he looks past the camera. His expression vaguely recalls Vladimir Lenin's on one of his ubiquitous pictures. This portrait of Brodsky now hangs in every editor's office in Russia. All this is quite ironic, since only twelve years ago his poems could not have been published in the Soviet Union, and instead of the Brodsky picture, the portraits of Soviet leaders were hanging on the same walls in the offices of the same editors.

Boris Shvartsman also took the famous photo of Anna Akhmatova in a white shawl, as well as the photo of her four "orphans" beside her open coffin on the day of her funeral.

Boris Shvartsman and I were neighbors before my emigration. In addition to the apartment where he lived with his wife Sofia, he also had a tiny room in a huge communal apartment on Voinova Street. Before the revolution, this apartment certainly belonged to only one family and the tiny room probably was used by a servant. Boris Shvartsman offered this room to Brodsky for "political asylum." In Russia, the question "Your place or mine?" was out of the question as a rule, because very few people had a place they could call their own [that is, without roommates]. Brodsky would invite girls to Shvartsman's room and escape the glare of his parents' disapproval. Most importantly, he found it a good place to work. It was in this cell that he wrote the "Eulogy of John Donne" and the poem "Isaac and Abraham." After his arrest, Rein and Shvartsman returned the belongings he'd left behind in the little room to his father. They found Brodsky Senior very sad and depressed. "Why does he write poetry? He should be doing something else." When Brodsky returned from exile he gave Shvartsman this poem:

AN EXCERPT
The house is before me, the house transformed.
Pilasters are not pilasters, the front door.

The room where I to you... Oh, no!
The room where you to me... Only with great
Difficulty can I find it today.
There's an excess of landmarks.
It reeks of *borsht* from behind the painted doors.
Water rattles through dirty dishes.
A Jew hounded by neighbors sits
Over little tubs in the dark.
Now "Photography" is there. Everywhere
Pieces of street lights, caryatids,
The moon over a legendary shelter.
Scraps of the Neva, a wooden grave marker,
Countless naked broads...
And this—if you wish—an echo.

Yuri Tzekhnovitzer, the son of a famous literary critic, lived in an apartment building on a bank of the Neva near the main Admiralty complex. This is the most beautiful and desirable neighborhood in St. Petersburg. Right under the windows is the Neva, and on the other side, the Academy of Science, Kunst Camera, and the Twelve Colleges of Leningrad University. The apartment was grand and impressive. Ceiling moldings, bronze candelabras, beautiful antique furniture made of Karelian birch, expensive artwork, glass bookcases, a copy of Pushkin's death mask. A collection of top hats hung on a stand in the foyer. In other words, the place gave no hint of the Soviet reality just outside. Entering the apartment was like entering the nineteenth century.

Yuri, a talented artist and architect, was a noisy, bearded bon vivant and a popular host. On November 7, when the whole country was celebrating the anniversary of the October Revolution (it started on October 25, 1917 according to the Julian calendar that was used in Russia before the revolution; when Russia switched to the Gregorian calendar later, the date became November 7, but the name stuck; nobody worried about this little absurdity), we were partying at his place because it was his birthday. It looked like we were celebrating with all the Soviet people, but we were really there for a different reason.

Brodsky reminisced about "Tzekh's" place many times. In

1988, after meeting with Rein in New York after a 16-year separation, he had this to say: "I had a moment of enlightenment once when standing across the street from Tzekhnovitzer's place. I remember this moment very well. If I have ever had any revelations in my life, this was definitely one of them. I was standing with my hands on the granite embankment, my hands were hanging slightly over the water, the day was gray, I wasn't thinking about whether I was a poet or not, I never have these thoughts, but I remember I was standing there with hands over the water, people around me were fishing and strolling, the Palace bridge was on my right, I was watching the water move towards the bay, there was space between my hands and the water, and I thought to myself, the air between my hands is moving in the same direction as the water, and instantly it dawned on me that at this very moment no one else had this same thought, and I realized that something had happened here. A moment of enlightenment that something specific was happening in my head...well anyway, our whole life, when going into Tzekh's place, and putting on a top hat, with all the books and girls around..."

The fifth group of friends, which later connected with the first, consisted of Gennady Smakov and a few Italian graduate students who were studying in the Leningrad University. Brodsky was friends with "our Italians" his whole life and at least part of their story deserves to be told.

The Italians entered our lives in 1965. They came to Leningrad to study Russian Literature. It surprised us that they, so different from us by upbringing and life experience, turned out to be so close to us spiritually. They liked the same art and music. They fell in love with the same books, they knew by heart the same poems. And they were "wounded" as we had been by Russian literature. Among them, Brodsky became good friends with Gianni Buttafava, Fausto Malcovati, Silvana DeVidovich, and Anna Doni. Unfortunately, Gianni seldom came to our house. I know about him mostly from things that Brodsky said. Gianni translated Brodsky's poetry into Italian, and Joseph was very fond of him. Gianni's early death was a big blow to Brodsky. We saw the other three in Leningrad pretty often. The beautiful Silvana seemed like a movie star to us, maybe because she had the same name as movie star Silvana Pompanini, who was quite popular at the time. We knew almost nothing about her family. Of Anna Doni we only knew that she was a Venetian, and of an aristocratic family. Anna had blond hair swirling around her shoulders, angelic facial features, and a great body. She was in her early twenties. Her Catholic family, the suspected but unproven descendants of the Medicis, was very religious. The children had been brought up strictly: drinking, smoking, and nightly outings were out of the question. Besides, she was shy, and embarrassed to speak Russian, although she knew the language well. It seemed to her that her Russian was too academic and artificial. She wanted to know idioms and slang and memorized the poems of Galich, Vysotsky, and Okudzhava (the most popular bards of the time). Once Rein showed her how "real people" drank vodka. They didn't use cups or shot glasses, but drank "*iz gorla*"—straight from the bottle. He sang her some popular modern songs whose words Anna eagerly wrote down and memorized. A few days later at someone's birthday, Anna grabbed a bottle of vodka, threw her head back and started to drink from the bottle as her teacher had suggested. By the early morning hours she was dancing on the tables... When at a seminar a professor asked foreign graduate students what modern Russian songs they knew, Anna Doni raised her hand, and with a clear loud voice sang a song popular among conscripted soldiers:

It is miserable, hungry, and cold
There are no walls around,
Where could we find a loose broad
That would fuck every one of us?

I do not exaggerate in saying that Fausto Malcovati was fabulously handsome. Well educated and well mannered, he was the son of a Milanese gynecologist, and the second of four brothers.

All "our Italians" were courageous dealing with the peculiarities of Soviet life. Their bedbug-ridden dormitories elicited no complaint, nor did the lack of hot water for showers, or the long, cold and sunless Leningrad winters without fresh fruits and vegetables. We understood how unpleasant it was for them and tried to brighten their lives by inviting them to dinners of "fettuccine and linguine," as we designated our thick noodles with tomato sauce.

"You have no idea how much we value your hospitality," Fausto would say. "When you come to Italy…" We would giggle and not let him finish the sentence.

At the time, the ordinary Soviet citizen could only see Italy in Italian movies. One could not even dream about going there in person… But in 1975 the wheel of history creaked and budged a little. We emigrated from the USSR and, waiting for visas to enter the United States, found ourselves in Italy among majestic ruins, marble fountains, and Michelangelo's masterpieces. The hotel where we put up had no phone so the first day I ran to the central rail station Termini, only a few blocks away, to call Fausto in Milan.

"You are in Rome? But that's impossible!" His languid voice showed his excitement. "I'll immediately call Anna and Silvana and we will try to come to Rome for the weekend. Where are you living?"

"Nowhere at the moment. Well, in the Hotel Cipro. But we have to find an apartment and move in two days. By the time you come here we will be someplace else."

"We will find you."

From Termini to Cipro is a ten-minute walk. As soon as I returned to the room I heard a knock on the door. We had no acquaintances in Rome. Frightened by stories of immigrants being robbed in their hotel rooms, we didn't open the door. Somebody behind the door appealed to us in Italian and then we heard receding footsteps. We opened the door a crack and saw a basket of divine scarlet roses with a card pinned to it. *Benvenuti in Italia, Fausto.*

We felt like complete idiots. Since we were, as I've indicated above, ordinary Soviet citizens, we had no idea that it was possible to order and send flowers anywhere in ten minutes.

A few days later we rented an apartment on Piazza Fonteiana. And our old Italian friends soon burst into our new Italian home with bags of delicacies, bottles of wine, and a determination to make our lives in Italy happy and carefree.

In Leningrad we had talked incessantly about literature and

almost never about politics. It went without saying that we saw world events from the same outlook but from different ivory towers. So it turned out to our amazement that after our third bottle of Chianti, Silvana began passionately defending Marxism/Leninism or Marxism/Trotskyism or Marxism/Maoism or some other form of Marxism. We went hoarse arguing till two in the morning.

The next day the landlady threw us out, saying that she had rented the apartment to a nice family and not a political club.

So we ended up on the street. And we'd be there still if it weren't for Irina Alekseyevna Ilovaiskaya, bless her memory. At the time, she was not yet the chief editor of *La Pensée Russe* in Paris, but worked in Rome. Someone told her our story, and since her children were in Switzerland, she gave us the key to their apartment. "Stay as long as you want," she said. We spent four magical months in the center of Rome on Gaeta Street. Soon Fausto came again to visit.

"You look terrible," he said. "You desperately need rest. Go and lounge on the beach and forget about your problems."

"Yes, he'll eat it, but who will give it to him?" I was alluding to an old Russian joke.

[A father and son go to a zoo. They walk by an elephant and the father reads out an explanation on the wall, "An elephant will eat half a ton of cabbage and carrots a day." An old babushka overhears this and says, "Yes he'll eat it, but who will give so much to him?"]

"Go down to Ischia," Fausto said, not understanding my joking reference.

"Isch-what?"

"Ischia, an island in the Bay of Naples. We have a little country house there. Unfortunately I can't go with you in the middle of the semester. But my mother is there now and she'll look after you."

Fausto bought us tickets to Naples and jotted down the address.

In Naples we boarded a slow ferryboat. I remember turquoise waves, the salty taste of sea spray, dazzling bursts of sun, and the misty contours of the small island of Prochida as we slid by. Then Ischia Porto glimmered up ahead. We saw a round harbor with cheerfully bobbing yachts and tiny fishing boats. Behind it rose white flat-roofed houses amid tropical greenery: palm, fig, eucalyptus, almond, and pomegranate trees. Over it all towered Monte Epomeo, the most majestic of the fifty volcanoes that had once erupted on this eighteen-square-mile island.

A line of funny-looking canopied motorcycles—the local taxis—stood idling by the pier. When I handed the address to one of the drivers, his face lit up: "*Casa Malcovati! Certamente Signora! Con piacere!*" We rode down a narrow street flanked by huge pine trees, then sped to the sea. No more than five feet away from the precipice our driver took a sharp right and announced: "*Casa Malcovati!*"

Before us lay a fortress, three sides of which went straight down to the sea, where high waves smashed against thick stone walls. Hesitantly, we tried the door's knocker—an iron lion's head with a heavy ring between its teeth. The door opened to reveal a noble-looking signora with gray, beautifully done hair, wearing a black dress and lace shawl. "Vera Malcovati," she said with a bow. "*Benvenuti a Ischia!*"

There were thirty-four rooms on three floors, Signora Malcovati explained as she gave us a tour through "the little country house." Happily, our bedroom faced the sea. I opened its glass doors and descended a few wet stone steps to a huge, shiny black rock that rose from the sea like a sleeping hippo.

Over dinner Signora Malcovati said, "Fausto asked me to leave you alone and not to hover over you. Take walks, sunbathe and swim, go shopping, eat in any restaurant, but don't even think of paying. Just say that you are guests of the Malcovati family."

"We are eternally grateful," I said, barely holding back tears. "I don't know how we could ever repay you for your hospitality."

"There's nothing easier," laughed Signora Malcovati. "When you become rich Americans and when Fausto goes broke and knocks on your door, invite him to McDonald's."

Fausto is now a professor at the University of Milan, he still isn't broke and hasn't yet knocked on our door in search of food and shelter.

The house was filled with unusual things. The main hall housed collections of antique umbrellas and canes. The dining room had stained glass windows, and there were oak cabinets with ornate carved designs and wine bottles inside that had been fashioned to resemble the busts and faces of eighteenth-century European monarchs. The library had arched ceilings and was lined with rosewood. I found many books in English, French, Russian and Italian, and beautifully illustrated books on the history of Ischia, Sorrento, and Naples. There were ancient maps and atlases of Italy. Everything in the house was solid and elegant without showy luxury or styles to be found in fashionable magazines—what in my family was called "the glittering worthlessness of courtesans."

We saw Signora Vera Malcovati every day but only for one or two minutes. She would come into our kitchen in the mornings to ask us how we had slept and if we needed anything. In the evenings she'd ask us how our day had gone. We were thankful for her tact—for not having to tell her the story of our lives in a broken foreign language, puffing up and depicting ourselves as victims and dissidents. In this old fortress in the middle of the sea where everything breathed dignity and nobility, I realized how tortured and distraught we had been during the last few months in the Soviet Union by the perpetual fear, the endless slights, the Kafkaesque senselessness of our Soviet existence. And instead of sunbathing, and swimming, and walking around this incredible island, I sat in the library and cried about my fate. Later I understood why. Life on Ischia was a pause. It was obvious that all my energy, the whole force of my body and soul, had been focused on survival. Here where it was calm I was experiencing my life's first depression.

I am describing Ischia in such detail because Brodsky loved it so much. On one of his frequent visits to Fausto's home he wrote:

Casa Malcovati is full of glory,
Only that its beds are too small I am sorry.

In 1993 Brodsky came to Ischia for the last time with his wife Maria and their young daughter, Anna. On this last visit he dedicated to Fausto the poem "Ischia in October."

Once a volcano seethed here.
Then a pelican pecked his breast.

33

Virgil lived not far away
And W.H. Auden drank his wine.
<...>
Daughter and wife gaze from the balustrade
Looking for the piano
Of a sail or a hot air balloon—
Frozen toll of a bell.
<...>
We are here, the three of us, and I'll bet
That together we see three
Times the blue you saw,
And all of it unmoored, Aeneas.

But Ischia has distracted me. It's time to return to the '60s in the Soviet Union.

In mentioning Brodsky's friends earlier I've given the names that most readily come to mind. The list is incomplete, then, but not out of spite. Forty years have passed and, as my old nanny used to say, "it's beginning to show." I apologize to those who are not mentioned here, hoping to prevent hurt feelings.

The fact of the matter is that Brodsky got bored easily talking to the same people. That's why he had thousands of friends and seldom spent an evening in one house. Usually he managed to be with many different groups in the course of one day, and he always fretted that something more interesting was going on someplace else. He went through people the way whales go through plankton.

3

Life before Brodsky

FOR RUSSIANS, THE SECOND WORLD WAR officially ended on May 9, 1945. The Soviet Government would not declare war on Japan until August 9, 1945, the day of the Nagasaki atomic bomb. The May date may have seemed appropriate to celebrate the end of what was called the Great Patriotic War in part because of the great patriotic celebration that took place a month afterward, when soldiers from the Leningrad front returned home. They marched through all the major streets of the city. Unusual for Leningrad, it was a hot and balmy day. The huge crowds of Leningraders streamed outside to greet the returning soldiers. First came the infantry, then the cavalry. Thousands stood along the sidewalks and laughed and cried and offered candy, flowers and even ice cream to the soldiers. Children were presented to soldiers on horseback by their mothers and given a ride for a block or two. The kids were ecstatic.

Mother, Father and I stood on the Liteiny Prospekt near the Liteiny Bridge over the Neva River. My parents had tears in their eyes but I was too little to be moved in the same way... Another family stood next to us. A man in a naval uniform, a short, plump woman in glasses, and a little red-haired boy about five years old. He wanted a ride on a horse and was nagging his parents nonstop. The mother was saying, "You're still too little, Osya, all those kids who are riding are at least ten years old."

For no apparent reason the memory of this nondescript family stayed with me.

Many years later Brodsky and I were reminiscing about our childhood. Naturally, each was remembering his own. I told him about how I had stood near the bridge that day.

"I was there too!" he said. "Do you think we were standing together?"

All of a sudden, I clearly recalled the little kid who wanted to ride a horse. "Possible, but then, at my age I wouldn't give the time of day to such small fry as that little red-haired boy." I am not sure whether that was really the Brodsky family next to mine that day, but the very possibility of such a coincidence gave me the feeling that our paths in life had been fated to intersect.

As an adult, I met Brodsky the summer of 1957, I guess. Again, I'm not sure, but I think I did because when we were formally introduced the first thing he said was, "Hey, haven't we met before?" Sounds like a pickup line, I remember thinking. But a prior meeting was possible. In the summer of 1957, both of us had worked for the same geological consulting firm in neighboring areas. He was at the White Sea, and I was in Northern Karelia. It is quite possible that we saw each other in the office before we went into the field, or right after we returned home, at the meetings held for field geologists. But officially I met Joseph at my friend Galina Dozmarova's wedding in 1959.

As Brodsky's Pimen, or official recorder of events, let me try to depict that wedding day. The bride, Galina Dozmarova-Kharkevich (nicknamed Galka) was my college friend. She looked exotic. If you saw her once, you would never forget her. She had an unruly shock of chestnut hair quite like a haystack. Her stubby nose was turned up slightly, and she had a big, sensual mouth. Imagine her with a guitar in hand, singing—a cigarette in the corner of her mouth, green eyes squinting because of the smoke—but with perfect pitch and a low, raspy voice that would be called sexy today. There was much more to recommend her, of course: she was a great track and field athlete and had a beautiful figure. To make a long story short, there were many who were madly in love with her.

Galka was, and still is, a person who was created to comfort and to soothe people's emotional traumas. Who hasn't cried on her shoulder? She gave everyone money for a drink, or for a little bit of food or for life. The homeless slept over, and the hungry ate. There was a time when Brodsky couldn't have managed without her. There should be a bronze plaque on the wall of her old dwelling inscribed thus: *Behind these stone walls lived a real friend.*

Galka's heritage was replete with murky legends. It was said that her mother was a Gypsy who had been an ace fighter pilot during the war and received the highest Soviet decoration for bravery: the medal of The Hero of the Soviet Union. Gypsy and ace fighter pilot is not a trivial combination. But when it was revealed that Galka's mother, Raisa Pivovarova, was, in fact, a fighter pilot, and not a Gypsy but a Jew, eyebrows were raised even higher. In 1942, Raisa was injured and lost her hearing. She stopped being a fighter pilot and assumed less glamorous duties, but Galka's romantic origins had been established. However, I do not remember that she mentioned her father even once.

Strange, but I also don't remember where her husband, Tolya Michailov, came from. Her wedding day was the first and last time I ever saw the man. And in the past forty years I have only heard about him once. No, not from Galka, but from Brodsky. Once in New York an uncharacteristically enthusiastic Brodsky described how he met Tolya Michailov at one of his literary readings in Prague.

"After my reading, an older, bald guy came up to me and said, 'Joseph, of course you don't remember me. I'm Tolya Michailov.' I said, 'Of course I remember you, I recognized you right away.'"

Then I said to Brodsky, "Thirty-five years later, how could you recognize him? You'd only met him once."

"By his sweater, it was the same one he wore at his wedding," Brodsky said. "Tolya became a successful physicist in Prague, and we happily spent a few hours together. He surprised me with an invitation to an expensive restaurant."

"What's so surprising about that?" I asked.

"I'm the one who always invites people to a restaurant."

So it was that I had no more information about Tolya than those few words from Brodsky many years later. But serious "keeping of the historical record" requires serious research. So I emailed Galka again with a few questions: Where did Tolya Michailov come from? Why did you marry him? How long were you together? Why did you divorce?

In two hours I received this illuminating reply:

"Tolya Michailov is five years younger than I am, his mother is from an aristocratic family, a translator of Japanese; the father was of peasant ancestry and a communist activist. I met him on an expedition in Southern Yakutia, near China. I was afraid of the war and wanted a home with children. I had three suitors. Genka Shteinberg—a flaccid romance that lasted many years. Goshka Sheelinsky, an intellectual from an academic family. And, of course, Tolya. Handsome as a Greek God, and madly in love. Watching him was a pleasure, like being in the Louvre, and that proved to be the decisive factor. The other suitors understood my aesthetic sense. After five months of exhaustive field work, I returned to Leningrad and we rented a room at Kolomenckaya 27. I needed only two months to sort everything out. I nicknamed him the 'sexual eccentric' and decided I'd had enough. Then I was touched by the big tears on his beautiful face and his attempt to throw himself under a train at the 'Moskovskaya' metro station and I extended our union for another two years."

The pre-Tolya and the post-Tolya romances are more memorable and both involved friends of Brodsky.

The hero of the pre-Tolya romance was Genka, or, more officially, Genrikh Semyonovich Shteinberg, another fellow student at the Leningrad Mining Institute, who later went on to become a fearless conqueror of volcanoes and hearts alike. He is currently a member of the Russian Academy of Science and the director of the Institute of Volcanic Studies. He was probably the first man to risk his life by going down the crater of an erupting volcano to do research and collect samples. There are amusing similarities between him and Brodsky.

Joseph Brodsky couldn't stand intellectual superiority and at the least sign of it, girded himself for combat and spent all his energy defeating his opponent. Genrikh Shteinberg couldn't stand to be shown up in any way, but he could only prove his superiority physically by demonstrating bravery, heroism, or machismo. If one could combine the powerful energies of Brodsky and Shteinberg in one individual, the result would be a true superman who should be cloned to help tired mankind to survive. Genrikh Shteinberg has already been immortalized in literature by the famous Russian writer Andrei Bitov, who described Shteinberg's heroic deeds in his novella *Journey to a Childhood Friend*. One of the heroic deeds, namely Deed Number 6, was not described accurately. Unlike Bitov, I witnessed this deed with my own eyes and it is my duty to correct the historical record [see *The Leap from the Swallow's Nest* below].

Dozmarova's other lover, Yuri Kukin, who later fathered her daughter Masha, is a very popular bard. Brodsky liked his songs and sang them when in Russian company on both sides of the Atlantic—after three or four shots of vodka. His two favorite Kukin songs are these:

PARIS

Why are you whistling, my friend?
Is Paris bothering you?
Look, look, the Taiga surrounds you.
You had better put wood on the campfire
Listen to the silence
Paris is far away,
And you are here, on the devil's horns.

It's not like the Place Pigalle here,
One has to pretend to be cheerful,
Nobody is surprised by your grief
We have Montmartre by campfire,
Yesterday, today and tomorrow,
Please, stop thinking about Paris.

Just wait a little bit,
Rainy days will start,
And there will be no place to run to.
There is no bistro here,
There is tea instead of cognac,
And please, stop thinking about Paris.

The mountains are covered by haze,

Try to think about your business
And not about Paris,
Stop longing for Paris!

CHASING FOG

Understand, it is strange, it is very strange.
But I am such an incurable oddity.
I am chasing fog, I am chasing fog
And I can't cope with myself.

People are after business, people are after money,
People run from trouble and from grief.
But me, I'm after dreams,
For fog and for the fragrance of the Taiga...

Understand, it is simple, very simple,
For one who has gone there once.
Try to imagine keenly, very keenly
The sun and mountains, the silver firs and songs and rain.

Never mind that my suitcases
Are full of memories, sadness, depths....
I am still looking for fog, I am chasing fog,
I am chasing dreams and the fragrant Taiga.

And now – the story of the Legendary Deed of Genrikh Shteinberg.

THE LEAP FROM THE SWALLOW'S NEST

In summer of 1955 I was sent to the Crimea to participate in a geological survey with a group of students from the Leningrad Mining Institute. When we had finished our field work in August, we decided to spend our vacation together right there in the Crimea, at one of the beautiful vacation spots on the Black Sea. There were eleven of us. Besides geologists and geophysicists, there were two young men who had nothing to do with geology.

The first was Victor Shtern, future professor at Boston University, with whom I'd become romantically involved before leaving for summer field work and to whom I would be married a year later. [For the record, we are still together and on speaking terms even though we disagree on almost everything.]

The second was the poet Evgeny Rein. In the future, Brodsky would call him his teacher and spiritual guru. My friendship with Rein is another story.

In Yalta the eleven of us rented one room with three beds. I have no memory whatsoever of who slept with whom in which bed and in what order. In fact, it is of no importance, since by "slept" I mean actual sleep and not what one might think at the tail end of the sexual revolution. In those years, we were too chaste for "group recreation."

After hanging around Yalta for a week, we decided to go to Sochi, another Black Sea town, on the boat "Russia," which was rumored to be a former German cruise ship and to have belonged at one time to Hitler himself. We took stock of our resources and found them so meager that we could forget about staterooms. We could only afford tickets for the deck. Dozmarova had no resources at all. There wasn't enough for her even if everyone contributed, and her trip was in jeopardy. Then Genrikh Shteinberg came forward wearing a mysterious half-smile: "Don't worry about the money. I have a plan."

Before I reveal his plan, a word about "*Lastochkino Gnezdo*" (The Swallow's Nest).

"The Swallow's Nest" is the name of a miniature romantic castle built on the south shore of the Crimea, on the very tip of a huge impregnable cliff ("Aurora's cliff"), where it appeared to overhang the Black Sea about 200 feet below. During a devastating earthquake in 1927 it was half destroyed and for the next fifty years was unavailable for tourists. But it was surrounded by resorts and sanatoriums, mostly for military personnel. Consequently the beach under the huge rock was littered with specimens of the rich military high command who were dying of boredom.

Genrikh's plan was to go to the Swallow's Nest and walk among those fat half-naked military types, letting it be known that he was willing to jump off the Swallow's Nest for money.

The warriors would get excited and start betting. Genrikh would jump and ... Dozmarova would go to the Caucasus.

Genrikh disappeared in the morning. We had no idea where he went because he adamantly refused to take anyone along. He returned about four in the afternoon, but for some reason did not go home. He was discovered by chance at the Yalta post office, claiming to have just wired money to his parents.

"Why do your parents need your money? Where'd the money come from? Did you really jump? Nothing smashed or broken?" Genrikh replied by lifting his shirt and baring his chest and stomach, which were generously smeared with iodine. Iodine also covered his neck, knees and other parts of his anatomy. We made clucking noises and demanded details. He waived us off, apparently not wanting to boast of his heroic deed. But we persisted and, finally, he gave in.

According to him, on the beach at the Swallow's Nest he had struck up a conversation with a sunbather. One thing led to another and Genrikh said that for two thousand rubles he'd jump off the cliff. People gathered around. Some tried to talk him out of it, others urged him on. After a while bets were placed. Genrikh jumped, hurt everything that could be hurt (see the places smeared with iodine) and lost consciousness. He was fished out of the water and resuscitated by the lifeguard on duty. He had survived...

And what do you think? The cheap bastards at the beach did not hand over the promised sum, neither in an envelope nor on a plate. Instead, they started shouting, "Everybody who saw the guy jump off the Nest? Come on, give as much as you can!" Not many volunteered, and Genrikh, having just regained consciousness, had to approach everyone for a "pathetic handout." It came to about 600 rubles.

"To hell with the pain," Genrikh said. "It was the humiliation I couldn't stand."

The same lifeguard put him on a bus. On the way back, Genrikh's mind somehow became clouded. He said that he opened the bus window and began tossing out the damned money. He didn't have time to toss it all out because the bus arrived in Yalta, so he sent what was left to his parents in Leningrad.

"But what about Dozmarova's ticket?" we wondered.

"She is not worthy of this..." I don't remember exactly what she was not worthy of—his suffering, his torment, or just "too much honor."

Somehow we scraped together enough money for her ticket and set off the next day on the fourth deck of the "Russia." During the day it was hellishly hot and the sailors who hosed the deck, hosed us too, at our request. At night there was a pouring rain, and the same sailors covered as with a tarpaulin. In the morning, as they say in novels, "The sun shone brightly, the sea sparkled." Twenty minutes before arrival in Sochi, Genrikh announced that he was going to jump into the water off the deck of the "Russia." But only on the condition that we, rather than he, should take up a collection from the passengers. We tried to talk him out of it but he persisted, went up on deck and began warming up. He was stretching, doing pushups and sit-ups until the boat docked. It was too late to jump.

Epilogue: Before leaving Yalta, suspicion got the better of Victor and me and we asked our friend Vitaly Purto, who was staying in Yalta, to go to the Swallow's Nest and ask if anyone had jumped lately.

Two days later, the following telegram awaited us at the Sochi post office: "The last jump off the Swallow's Nest was a drunk sailor jumping for a gold watch in 1911 stop He fell to his death stop Vitaly."

4

A Spiritual Guru

I MUST GO BACK to 1953 to introduce the reader to the future spiritual guru of Brodsky. At the time I met him he was no guru yet, and Joseph was only thirteen and had not begun to write poetry.

That year I was a senior in high school. In March 1953, Comrade Stalin, "our father, leader and teacher," died. Today, this does not sound like a big deal. Cesar, Nero, Attila the Hun, Ivan the Terrible died, so it was only natural that Stalin would eventually die, too. And yet it was most unnatural. I do not know what the subjects of Cesar, Nero, Attila the Hun or Ivan the Terrible were told, but the inhabitants of "one-sixth of the world's dry land" were told in no uncertain terms that their Leader was different. His wisdom was boundless. He personally planned our industrial progress. At his direction small private plots had merged to become the state's huge collective farms. He had even written books depicting the demise of nationalism in Russia and explaining what we should think about the laws of language. This "Father of Nations" and "Best Friend of Soviet Athletes," as he was commonly called, was always awake, never slept. No official ever made any public contingency plans for Stalin's death. Indeed, it seemed clear that he was immortal, or at least that the rest of us would die before he did. And now he was gone.

This tragic event almost cost me the chance to earn a high

school diploma.

Having gathered in the great blue hall of my high school (where my mother had been a student also, in her day), we were expected to drown ourselves in grief. Sobbing students and teachers filled the place. Some were choking on their tears, some were crying so hard they got the hiccups. At that age, I already had trouble displaying my grief in public. Instead, I started to giggle, and I couldn't stop. I got kicked out of the hall, and the next day I was kicked out of the Comsomol, the youth organization that conditioned its members to Communist ideology. Without a membership in this organization, one could hardly expect to get ahead in life, or even to be admitted to college. The day after that they were going to kick me out of school as well, but my mother managed to procure a doctor's note to the effect that "Ludmila suffers from various neurotic anomalies as a result of childhood trauma. These anomalies manifest themselves through improper emotional displays: laughter from sorrow, and tears from happiness."

Incidentally, at this tender age Brodsky too had little admiration for the great Comrade Stalin. He referred to him as a "Gutalin." "Gutalin" is the shoe polish commonly used by street shoeshine specialists who were mostly Georgians (or looked Georgian)—and Stalin was Georgian. Calling him "Gutalin" might be in poor taste, but it showed a lack of fear of the KGB.

In the summer, while I was preparing to take college entrance exams, Father and I went for a week to Zelenogorsk, a little resort town on the Finnish Bay that was called Terijoki before Stalin seized it in 1940 from Finland along with the rest of this wonderful resort region. We were relaxing on the beach when a middle-aged woman and her son lay down next to us. The son was a brunet with thick lips and well defined facial features. He leafed through a chemistry textbook wearing an expression of terminal boredom. When the woman went swimming he quickly grabbed another book from under the towel and became engrossed in it.

When she returned, we heard her angry voice. "Zhenya, how many times must I tell you the same thing? Only textbooks! Only chemistry! Pass your exams and read all the poetry you want after that."

"Do you admire the democratic tendencies of our family?" my father told me, laughing. "Or maybe I'm just an uncaring, bad dad?"

Soon, the lady stood up, wrapped herself in a beach towel, and began to change from her bathing suit to dry clothes, a common procedure at a "wild" beach that had neither lifeguards, nor bathhouses, nor even changing stalls. She said, "Let's go, already, Zhenya," and they left. I looked wistfully after them, sorry that I had not managed to introduce myself. There was something intriguing and dramatic in the young man's face.

"Look," said my father, "the mother left her bathing suit." I jumped up, grabbed the bathing suit and caught up with the mother and son on the woodsy path leading to the highway. I got smiles, gratitude, and more smiles...but visiting cards were not exchanged.

We were formally introduced a year later at my friend Mirra Meilakh's birthday party. I was a student at the Mining Institute at that time. Mirra was studying Russian Literature at Leningrad University. Her Russian mother was a biologist, and her Jewish father was a literary scholar who published unexceptionable books on the virtues of Socialist Realism, the great role of Lenin in Russian literature and the like. He was very successful in his loyal service to the regime and quite famous, and Mirra Meilakh was one of very few lucky people whose family had a two-story "dacha" in Komarovo [another resort town taken from Finland]. Mirra and her parents always welcomed guests, their food was excellent, and our young company loved their parties, dinners, teas, or just long conversations on the veranda over tea and biscuits.

Mirra's brother, Misha, was ten years younger and was not welcome at our "adult" parties. On the day of the birthday party, he was ordered not to leave his room because he had contracted a severe case of tonsillitis. When I stopped by to check on him, he was sitting in his bed with a thick compress over his neck. With obvious disgust he was drinking hot milk, a traditional Russian medicine against almost all illnesses. From under the pillow, the nine-year-old boy pulled out a "love note" that he had prepared in advance. The note said: *In this house, nobody takes me seriously; meanwhile, I like jazz very much. I would like to always sit close to you and listen to records."*

Today, Mirra lives in Boston. She became Russian Orthodox and is deeply involved with the local Russian Orthodox community, visiting the sick, taking care of the poor and mentally unstable and the like. Misha grew up, learned yoga (very few could learn it at that time in Russia because it was considered ideologically harmful), befriended many foreign visitors to the Soviet Union (few dared to do it then), and the government punished him by sending him to Soviet labor camps for seven years. Now he is a Professor of Russian Literature in Strasbourg.

The day before the birthday, Mirra told me who was coming. In that list of names was one from the Technological Institute. Mirra said that he was a guy "who knows more about Russian poetry and literature than anyone on the planet." "More than I?" I asked haughtily. My question was met with sardonic laughter.

The guy from the Technological Institute who "knew more about Russian poetry and literature than anyone on the planet" turned out to be the young man from the Zelenogorsk beach— Zhenya—or more formally, Evgeny Rein.

It was true, his head was stuffed full of literary facts and names, though my father later doubted Rein's abundance of knowledge. "The bum knows everything but his facts aren't right."

We appealed to each other, Rein and I. He even had a romantic interest for some time. But it was a lazy interest and not well focused. I still remember some midnight phone calls in which he tried to win me over with poetry. "Listen to what I have dedicated to you," he growled happily. "You were most lovely, tender and exquisite; Do not send me away..."

After hearing this I said, "Rein, don't take me for an idiot, that's an Aleksandr Blok poem."

"Okay. Fine. And how about, 'You are not always proud and aloof, and you do not always turn me away. Very quietly, tenderly, as in a dream, sometimes you come to me.'"

"And that's Gumilyov, from the 'Fireside' collection."

"Well damn you then, good night."

I remember when I first came over to Rein's place. On the table, covered by a starched, ornate napkin, lurked a cheesecake.

Next to the plate lay a note: *Zhenya, appreciate my unlimited kindness. I baked this masterpiece for your "lost Lenore." For this, you are going to take out the garbage and fetch the potatoes for the next two weeks without a peep. If she doesn't come, don't you dare eat the pastry yourself, Grisha and Sonya are coming tomorrow. Kisses, Mother.*

Zhenya lit candles, I sat at the piano and improvised some gypsy melodies.

"Oh, Chopin, my favorite composer," he howled. Zhenya was musically deaf.

"Chopin" impressed him so much that he threw himself in my arms, and one candle from the piano fell into my lap. I was furious and left without trying the divine cheesecake.

Anyway, the romance with Rein fell apart, and turned into a friendship that flourishes still. Today, fifty years later, many think that Evgeny Rein is the greatest living Russian poet.

Besides, Rein turned out to be the best storyteller in the world. His "absolutely, swear to God, truthful stories" are bizarre and hilarious, witty and absurd fables. For many years, his friends asked him why he was wasting his time and energy entertaining people at parties instead of writing a collection of stories. Rein dismissed the idea by casually waving his hand.

Once I asked him to give me one of his stories as a birthday present and let me have a free hand with it. "Sure," he said, "be my guest."

I wrote the story, adding details and vignettes and polishing dialogue, but sticking to the main story line, then published it in Russian in a collection of my short stories and in English in *The Boston Globe Magazine*. Here it is:

THE PREMATURELY GRAY WOLF-PUPPY

Once upon a time, Sir Harold Macmillan, Prime Minister of Great Britain, made an official visit to the Soviet Union. The Soviet Politburo, the Old Guard, gathered around the British airplane in full pomp and regalia. Their seal and muskrat fur hats were powdered with newly fallen snow. Both national anthems echoed (GOD SAVE THE QUEEN and UNBREAK-

ABLE UNION OF THE FREE REPUBLICS) flags flapped, faces grinned, cannons saluted and cameras clicked and buzzed. Everything was according to protocol.

First Mr. Khrushchev made his speech, then the British Prime Minister took his place and spoke words appropriate to the occasion. Suddenly he stepped back from the microphone and, as if mesmerized, stared at something intensely. Everyone's eyes followed Macmillan's, but saw nothing except a few modestly dressed reporters and photographers. The British Ambassador bent his head to Macmillan and whispered, "Anything wrong, Sir? Are you all right?" "Everything is fine," Macmillan mumbled, "I'm just curious about that gentleman over there." He pointed with his chin, "Would you kindly find out his name for me, please?"

The Ambassador whispered to the translators, the translators murmured to some other men, and all the while the transfixed Prime Minister could not stop staring.

"The man is Mr. Chaim Frankel, an assistant photographer from the newspaper *Pravda*," the ambassador reported to Macmillan.

The Prime Minister smiled, stepped forward, and, breaking all the traditions of diplomatic etiquette, approached the reporter. "How do you do, Mr. Frankel?" he said, extending his hand. The color drained out of Frankel's face, which expressed sheer fright. Comrade Frankel was an ordinary Russian Jew. He was neither much of a coward nor much of a hero. This special attention meant only great trouble. He could be now accused of thousands of crimes, among them of being a traitor and a British spy.

"Tomorrow we are giving a reception at the British Embassy," Macmillan continued, "and I would be more than happy to see you among my guests, if you have no other plans. I have something very important to discuss with you."

Frankel almost fainted. "I'm looking forward to seeing you," Macmillan repeated once again, shaking Frankel's cold, limp hand, and moved along the honor guard.

There was nothing significant about Macmillan's limousine trip into the city. Unfortunately, we cannot say the same for comrade Frankel's. He was surrounded by a thick ring of secret agents who whisked him off to Lubyanka, the main office of the KGB.

"Would you be so kind to explain to us the particular interest of Prime Minister Macmillan in you, comrade Frankel?" General Markov grumbled hoarsely. Grudgingly, he had gotten up from a sickbed and had brought along his terrible flu. "What the hell does he want you for?"

Frankel cried, swore and vowed, "I never in my whole life, since I was born or even before, laid an eye, or an ear, or a nose on this Minister. I don't know how to spell his name! And, besides, what would a simple man like me have in common with him?"

"This we will certainly find out." The interrogation lasted several hours during which it became clear that no matter how long or much they twisted or mangled him, Frankel could say nothing more.

The photographer was brought home after midnight. His spouse fed him nitroglycerin, put him to bed and went into the kitchen to weep. The next morning, Frankel called his editor's office and said he was sick. The staff was not surprised at all.

The guests began to arrive at the British Embassy at 5 p.m. Macmillan greeted them half-heartedly, looked around the room and finally asked his ambassador, "Have you seen Mister Frankel?"

The ambassador turned to the secret agents who were masquerading as busboys and waiters. In fifteen minutes, six men broke into Frankel's apartment and ordered him to get out of bed. Frankel cried, clutched intermittently at his heart and at the bedposts, and then again at the heart as they dragged him into the street, all the while dressing him in a necktie and jacket. His wife hysterically wrung her hands as they pushed him into the official car.

As soon as the trembling Frankel arrived at the Embassy, the Prime Minister spotted him, abruptly stopped his conversation with the Soviet minister of Foreign Affairs, and greeted Frankel across the entire length of the reception hall. Translators and guests gathered around Macmillan and Frankel. Somebody put a glass of champagne into Frankel's shaky hand.

"Thank you so much, Mr. Frankel. It was frightfully nice of you to sacrifice your evening and come to see me. I was afraid that I wouldn't have another chance to chat with you. I appreciate your kindness very much... The matter that I wish to discuss with you is something awfully important to me, indeed... But let me get directly to the point. Where did you buy your fur hat?"

"What hat?" stammered Frankel.

"The hat that you wore yesterday at the airport."

"I don't know. Wait, I'm sorry, I do know! Yes, I do remember! At a flea market in the Far East, in Magadan. I was there three years ago... But, why? Something's wrong with it?"

"Oh no, nothing wrong, on the contrary. Let me explain," said the British Prime Minister. "I am not sure if you're aware of it, but your hat is quite unique. It's made of the rarest fur of all— that of a prematurely gray wolf puppy. My father presented just such a hat to me a long time ago, and my father was a splendid connoisseur of fine furs. 'Take care of the puppy hat,' he charged me, 'that hat will be your talisman and will always bring you good fortune.' But two years later, in Brussels, in the airport, my suitcase was lost together with the gray wolf puppy hat inside. Since then, despite all of my efforts, I have been unable to locate another one quite the same until now. I am not ashamed to admit that I am a rather sentimental and superstitious chap. Mr. Frankel, do me a great personal favor! Please, sell me your hat. I will be happy to pay any price you quote."

Frankel heard a soft squeak. The wheel of European history was cranking. "Please, don't mention money. It would be my great pleasure just to give you my hat." (Frankel almost said 'This lousy stinking hat,' but checked himself.)

"I cannot accept such a present." Macmillan regretfully declined.

"Yes, please," Frankel protested, "it's a great honor." He turned around and ran to the cloakroom.

"Dear Mister Prime Minister," Khrushchev said with a broad smile, "I'm afraid you're forgetting your position as our most welcome guest of honor. You don't need anybody's hat (Khrushchev almost said, 'some dirty Jew's lousy stinking hat,' but checked himself). Tomorrow we will present you with five new hats like that."

"I don't think you could accomplish this, sir. During all these years, I've made inquiries of fur companies in Canada, Japan,

Sweden, Norway, the United States and Australia. Nobody, but nobody could find such a hat."

"You never asked us, which is very unfortunate. We would have saved you a lot of time and trouble. Actually, we have plenty of them, as many as you want. I promise that tomorrow we will wrap you in them from head to toe."

Everyone smiled at that most witty and proud speech.

"Gentlemen, 'plenty of them' do not exist in the world," explained Macmillan patiently. "Apparently, you are talking about a gray wolf. Plain gray wolf has a decent fine fur, but gray wolves are commonplace and not a rarity at all. This, however, is the fur of a wolf that turned gray when it was just a cub, and later its black hair grew in and mixed with the gray. It is biological nonsense, but a marvelous fur...Quite unique."

At that moment, Frankel appeared, stretching his hands out, presenting his hat to the Prime Minister.

The Soviet leaders looked with disgust at the sweat-stained lining of the grubby hat. "Don't you dare give it!" Khrushchev gritted his teeth as he spoke. Then, with a charming smile, he turned to Macmillan: "Please take my iron communist word, Mr. Prime Minister. I swear to you that your dream will come true no later than tomorrow."

The well-mannered Briton had the good taste not to insist. He helplessly gave a long, last, loving look at the treasure slipping away and thanked Frankel cordially. Then Macmillan stepped back into the political arena. As for the forgotten Frankel, he went back to the cloakroom, struggled into his shabby coat and hat, and took the streetcar home.

The next day Harold Macmillan was leaving the Soviet Union. All the night before, the Soviet government was busy discussing how to arrange the presentation in the most solemn and prestigious way. A new ministry was formed especially for this occasion: The Ministry of Young Beasts' Fur. The final decision was to present the gift just as its famous recipient was boarding the airplane.

At the very moment when Harold Macmillan was embracing Nikita Khrushchev, a shiny black limousine raced up and stopped one yard from them. The just-appointed head of the Ministry of Young Beasts' Fur (Y.B.F.) jumped from the car holding a scarlet box with white ribbons and bows.

"Let's open it, gentlemen, and you will see that we are not full of what you call 'bull,'" said Khrushchev.

The freshly minted minister undid the ribbons and lifted the cover. Five gorgeous hats lay in the box. A gentle breeze riffled the noble gray fur.

A shadow fell over Macmillan's face and tight wrinkles appeared at the corners of his lips.

"It's exactly what I was afraid of, gentlemen," he said glumly. "These are beautiful hats, but made from plain gray wolf. I have a whole collection of them. I was dreaming of THE hat, made of prematurely gray wolf puppy. Forgive me, please, but it's difficult for me to hide my disappointment."

He shook hands with all those assembled and slowly walked up the airplane steps. The Minister was left holding the box.

Afterwards political observers and reporters all over the world have noticed that relations between the Soviet Union and Great Britain became chillier. Even today one can feel the frost.

By the way, do you care to know what happened to Comrade Frankel? Nothing special. He was simply fired from *Pravda* the very next day. [End]

I could not have published this story in Russia. In any case, I wrote it in 1977, a year and a half after coming to the States. It was one of the first stories I published here. Brodsky read it and made a few flattering comments, encouraging me to write in English. In 1997 Rein published the story about the gray wolf's hat in his collection of memoirs, *I Am Bored Without Dovlatov*. When I confronted him with accusations that he gave this story to me and should not have published it, he simply said: "What's the big deal? You wrote it twenty years earlier and, besides, your version is better."

Brodsky met Rein in 1960 and they became inseparable. Rein played an important role in Brodsky's life—for example, it was Rein who introduced Brodsky to Anna Akhmatova. And Brodsky recognized Rein's talent and importance, calling him his guru and mentor in various interviews many years later. Rein was not the only mentor, of course. Brodsky also counted Mandelshtam and Tsvetayeva as such, as well as Frost and Auden. But Rein was the first, and only to Rein would he read his new poems as soon they were written. In 1987, when Brodsky received the Nobel Prize, he publicly recognized Rein as one of few people who had influenced him. Brodsky dedicated several poems to Rein, including one of his best early poems—*Christmas Ballad*—and much later, a part of "The Mexican Divertimento."

CHRISTMAS BALLAD
for Evgeny Rein, with love

There floats in an abiding gloom,
among immensities of brick,
a little boat of night: it seems
to sail through Alexander Park.
It's just a lonely streetlamp, though,
a yellow rose against the night,
for lovers strolling down below
the busy street.
There floats in an abiding gloom
a drone of bees: men drunk, asleep.
In the dark capital a lone
tourist takes another snap.
Now out onto Ordynka turns
a taxicab, with sickly faces;
dead men lean into the arms
of the low houses.

There floats in an abiding gloom
a poet in sorrow; over here
a round-faced man sells kerosene,
the sad custodian of his store.
Along a dull deserted street
an old Lothario hurries. Soon
the midnight-riding newlyweds
sail through the gloom.

There floats in outer Moscow one
who swims at random to his loss,

and Jewish accents wander down
a dismal yellow flight of stairs.
From love toward unhappiness,
to New Year, to Sunday, floats
a good-time girl: she can't express
what's lost inside.

Cold evening floats within your eyes
and snow is fluttering on the panes
of carriages; the wind is ice
and pale, it seals your reddened palms.
Evening lights like honey seep;
the scent of halvah's everywhere,
as Christmas Eve lifts up its sweet
meats in the air.

Now drifting on a dark-blue wave
across the city's gloomy sea,
there floating by, your New Year's Eve—
as if life could restart, could be
a thing of light with each day lived
successfully, and food to eat,
—as if, life having rolled to left,
it could roll right.
(translated by Glyn Maxwell)

Even now, in Russia, the names of Brodsky and Rein are often mentioned together.

Thirty years after they met Brodsky wrote:

"Rein is the most gifted Russian poet of the second half of the twentieth century. Few among his compatriots would dispute the depth of the despair and exhaustion that darkened his poems."

But in the sixties, Rein's poetry could not be published. In 1963 he counted himself lucky to have *me* as his first publisher. I typed five copies of his sixty-two poems on my typewriter. We bound the pages and created five books. The cover was of red cloth, with designs sewn in with black thread. On the first page we pasted a photograph of Rein smoking a cigarette with a glass of wine in front of him. And this was all the poetry Rein was able to publish over the next twenty-five years. Not that his poems were anti-Soviet. They described his internal life and emotions, which did not jibe with the optimism of officially sanctioned poetry (praising the Soviet way of life, success in work and study, and the like). Officials in the government's publishing house sensed Rein's internal freedom and went nowhere near this poetry. Recognizing Rein would have courted trouble for "lack of vigilance"—endangering young minds because of sloppy selection criteria.

On different occasions, the KGB confiscated four copies of my edition. Well, these books were fair game: they did not have a magic permission number (denoting the censor's approval) on the last page. This was what we called "*samizdat*" (literally, self-made literature) and it made one liable to prosecution under two articles of Soviet criminal law: for the manufacture and also for the distribution of anti-Soviet propaganda. The government did not prosecute all the instances of *samizdat*, but the danger was always there: every piece of uncensored writing could at any moment be interpreted as anti-Soviet. The *samizdat* was of course very inefficient; it was later augmented by "*tamizdat*" (literally, "publishing over there," where "over there" meant in the West). For reasons that a normal person would never comprehend (at the very moment when one comprehends this reason, one ceases to be a normal person) the Soviet government viewed publishing abroad not as a sign of recognition, international cooperation and expanded understanding, but as an act of disloyalty, betrayal, and duplicity on the part of the author.

I have the one surviving copy of Rein's book. It sits on my shelf next to many other collections of his poetry that were published twenty-five and more years after I "published" the first five copies on my typewriter.

One of the poems from this first ill-fated *samizdat* collection was entitled "The Rooms." Brodsky liked it best of the poems from this book.

> I visited these rooms
> With their random furniture,
> Original lost masterpieces,

As if I had never been there.

Not so: I was in these rooms,
Took off my shoes, stroked someone's hair,
Managed ten words
Imbued with feeling.

Next I moved tables around,
Put one almost at the exit—
Patched and crooked tables—
What was the profit in it?

And the girls, fond of fabrics
That astonish the eye,
Arranged on their bodies
To be crudely stunning,
Having forgiven the table-moving
And some other escapades,
Did not demand good lighting—
For what was the profit in it?

In the mornings, coming out into the squares,
Carried off by a truck,
Called to earth from the bed of it
With shouts of "Get off, now!
We need you! Listen…"
And the rooms, how were the rooms?
They were renovated, they were despaired in;
What have they become—what were they to start with?

My favorite poem from that collection was the one entitled
"My Neighbor, Kotov." In it, Rein played with fire.

In a communal apartment lived Kotov, our fellow citizen,
A shrewd man, missing a finger.
This room on the left he took from someone in a lawsuit,
He sued, the other died, but Kotov remained.

Every evening in the kitchen, he publicly washed his feet

And interpreted news stories from *Izvestia*.
And of those who cooked, washed and listened there
Asked many questions—everything was known to Kotov.

He rarely got drunk. Alone, he poked around—
Scared us when we heard him prowling...
He found meaningless and lonely vases,
Sang limericks, crushed shards of Wedgewood china.

He sat alone on the balcony, swearing and smiling.
Smoking and shaking ashes on the heads of passersby...
Never got letters, was frightened by receipts and telegrams,
And put "A.M. Kotov" on a separate mailbox.

In the summer, I moved away. If I'm stopped and told:
"Remember Kotov? Well, he is a murderer,
Or a thief, or a secret agent..." I will believe it. I have stored
up
A dark stain of dislike. I cannot defend Kotov.

Behind his plywood wall he remained eerily opaque.
What was he hiding? And how to defend him?
Yet once I saw: from the best Saxon china
On Kotov's balcony, stray birds were drinking.

This poem is a brilliant depiction of the Soviet Man, a.k.a
"*sovok*" (which also means "dustpan") in the modern slang. It
deserves a place of honor in the Soviet Encyclopedia as an
ethnographic field guide.

Here is Rein's poem "Beneath The Coats of Arms" (translated
by Robert Reid) that depicts different feelings:

Everything's coming true: awning, glass of Heineken,
And the boozy grin on that tailor's dummy
That's looking at me from the shop next door,
Bad luck, ruin, Russia, Europe...
There on the town hall gleam the arms of Totterdam,
Which is why I stubbornly say again and again:

"I want nothing, know nothing, stop it."
Bad luck, ruin, blockade, annoyance.
Give me everything back, accursed demos of the day,
Renew my flesh, deceive my reason,
May my scars and stigmata crust over,
Oh God, Oh God, you can see that we're not to blame!
Give me that sly Leningrad stink,
Take me back to that beer bar on the Fontanka,
Let Dima, and Tolya, and Osya take their seats.
And then I will say: "Success, success!"
Curse you, wench, longing and poison,
My eternity's on the left, yours on the right.
So let's whisper something in secret,
Take a farewell look beyond the Moika, beyond Lethe,
Beyond the crowds of seraphim, Mohammed and Buddha.
You won't forget me, I won't forget you.
There, beyond eternal time, beyond Einstein's gloom,
Every man once more is good-looking, and awkward, and
partial
To having the last word—that it's useless to utter—
And to the runner on the first snow, that passes over your
skin.

In this poem, Fontanka and Moika are two of the numerous artificial canals that crisscross Leningrad; Mohammed and Buddha are exactly who you think they are; finally, Dima, Tolya, and Osya are Dmitri Bobyshev, Anatoly Naiman, and Iosif Brodsky—young poets who played such a big role in Rein's life. In the foreword to the 1991 collection of Rein's poetry entitled "Against the Hands of the Clock" Brodsky wrote:

"If heaven exists ... then there is a chance that the author of this book and the author of this foreword will one day meet each other there, provided that they overcome their lives. If not, then the author of the foreword will remain thankful that he had the chance to meet the author of these poems under one book cover."

In February 2003 Evgeny Rein visited with me in Boston. For three days he read his poetry non-stop and his voice boomed like a church bell. During this visit in my home, in a way that I was pleased to think symbolic, he received word that he had been awarded the Pushkin Prize, that highest of honors and most coveted of awards for achievement in Russian literature.

5

The Hero's First Appearance

DOZMAROVA'S WEDDING took place on May 20, 1959 in a small (140-square-foot) room on 27 Kolominsakaya Street. The guests were mostly geologists and geophysicists as well as poets from the Mining Institute's literary club. At the time it was dangerous, especially for poets, to be involved openly in literary pursuits. Many elected to study the sciences instead, and the Mining Institute's literary club was one of the most talent-rich in Leningrad.

Among the familiar "geological" faces I noticed a sprinkling of strangers. There were ten chairs for the thirty people present. I arrived late, and all the chairs and all the laps of those sitting on the chairs seemed to be taken. Nor was it possible for me to squeeze in between them. A stranger, an unkempt, red-haired young man in a plaid shirt and jeans, was the only person with a free lap. No, he didn't give me the chair, but squinting slightly he said, "Madame, swear to god, I've met you somewhere before," and pointed to his knees. "They're free, if you are not averse." I sat down in this stranger's lap and he immediately began fidgeting and whispered in my ear, "Row, row, row your boat, gently down the stream—" I managed to jump off before he got to "throw your teacher overboard and listen to her scream."

Looking around for a place to sit I pulled out a cigarette.

That very second, the young man in the plaid shirt jumped out of his seat, grabbed a match, lit it off his backside and offered it to me. Other guests were delighted by this circus trick and more matches were offered. "Oska, light another, light more!" Some guests began trying to light matches off their own pants, but no one could do it. I am not sure whether his secret was in the material of his jeans, or in its tension around his thigh, or in the static electricity of his body, or in a special quick movement of his hand.

That evening, Brodsky was in high spirits. He was filled with jokes, good ones it seemed, as everyone was giggling. I don't remember any of them, but a gesture of his was burned into my mind. After telling a joke, he'd blush, hunch over, and grab his chin. In so doing he gave the impression that shyness and aggressiveness were at war within him. In retrospect, the young Brodsky's reputation for aggressiveness might have been unwarranted. I think it is more likely that he lacked social skills and had never made the effort to polish his behavior.

We left the wedding together. It was getting close to the time of white nights and at three in the morning Leningrad was drowning in iridescent purple twilight. When we came upon an available taxi, I said "Let me take you home Joseph, and then I'll be off myself."

"How could it be otherwise?" my cavalier wanted to know.

"How could it be otherwise? You could take me home first," I said.

"That would never have occurred to me." He snorted and got into the car.

In the summer of 1959 Galya Dozmarova began working in the Far East Geological Expedition, and left for a field job in Yakutya. She was the one who cleared the way for Brodsky to join the expedition.

I don't remember Joseph complaining about his health at that time, but even then it was somehow known that he had a heart condition. Before he left for Yakutya, Dozmarova warned the expedition leader to pay special attention to him. The warning was not ignored and he was treated gently as a result.

In 1960, the next summer, he bolted (according to him) in the middle of a field job. He explained his reasons for leaving differently to different people. To me, he said that the mosquitoes got to him. He gave Yakov Gordin a better-sounding explanation: that the female expedition leader had annoyed him by treating him with excessive attention.

Thanks to Dozmarova, a lot of interesting people ended up in Yakutya, including the poet Leonid Aronson (who soon committed suicide), Yefim Slavinsky (who was later falsely accused of drug use and who now works as a journalist at the BBC), and Vladimir Schvejgolz (who later killed his lover). I'm mentioning these people because they became forever tied to Brodsky in a famous (and fateful) newspaper article that appeared four years later, in 1963.

…Years later, when trying to document the stages of Brodsky's creative life, I asked him many times when he wrote his very first poem. He would always shrug. "I don't know, I don't remember."

"But do you remember what the poem was?"

"If I recall, I'll tell you."

I never did learn about his very first poem. According to him, Brodsky started seriously playing around with poetry when, at age sixteen, he had accidentally read a collection by Boris Slutsky. Later in the expedition to Yakutya he heard the poems of Vladimir Britanishsky, one of my colleagues from the Leningrad Mining Institute. Once in New York, Brodsky awed me with his incredible memory. He recited by heart an excerpt from Britanishsky's poem "Nature," published in 1961 in a modest collection entitled *The First Encounter.*

"Luxuriant nature shines in splendor,
At first glance – decorative,
At second glance eaten up,
At third glance – dull."

"I thought I could do it better," said Brodsky.

[Curiously, Britanishsky himself forgot this poem and later categorically denied authorship.]

The earliest published poem of Brodsky was dated 1957.

Farewell,
Forget

And don't judge me.
Burn my letters,
Like bridges.
Be brave
In your path
Let it be simple
And straight.

In 1958 he was already well known in literary circles for his poems "The Jewish Cemetery near Leningrad" and "Pilgrims." Still, to the question "when did you finally realize that poetry is your calling?" Brodsky would answer according to his mood: "I still don't know if it's my calling," or "since last Saturday," or "relatively recently."

The most sensible answer was given to Rein. To Zhenya's question, "What pushed you towards poetry?" Brodsky answered, "In 1959, in Yakutsk, when walking in that terrible city, I went into a bookstore. I snagged a copy of poems by Baratynsky. I had nothing to read. So I read that book and finally understood what I had to do in life. Or got very excited, at least. So in a way, Evgeny Abramovich Baratynsky is sort of responsible." [Baratynsky, a 19-century contemporary of Pushkin, brought new forms of expression into Russian poetry, but Pushkin's "smooth" poetry was more widely known, and today one needs a sensitive ear to recognize Baratynsky's worth.]

It's a good guess, then, that Brodsky's earliest sense that he had found his calling was in Yakutya in 1959 or 1960.

Two days before he emigrated, Brodsky left Victor and me a memento of himself from the Yakutsk period—a small photograph of himself at the airport there. The airport is in the background and he is standing alone with his legs spread and his hands in his pockets. There was a little note on the back. *An airport where I will never again land. Don't grieve for me.*

As it happened, Brodsky's "Geologic Period" lasted from 1957 to 1961. In the next few years I managed to hire him as an assistant at the Irrigation Project Institute where I worked at the time. The pay was laughable, but it was better than nothing. I remember one project that was called "On the Conditions of the Irrigation and Drainage Canals in the Northwestern Soviet

Union." We bounced around the Leningrad Province examining kilometers of canals, checking their embankments—which looked terrible. They were falling down, coming apart, had all sorts of strange things growing in them. I would describe them and Joseph would photograph them. Joseph was a first-class photographer; it was probably hereditary. His father, Aleksandr Ivanovich, had let him use his equipment. In any case, when I presented my project, I was praised for the "beautiful pictures that brilliantly confirmed the descriptions of canal conditions." It is quite possible that these reports with Brodsky's photographs are still lying around somewhere on the dusty shelves of the Institute.

We even had the crazy idea of making a few rubles by writing a script about the stability of these irrigation canals for a documentary movie. Brodsky came up with a catchy title— "Catastrophe Averted"—meaning that the dilapidated canals weren't going to bury anyone. But the next day the idea for the project died due to the incredible dullness of the material. It was during these trips, however, that I was privileged to hear the poems "The Hills" and "You Will Gallop in the Dark." Brodsky read them aloud to me between two train cars as we were going towards Tikhvin. To this day, forty years later, I can see before my eyes the jittery image of that dirty little space between cars, with cigarette butts on the ground and Brodsky's voice over the groans of the old train.

Joseph wasn't a bad storyteller. He also knew bits of trivia about everything. On those journeys, the 22-year-old Brodsky enlightened me, a married woman and a mother, about sexual practices in Central Asia. He would vividly and passionately describe how the shepherds would fulfill their sexual fantasies, putting a sheep's hind legs into their high Russian boots, so that the animal couldn't run away, and they could...

Since I didn't want to seem a backward provincial, I reacted to these stories with a knowing laugh even though the erotic exploits of these shepherds had shocked me greatly and even figured in my dreams.

But Brodsky was no longer able to go on long geologic expeditions, even though I tried to set him up with employment opportunities many times.

From the time he was a young boy, Joseph had possessed a

unique ability to tune out the real world completely. At such times he was absolutely involved in his own thoughts, never paying attention to the reactions of his companions or giving a thought to their intellectual capacity. It was probably this quirk that prevented him from having a decent career in geology.

Once Brodsky asked me to set him up as a technician on one of the geological expeditions. A short story I wrote some time ago will serve to explain what happened when he went for an interview.

BRODSKY THE GEOLOGIST

Once upon a time, long before Joseph Brodsky became an established, modern poet, a laureate of the MacArthur Foundation for Geniuses, an American poet laureate, a Nobel Prize winner, and a cavalier of the Légion d'Honneur, and even before he had published a single line, he made his living by doing odd jobs à la Jack London and Maxim Gorky. He worked at a military plant, in a morgue, in a boiler room, and on geological expeditions.

Since I also worked as a geologist at that time, we became colleagues, a fact that still fills me with understandable pride.

However, in 1964 the Soviet authorities became "concerned" that Joseph hadn't earned enough to support himself. Having proven this unfortunate fact at two separate court trials, one open to the public and one closed, and after checking him into a mental hospital, the great government of the mighty Soviet Union exiled him to the Norenskaya village in the Arkhangelsk region near the Arctic circle, where, they figured, the young poet would be able to make ends meet by shoveling manure.

After a year and a half, thanks to international pressure, Joseph Brodsky was allowed to return to Leningrad. It was then that Brodsky asked me to help him find a job, preferably in a geological expedition. I talked to my boss, a dreary fellow by the name of Ivan Egorych Bogun, and he wanted to personally interview the prospective employee.

I called Joseph. "You have an interview tomorrow at 10 a.m. sharp. Please, dress neatly, don't forget to shave, and show some enthusiasm for geology."

Brodsky showed up at 11:30 sporting three days of red stubble and wearing a flannel shirt with a few buttons missing and a pair of canvas trousers that had never been touched by an iron. He certainly was no dandy in those days, as he would sometimes appear to be in the West when his lifestyle demanded a tweed jacket, or even black tie and tails.

Alas, without waiting for an invitation, Joseph Brodsky flopped into a chair and blew the smoke of his deadly "Prima" cigarette right in the face of nonsmoker Comrade Bogun.

Comrade Bogun wrinkled his nose and waved his hand in front of his face to disperse the smoke. Joseph didn't get the hint. They then had a conversation along these lines: "Your friend Ludmila tells me you love geology, dream of working in the field, and will be an indispensable worker." (Thus Ivan Egorych, amiably.)

"I can imagine . . ." Brodsky muttered and blushed. (In his youth he was often painfully shy.)

"This year we have three expeditions: to Kolskij Peninsula on the North, to Magadan on the Far Northeast, and to Central Asia. Where would you most like to go?"

"It makes absolutely no difference to me," Brodsky mumbled and grabbed his chin.

"Well then," Comrade Bogun frowned slightly, "what do you like better—cartography or exploration for useful minerals...?"

"Couldn't care less," interrupted Joseph. "Anything to get out of here."

"And yet...what would you prefer to do? Gamma-ray logging, perhaps?" said the boss, not giving up.

"Gamma, beta, delta. . . its all the same to me," countered Brodsky.

Comrade Bogun pursed his lips. "Well, then, which area of geological work interests you?"

"Geological?" Brodsky answered back and let out a giggle.

Bogun lowered his glasses to the tip of his nose and looked intently over them at the poet. Under his gaze, Joseph got awfully embarrassed. He turned beet-red and began to fidget in his chair.

"Allow me to ask," Bogun went on in an icy tone, "if there is anything at all in this life that interests you?"

"But of course!" Brodsky said animatedly, "Very much so!

More than anything I'm interested in the metaphysical essence of poetry." Bogun's eyebrows shot up to the top of his forehead. But Brodsky didn't notice these subtle visual cues. "You see, poetry happens to be the highest form of the existence of language. Ideally, poetry is the negation of mass and the laws of gravity by language. Thanks to poetry, language aspires to the very beginning of time when there was the Word."

At last, Joseph was in his element. He positioned himself more comfortably in the chair, lit yet another cigarette, and deeply inhaled.

"You see," Joseph said in his most confidential tone, "All the tercets, sestets, and decasyllables that make it deeper and richer expand the understanding of the echo that is the Word. They only seem to be artificial constructs of the poetic form. Am I explaining it clearly?" It seemed Brodsky had just noticed Bogun's existence. The shocked Bogun didn't respond. Wearing a hunted look, he had pulled his head back and seemed to have no neck. Meanwhile, Joseph was singing like a nightingale. "I'm very interested in Latin. I'm exploring the different genres of Latin poetry, especially the iambic and lyric. Remember the short poems of Catullus? He often used iambic meter. And he also liked to use the hendecasyllable as a medium for love poetry. Let me give you an example..."

The stupefied Bogun didn't give Joseph the chance... He half rose from his chair, muttered "Excuse me" and signaled to me with his hand.

"Please, see your friend to the elevator."

While escorting Brodsky out of the office, I turned to see Comrade Bogun gazing after me with an insane look in his eyes and twirling his finger at his temple.

6

The Golden Days

FROM THE BEGINNING OF THE SIXTIES till he left for the West (except during a year and a half of exile in the village of Norenskoe in the Arkhangelsk region in the far North of the country), Brodsky used to come over to our place once or twice a week. We would often have guests in the evenings, but Joseph would stop by alone in the middle of the day without so much as a phone call or prior warning. It certainly wasn't a common Russian custom to visit friends this way, and such visits were only tolerated because of the visitor's extraordinary need and ability to communicate his ideas.

We lived two steps away from New Holland, a St. Petersburg neighborhood that Brodsky loved. He was drawn to the industrial landscape of the old naval quarter—haunted by it. The frames of half-built ships, the rusted construction equipment, the giant cranes that looked like dinosaur skeletons. After brooding in New Holland he'd come to our place to warm up, have a bowl of soup, a shot of vodka or a cup of tea, depending on the time of day—and he'd read his poems. If Victor and I weren't home he'd read to my mother and they'd talk about the poets and writers who were the glory of Russian literature in the twenties.

Joseph and his friends, all our friends, loved our house. By the Soviet standards of the time, we had a large non-shared apartment with unusual features: fourteen-foot ceilings, oval

Petersburg windows, balconies and arches. Still, the living room doubled as my mother's bedroom. She had painted the ceiling in it a deep purple as a nostalgic remnant of her avant-garde youth. A friend of my parents, the director of the Leningrad Public Library, Lev Rakov, wrote the following ditty as New Year's wishes.

> May you have fewer purple ceilings
> And more tasty pastries.

The apartment was furnished with beautiful mahogany pieces that had escaped being used as firewood during the Siege of Leningrad. We were not permitted to take any of them with us to America. The composer Solovyov-Sedoy and the poet Sergei Mikhalkov bought them for a song. Mikhalkov bought the two mahogany bookcases with glass doors that almost reached the ceiling. During my childhood, when I'd play hide-and-seek, I would squeeze between them and become invisible. In one were encyclopedias and Russian and European classics; the other held a unique collection of Russian poetry from Kantemir and Zhukovsky to the present day. Many of the books were signed first editions.

We were also denied permission to take these rare and valuable books with us when we emigrated. In 1975 we were only allowed to take books published after 1961. One might wonder why the authorities cared about books published earlier. Most of them were filled with Soviet propaganda anyway, but that was beside the point. The authorities cared, and we did not challenge their rationale, but neither did we play by their rules. When it came time to leave the country, quite a few of our books went abroad illegally with the help of our Western friends.

Though Brodsky stopped at our house often, his intellectual hunger wasn't satisfied by our family alone. His mind needed constant high intellectual and spiritual voltage, and lack of it was to him like a lack of oxygen. Here is another story of mine that became the subject of dinner-table conversation, not only when the participants became accom-plished literary figures, but much earlier, while they remained aspiring writers who hadn't yet tasted public recognition.

SOLITUDE

In the early sixties I was working as a geologist in an enterprise with the unpronounceable name of "*Lengiprovodkhoz.*" It was located at 37 Liteiny Prospect. This building had an elegant entrance that was immortalized by the great Russian poet Nekrasov in his poem "Contemplations at the Main Entrance." Once it had really looked impressive. But when I came back to St. Petersburg in the summer of 2000 I found this beautiful entrance so dilapidated that it looked as if someone had thrown a bomb at it.

True, to get to the hellhole where I worked we didn't use the beautiful entrance, but had to go through the back door in a cement courtyard, past a VD clinic, a boiler room, and a school for hunting dogs. Yet our shabby courtyard had its attractions— namely a ping-pong table.

Brodsky lived two blocks from my work in the Muruzi house located at the corner of Liteiny and Pestelya street. In the summer, he would often drop by during my lunch hour for a game of ping-pong.

One day, a few minutes before lunch, I heard angry male voices coming from the courtyard. I couldn't make out the words but someone was arguing. When I looked out my window I saw the following scene:

A disheveled Brodsky was sitting on the ping-pong table, energetically swinging his paddle and trying to prove something to our mutual friend, the poet Anatoly Naiman. Naiman, pale, with trembling lips, was running back and forth along the table and suddenly, stretching out his hand toward Brodsky, let out a blood-curdling scream. I couldn't make out the words from the third floor, but it sounded like a condem-nation, or even a curse. Brodsky, looking serene, put down the paddle and placed his hands on his chest à la Napoleon, and spat at Naiman's feet. Naiman stiffened for a second and then ran forward trying to knock down the table with Joseph on it. But Brodsky, with his greater mass, grabbed Naiman by his shoulders and pressed his head against the table. I tumbled downstairs and ran to them.

"One feels fear of death because one is estranged from

71

God!"—Brodsky howled, knocking Naiman's head against the table. "It is the result of our separation, abandonment and total solitude. Can't you understand something as simple as that?"

As it turned out, the young poets had been wandering about since early morning along the New Holland embankments, reading poetry to each other. Then they talked about the solitude of the creative individual. Then they complained bitterly about their own solitude. This rather philosophical contemplation had become a personal and passionate discussion when they started to compare who was suffering more from solitude and abandonment. Toward noon they became very hungry, and neither of them had any money to buy lunch. Their moods had turned dark.

While trying to figure out which one of them was more miserable and lonely, Brodsky's existential mood had finally clashed with Naiman's transcendental trajectory, and in the courtyard of *"Lengiprovodkhoz"* the young geniuses started fighting, unable to divide solitude fairly between the two of them. [End]

It was the fall of 1961. Brodsky wouldn't leave his house for days at a time. He was madly, thirstily writing his poem "Procession." He needed listeners immediately. Since for an eight-hour period each day I was only two blocks from his house, I was always ready to drop my boring water tower projects, run over and hear another chapter. Joseph would call around noon, counting on my lunch break. Then his mother, Maria Moiseevna, would take the phone and confirm the invitation. "You should definitely come over, dear. I just baked a mushroom pie."

The Brodsky family had one rather big room in a huge communal apartment where four other families lived. Iosif's parents had partitioned the room to provide Joseph's quarters, which they proudly called a "half-room." From floor to ceiling, it was filled with books and manuscripts. A bed, a chair and a hi-fi occupied the rest of the space. The parents' part of the room served as their bedroom, dining room and living room...

Our lunch would stretch out to two hours. In his half-room cluttered with books, I was witness to a miracle. Called to life by the slightly nasal, almost sing-song voice of the author, the heroes of "The Procession" solemnly passed before my eyes...

Among them were Harlequin, Colombine, the Violinist, the Cry, the Poet, Count Myshkin (from Dostoyevsky), Don Quixote, the Devil, Hamlet, the Thief, the Happy Man, the Tired Man, the Lovers...

...Straight ahead, my Fatherland,
Where we are driven by brave swindlers,
Where we are prodded by vicious ideas
And a chorus of apoplectic leaders.
<...>
To see again the golden park paths,
The sunset, more scarlet than flames,
The rustle of branches, leaves like wreaths,
And someone's weak gaze from afar?
And the blue expanse over the Neva,
And the blue sky over self.

Or from the romance of Count Myshkin:

To come to the Motherland in a carriage,
To come to the Motherland in despair,
To come to the Motherland for death,
To die in the Motherland with passion.

Or
This cry is for every one of us,
This city falls from our eyes,
In flight along the boulevards
Under the crumpled moons of streetlights.

This is a cry for one's own fate,
These are tears for oneself,
These are wordless sobs,
A funereal tolling of bells.

....

It's always thus: when you look back,
Your past life is a crowd,

73

Unknowable, bizarre perhaps,
And when death comes, as if for the first time,
No one, no one knows us.

At night I would often dream about the heroes of "The Procession." Next to these protagonists other characters would appear, but they were always influenced by the images of "The Procession." I had one of the dreams so often that I even told it to Brodsky.

This is the dream.

COZEBRA

I am leaving my house on the Moika. I think it's night, but it's fairly light out, so it should be a white night, sometime in the middle of summer. Our street is completely empty. I walk out onto Morskaya Street, where presumably one could find buses and people and cars, but there too, not a soul is to be seen. The windows of all the houses are wide open but no lights can be seen within. I panic and fly into a phone booth. I call one person, another, and another—all I hear is ringing, no one answers. I run across St. Isaac's Square onto Nevsky Prospect and into the open doors of the Hermitage Museum in the Winter Palace. Surprisingly, there is no guard at the entrance. I'm running through the empty regal halls of the Winter Palace, yelling and calling out, but no one answers. Only my echo is dying in the faraway rooms and in the "Gallery of 1812" the war banners are waving gently among the portraits of the heroes of the Russo-French War, with Napoleon.

I run out onto the square in front of the Winter Palace again, not a soul is around. And then, all of a sudden, dust devils come spinning out of Arch of the General Headquarters building—more and more of them, as if being pushed forward by a hurricane. They are lifting upwards as if in the vortex of a tornado. Behind them, I see a mob running at me—men, women with children in their arms, old people, and all of them have a crazed and fearful look. I try to stop one and then another, I grab one man by the arm, I'm asking what happened but no one answers. One turns to me in terror and points to the General

Headquarters Arch. Then everything suddenly disappears. No dust, no people. On the asphalt—one child's sandal, a pair of broken glasses and a handkerchief.

From the arch I see a stroller on high wheels slowly roll out. Nobody is pushing it, it's going by itself. I see an old woman sitting inside. Either she's a midget, or she's legless, but she fits into the stroller in her entirety. She's rolling with her head held high. She's got salt and pepper snakelike curls, a wrinkled face, a strong chin, and wide-open coal-black eyes. She has a bumpy nose reminiscent of poet Akhmatova's and a beauty mark on her upper lip. Her face is calm and her beautifully drawn lips look ready to smile ironically. Her whole body is wrapped in a white sheet whose ends are almost touching the ground. She's approaching, but paying no attention to me. She rolls by so close that I feel the tips of the sheet brush past me. And from this gentle touch my feet buckle under me from horror. "Is it you, that everyone is running from?" I ask. The old woman regally nods her head. "But why? Why is everyone afraid of you?" The woman had already slowly rolled by, but she turned around with her mysteriously ironic look. "What, you don't know?" She has a low, almost raspy voice. "I am—the Cozebra."

Then I wake in terror, covered in cold sweat.

"Cozebra?" asks Brodsky. "Cozebra, Cozebra, Cozebra," he mutters and shrugs his shoulders. "Not bad, I like the concept. She could have definitely been in my procession."

Thirty years later, in 1991, I read his magnificent poem "Portrait of Tragedy" and was struck all of a sudden by the resemblance between the face of tragedy and the Cozebra image of my youth.

Let's look at the face of tragedy. Let's see its creases,
It's aquiline profile, its masculine jawbone. Let's hear its rhesus
contralto with its diabolic rises:
the area of effect beats cause's wheezes.
How are you, tragedy? We haven't seen you lately.
Hello, the medal's flip side gone lazy.
Let's examine your aspects, lady.

....

Ah, but to press ourselves against her cheek, her Gorgon
Coiling hairdo!......................

(Translated by Brodsky. First appeared in *The New Yorker* in 1996.)

Looking back, I have to say that we all agreed that Brodsky
was talented, even very talented—but we didn't think of him as
an outstanding genius. In our circle, everyone wrote poetry, and
almost everyone was a genius. And we all took for granted this
unbelievable mixing of images—our 21-year-old redhead in torn
jeans with whom we gossiped, drank, hung out, and the creator
of the spellbinding "Procession." Even today I think of this early
poem as an incredible work of literature. It's too bad that in his
final years Brodsky used to wince and make a face at any mention
of "The Procession."

It is a small wonder that Brodsky impressed sophisticated
young intellectuals who would not blink in the face of his poetry's
complexity. But what would uneducated people say? The
following example doesn't have statistical significance (whatever
statistical significance might mean in poetry). However, I can't
help but recall it. When the Soviet government was trying to
justify sending Brodsky into exile with forced labor on the farm,
one of the reasons was that "plain" readers found his poetry
meaningless and hard to understand. Had it been easy to
understand, well, the government might have tolerated Brodsky's
"antisocial" behavior better.

THE VOICE OF THE PEOPLE

Uncle Grisha, an uneducated relative of my nanny Nulya,
was the first to tell me that "Brodsky is, in fact, not like us. He is
cut from a different cloth." Nulya's relatives would often come
to the city from rural Russia to buy essential goods. Village stores
had empty shelves. All one could buy there was vodka (if one
was lucky), eggs, and slogans and portraits of communist leaders
(buying these required no luck). So Nulya's relatives were often
in our house. They came bearing gifts: dried and salted
mushrooms that they had picked and salted themselves; wild

berries. And they left our home with sugar, bagels, sunflower oil, and other goods. When we could, we would give them clothes.

On the day in question, Uncle Grisha's mission was to get a cassock for a close friend of his, a priest. "The Father conducts services in rags." I spent all day running from store to store looking for material and finally found a beautiful scarlet brocade with a gold design. Uncle Grisha gently felt the cloth and said, "no one in Russia will have such a gorgeous cassock."

That very evening, my friends gathered at my place and Brodsky brought new poems to read. Uncle Grisha stood in the doorway of the living room and absolutely refused to come and sit with us. He stood that way in the doorway without moving for two hours. Joseph read a lot that evening, with an agitation that was unusual, even for him.

You are my woods and my water! Who will make a detour and who, like a draft,
Will cleave to you, who will speak directly and who make hints,
Who stand aside, place palms upon your shoulders,
Who will lie on his back in a freezing brook.
Do not force me to leave, to sort everything out,
Because this isn't a life, this constant pain
That cleaves to you, so that you are deaf to the coming of spring;
Only treetops incessantly whisper in the dark,
Like a pendulum of sleep.
(translated by Katerina Simons)

When Brodsky blurted out his lines, Uncle Grisha crossed himself. I started to inadvertently follow him with my eyes. He kept crossing himself and was whispering something under his breath after every line of Brodsky's "From the Suburbs to the Center."
It means there are no partings.
It means we needn't ask for forgiveness
From our dead.
This means the winter will not return.
Only one thing is left:
To walk the earth without discontent,

It's impossible to fall back.
To get ahead—only that is possible.

Then we drank and chatted. We invited Uncle Grisha to join us, but he refused and shut himself up in Nulya's room.

The next morning, when Uncle Grisha was dipping a *sooshka* (ring-shaped cracker) into his tea and sucking on it with his toothless mouth, I asked him whether or not he liked the poetry. "I don't understand poetry. I've only had four years of school. But the issue isn't the poetry, it's the thoughts...your Joseph spoke so many thoughts last night, most of them wouldn't have even occurred to another person even if they lived to be a hundred. And the way he read, it was as though he was praying. Does he believe in God?"

"I don't know, Uncle Grisha, I never asked."

"He ain't the only one," Nulya told him. "They got other folks who write too."

Uncle Grisha shook his head disbelievingly. "There ain't no other folks who write like that. Naw, he ain't a simple person. But he's gotta believe because God made him special and blessed him with thoughts. It seems to me, He gave him a mission to preach His thoughts. If only he doesn't take the wrong path." I was sure that Uncle Grisha meant to call him "Chosen," but didn't quite find the words.

A while ago, in Brodsky's *The Big Book of Interviews* I read an interview he gave to Dmitri Radyshevsky. The reporter's last question was, "When you think of the Almighty what favor do you ask of him?" "I don't ask," Brodsky said. "I just hope that He approves of what I do." If Uncle Grisha were alive, he would have been happy to hear such an answer.

Today it seems to me that the early sixties was the most important time of our lives. This is true not only in the sphere of social consciousness, but in personal relationships as well. We had a few married couples in our circle of friends. Tolya Naiman was married to Era Korobova, Zhenya Rein was married to Galya Narinskaya, Victor Shtern was married to Ludmila Davidovich, Bobyshev was married to Natasha Kamentseva (but for such a short time it's almost not worth remembering; he was soon single again).

Brodsky remained a bachelor. He was always infatuated with somebody, often with more than one woman at a time, transfixed by the beauty and charm of each, unable to choose.

He loved Rein and his wife Galya the most. He was even slightly in love with Galya (as were other members of our group). Brodsky's relationship to the Reins can be judged by the dedication of the poem "The Procession." He gave Galya a copy of his poem as a birthday present. I don't remember why I have it now.

"Galya, on your birthday, in these happy years when everything is wonderful remember me, regards to Zhenya as always, I will love you both all my life. Galya, this 'Procession' belongs to you more than to anybody else. -J. Brodsky"

Here I want to clarify a bit the conventional wisdom about Brodsky's unjustified and unwarranted sharpness, unyieldingness, and readiness to laugh at another's expense. It's true, and at the same time it isn't. With his close friends whom he really loved, he was gentle, kind, and tender. Galya Narinskaya and Zhenya Rein fell into that category. Galya was also my closest friend of many years. When I was emigrating from Russia, I wrote up a list of people with whom it would be especially painful to part. Galya was number three on that list.

Rein brought her from Moscow to Leningrad and introduced us at some event at the House of Writers. I was massively pregnant at the time, round as a bagel, with swollen feet and a puffy face. The sight of this elegant beauty with a long cigarette between her fingers, in a perfectly fitting terra-cotta dress and spike heels, crushed me. Victor later said that I'd even gone yellow, probably flooded with bile. I said hello in an icy tone and proceeded to ignore her. And secretly swore to call upon all the poisonous sarcasm in my arsenal to obliterate this "arrogant upstart from the capital."

On the way home we took the same trolley from the House of Writers and sat next to each other. The men hung over us. I sulked, getting ready to loathe her utterly, but then Galya caressed me with the look of her bottomless jet-black eyes. "Rein told me so many good things about you and I am happy that we've finally met," she said. "I don't have anyone in Leningrad.

And I felt right away that I could trust you... I hope so much that we'll be friends."

I was speechless. The poisonous cobra inside me curled up at her feet like a kitten, and... I loved her for the rest of my life.

God favored Galya Narinskaya with intelligence, an easygoing nature, a great sense of humor, boundless charm and unerring literary taste. Her kindness and equanimity created around her a "zone of repose."

Galya had graduated from the Moscow Petroleum Institute (having gone there probably for the same reason that I had gone to the Leningrad Mining Institute), and worked in that field for about a year. Somewhere I have a touching photograph— Narinskaya in a mine, wearing a miner's helmet, holding a lantern. But this image was not typical of her. I see her sitting in the kitchen with her legs crossed, in tight-fitting jeans, with a goddess-like figure, a cigarette in her mouth. On the table among the piles of plates—an English novel, across the table—one of the "singers of the magical Akhmatova chorus" with burning eyes and a poem in his hands.

In the early sixties, as Brodsky wrote to the Reins, "everything was wonderful." Galya and Rein appeared to be a happy couple, unlike Naiman and his wife Era, who never seemed to be in harmony. Yet at some point both the Reins and the Naimans got divorced. Naiman obtained his happiness by taking Galya away from his best friend, Zhenya Rein. I understand that what I am saying sounds anachronistic. After all, Galya was a modern woman and was not somebody who could be "taken away." All her life she did pretty much as she pleased. So one could blame her for playing "musical chairs" as much as Naiman, but somehow all of us thought about this in terms of Naiman's actions, not in terms of Galya's.

Joseph Brodsky, being an old-fashioned moralist (except in respect to his own behavior), strongly disapproved of this shift and even temporarily broke off his friendship with Naiman. The friendship was later restored, but the old cloudless trust never returned.

During this time in the sixties, the very air of our home was filled with poetry, so many poets gave readings there. During the late fifties and early sixties, Gleb Gorbovsky was an extremely popular Leningrad poet. Songs written to the words of his poems were so well-known they were considered folk songs and were sung on geological expeditions and by college students on work brigades when instead of spending September in classrooms they were sent to farms where they would harvest cabbage or potatoes or build dams and roads. And they were sung at student parties, that is at gatherings of more than three persons between 17 and 30 years of age. Even now, 40 years later, if you wake me up in the middle of the night, I will still sing with feeling "Night Streetlights," "Ah, you, Breasts," or "On the Couch."

I remember one poetry reading at our home where Gleb Gorbovsky was the main attraction. The guests had already gathered, when Brodsky, Rein and Gorbovsky showed up with an unknown poet from Moscow who was, in Rein's words "a genuine genius." (Or as Nulya informed me, having let them in, "Zhenka and Oska with two guys who have had one too many.")

Gorbovsky volunteered to read first. The poems were rolled up in a tube and stuck out of his pocket. He made an attempt at reading, but was too drunk to put two words together. So he gave the roll to Rein and said, "You go ahead." Rein began to read... I still remember some of the poems:

God's little birds' mysterious babble.
The cage of life, the seeds of love.
No, from the sky, like a widowed swan,
I will not throw myself—do not expect this.
Goodbye, old galoshes,
I'll be sorry if you are through,
If you, heavy with your burden,
Will sometimes make a mistake.
Inevitably resonant valleys
Will be overgrown with iron grass.
We drank everything but shoe polish,
We drank longing, we drank living water.
I am sick of everything, even what I love,
Goodbye, funny faces of pages!
It wasn't wine that wore out my heart –
But the mysterious babble of God's birds.
(translated by Katerina Simons)

And the poem "Boredom" was worthy, I thought then, to be the hymn of our generation:

I fear boredom, I fear boredom,
From boredom, I could kill.
From boredom, I am more pliable than that bitch of yours.
Give me a bomb—I will bomb,
Got a crowbar?—I'll knock out a rail,
And throw a train full of meat from the bridge!
I will drink your blood from boredom,
My girl, pink beauty...
Boredom, boredom will eat a man,
Cut off the light in the apartment.
I am the son of the twentieth century,
I am the gardener of its slanders,
Tiller of corpses, baker of violence,
Wine pourer of deep tears.
From boredom I turn blue,
Like from gas! Boredom is a narcotic.
I sleep. Flies alight. Sting.
It is so boring that... you can hear it!
Like singing....
Shoot me, please,
It is I, the generation, that asks.
(translated by Katerina Simons)

The poems were wonderful and everyone admired them. Especially Gorbovsky himself. He would wave his arms, gaze at his audience with misty eyes and exclaim, "What the hell! That's me! Not too shabby!"

"Moscow's genuine genius" expressed his admiration with a long string of colorful obscenities. Gorbovsky gave a start. "What the fuck do you think you are doing, cursing in a respectable home? Here are paintings, furniture, an older lady," He pointed his finger at Mother. "Hey, Zhenka, Oska, get him the fuck outta here!"

He tried to get up himself to get the guest out, but fell back in his chair. Rein started to move in on the Moscow poet, rolling his eyes in a terrifying way, and the poet took off and rolled down the stairs. I have never learned the name of "the genuine genius."

Warm Khrushchev winds were blowing through Russia and the Cultural Thaw was in full bloom when a French industrial exhibit opened in Sokolniki in Moscow. I don't remember for sure, but I think it was 1961. Usually a Sokolniki exhibition would boast of the outstanding achievements of miners from the Ukraine, of cotton harvesters from Uzbekistan, and other important manifestations of selfless efforts for the benefit of the country that was trying, in Khrushchev's words, to "catch up with and overtake" the West. A French exhibit was not to be missed, so I began to call friends to find someone to go with. Brodsky responded. We went together and then separated—we were excited by different aspects of life. You could not drag him away from the book pavilion, while I was stuck at *"La Mode d'Aujourd'hui."* Black walls, recessed blinking lights, everything foreign: Balenciaga and Dior tickling your nostrils, Yves Montand pouring into your ears and the goods on sale.... Brodsky could have described it, but Brodsky was criminally indifferent to fashion, or so I thought. But there were other opinions. The young dandy Zhenya Rein (a regular at secondhand shops, the only places where one could buy foreign clothes, for which he felt boundless love) claimed that Brodsky's attitude to clothes escaped my notice. His love for blue Oxford shirts, for example. Zhenya claimed that Brodsky used to own one in Leningrad when nobody else did and that he never parted with it. When the collar wore out and the shirt was no longer presentable, Brodsky became quite forlorn. However, the resourceful Rein advised him to have it turned and thus brought it back to life.

At the French exhibit, Brodsky spent all his time in the book pavilion. Unfortunately, the bookstands were empty after two days. There were no foreign bookstores in Russia and one could not buy foreign books by mail order. Some research libraries had foreign books, but to borrow them, one had to present an official request from one's employer explaining why this book was needed for a specific project. This is why everything was stolen from the book pavilion, and the pavilion had to be closed. The exhibit director's reaction was quintessentially French: "What a remarkably cultured country," he said. "Even thieves here are interested in art."

The restaurant Maxim's was among the exhibitors here. The menu featured lobsters. The two of us didn't have enough money for one lobster claw, but Brodsky said firmly that it is impossible to go home to "Peter" without trying the lobster.

I suggested we walk around the exhibit looking at the floor; maybe we'd find a tenner. I had this idea after Rein told me how to scrape together enough money for ice cream.

"You walk along Nevsky from the Palace Square, staring at the ground and saying, 'I really want some ice cream. I desperately need ice cream. More than anything in the world, I want ice cream. I crave ice cream the way I've never craved any woman. I will die if I don't have some ice cream this minute...' The money will start showing up. By the time you reach the ice cream shop across from Marat Street, you will have found the needed amount. The important thing is to convince fate."

By the way, I remember how Victor and I and Brodsky and his girlfriend Marina ordered some ice cream with nuts in that shop. Two scoops each. And how Joseph went to complain that his portion didn't have any nuts at all, and how the countergirl showed him the empty bin, shouting, "How am I going to get nuts for you? Give birth to them?"

Joseph rejected the idea of looking for money on the floor. He would make a few phone calls and tomorrow we'd have the money.

He did get the money. But when we walked up to Maxim's, the line was longer than for Lenin's mausoleum. Besides, somebody shouted from the door in Russian, "Don't waste your time standing in line. We are all out of lobsters."

We all liked to have fun, to eat and drink, and the tragic poet Brodsky did not love "the good things in life" any less than the rest of us. But for some reason, it was my vanity that was singled out by my friends for constant teasing. "You are so materialistic," Naiman used to say, having stuffed himself with meatballs at my dinner table.

Unfortunately, the Russian calendar was not rich in holidays. To be sure, there were holidays: the Day of the Soviet Army in February, International Women's Day in March, the International

Workers' Festival in May ("festival" denoted two free days in a row), the October Revolution Festival in November, the Day of the Stalin Constitution in December. We celebrated these holidays all right, with parties, drinking and fun... Still, we were never celebrating the official reason for the holidays, only the occasion for drinking and fun.

April 30th and December 31st were therefore "sacred" dates. The former is my birthday, the latter New Year's Eve, and neither day belonged to the official calendar. We could celebrate them because of their meaning, not because they were ordained by the government. On January 1, still with a hangover after celebrating New Year's, I would begin to consider whom to invite to my birthday party, and on May 1, the day after the birthday, I would began to poll friends about where to celebrate New Year's Eve. The success of a party of course depended on the strategic seating of guests. Someone was always in love with someone, someone was always offended by someone, and a certain person could not for the moment stand a certain other.

In other groups irresponsible chaos reigned and key moments were left to chance. Once I was visiting a sick aunt in an overcrowded communal apartment. The neighbors in the next room were celebrating something—we could hear shouting, screams, music and stomping. Suddenly, amidst the racket, a woman's voice plaintively asked, "And who-o will sleep with who-o?" Apparently there was no response, since the curious voice continued to whine, loudly and persistently, "No, you must tell me, who is going to sleep with who. I must know who will sleep with who." Finally, the annoyed voice of the hostess could be heard, "Stop bugging me. Everyone will sleep with whomever they want."

In our house, this kind of self-determination was not permitted. After all, if you leave guests to their own devices, who knows what might happen. Once, because of a lapse in attention, I seated Genrikh Orlov next to Brodsky's girlfriend Marina Basmanova. First Genrikh lightly put his arms around Marina's shoulders, then he covered her hand with his. Joseph, sitting to the left of Marina, did not approve and stuck a fork in Genrikh's hand.

Several parties later, this episode was repeated, the only

difference being that now Marina Rachko was in the role of Marina Basmanova, and the jealous defender was her husband Igor Yefimov. Genrikh Orlov was the same. Maybe even the fork was the same.

To minimize accidents of this kind, guests in our house usually took their seats according to place cards on their plates. The card inscriptions had to rhyme. The rhyme did not have to be perfect, but it had to be there. The inscriptions' veracity or even simple politeness were incidental, considered important neither by the hostess (the author) nor by the guests (the readers). For example:

"Toy terriers stick out from a clutch – These are Tolya and Era."

"Glum and somber, like an orphan – Joseph Brodsky dragged himself here."

"Cannot live without pel'meni and foreign rags – or Rein, Evgeny."

"This is not a painting by Renoir – This is Marina Zhezhelenko."

Etc, etc.

"Why do people tolerate this stupid gibberish?" Mother shrugged.

"Because, though the form is imperfect, deep meaning shines through." Father's sarcasm was boundless.

I remember how Brodsky scared everyone during the banquet in honor of my dissertation defense. As Nulya liked to say, "everyone had had a few" and Oska was smashed. Our dining room was small and the banquet was held in the living room with tables pushed together. Our apartment was on the second and a half floor, rather high, because of the aforementioned four-meter ceilings in our building. The dining room gave onto the balcony, where people took turns smoking. Suddenly, someone was knocking on the living room window from outside. Brodsky had come out into the balcony, climbed over the side railing and was standing on the ledge. He was holding on to the molding with one hand and with the other was pantomiming to have a glass of vodka passed to him through the opening in the window. So he was playing a dashing and reckless Dolohov from *War and Peace*. Mother covered her face with her hands. Everyone jumped up and stood frozen. It was too scary to shout, impossible to go after him. Joseph stood, swaying a little, I don't know if he did it on purpose to scare us. Three minutes must have passed but it seemed like eternity. Finally, hugging the wall, he made his way to the balcony, climbed back over the railing and entered the room with a "What, is something the matter?" look.

We wrote occasional and non-occasional poetry to one another. Sad to say, in those years it did not occur to us to save them. Most are lost forever, and only a few have survived. I was presented with these verses for the Ph. D. dissertation banquet:

Joseph Brodsky –
To Ludmila Shtern
Upon the defense of her dissertation.

A guest without a ruble is a turd and a scumbag
When alone, more so en masse.
But is a hero when he has
A few words in his pocket.
Ludmila, for how many years
Around you like a damned horde
We buzzed, swarmed, rooted
And, crudely speaking, stank.
<...>
Friends from all over, salivating,
Drooling wellwishers flying in
And trumpeting your heroic deeds.
I pray to God I will lie in my grave
Like Vit'ka, next to you.
(translated by K. Simons)

Unfortunately, the middle is lost. About 20 years ago, when Brodsky first mentioned that he saw me fit for the "Pimen" role, I tried to recover some of the old poems. I turned to the author for help. After all, getting a Ph.D. was an important event in my life. "Do you really think I remember that drivel?" the poet replied courteously.

As a matter of fact, it later turned out that I was not the only one to whom Brodsky began his congratulations with a variation on the theme of "A guest without a ruble..." "Almost an Ode on September 14, 1970" which Brodsky wrote for poet Kushner's birthday begins the same way. In my opinion Brodsky wasn't stealing from himself. Rather, ideas that lay near the surface of his consciousness popped up easily, that's all.

I am comforted that "my" congratulation had been written first. I defended my dissertation on June 7, while Kushner's birthday was on September 14, 1970.

And here are verses by Sergei Dovlatov dedicated to my visit to him during his sore throat. The inclusion of these lines is not so much to demonstrate my intimacy with their author as to reveal the way we wrote to each other—Dovlatov no less than Brodsky:

Among all other objects
Dalmetov[1] stands apart
In his incomparable beauty
Unappreciated by you.

It is surprising and dear,
That Ludmila came to me.
Gave me milk,
And dissolved the lump in my throat.

For this I give you Toulouse[2]
Incomparable Frenchman,
Let this Toulouse
Strengthen our ties.

---

[1]Dovlatov's name was frequently mispronounced by those who did not know him well, and he frequently referred to himself with the misnomers.

[2] "Toulouse" here is a book containing reproductions of Toulouse-Lautrec's paintings; it bore the stamp of the Hermitage, indicating that it had been stolen from the state's collection and given to me. A very bold thing to have done!

7

Pasik

IN AN ODE DEDICATED TO MY MOTHER on her birthday Brodsky wrote about our home: "...there the sight of Pasik moved me..." Who was the mysterious Pasik and why did the sight of him move the poet?

Mother won the two-week-old kitten in a game of Preference. This was remarkable because Mother was not, to put it mildly, a good card player. She usually played cards with some old friends, who took turns. These card games were accompanied by gossip, jokes, and discussion of the latest art news. By this time, all these friends of Mother's had become well-established academics, professors of literature or foreign languages, and only Mother remained a free spirit. She did not have the discipline for an academic career. Nor did she have the patience to calculate the consequences of each card move. The way she played her cards often produced loud screams from her partners who could not understand how Mother could not see the obvious (and disastrous) results of her actions. But this time around Lady Luck was on Mother's side: she won big, and was offered a kitten in lieu of money. Like any two-week-old kitten, he was adorable and aroused warm feelings in all who saw or touched him. Mother was happy with her prize and announced a contest for the best name. The term "Pass," from the card game, was suggested by Brodsky and unanimously approved with the addition of the diminutive "ik." The names of Russian cats often contain letters 'k' and 's' because Russian cats are sensitive to these sounds. (When we emigrated, I was surprised to learn that American cats are totally indifferent to them.) Iosif adored his "godson." Cats in general were his favorite animals. Whenever he could, he had a cat around the house. He loved to keep a cat on his lap, and some of the best pictures of him are with a cat. Once he said: "Have you ever noticed? Cats don't make a single graceless move."

Asked who he would like to be in the next life, or in what guise he would like to return, Brodsky would reply unhesitatingly: "a cat, of course; as a cat."

When Pasik grew up, he became a fluffy, ash-gray cat without a trace of any other color. Pasik's dignity was regal. His eyes, green and round like gooseberries, were imperturbable and indifferent as they looked at the world. Never, on principle, did he come when he was called and he even turned away contemptuously when someone shoved a piece of chicken or fish under his nose, seeming to shrug his cat shoulders as if to say: "Because of this bit of nonsense you dare to disturb me?" Not that he loathed human food and preferred cat food. There was no such thing as cat food in Russia, and every cat (or dog or whatever pet you could afford to keep in your apartment) was perfectly happy to subsist on human food. Indeed, that very piece of chicken "accidentally" left on the floor would disappear in the blink of an eye. The main thing was to play the game by the rules—not to see or hear. Image was more important than reality.

As with subtle, delicate natures everywhere, Pasik was full of contradictions. Although he did not respond when his name was called, neither did he run away, and when picked up, even by a stranger, did not struggle but melted, exhibiting a complete paralysis of will power. He could be manipulated into any position: thrown over the shoulder, wrapped around your throat as a fur collar, or placed on his back with a newspaper between his paws and a pair of sunglasses on his nose. In that pose he would lie still for hours, days, or centuries.

Iosif used to say that Pasik pacified him like a tranquilizer and the poet even tried to rename him "Bromide." But the Russian word for "Bromide" (Brom) sounded too much like the Russian word for "Thunder" (Grom), and that reverberation did not suit this cat's bucolic nature. Also, as I mentioned earlier, the names for Russian cats have to include at least one s-sound. Most Russian cats will come to you, a total stranger, if you say "kiss-kiss-kiss" loudly enough. Anyway, the new name did not stick.

On the Eve of 1963 I decided to create a New Year's literary magazine, dedicated entirely to Pasik. Self-made magazines, newspapers and even theatrical productions (they were called "*kapustniks*," from "*kapusta*" for cabbage) were a necessary mode of expression in an environment where we were not allowed to publish our work. Some of us would do this kind of production because we did not belong to the party-approved establishment. Others managed to be accepted into the party-approved establishment but still could publish only what was acceptable to the party. Self-made magazines let us release our energy. We also had some fun parodying the style of official publications with their wooden language, suspicion towards anything of foreign origin, uncritical admiration for everything that had originated in the mother country and insincere appeals for contributions by the young and bright. This tongue-in-cheek mockery was not offensive enough to attract the attention of the KGB, but gave us the feeling that we were able to express ourselves. Circulation was of course severely limited, but who cared? With a few copies, you could reach most of your friends and enjoy their approval, and still hope to avoid the wrath of the KGB by remaining below their radar.

Any topic would do for such a magazine: the celebration of somebody's birthday, description of a vacation in a remote place, review of a new book by a notoriously official writer. Our cat Pasik was eminently qualified as raison d'être for such a magazine.

The poetry section of the magazine boasted contributions by the leading poets of Leningrad: Brodsky, Bobyshev, Rein, Naiman. My mother Nadezhda Kramova joined them not so much because she had a similar poetic stature but because she was close to the editor.

Well, things like that happen in official magazines, right? Why should I have displayed any scruples in deciding who to publish?

The critic's corner was taken by my friend the film critic Marina Zhezhelenko, who by that time was already working in the quite official Leningrad Research Institute of Cinematography. The Institute studied the history and current work of the world cinema and, most importantly, often showed modern movies not available to the general public. These movies were shown for the benefit of Institute researchers only, who were often magnanimous enough to invite their friends. Marina's friendship had kept me quite up to date.

The science section was headed by my husband Victor Shtern, who was a specialist in automatic control systems and in what later would become Computer Science (the word "cybernetics," appropriated at that time, could not be used officially because, as with genetics, it was ruled by the Communist Party to be an invention of bourgeois propaganda aimed at diverting the proletariat from its victorious struggle with the worldwide forces of capitalism).

As indicated earlier, I was the self-appointed Editor-in-Chief.

Unfortunately, during our emigration shakedown the Soviet customs officers going through the ton of letters, papers, and photographs that we wanted to take with us found and confiscated the three pages of Victor's essay which dealt with the model of a feline brain. In addition they tore off the photograph of Pasik (taken by Brodsky) from the magazine's cover. Either they had been struck by Pasik's beauty, or had decided that the cat's portrait was really a cleverly masked "secret Soviet factory plan."

In America I replaced the cover photo with one of a strange cat—from a Picasso reproduction.

Not so long ago my nanny Nulya sent me one old, bedraggled photo of our Pasik, but of course the quality of that picture leaves much to be desired.

And so...without further introduction:

PASIC No. 1
Preface

"PASIC" is the name of the new literary and political magazine, published by the future Steering Committee of the Leningrad chapter of the Soviet Writers' Union.

The mission of this magazine is to highlight a variety of issues in contemporary literature, art, science, technology, and social sciences.

The name "PASIC" has not been chosen randomly, but dictated by life itself, as it is created by

Poets
Actors
Screenwriters
Inventors
Critics

While gathering material for this very first, New Year's edition the editors decided to bypass an established tradition—that of calling upon veterans of the medium.

In this edition you will hear the voices of the young. Yes, our authors are young, they are not yet thirty. But they have a certain life experience, and, most importantly, an acute contemporary sensibility, boundless love for the Cat, and genuine interest in his destiny, hopes and aspirations.

The first section, "Poetry," is represented by the poets Dmitri Bobyshev, Iosif Brodsky, Nadezhda Kramova, Evgeny Rein, and Anatoly Naiman (hiding behind the pen name A. Chelnov).

They are not alike; all are profoundly original. An emotionally expansive ode by Brodsky stands cheek by jowl with the epic verses of Rein, flowing by like the swollen waters of his native river, calm and wide. A seductively graceful and elegant sonnet and an acrostic by Bobyshev peacefully coexist with them.

One might well be alarmed, however, by the offering of the undoubtedly gifted poet A. Chelnov. A note of pessimism and lack of faith in the glorious Soviet future of the Cat constantly crop up in his poetry. It makes one wish to give the poet a loving, fatherly rebuke, and help him to overcome these unhealthy leanings.

We wish to specially note the success of the youthful poetess Nadezhda Kramova. Her lyrical, intimate poems, permeated by tenderness, cannot leave unmoved the soul of our Cat, no matter how remote it might be from poetry.

All the authors, then, are working in their own unique styles. And this is gratifying and deeply symbolic, proving once again the unlimited possibilities of social realism—in particular, of its vanguard—and demonstrating the true, that is to say not counterfeit, freedom of Soviet creativity.

The second section, "Criticism," features a comprehensive overview of contemporary Western cinema by movie critic Marina Zhezhelenko. There is perhaps a certain regrettable tendentiousness and intolerance in the work of this young critic. The time is long past when one can groundlessly slander the Cat by ascribing non-existent evil deeds to it, without proof. We must not punish cats but educate them, and certain hotheads would do well to remember this.

The third section, "Science," is dedicated to technological progress. It features inventor Victor Shtern, enthusiastically proving that an electronic feline brain created by man can easily replace the brain of a living cat.

In conclusion, the editors of "PASIC" wish all their authors and readers a Happy New Year!

Ludmila Shtern, Senior Editor

Iosif Brodsky

AN ODE

Oh, blue-eyed, glorious Pasik!
Stay with me, stay but an hour.
Pacify my grumbling spirit
With your holy purring.
Allow me to pet you; that is
To glorify your fur and your valor—
I mean, Nature's triumph entire,
Oh, paragon of your breed!

O matrix of gray colors!
You are made for brave caresses.
You are so beautiful, so lovely,
Worthy of hymns and flattering songs,
Oh, Pasik! What sweetness, what delight,
A poet feels while looking
At this wondrous body! But such a feeling
Cannot be expressed in art.

Losing the gift of speech and writing
I moan: Where is thy chisel, Canova?
Shostakovich, where are thy notes?
Eliasberg, Rabinovich, Leo
Tolstoy?—where are you, Tolstoy?—we need a classic.
O blue-eyed, glorious Pasik,
You have lived to see an evil time.
O heavens! Where is the brush of Picasso?

Let Wajda drown in drunk despair,
Chaplin alone in the ocean.
Into the Pacific marvelous Pasik
Goes bravely! What is the problem?
Laughing, purring, and triumphing
Let's go together to Mokhovaya Street
And there, from Eiba, without fear,
We will get Averbakh's address.

My horse! I shall give up my specialty
Or, disregarding officialdom,
I shall speed by fastest plane
To Moscow, to Moscow, to the Ministers Union.
To beg, there in the capital,
For you, you round-faced beauty,
A good pension, and Picasso's brush,

And a kilo of the best cuts instead of scraps.

And, if I can sway them with my charm,
I shall get you a special diploma,
So as to compensate partially
Your plundered virility;
So that you could then yourself,
Rolling up this piece of paper as a symbol,
Flash it everywhere
Wave that thing all around.
Oh, Pasik! You are so beautiful!

[Eliasberg and Rabinovich: famous Russian conductors in the 50s and 60s; Eliasberg conducted the Leningrad Philharmonic Orchestra for the world premiere of the Shostakovich Seventh Symphony during the Leningrad siege. Ilya Averbach: a movie director and a close friend of the young Brodsky. Eiba: Averbach's first wife.]

Dmitri Bobyshev

ACROSTICH

Can you tell me who chose as his life's motto
A good dinner and hit the sack after,
The quietest sort of abstractionism
Patiently teaching us to understand concretely?
Abstraction, he learned from experience,
Said he: "I adore sour cream" and ate a mouse for dinner.
In sooth, who in his judgments has no equal?
Kindly read the capital letters to know.

A SONNET TO PASIK

I cannot stand those soft creatures.
But, suddenly I'm stopped half-way,
And must hurry my pen to catch up,
At least up to the fourteenth line.
I should sing of the silken locks,
But do not like to be coerced.
Are only flatterers happy
To serve, if not fame, then at least Mammon.
You know, Cat—examples are many
Of how touch-me-nots were attained.
I have kept my pen clean and was strict with it.
But not strict enough. To tell the truth,
For the sake of your mistress only,
Dearest castrato, I sing of you.

Nadezhda Kramova

THE LIFE OF PASIK THE CAT

You were brought home in the palm of a hand
Like a grey powder puff,
A little ball of yarn,
Unseeing, not brave, not wise.
In your innocent ignorance
You sat in dark corners
And I begged the neighbors:
"Do not step on the kitten."
You grew up cheerful and frisky,
Romped like a whirlwind around the house,
And were, soberly speaking,
The happiest creature in the world.
But once on a cold and rainy morning,
Obeying ancient customs,
I took you, poor Pasik, to the vet.
Weeping from pity,
I mangled your fate,
Took away all earthly delights—
Both animal and human.
And since then, holding a grudge,
Daily dreaming of revenge,
All your business, with an independent mien,
You have done in the wrong place.
Silently I have wiped up puddles...
Cleaned up mounds without a murmur...
Not suspecting it would get worse,
That you were readying a mighty blow.
You, ignoring my superiority,
Let fly, arching your back,
Upon my means of survival,
My only typewriter.

A. Chelnov (a.k.a. Naiman)

P. Sh.

Like you, burdened by fate,
I rub my crazy head
Against the grating of the stairwell.
There, Pasik, that's our freedom.

There, my friend, is our life: all day long
To loiter around a warm room,
To listen to dear women's mindless chatter
And to smile.

And our near ends
Will be so alike, dear Pasik;
Young lads will catch you,
Throw you into the cellar and turn out the lights.

And you will die, and I will die.
Not in the bed, but in the cellar,
Not in the daytime, but at night—so that by morning
The tenants' footsteps will sound overhead.

But for now, be well,
Sleep on a satin pillowcase.
My friend, I know how wonderful
Is the fate of cats.

Evgeny Rein

TO THE GREAT PASIK -
FROM HIS NEIGHBOR, KOTOV
[Kotov means "cat-related" in Russian]

Among luxurious terra-cotta arches,
Amidst great coziness,
In the apartment with hallways
He lives, gray and large.

Beautiful and insincere,
He slyly whispers,
Caresses one in a savage frenzy
Then surrenders his soft underbelly.

Some guests bring a small mouse
To honor him.
He scratches his armpit
And eats *satsivi* and chicken broth.

Stealing everyone's attention
With his unequaled beauty,
Nobody cares that a daughter
Of marriageable age is wasting away.

Or that the unhappy mother writes plays,
Or that the son-in-law has yet to get his Ph.D.,
Or that terrible events
Are haunting his mistress.

Pasik is a cat-emperor,
Pasik is a royal cat.
That's why in the terra-cotta home
Everything is upside down
Because next to the beauty and wisdom
Of his silver soul
Our successes, our setbacks
Are silly gewgaws...

He, like an ancient Greek philosopher,
Lives among cretins
And the titbits of human life
Observes askance.

I hope that the reader can feel in these poems the power of
creativity that drove us and the feeling of discontent that haunted
us. Of course, youth can have a hard time being accepted in any
culture. Often the young feel that they are up against a mafia of

older people who hold key positions and spare no sinister effort to prevent the young from breaking in. Our problems had little to do with age. It was not the older people who were taking away our right to express ourselves. It was the System telling everybody what was right, what was wrong, what was good, what was bad—labeling what we were doing as this or that, condemning us in perpetuity without right of appeal.

Still, when I remember those long-gone years, I think we had a wonderful time. We were friends. We worked together. We shared our ideas and accomplishments. We learned from each other. All that would change in the future. Different fates awaited us. Strong passions would tear us apart. Fame and obscurity would divide us through jealousy and condescension. Former best friends would become bitter enemies. And with all that, still—we had a wonderful time.

8

"Happy Birthday, Dear Iosif..."

NOSTALGIA HAS ME IN ITS GRIP when I recall the birthday celebrations of our youth. The most "fruitful" months were April and May. Mirra Meilakh was born April 1st, Marina Zhezhelenko - April 2nd, Bobyshev - April 11th, Naiman - April 23rd, Luda Shtern - April 30th, Galya Dozmarova - May 3rd, Galya Narinskaya [the first wife of Rein and the second wife of Naiman] - May 16th, Osya Brodsky - May 24th.

The most magnificent parties of all marked the birthdays of Mirra Meilakh and Osya Brodsky.

Mirra's usually took place in the resort area on the Finnish Bay that was annexed to the Leningrad region in 1939 after a short but bloody war with Finland. Finns who used to live there were sent to labor camps, and the resort area was adapted to the needs of the new masters. They gave new names to the towns and streets and purged the area of anything that recalled the previous owners.

The town of Komarovo, the former Finnish Kellomäki, deserves mention. In the fifties and sixties it became a favorite resort for the Leningrad intelligentsia. The Writer's Union had the Writer's Retreat there, and successful writers their personal country houses. The prominent scholars received a generous present from Stalin himself: two dozen country houses (*dachas*) that were called Academicians' Village.

Mirra's father, a well known literary scholar, who lived in harmony with the Soviet regime by writing books about Lenin's outstanding contributions to Russian literature, built a beautiful lilac mansion there, called by mocking well-wishers "Meilakh's Mound" [an allusion to the Malakhov Mound near Sevastopol that was a place of vicious fighting during the Crimean War in the 19th century and made famous by Tolstoy] or "Saviour-upon-quotes" [an allusion to the Saviour-upon-Blood, a cathedral that was built in St. Petersburg on the place where revolutionaries killed Tsar Alexander II, the one who freed the serfs in 1861].

Komarovo is surrounded by beautiful lakes and pine woods. In the beginning of April they are covered by snow, and Finnish Bay is still frozen near the shore. So on Mirra's birthdays we usually went skiing for a few hours and then had a real feast in the lilac mansion. Mirra's parents made guests welcome, fed them to bursting and plied them with spirits.

Today, fifty years later, Komarovo doesn't look so glamorous. For our generation, its cemetery rather than its dachas has become signatory. Anna Akhmatova is buried there along with many Leningrad writers and scholars—quite a few friends my age among them...

But let's go back to our youth. Unlike Mirra's snowy birthday's celebrations, Brodsky's birthdays are associated in my mind with warm, bright evenings, and a riot of lilac bushes on the Marsovo Pole (*Field of Mars*). This magnificent square is adapted to serve as a small cemetery for the communists who were killed during the Revolution and the Civil War. We always brought bouquets of white lilac to Iosif's mother, Maria Moiseevna, and she, before putting them into vases, picked out and ate some of the five-petaled blossoms for luck.

Most of Iosif's guests were poets and writers of varying literary talent and merit, but with one characteristic in common: nobody had been published or was even publishable. Their oeuvre circulated only through *samizdat*. Besides the ever-present Rein, Bobyshev and Naiman I recall Misha Yeremin, Lenya Vinogradov, Volodya Gerasimov, Lenya Stakelberg, Garrik Voskov, Volodya Uflyand, Lev Lifshitz (Loseff), Yefim Slavinsky, and Alesha Khvostenko, nicknamed "Khvost" ("tail" in Russian), always with his guitar and very striking in those years.

Iosif and his parents lived in a fairly crowded *"kommunalka"* [common name for a communal apartment]—Apartment 28 on Pestelya Street, 24, also known as the Muruzi house [the name of the former owner of the building].

This building had a long literary history. In the years 1899-1913, Dmitry Merezhkovsky and Zinaida Gippius, the famous literary couple, had lived there. Andrei Belyi, another famous Russian poet, lived there in 1905. In the 1920s, Nikolai Gumilyov (another famous poet executed later by the Cheka) was giving poetry seminars in the building, one of which my mother had attended.

The Brodsky family, as I mentioned earlier, occupied a room and a half (many years later, he would write a beautiful essay about his life with his parents). This means that the rooms in the apartment were divided by additional walls, and the trimmings and moldings near the floor and on the ceiling clearly indicated which walls were original and which were added. The birthday party always took place in the main room that served as the living room, dining room, and the parents' bedroom combined. This room reminded me of an aging noblewoman in reduced circumstances. High ceilings typical for St. Petersburg architecture were adorned with stucco molding—wreaths, flowers, curlicues. The main room was crowded with old-fashioned, cumbersome furniture "of good pedigree," which by modest Soviet standards, would be sufficient for a three-room flat. Behind the glass of a theatrically huge sideboard twinkled wineglasses and small English teacups. Except on special occasions, the dining table stood against the wall between two windows, and the greatest part of the room was taken up with an enormous bed, which seemed to us luxurious. It was covered with an intricately patterned, golden counterpane which came from somewhere abroad.

During festivities the bed was moved flush with the wall to the right of the door, and the guests were allowed to gather on it. Two additional tables would be borrowed from the neighbors, and placed end to end, crossing the room diagonally from the door to the window.

Iosif's parents Alexander Ivanovich and Maria Moiseevna were hospitable and gracious hosts. Maria Moiseevna was also a remarkable cook, and despite the family's humble means the tables groaned under the weight of pies, roast ducks, salads and various pickled foods.

At one of Iosif's parties, his twenty-second birthday to be exact, Victor and I did a monstrous thing. The idea was mine, and even now, more than forty years later, I cannot stop marveling at my own idiocy.

To this infamous episode I have dedicated a vignette entitled

SUICIDE

May 10, 1962, two weeks before Iosif Brodsky's birthday, there was a meeting of the young poets' group in which Iosif participated. The reading took place in the Red Drawing Room of the Writers' House. The so-called "Khrushchev thaw" had just begun—a spring of hopes and expectations. Things that used to be unthinkable, like this public reading, became possible. The room was completely packed. The atmosphere was tense; the very air seemed electrified.

...Much is written about the way Brodsky read his poems. But it is doubtful that any description can do justice to the strange, almost hypnotic effect created by his voice and intonation. Actually, there were no intonations. There was a certain nasal crooning (*sing-song*), with the voice dropping at the end of the line and, at the same time, the "voltage" going up with each new stanza. It sounded like a prayer or an incantation that caused a great many listeners to enter a trance or a trance-like state.

This explains why those who heard Brodsky read could not (and still cannot) stand it when his poetry is sung with a guitar accompaniment, or declaimed "with theatrical expression à la Kachalov" [the famous Russian actor]. And Brodsky himself became irritated when he heard alien intonations in his poems.

That evening Iosif read excerpts from the just-finished long poem "Zofya":

You, capable of hanging by a thread,
You, capable of lies and ennui,
You, capable of relations anywhere,
You, capable of disgrace and of stardom,

104

You, capable of polluting the bloodline,
You, capable of infection and of love,
You should not have left the light on,
You should not have left your footprints,
Acquaintances are not keeping your secrets,
Your feelings will hunt you down.
What could be more amazing to the eye
Than feelings that overtake us
And try to get at our throats?
I SUGGEST YOU BECOME A PENDULUM.

In the middle of this excerpt a certain Lev Kuklin, a poet himself, and a member of the Literary Club of the Mining Institute, got up. With the loud words "what gibberish" he stepped over legs and, stomping deliberately, went out into the hallway, slamming the door behind him. Bobyshev jumped up and ran after, with the intention of rearranging Kuklin's face. Other friends ran after them with the intention of not allowing it. For the love of Kuklin? Of course not, but out of a well-founded fear that any scandal would serve as an excuse for other such readings to be prohibited. There was some noise and heavy breathing for a time from out on the staircase, but Kuklin managed to get away unscathed.

Kuklin was a short, puffy-looking person with no neck and an inflated opinion of himself. While still at the Mining Institute he was hopelessly in love with a girlfriend of mine and even dedicated a poem to her, which for some reason I remember:

Nowadays we don't believe in dreams or fortunetelling,
We even laugh at a black cat,
But we still stand quietly, waiting,
Waiting for what the cuckoo will tell us.
The bird sang forty times in answer.
What are we to the cuckoo? She lives without loving.
This means I have forty years left,
Only forty years to love you.

After Kuklin's outburst during Brodsky's reading, Victor and I talked about what a decent person would do in Kuklin's place.

Apologize, probably. I said that Iosif would forgive him and Victor insisted that he would tell him to go...well, far away. And so our practical joke began: I decided to find out what Iosif would do.

We were invited to Iosif's birthday party for six o'clock. Before we left, Victor called him up and said in a disguised voice:
   - Hello, Iosif, this is Kuklin.
   - What do you want? growled Brodsky.
   - I really need to talk to you.
   - We've got nothing to talk about.
   - Old man, I know it's your birthday today. Can I stop by for a few minutes?
   - Not a chance!
   - Iosif, I want to apologize.
   - Consider it already done.
   - Iosif, I have to see you right away... It's a matter of life and death.
   - Go fuck yourself! barked the poet and slammed down the receiver.
   With the passing years, Iosif melted somewhat and had more and more difficulty saying "No" to people. If you were persistent, you could press him to do things he didn't necessarily want to do—like invite somebody for a drink in his home, or write a foreword to somebody's book, or recommend somebody for a teaching position, or write a reference for somebody, or introduce somebody at a public reading. He would dispense these favors and then torment himself for being soft and unable to withstand pressure. But that would be much later. Here, Iosif was firm and uncompromising.

   ...We were running late. Waited for the bus, but it never came... Walked to Nevsky Prospect on foot, finally got a taxi. Drove up to his house an hour past the time. Aleksandr Ivanovich was smoking on the balcony and, seeing us, yelled: "Come quickly, the ducks are getting cold."
   People were already sitting at the table, but Iosif was not in the room. He was taking something to the kitchen, or bringing something from the kitchen, we caught up with him in the hallway.

- How come you're so late? Iosif asked. Took you two hours to put on your makeup?

- No... You see... Someone called us about...

- Vit', don't... not now... Let's not spoil Os'ka's birthday.

- What happened?

- We'll tell you later.

- Out with it, immediately.

- You see... Kuklin... hanged himself.

Brodsky turned white and began to shake, pressing his fingers against his temples.

- Os'ka, what's the matter with you? (We were scared to death.)

- Damn! It's my fault, mine! It's me! Me! Iosif repeated as if feverish. He called me! He called me today!

Iosif was beating his head against the wall; it was unbearable to see. We cursed our idiocy.

- Os'ka, calm down, Victor cried. They resuscitated him!

- Is he alive? Just don't lie about it!

- Alive, alive! What else would he be!

- Where is he, in the hospital?

- Oh, hell, what hospital? He is at home.

- Thank God, said Iosif, slowly calming down, I'll go see him tomorrow... anybody know where he lives?

I imagined the scene—Brodsky visiting Kuklin. We had to confess immediately.

- Os'ka, forgive us! Forgive us, we're such idiots, for God's sake! We did not know you were so sensitive.

Iosif snorted: "Some damn jokes you've got..."

And the birthday party went on as usual...

About twenty years passed. It seemed that this episode had passed into oblivion. At any rate, I forgot about it completely...

...Brodsky had the habit of calling both the men and the women who were close to him "Kissa," "Koosya," "Sunshine" and "Bunny." "Kissas" were especially plentiful. His mother Maria Moiseevna, for instance, was "Kissa" as were almost all his friends from that time. And that is also what he usually called me. But once he called me up in Boston from New York before one of his parties and said: "How about you, snake, are you coming?"

- Now, that's interesting... What did I do to deserve being called a snake all of a sudden?

- Oh, you deserve it for Kuklin, you snake...You think I don't remember?

9

Epistolary Games and Others

IN THE EARLY 1960s no one from our circle had ever been abroad. Not that we did not want to go, but Soviet citizens could not go abroad like everybody else merely by asking for a tourist visa, buying a plane ticket, packing, calling a taxi, going to the airport, taking off. Of course Soviet citizens could do all these things but first and foremost they had to get an exit visa from their own government. To apply for an exit visa, one had to produce a letter of recommendation that said that one was an excellent worker who did whatever he did with enthusiasm and selflessness, was respected if not loved by his colleagues, and his (or her) political loyalties were firmly with the Communist Party. The letter had to be signed by the firm's director, and the heads of the local Party cell and the labor union. For the letter to be accepted for further processing, it had to state that the signatories of the letter were confident that the applicant was a mature person who would behave abroad as a proud citizen of the Soviet Union, that he would respond to any hostile provocation during his trip with candor and firmness, that he would represent his country abroad with dignity; finally, that the signatories would recommend said person for a trip to this particular country. Then the aspiring tourist went to a combined meeting of the representatives of his company's administration, Party and labor union. The decision to approve the recommendation, or not to approve it, was made only after all the pros and cons had been weighed. Since approval was politically risky, after it was obtained a letter was sent to the secret police for a thorough background check.

In due course the tourist was invited to another meeting, this time at the District Committee of the Party. There he was grilled with questions that would make it clear whether or not he was familiar with national and international political problems and whether his views were correct enough. After a few more weeks, a letter would come saying that you could come and get your exit visa, or that all your trouble was for nothing. Leaving close relatives behind always helped—they served as hostages in cases where a tourist decided not to return. Applying for a vacation abroad with one's spouse was hopeless. Most people did not even try to start this process: why bother if the result was known in advance? The opportunity to go abroad, even to a socialist country like Poland, was always viewed as a cherished, albeit rarely attainable, dream.

But despite this grim reality, having read a great deal of foreign literature (in translation, mostly), we dreamed of breaking out of the dull Soviet cage. We were crazy about mysterious "Western life" and simply delirious on the subject of America—American movies, American jazz, the American way of life. It was not about all things American being cool, even though they were. It was not that we valued things of foreign origin more than things of local origin, even though we did. It was about freedom. We dreamed about being free. On the streets of Leningrad, we could always tell a foreigner from a Soviet citizen, even if the latter was sporting American jeans, sneakers and clothes. Trying to verbalize my intuitive feelings, I came up with the following difference: "Foreigners behave on the street as if nothing bad could happen to them. They walk holding their backs straight, they make eye contact with strangers and smile at them without reason, they are ready to start a conversation on the street, they certainly look more friendly..."

Well, all kinds of things could and did happen to foreigners on our streets, but this was how I was struck by their behavior.

Consider the following story. Once in early spring, I went to the Hotel Astoria to visit my American friend, Anne Frydman. It was time for me to go home, but the weather had turned colder, and I had come to see Anne without a coat. So I called home and asked Victor to bring my coat to the Astoria—we lived about ten minutes on foot from the hotel. When Victor was crossing the square in front of St. Isaac's Cathedral—the very center of the city—he was stopped by a policeman. The policeman thought it was suspicious: why does this man wear a coat and carry another one in his hands? To the policeman the most natural explanation was that the coat was stolen. Never mind that Victor wore glasses, was dressed quite decently and in general looked more like a famous violin player than a petty thief. The policeman stopped Victor, asked for ID, inspected it thoroughly (and the Soviet ID describes not only the name, home address and date of birth, it also describes ethnic origin, marital status, and place of employment), conducted a thorough interrogation, and finally let Victor go. This is why America existed in our minds as a country where everything was perfect.

So we were dreaming about America. Movie director Ilya Averbakh was crazy about westerns, Brodsky and Naiman about jazz, Misha Petrov and myself about detective stories, and all of us together about Hemingway, Faulkner, Steinbeck, Truman Capote, Tennessee Williams...

We wrote each other letters in the styles of our favorite writers, and made up imaginary play-scenarios with ourselves as characters. We had just read Truman Capote's *In Cold Blood* and were fascinated with the idea of a perfect murder. Had we brains and craftiness enough to commit an ideal murder? Not a Russian, Dostoyevsky-style murder, such as when Raskolnikov killed an old lady for money and became conscience-stricken, but an American murder without motivation and without guilt. Could we commit an unsolvable murder? Without clues, with watertight alibis for all the participants?

Who would we kill? While thinking it over, the first candidate who came into the minds of the five participants (that is, Averbakh, Brodsky, Bobyshev, Petrov, and me) was Tolya Naiman. Actually, in those faraway years we didn't have any reason to murder Naiman. The good reasons appeared much, much later, but we had by that time become grownup people and had stopped playing dangerous games. So Tolya Naiman is still perfectly alive...

Unfortunately, forty years later I am unable to reconstruct the exact plot but it was, I assure you, quite cunning. Naiman was to be invited to Bobyshev's house, then Petrov (the only person in our group who had a car) would appear to suggest spending a leisurely day in the country; then they would drop by Brodsky's and Averbakh's; then they would pick me up from a certain doorway on an empty street, after which we would call or show up at many acquaintances', switch the car's license plates twice—in short, would do many things as a result of which Naiman's corpse would end up in the trunk of Petrov's car, later to be thrown into the Oredezh river near the town of Viritza. I don't know why we chose this particular little town. Maybe because it was the site of a Nabokov family estate before the Revolution. To make sure our plan was air-tight we related it in detail to my father, a law professor, so he could admire our inventiveness and verify that there was not a weak link anywhere.

Papa agreed that it was not badly thought out and that technically speaking the plan looked lovely, but that it was impossible to implement because we were "intelligentsia" with tender consciences and would definitely blow it... Probably right at the beginning of the escapade.

"With a nervous system such as yours you cannot commit unmotivated murder," said Papa. "The minute you start asking each other why or for what purpose you are killing Naiman, your consciences will go into overdrive. You'll start feeling sorry for him and it will be all over. Better think about robbing the rent collector."

In his novel *B. B. and Others*, written a few years ago, Naiman deftly touches upon this episode. The narrator's name is Aleksander Germantzev, Misha Petrov appears under the pseudonym Mirosha Pavlov, and I am featured as "a mutual acquaintance."

I have taken the liberty to quote from *B. B. and Others*:

"Mirosha Pavlov gave me rides in his car from time to time... We were friends, but once he and Ilya Averbakh spent a whole evening talking with the father of a mutual acquaintance, who was a well-known legal expert, about how to organize a murder of, say, Tolya Naiman, so as to leave absolutely no clues. Well, not seriously, of course, only as an example..."

Further on there is a bit about how when Naiman finds out about it he'll be flattered...

Neither we, nor Naiman thought about this in real terms; it was a game that let us explore the motives of foreign literature, to think about life in faraway lands—again, not in real terms, but in terms of symbols and symbolic acts.

10

Marina

THE LOVE STORIES OF OUR YOUTH were worthy of *The Decameron*. Affairs and breakups, betrayals and adulteries, marriages and divorces—Pierre Chaderlos de Laclos with his *Liaisons Dangereuses* had nothing on us! Some got off with minor scratches on their hearts, others got badly scarred... I think that the painful love affair and breakup of Joseph Brodsky and Marina Basmanova was the most significant and tragic episode of his life.

In those years, Marina was tall, statuesque, with a high forehead and soft features, dark-brown shoulder-length hair and green eyes. On a copy of *Urania* that he sent from the U.S as a gift to his friend Yakov Gordin in 1978, Brodsky wrote:

Accept a green tome, Yakov.
Green is the color of the local money,
It is the color of the Prophet's banner,
And of Basmanova's eye in anger.

Very thin and pale—blue veins showing at her temples—with a somewhat lethargic manner and a quiet voice without inflection, Marina seemed anemic. At the same time, some saw a mysterious quality in her paleness, her passivity and lack of emotional expression.

Marina was an artist by profession. I think she was a book illustrator. Although I have known her since 1962, I cannot judge her talent. I have never seen her work. Forty-something years ago, Brodsky spoke enthusiastically of her talent for painting and her musical ability. But then he admired everything about her, and could not have been objective.

I often saw Marina at the Symphony, usually without Joseph, who was not a regular at the Symphony in those years, though he already knew Mozart and Haydn well. The Concerto Grosso was often playing in his "half-room" both during the creative process and during a visit from one or another of his girlfriends.

Marina lived on Glinka Street, a few blocks from our house. She and Joseph often came to visit us together, but I never managed to engage her in a serious conversation or learn her opinion on any question on "life and the universe and everything." She readily discussed films. I remember that her favorite actress was Maria Casarès in *La Chartreuse de Parme*.

Despite many attempts, no one in our group managed to become friends with Marina. Maybe Bobyshev was an exception, if their relationship could be termed "friendship." She seemed very shy. She did not shine with her wit, did not take part in verbal jousts, wherein we sharpened our tongues against each other. Sometimes she would not say a single word or open her mouth during the course of an entire evening... Or maybe she would say, "All right, Iosif, let's go." But occasionally there was a wild expression in her green eyes. Then one would wonder if there were deeper waters and what was in them.

Relations between Joseph and Marina were quite tense even during the heyday of their romance. During the idyllic days, after many hours of wandering around in New Holland, that dilapidated part of St. Petersburg where Joseph liked to take long walks, Joseph and Marina, frozen, would drop by to get warm and have a cup of tea. During the stormy days of their relationship Joseph came alone, ruffled and miserable, and we did our best to calm and comfort him. My nanny Nulya had the best recipe for calming him: "Sit Osya down to peel potatoes for dinner and he'll forget himself."

Once Joseph came in the middle of the day without a phone call, his pale face and wild expression attesting to another breakup. But it wasn't just his bizarre expression. His left wrist was tied with a dirty bandage—not a sight for those with weak nerves. He said he had tried to cut his wrist. We did not dare ask him anything and he did not offer explanations—just grimly ate a bowl of soup and left.

Soon they had reconciled their differences and were coming to visit again with smiles and flowers. On such days Brodsky glowed from within. He could not take his eyes off Marina and admiringly followed her every gesture, how she tossed her hair, how she held her cup, how she looked in the mirror, how she sketched something in her notebook...

After they left, we naturally gossiped about them. Nulya always had the last word: "Did you see how her eye burns? I tell you, she is a witch and has put a spell on Osya... He'll cry lots of tears over her yet."

And, indeed, after a while, the grim scene would recur. The crazed look, the trembling lips and dirty bandage on the left wrist. Then Victor applied shock therapy. "Listen, Osya," he said, "stop frightening people like this. If you ever really decide to commit suicide by slashing your wrists, ask me to explain how it ought to be done. It's not difficult at all." We saw no more bandaged wrists after that.

The turning point of their relationship was the New Year's Eve of 1964 at the dacha of our friends the Sheinins in Komarovo. There events took place that would influence the course of Brodsky's life. Actually, the dacha did not belong to the Sheinins. At that time few of us had the money or connections to have a dacha all to ourselves. Mirra Meilakh was an exception, but her dacha did not belong to her either, it belonged to her parents. The Sheinins' dacha belonged to the government, like most of the other houses in this resort area. The government rented out rooms or the whole dacha for a very reasonable rent for a few months to qualified applicants. The Sheinins were qualified: Alik headed a chemical modeling lab in a metallurgical research institute, Galya taught English. Next year our family also rented a dacha (well, one room out of three, and during the winter: we did not have enough clout to get a dacha or even one room for the summer).

Brodsky himself was in Moscow at the time. He had gone

there because the Leningrad KGB was already closing in on him, and his friends felt that in Moscow he could stay ahead of the game for a while, at least until the Leningrad KGB found out where he was and got in touch with their Moscow counterparts.

Victor and I celebrated that New Year at our friend's, architect Yuri Tzekhnovitzer's, mezzanine apartment on the Neva embankment, and were not at the Sheinins' party. The next day, January 1st, I left for Moscow on a business trip and thus found out what had happened at the Sheinins' dacha only when I returned the following week. Though it may look like I am going to give you an eyewitness account of an event that I did not witness, do not be disappointed. There were several eyewitness accounts, as is usual in such cases, and I am familiar with all of them.

To assure the authenticity of my story, I asked the hosts, Alik and Galya Sheinin, to recall who lived at the dacha, who celebrated that fateful New Year and what actually happened.

This is what Galya Sheinin wrote me:

"This famous dacha was on the border between Komarovo and Zelenogorsk. Even now one can see it in the spaces between pine trees when passing by on the Primorsky Highway. That year, seven of us rented the second floor. Evsei Vigdorchik, Dima Bobyshev and Garik Prilutsky had the biggest room. Vika and Misha Belomlinsky had the second room and we had the third.

"At that time we talked and wrote to each other mostly in verse form. For instance, the bathroom (actually, there was no bathtub, just a toilet of the outhouse kind, without running water) had an elegantly illustrated poster:

How did they write poetry of old?
Street, drugstore, and streetlight.
And here, after half a century—
Poster board, hole, toilet.

["Street, drugstore, and streetlight" is a line from a famous poem by Aleksandr Blok about the futility and lack of fundamental changes in Russian life.]

"Sometimes they were diary entries, usually in a form of an epigram, for example a poem by Irina Komarova:

117

Here was the poet Victor Sosnora
He drank coffee and ate Roquefort-a.

"More often, the genre was used for scathing criticism: For example, it was written to Bobyshev:

A friend of perversity, a master of drunkenness,
A hater of permanence,
And looking closer, a hypocrite and a boor.

"This was followed by a long text with dubious puns on the names of the ladies staying there [Galya Sheinin, Mika Gilio and Vika Belomlinsky].

Bobyshev came back with:
Quiet, Sheinins, rein in
Your games forthwith.
Here, behind the wall slumbers Dmitri,
A chaste and pure youth.

"There were more intense clashes, even violent ones. Once the men put the drunk and disorderly Bobyshev to bed by force. Waking up in the morning he did not calm down, but threw a rather heavy ashtray at Evsei. He called Galya Sheinin and Lilya Druskin whores and shouted to Alik, "Hey, you, blue!" [Russian slang for homosexual.] (He later made an excuse that he meant Alik's blue shirt.) He got a black eye while being subdued.

"Before the New Year's Eve party, Bobyshev warned that he was bringing a girl. The girl turned out to be Marina Basmanova. Bobyshev explained that Joseph had asked him to take care of Marina while he was away.

"We welcomed her warmly, but the friendship did not work out from then on. Marina was quiet all night, smiling mysteriously like Mona Lisa, while everyone around her was having noisy fun and paying her no attention. By morning, having gotten bored, she set fire to the window's curtains wearing the same mysterious smile. The flames were substantial and she commented, "How beautifully they burn." From what we saw, it became clear to us that Bobyshev's caretaking had gone too far.

"In a few days, Misha Petrov gathered everyone together in his apartment and called for a boycott of Bobyshev and for his expulsion from the dacha. I am ashamed to remember the expulsion scene. We arrived at the dacha where Bobyshev was alone. Reading of the sentence was delegated to poor Alik Sheinin. Behind his back, Vika Belomlinskaya was beside herself with indignation. Misha stuttered, as always, and I, Galya Sheinin, mumbled something.

"Bobyshev behaved with great dignity. He asked, 'Will you allow me to collect my things?' When leaving, he added, 'You are wrong, guys.'

"I remember clearly that our idea of boycotting Bobyshev was not guided by moral considerations, but by the fact that the 'triangle' had an influence on Brodsky's arrest."

[end of Galya Sheinin's letter]

This account covers all the major points of the story. Yes, it was not nice to sleep with a friend's girlfriend, but if that happened, we would not think much of it. However, at this time Brodsky was especially vulnerable, and what was all right during "normal" periods of one's life (whatever that means) was not all right toward Brodsky at that time. Also note that everybody turned against Bobyshev, not against Marina. This does not mean that all of us were male (or female) chauvinist pigs. We all thought that Marina's contribution to this betrayal was not less than Bobyshev's. However, we tacitly assumed that, being Brodsky's girlfriend, Marina had the inalienable right to torment him, cheat on him, drive him to suicide, or break up with him as she wished. Being Brodsky's friend, Bobyshev did not have the right to do anything that would tip Brodsky off balance.

...Brodsky was in Moscow at that time. In Leningrad, the KGB was hard at work building a case against him, and it was clear that returning home in the foreseeable future was out of the question: an arrest inevitably waited for him in his native city.

I arrived in Moscow on January 2nd, and that same evening visited our friends Evgeny and Galya Rein. Joseph was there. We sat down to dinner and began discussing who spent New Year's Eve where, how and with whom and "how everything was."

I described our evening at the Tzekhnovitzers' (it was also somewhat wild, but I will spare you the details) and also listed those I knew to have been at the Sheinins' dacha, including Misha Petrov, the Belomlinskys, Bobyshev and Marina Basmanova. Because of my precipitous departure for Moscow I had no idea what had occurred there.

But having heard that Bobyshev and Marina celebrated the New Year together, Joseph became glum, as if he felt that something was wrong. He sat in silence for a few minutes and then was suddenly in a rush. He put aside a full bowl of soup, mumbled that someone was waiting for him and left. We did not become worried at the time because sudden changes in mood, as well as sudden appearances and disappearances, were characteristic of Brodsky. But in this case, we were wrong not to be vigilant. A day later, against common sense, Joseph left for Leningrad and was arrested there on February 13th.

As soon as Brodsky returned to Leningrad, Bobyshev came over to explain himself. The substance of the conversation was known only to them, but speculation was rampant. This private drama became quite public. Most people thought that Bobyshev had explained his behavior as the result of sudden, irresistible feelings for Marina. But later events cast some doubt on the reality and depth of these feelings.

This New Year's Eve story terminated the relationship between Brodsky and Bobyshev. It was the first (but not the last) time our circle was torn asunder. However, Brodsky and Marina made up and their relationship continued. After Brodsky was arrested, tried, and sent into exile, Marina visited him there. She bore Brodsky a son, Andrei.

When we, the Shterns, learned what had happened at the Sheinins, we joined them, and the Petrovs and the Belomlinskys, in condemning Bobyshev and excluding him from our lives for many years. And again: he was not shunned because of some strict moral code, but because he was indirectly responsible for what happened to Brodsky... To some extent, it was a matter of choice between the two. Brodsky was not a Gospel follower who would "turn the other cheek." He was very much a man of flesh and blood who would "take revenge and bear a grudge." One could not socialize both with Brodsky and with Bobyshev at the same time. Brodsky would not tolerate it.

Yet I dare to speculate that even without Bobyshev's intrusion the relationship between Joseph and Marina did not have a future. Despite their attempts to make a life together, despite Marina's following Joseph into exile and the birth of their son Andrei, the union was doomed. They were very incompatible in terms of their personality, temperament and "energy resources." For Marina, Joseph was difficult—too intense and neurotic; too high-voltage for her to deal with.

In the poem "Kellomäki" Brodsky wrote:

> ... Probably you could state
> that you simply were trying to dodge the great
> metamorphosis, much as those smelts did
> (Translated by Brodsky)

The highly negative attitude of both sets of parents also contributed to the constant tension between the two. Joseph often complained that Marina's parents couldn't stand him and didn't let him into the house. He called them "hereditary anti-Semites." To Russian eyes, a Jew looks very different from an ethnic Russian, even a totally secular Jew in modern clothes, who lives exactly the same sort of life as any Russian. There are of course exceptions (the offspring of mixed marriages or adulteries) but as a rule, I could always tell the difference between a Jew and a non-Jew on the basis of facial features alone. So could most Russians, Jewish or non-Jewish. There is no doubt that Joseph looked a quintessential Jew to Marina's parents, and that his looks were repugnant to them. There is no doubt that they did not hesitate to express their feelings to Marina. Not that Marina would listen to everything (or anything) that her parents had to say. Still...

In their turn, Brodsky's parents greatly disliked Marina. They didn't hide it and repeated bitterly, "She is so cold and distant, what can they have in common?" The metaphorically inclined Aleksandr Ivanovich added: "It's as if, instead of blood, she has diluted milk flowing in her veins."

When their son Andrei was born in 1967, Marina refused to

give him Joseph's last name and registered him as Basmanov rather than Brodsky. Joseph was in despair. We called our lawyer friend Yakov Kiselev to ask if Marina could be "forced" through legal channels. The answer was that she could not.

We comforted Joseph, trying to explain that Andrei did not become a Basmanov out of spite and not because of the burning anti-Semitism of her parents. It was simply that, in the Soviet Union, a person with the good Russian name like Basmanov could survive easier than a person with the Jewish name Brodsky.

The full Russian name consists of a first name, a patronymic that derives from the father's name, and a last name identical to the father's. According to Russian tradition, then, Brodsky's son should have been called Andrei Iosifovich Brodsky. To add insult to injury, Marina did not even bestow the right patronymic upon their child. Marina registered Andrei as "Osipovich," not "Iosifovich." We were joking that she had evidently divided the paternity between Brodsky and the late great Russian poet Osip Mandelshtam. "Can my son at least be 'Iosifovich?'" Brodsky persisted, but to no avail. Soviet law makes the mother the only source of information about the child's paternity.

In the beginning of the nineties, Brodsky invited his adult son for a visit. Joseph had not seen him for about twenty years, though all this time he had supported him financially. He was very nervous before Andrei came. What would he be like? What would he love? What did he live for? Would they understand each other?

Joseph was concerned about Andrei's health and asked me to get Andrei an appointment with a good gastroenterologist in Boston. I found a "star GI specialist," and managed to arrange an appointment... Joseph was grateful, admired my effectiveness, but Andrei did not show up for the appointment.

To all questions about how they met, whether they would become friends, did Andrei remind him of himself as a young man, and so forth, Joseph replied gloomily, "Our relationship didn't work out."

Brodsky called us before Andrei was about to leave for Russia and asked for advice: should he or should he not buy his son a video cassette recorder?

"Of course you should, what's the problem?"

And suddenly Brodsky said in a querulous old man's voice,

"The problem is that he is lazy and won't do a damn thing. Not interested in anything. Marina had to take him to school in a taxi to make sure he got there. Doesn't want to study at all..."

"Well, well," I replied, "this is no surprise in light of who his father is." It seems he never did buy a videocassette recorder for his son.

I saw Andrei at Brodsky's funeral. The outward resemblance was striking. He had the same red hair and freckles, but he lacked his father's intensity, strong presence, internal energy and magnetism.

...Marina occupied a huge place in Brodsky's life. He never loved anyone the way he loved Marina Basmanova. For many years, inescapable longing for her tormented him. She became his obsession and the source of his inspiration. Once he confessed that Marina was his curse.

More than thirty of his works are dedicated to Marina, including "Izaak and Abraham" and "New Stanzas to Augusta."

However future biographers will judge Marina's behavior, we must be endlessly grateful to her: Russian literature was enriched by love poetry of the highest caliber.

Muffled somehow, haughtily,
every sentence you hear,
thanks you for not perishing,
because the dreams that walled you in
rage now behind my back,
and swallow the horsemen of Egypt.
(*"Sonnet"*, *1964*, *Norenskaya*)

* * *

Yes, this heart rushes toward you—,
harder and harder, farther and farther.
A falser and falser note creeps into my voice.
But you will set this down to fate,
a fate which does not ask for blood
but wounds me with a blunted needle.
And if you are hoping for a smile—
just wait, I'll smile! My smile will float
above me like the grave's long-standing

roof, lighter than woodsmoke.
* * *

(*"New Stanzas to Augusta,"* 1964, translated by George L. Kline, from the *Selected Poems*, p. 61))

Three years later, in 1967, Brodsky writes:

...The next to the top floor
feels the dark sooner
than the surrounding landscape;
I will hold you
and wrap you in a raincoat,
because in the window
there is rain – which can only be tears
over you and over me.

It is time for us to leave.
A silver thread
cleaves the glass.
Our time ran out forever
a long time ago.
Let us change our habits.
We are fated to live from now on
by the pocket-watches of strangers.

Brodsky saw Marina for the last time before his departure from the Soviet Union in 1972. In the West, he started a new life, full of new impressions, new people, and new interests. But the pain of loss did not diminish.

The collection of poems *A Part of Speech* written in 1975 contains poems dedicated to Marina that are full of sharp and desperate longing.

From nowhere with love the enth of Marchember sir
Sweetie respected darling but in the end
It's irrelevant who for memory won't restore
Features not yours and no one's devoted friend
Greets you from this fifth last part of earth
Resting on whalelike backs of cowherding boys

I loved you better than angels and Him Himself
And am farther off due to that from you than I am from both
Of them now late at night in the sleeping vale
In the little township up to its doorknobs in
Snow writhing upon the stale
Sheets for the whole matter's skin-
Deep I'm howling "youuu" through my pillow dike
Many seas away that are milling nearer
With my limbs in the dark playing your double like
An insanity-stricken mirror.

* * *

You're forgotten that village lost in the rows and rows
Of swamp in a pine-wooded territory where no scarecrows
Ever stand in orchards: the crops aren't worth it,
And the roads are also just ditches and brushwood surface.
Old Nastasia is dead, I take it, and Pesterev, too, for sure,
And if not, he's sitting drunk in the cellar or
Is making something from the headboard of our bed:
A wicket gate, say, or some kind of shed.
And in winter they're chopping wood, and turnips is all they
live on,
And the star blinks from all the smoke in the frosty heaven,
And no bride in chintz at the window, but dust's gray craft,
Plus the emptiness where once we loved.
(Translated by Daniel Weissbort)

From the time of Marina Tsvetayeva, Russian poetry has not
had verses full of such pain and inescapable sorrow.

In New York, Brodsky rarely spoke of Marina (at least to
me). And when he did mention her name, it was always with a
kind of mocking, ironic expression. Maybe because of this, I
remember particularly one evening in October of 1981. Our
mutual friend Gennady (Genna) Smakov had organized one of
his "gastronomic festivals." (Later, I will say more about this
very dear friend of mine.) After the guests had left, the three of
us stayed to talk. At the moment, Smakov was in love with a
half-English/half-Indian man named Chinko and complained
about this blue-eyed beauty. Chinko, a mediocre ballet dancer,

behaved like a spoiled prima donna and was wearing Genna out both financially and emotionally.

Both Joseph and I were recalling the time a certain married lady who was known for her weakness for Brodsky, the wife of poet B., living in Boston, one day descended upon Brodsky on Morton Street in New York and announced that she would stay with him forever.

"Note, please, without any warning," said Brodsky. "She rang the door, walked in with her suitcase and said, 'As you wish, Joseph, but I cannot live without you.'"

Joseph helped her out of her coat politely, sat her down in a chair, then locked himself upstairs and called me in a panic asking what to do. I was well-acquainted with this lady and her husband, whom I called and asked to come from Boston to New York to get his wife immediately and take her away together with her suitcase—which five or six hours later he did. And while the husband was on his way, Joseph sat in the locked room, while the lady howled at the door.

We finished remembering and laughing and suddenly without any connection to this story, Brodsky said, "It's funny, but I am still ill with Marina. A chronic case, you know." And he read us such a sad poem that Smakov and I were both in tears:

SEVEN STROPHES

I was but what you'd brush
with your palm, what your leaning
brow would hunch to in evening's
raven-black hush.

I was but what your gaze
in the dark could distinguish:
a dim shape to begin with,
later—features, a face.

It was you, on my right,
on my left, with your heated
sighs, who molded my helix,
whispering at my side.

It was you by the black
Window's trembling tulle pattern
who laid in my row cavern
a voice calling you back.

I was practically blind.
You appearing, then hiding,
Gave me my sight and heightened
it. Thus some leave behind

A trace. Thus they make worlds.
Thus, having done so, at random
wastefully they abandon
their work to its whirls.

Thus, prey to speeds
of light, heat, cold or darkness,
a sphere in space without markers
Spins and spins.
(From *Urania*. Translated by Paul Graves. First appeared in
Western Humanities Review, Spring, 1988)

A year later, Brodsky dedicated to Marina a poignantly
nostalgic poem "Kellomäki" (as explained earlier, an old name
for Komarovo). Here is a verse from it:

...Did it really happen, all that? And if yes, why
now disturb the peace of these has-beens by
recalling details, testing shadowy pines by grip
—aping the afterlife (often accurately) when asleep?
Only those who believe (in angels, in roots) will rise
again. And what honestly could Kellomäki prize
as such, save its rail and its schedule of tin-plate links,
whishing from nonexistence, by which these things
would be gobbled up five minutes later, along with blurred
thoughts of love, plus those who jumped aboard?
(Translated by Brodsky, first appeared in *The New Yorker*,
January 26, 1987)

The same year Brodsky dedicated "The Elegy" to Marina:
"Even now, remembering your voice, I feel excitement."
(1982.)
...And, it seems, this was the last poem dedicated to her...

Another seven years passed. Perhaps his feelings cooled
somewhat. In 1989, Joseph Brodsky addressed the most
important, the most beloved woman of his life with these verses:

BRISE MARINE

Dear I ventured out of the house late this evening, merely
for a breath of fresh air from the ocean not far away.
The sun was smoldering low like a Chinese fan in a gallery
and a cloud reared up its huge lid like a Steinway.

A quarter century back you craved curry and dates from
Senegal,
tried your voice for the stage, scratched profiles in a sketch
pad,
dallied with me—but later alloyed with a chemical
engineer and, judging by letters, grew fairly stupid.

These days you've been seen in churches in the capital and in
provinces,
at rites for our friends or acquaintances, now continuous;
yet I am glad, after all, that the world still promises
distances more inconceivable than the one between us.

Understand me correctly, though, your body, your warble,
your middle name
Now stir practically nothing. Not that they've ceased by
burgeon;
but forget one life, a man needs at minimum
one more life. And I've done that portion.
You got lucky as well; where else, save in a snapshot perhaps,
will you forever remain free of wrinkles, lithe, caustic, vivid?
Having bumped into memory, time learns its impotence.

Ebb tide; I smoke in the darkness and inhale rank seaweed.
(Translated by Brodsky. First appeared in the *The Times Literary Supplement*, February 1, 1991)

Of course, it is a very strong and significant poem. It seems to summarize the most important and possibly the most painful period in Brodsky's life. And yet... The lines "dallied with me—but later alloyed with a chemical engineer and, judging by letters, grew fairly stupid" seemed to me not only excessively cruel—they seemed unworthy of his love. Joseph often talked about "taking the high road" as a paradigm for noble behavior, and here he seemed to be unable to do that.

I did not dare to express my opinion to Brodsky either in person or by phone. I don't think he would have listened, anyway. But these lines bothered me, so I wrote him a letter:

"Joseph, forgive me or curse me, but I cannot stay silent. What did you proclaim to the world in this poem? That you finally stopped loving M.B. and got free a quarter century later from her charms? That you are cured of your 'chronic illness?' And in honor of this event, you hit her in the solar plexus?

"Why would an independent free spirit spit across the ocean in the face of the woman whom he had loved 'more than angels and Himself?'

"In poetry, great feelings are expressed by great lines. Remember Pushkin?

I loved you once: of love, perhaps, an ember
Within my soul is not extinguished yet;
But let that be no prompting to remember,
Or be a cause of sadness or regret.
I loved you once, quite hopeless, dumbly tender,
By jealousy and diffidence oppressed;
I loved you once with such complete surrender
As may God grant you may again be blessed.
(Translated by Alan Myers. *An Age Ago*. A selection of Nineteeth-Century Russian Poetry. Farrar, Straus and Giroux, NYC 1988)

"That's who took the high road.
Yours L.S."

129

No reaction followed this *démarche*.

Actually, it was pretty stupid of me to remind Brodsky of the immortal lines by Pushkin. He had them in mind without my help, though at a different time and for a different reason. In "Twenty Sonnets to Mary Stewart" written in 1974, Sonnet VI sounds as follows:

> ...I loved you. And my love for you (it seems,
> it's only pain) still stabs me through the brain.
> The whole thing's shattered into smithereens.
> I tried to shoot myself... But using a gun
> is not so simple. And the temples: which one,
> the right or left? Reflection, not the twitching,
> kept me from acting. Jesus, what a mess!
> I loved you with such strength, such hopelessness!
> May God send you in others – not a chance!
> He, capable of many things at once,
> Won't – citing Parmenides – reinspire
> The bloodstream fire, the bone-crushing creeps,
> Which melt the lead in fillings with desire
> To touch—"your hips," I must delete your lips.
> (Translated by Peter France with Brodsky, first appeared
> in *London Magazine* October/November 1988)

Here is another example. Brodsky published the poems to Marina written from 1962 to 1982 as a separate book. When Genrikh Shteinberg came to America on a business visit in 1989, Brodsky gave him a copy of this book. This was the same Genrikh Shteinberg who allegedly jumped from the Sparrow's Nest in the Crimea in Chapter Three of this memoir. He became a prominent vulcanologist, found rare and important metals in volcano gases in Kamchatka, and became one of the first humans (if not the first) to descend into the crater of an erupting volcano. Brodsky wrote the following dedication on the book that he presented to Shteinberg:

> While you were busy studying the lava,
> I was fooling around with an easy lay.

10: Marina

And now please accept, oh hero of Kamchatka,
The imprints of that foolishness.

So much for the poet's immortal love.

11

They Try the Poets There

ON A COLD AND RAINY EVENING on November 29, 1963, a friend
called me up and said only: "Read today's '*Vecherka*'" before
hanging up. I went out to get the newspaper ('*Vecherny
Leningrad*'—'Leningrad in the Evening'), and began reading it
right there by the newsstand in the rain. There was a large article signed A. Ionin, Ya. Lerner, and M. Medvedev, under the
title "Drone from the Literary Fringes."

"Some years ago on the fringes of Leningrad's literary circles
there appeared a young man who called himself a poet.... Friends
called him simply Osya, but in other places he was addressed by
his full name—Iosif Brodsky. He attended the meetings of the
association of young writers but then he decided to climb
Parnassus on his own. And what entitled this arrogant youth to
enter the realm of literature? He had a couple of dozen poems to
his name, all written down in a thin school notebook, and all
revealing the author's deeply flawed outlook on life. "Cemetery,"
"I will die"—these are the titles of his poems. In them he imitates
other poets who preached pessimism and distrust of human nature
and his poems are a mixture of decadence, modernism, and simple
gibberish. Crude plagiarisms, to be sure, since Brodsky could
not create anything on his own—did not have the talent or the
knowledge; lacked the culture. Anyway, what can you expect
from a half-educated individual who did not even finish high

132

school? ...This alleged poet has neither a real job to support himself, nor any knowledge about literature...

"... But we have not yet told you the most important thing. Gibberish, graveyard/funereal subject matter—these are only one part of Brodsky's supposedly innocent little games. Yet there is more: 'I love an alien motherland.'

"As you can see, this pygmy arrogantly climbing Parnassus is not so harmless. Confessing that he 'loves an alien motherland' Brodsky has been extremely frank. Truly, he does not love his Fatherland nor does he conceal that fact. More than that—he has for a long time been cherishing treasonous plans against the Motherland: to escape abroad!"

The end of the article left no doubt about the real purpose of this publication. It was not about literary criticism or exchange of opinions. It was a call for action.

"Clearly it is time to stop babying this near-literary parasite. There is no place in Leningrad for such as Brodsky.... Not only Brodsky, but all who surround him are treading the same dangerous path. Let the near-literary spongers like Iosif Brodsky be dealt the harshest rebuff, so that he will no longer muddy our clear waters!"[1]

This was not an empty threat. Articles like this were not published in Soviet newspapers just to express someone's personal literary opinion. They played an important role in supporting what in the Soviet Union was considered a just course in the management of the arts. First, a Party boss or KGB official would decide that someone had overstepped the bounds of acceptable behavior. Next, a newspaper would publish a "signal" describing how low this person had fallen. Often, the same newspaper would publish letters from readers (whose only knowledge of the subject came from the article they had read in the self-same newspaper) expressing their "horror" and demanding a punishment. Next, the police and court system "responded to the signal" and doled out a legal punishment, using the newspaper article and the readers' letters as admissible evidence. Finally, a new batch of letters from the readers arrived expressing their complete satisfaction with the justice dispensed.

November 29, 1963, was the black day that marked the beginning of Iosif Brodsky's persecution. Other events followed:

his arrest and two trials, his exile into a faraway village in the Arkhangelsk region with forced labor, his return home, and finally his exile from the country. Before I describe all this some obvious questions require an answer. Why was the Leningrad administration, why were the party bosses and all the powerful apparatus of the Soviet system so eager to destroy this 24-year-old poet? He hadn't killed anybody, he hadn't stolen anything, he hadn't tried to overturn the Soviet regime and hadn't even written any anti-Soviet poems. What kind of threat was he to society? Why persecute Brodsky—but not the other writers and poets who were also trying to find their way under the watchful eye of the party? How was he different?

In the context of Russian history, Brodsky's story isn't that unusual. For at least two hundred years, the Russian public, government, and literary establishment had all agreed that a writer was more than an artist who wanted to entertain the public in his quest for personal fame. The artist was to teach an eager-to-learn public what was right and what was wrong. The government had the duty (and the right) to see that this influence was not seductive or subversive. Censorship of the printed word was deemed a very good idea. Who knows what an irresponsible writer might write? Most of the time, censorship would not turn up anything serious: many Russian writers shared the values of the government and were willing to produce books that would not challenge them.

There were a few exceptions, of course—mostly writers who were infected with the ideas of liberal French philosophers and other Western thinkers. These writers also wanted their books to influence their readers' minds, but wanted to have an influence that ran counter to the government's. At the end of the Eighteenth Century, Catherine the Great crushed the writer Radishchev, who had portrayed the misery of Russian serfs that he had observed while traveling from Petersburg to Moscow. He was first sentenced to death. Then, as an act of clemency, the execution was commuted to 10 years of exile in Siberia. At the beginning of the Nineteenth Century, the poet Pushkin got himself in trouble with the censor, was exiled from Petersburg and sentenced to house arrest in the country. Since his talent was heads and shoulders above all other Russian writers of the time, Tsar Nicolas the First did him a special favor—became his personal censor. Indeed, the tsar read Pushkin's manuscripts and made his life miserable demanding changes and corrections. In the second half of the Nineteenth Century, Dostoyevsky was sentenced to death for his participation in a society of free thinkers. The sentence was commuted, but not before Dostoyevsky had been escorted to the city square where he witnessed the execution of several of his comrades, was blindfolded in front of a firing squad, and heard his death sentence read aloud. After ten years of hard labor and compulsory army service, Dostoyevsky was under severe censorship for the rest of his life. With time the punishments became milder. At the beginning of the twentieth century, Tolstoy was "only" excommunicated by the Russian Orthodox Church.

However severe, tsarist government concerns for the ideological health of Russian society were nothing compared with the paranoia of the Bolsheviks. They exterminated whole segments of the Russian population who could not accept Communist ideas (such as the nobility, the clergy or anyone who owned income-producing property or employed hired hands). It took the Soviet government and its security apparatus many years and several purges to do the job, but do it they did.

The rest of the population had to undergo indoctrination. It started in nursery school and continued through elementary school, high school, college, working years, and retirement. To make sure that no alien influences would corrupt people's minds, all means by which news and information could be disseminated were brought under tight government control. One could not Xerox a scrap of paper by going to a corner shop. To copy a business document, one took it to the company copy center after obtaining both business permissions and security clearances: access to copy machines was more tightly guarded than access to bank accounts. If one had written a scientific paper, a committee of colleagues had to certify that it would not provide foreign readers with knowledge that could jeopardize the security of the state. In the Soviet Union, all printed matter—books, newspapers, street posters, even movie tickets—had to carry a permission number in small print. It was the censor's permission, but it did not say "censored." The censorship itself was a state secret. The censors had a list of topics that could not be discussed in print, but the list itself was classified.

When World War II started, the government confiscated all radio receivers and installed a huge network of PA systems to broadcast government-controlled news, talk shows, and concerts. For those who could not afford a newspaper, there were stands on each street corner where the daily newspaper was glued over yesterday's. When the war ended, radio receivers were again allowed. To prevent the public from listening to the BBC, the Voice of America or *Svoboda* [Radio Liberty] broadcasts in Russian, jamming stations ["*glushilki*"] were placed around large cities. This made listening to these "hostile lying voices" not only futile but dangerous: from the jamming noise in your room, your neighbor could easily guess what you were trying to do.

Art played an important part in all this. Movies, paintings, and songs had to show the glorious past and the exciting present, extol the delights of manual labor and say that everything would be all right despite temporary hardships. Writers were expected to be "the engineers of human souls." Official writers were paid generous royalties. The Union of Soviet Writers had branches in all major cities, and its members received government dachas, better apartments, paid-up stays at resorts closed to the general public, permissions to travel abroad and other perks. In their novels and poems, writers had to sing the praises of "new, socialist humans." Those who did not were punished. Brodsky was not the only one, and he was not the first.

World-famous Osip Mandelshtam and Isaac Babel died in the Gulag as unnamed prisoners. Marina Tsvetayeva was silenced (without much public discussion) and committed suicide. Mikhail Zoshchenko and Anna Akhmatova were condemned in a special finding of the Central Committee of the Communist Party in 1946. Though not arrested, they were barred from publishing and lived in poverty. Their names were crossed out of the 1952 edition of the fifty-volume *Great Soviet Encyclopedia*.

Boris Pasternak's *Doctor Zhivago* could not clear the censor. After much anguish (he knew it was very dangerous), he published the book abroad in 1957. This act—mundane in any other country—was labeled treason in Russia. The Nobel Prize that was awarded him in 1958 did not help but made things worse. The Soviet Union viewed the award as a slap in the face. The

Union of the Soviet Writers expelled Pasternak and it even had the nerve to petition the government to strip Pasternak of his Soviet citizenship. Those who read about him in the newspapers were writing letters like the following: "I have not read Pasternak's book, but now that I know how horrible it is I demand that Pasternak be punished." Some official writers were not ashamed to sign letters calling for Pasternak's execution. Eventually, Pasternak succumbed to all the pressure and published in the Party newspaper *Pravda* a letter saying that he refused to accept the Nobel Prize. Nothing was gained by this, however.

Pasternak was not an obscure youth, he was a master with fifty years of experience, a famous, internationally known poet. Yet nobody published even one letter in his defense. Ironically, we called this period "the vegetarian era"—Stalin died in 1953, he was denounced by the Party in 1956 (though only to private Party audiences and not within earshot of the general public), and Pasternak was not even arrested. They let him die in his own bed.

It was different with Brodsky. There were people who felt that they could risk their reputation, security and well-being and raise their voices for what they felt was right. In this sense, Brodsky was the first. Probably Brodsky was not the only one who did not want to write poetry that would be acceptable to the Union of Soviet Writers, but he manifested the unique combination of traits that made him an ideal target for Party rage despite the fact that nothing of his had yet been published.

The "*Vecherka*" article said that he wanted to make it on his own, outside the young writers' association. In the Soviet Union, this was a sign of rebellion not to be tolerated: he wanted to circumvent the accepted system of training and supervision. The same message is being sent by the assertion that he didn't finish high school. This was no Bill Gates who was free to decide whether he should continue studying at Harvard or go into business: in Russia, an attempt to avoid indoctrination in school was a clear sign of rebellion. The article said that Brodsky's poetry was pessimistic, that he wrote about cemeteries and death. In Russia, this was no private matter either: the poet had to lead the readers to new achievements; if he did not, he was indeed a drone.

The "*Vecherka*" article said that Brodsky did not hold a job: another grave accusation. In Russia, holding a salaried job was not a matter of preference, it was a social duty. Entrepreneurial activities such as private contracting or services (especially, buying and selling) did not qualify. Earnings from these activities were called "non-work-related income" and made you liable for prosecution. In 1961, to combat any private activity, the government passed a law entitled "On intensifying the struggle against individuals avoiding socially useful work and leading an antisocial, parasitic way of life." People sentenced under this law were not permitted to live in metropolitan centers. They were exiled to remote villages and forced to accept manual jobs there. One wonders what people who lived in those remote villages and had manual jobs thought about this "punishment"— that is, the characterization of their day-to-day existence as suitable for criminals who were doing time.

Finally, the "*Vecherka*" article accused Brodsky of treason. Never mind that the issue was merely his desire to live abroad. For a Soviet citizen, this was tantamount to the statement that life in the Soviet Union was less attractive than life abroad. This ran against every tenet of Soviet propaganda and could not be tolerated. It was not even about the law of 1961. For this, one could get a prison term or even a death sentence.

We see that the accusations were serious and, from the accepted Soviet point of view, they were valid. Brodsky was indeed different from other young poets. He felt free in this country of rigid regimen. He was making decisions such as not to continue his official education, not to hold a steady job, ignoring the official channels by which he could get into the Writers' Union, writing poetry that ignored official Soviet ideology. This total freedom was indeed unique. All our friends were trying to do at least something that let them pass as obedient Soviet citizens—studying in colleges, working as engineers, researchers, teachers, journalists and the like. Brodsky was different. Small wonder that the Leningrad KGB and party administration felt that he was dangerous. He wasn't their "Soviet breed," he was *l'étranger.*

In his keenly clairvoyant poem "From the Suburb to the Center" the 22-year-old Brodsky wrote:

Thank God, I am a stranger,
I blame nobody here.
One knows nothing.
I go in a hurry, I pass by.
How easy I feel now,
because I didn't part with anybody,
thank God, I was left without a motherland.

This is a pretty explosive statement in a country where the lack of allegiance to one's country was equated with the loyalty to the enemies of the country. Although Brodsky didn't commit any antisocial acts, his thoughts were "different," he was a free person in a country of slaves, and his fierce independence was an organic part of his nature and his character. This independence could be traced to his earliest poems and verses. They were circulating in *samizdat,* bearing the fresh wind of freedom (or a frightening contagion in the minds of certain officials who stood guard over the people's sensibilities).

So that's how it began. Two weeks after the article, the Leningrad chapter of the Union of Soviet Writers discussed it. One of the authors, Lerner, made the presentation. He stressed that Brodsky was at the center of "antisocial elements" such as drunkards, drug addicts, dealers in clothes bought from foreign tourists—that he socialized with American tourists, dealt in foreign currency, subscribed to anti-Soviet and Zionist views. Anyone who defended such a person would also be tacitly insisting that these accusations were unimportant. The frightened writers voted for the motion to ask the Leningrad government to prosecute Brodsky under the 1961 law.

Brodsky went to Moscow to stay with friends. Several prominent figures such as writers Akhmatova, Marshak, Tchukovsky, composer Shostakovich, journalist Vigdorova pleaded with Party bosses and the Attorney General. This was one of the remarkable "firsts" for Soviet culture but it brought no results. When Marina's betrayal compelled Brodsky to return home, the Kafkaesque "process" rolled along.

On February 13th Iosif was among the guests we had invited to our home. I remember that he was going to stop first at Sergei Slonimsky's [Sergei is now a famous Russian composer] who lived halfway between Iosif's place and ours, and bring him along. All our guests had already arrived. We were hungry and tired of waiting, and still they did not come. We called Slonimsky. He said that Iosif had never showed up and that he did not know whether he should wait longer or not. We decided not to wait. We called Iosif. Aleksandr Ivanovich said that Osya had left a long time ago. Perhaps he had gone to a different get-together, I thought—that had been known to happen.

Brodsky did not show up, but Aleksandr Ivanovich called the next day and said that Osya had been arrested and kept at the Dzerzhinsky police station. In his interview with the writer Volkov, given in the nineties, Brodsky spoke but two sentences on the subject of this arrest:

"They hassled me in the street and took me to the police station. They kept me there for maybe two weeks."[2]

But I remember the more detailed story of the arrest that Iosif told Aleksandr Ivanovich and Aleksandr Ivanovich repeated to me: as soon as Iosif left the house, three bozos came up and started bothering him—asked him if he was Brodsky, began spouting anti-Semitic bullshit, and imitating the burr in his speech [a common Russian way to taunt a Jew]. Iosif punched one of them. Then they twisted his arms behind his back and bundled him into a car.

Brodsky asked the police to notify his parents so that they would know that he was alive, but they refused. He asked for paper and pen to write a complaint to the district attorney, but this request was refused also. During his first five days in solitary confinement, no visitors (including his parents) were allowed. Jailing Brodsky and keeping him locked up in solitary confinement without bail was in violation of Soviet law. Protests did nothing to free him, however, and the first hearing took place February 18 in the district court on Vosstaniya Street. Quite a crowd collected at the entrance. The quickest ones (my husband and I among them) managed to get in and up the stairs, but only a few were allowed into the courtroom. The stairs were dark and full of junk, people stood along two flights, some hugging the railings, some the walls. Positioned thus we awaited the end of the session.

Another "first" was a transcript of the hearing made by an independent observer, the journalist Vigdorova. Previous political trials had left no unofficial records—only records that conveyed what the government wanted the public to know. Thus the government not only stripped accused citizens of their basic human rights, but also counterfeited their place in history. During this trial, the judge Savel'eva also ordered Vigdorova to stop recording and threatened prosecution if she did not. Vigdorova was one of the most vocal defenders of Brodsky. She pleaded on his behalf in the corridors of power, crying out for justice. In the courtroom, she resorted to deception and continued taking notes while looking straight at the judge.

Thanks to Vigdorova's courage and persistence both our contemporaries and our descendants will know the truth about what happened in these courtrooms and about those who were trying to sink the poet, and about those who tried to save him. Her transcript was circulated in *samizdat* and was leaked to the West. This played a significant role in creating external pressure on the Soviet government to release Brodsky. We had no idea how the Soviet government would punish Vigdorova for "slandering" the Soviet system (the standard accusation for any free speech in Russia). Several writers, eager to please the government, proposed expelling her from the Union of Soviet Writers, opening the way for further persecution. Tragically, Vigdorova was diagnosed with cancer soon after the Brodsky trial and died before he was released.

The transcript shows how far Brodsky was from the judge's idea of a Soviet citizen. (The segments given here were translated by Yefim Etkind.)

Savel'eva: What is your work?

Brodsky: I write poems, I translate. I believe...

Savel'eva: There will be no "I believe." Stand straight! Don't lean on the wall. Look at the Court. Answer the Court as directed! (To me: immediately stop writing! Otherwise, I will throw you out!) Now, do you have a permanent job?

Brodsky: I thought that I had permanent work, yes.

Savel'eva: Answer precisely!

Brodsky: I wrote poems. I thought that they would be published. I believe...

Savel'eva: We are not interested in "I believe." Answer: why were you not working?

Brodsky: I worked. I wrote poems.

Savel'eva: This does not interest us. We are interested in what firm you were connected to.

Brodsky: I had agreements with a publishing house.

Savel'eva: And in general, what is your specialty?

Brodsky: Poet. Poet and translator.

Savel'eva: And who decided that you are a poet? Who put you in the ranks of the poets?

Brodsky: Nobody. (Without challenging.) And who put me in the ranks of mankind?

Savel'eva: Did you study for this?

Brodsky: Study for what?

Savel'eva: To become a poet. You never tried to finish college where they prepare... where they study...

Brodsky: I didn't think that this was a matter of education.

Savel'eva: And if not through education, how is it?

Brodsky: I thought... well (perplexed), I thought it came from God.

Savel'eva: Do you have any petitions to this court?

Brodsky: Yes, I would like to know what I was arrested for.

Savel'eva: This is a question, not a petition.

Brodsky: Then I do not have petitions.

At the end, the judge decided to show mercy towards the defendant. She interrupted the trial and ordered that Brodsky be sent to a prison psychiatric clinic to evaluate whether "sending him to remote places with forced labor" was contraindicated for any reason. However, the motion to free him on bail so that he could go to the clinic from his home was denied.

Before they took the accused out of the courtroom, policemen shouting that the stairs had to be cleared rudely pushed us out into the street. A windowless Black Maria drove up and parked, blocking the sidewalk, with its back doors flush with the doors of the district court building, so as to prevent the accused from seeing through the four-inch gaps between the two doors. Cops lined up on both sides. Curious passersby were asking: "Who they got?" and "What they got him for?" Some said for knife-fighting, some said that the guy had been handing out anti-Soviet flyers... I heard one granny explaining that "It's the guy who pinched a sweater from the Passage Department Store."

We were already out on the street and did not see Brodsky as he was taken out of the courtroom. But our friends who managed to stay on the stairs said that Iosif was led out with great speed, led down the stairs almost on the run, and bundled into the car "from door to door." (Later Brodsky said that the guards in the Black Maria were sympathetic, let him have a smoke, and asked him to write a poem about them some day.) Our friends told me that the judge was surprised when she saw such a crowd. She said, "I do not understand why so many people came here." Somebody said, "But it is not every day that a poet is put on trial," and the judge answered: "It is all the same to us, poet or no poet."

The psychiatric evaluation confirmed that Brodsky could stand trial, exile, and forced labor. At that time we did not know that the government demanded the cooperation of psychiatrists in suppressing dissent, and we did not understand what horrors Iosif went through.

The second trial took place in a builder's club, on Fontanka, near the City Courthouse, on March 13, 1964, a month after his arrest. This unusual site was chosen so that workers the government had invited to the trial would feel at ease. Some of these workers served as witnesses for the prosecution, others played the part of the public, spontaneously booing, laughing, applauding and sneering at appropriate moments. The presence of the public and their use as a kind of chorus, however, may have made this trial the first of its kind. In arrogance and shamelessness these proceedings constitute some of the most disgraceful pages in Soviet history of the sixties.

The court calendar posted in the hall said, "Trial of the parasite Brodsky." So much for being presumed innocent until proven guilty. Guilt had to be presumed, or so it seemed, before the trial could begin.

We managed to get a few places in the fourth row. Next to my husband Victor, mother and myself sat the film director Ilya Averbakh. Victor held a photo camera in his hands. A policeman noticed it and barked an order: put it away immediately or he would take it away.

The air in the crowded hall was electric. It felt as if lighting a match would have been enough to blow the whole builder's club to smithereens. Cops were posted on each side of every row and noticed every movement. Averbakh put a notebook on his knees, fencing it off with his briefcase, and tried to take notes, but in a few minutes the very same cop popped up at his side and tore the notebook out of his hands.

Brodsky stood half-turned to us. He was wearing an unbuttoned dark-gray coat, corduroy trousers, and a reddish-brown sweater. He was very tense, but behaved with great dignity and calm.

Many years later, in New York, I asked Brodsky why was he so unperturbed, as if events were happening not to him but to someone else.

"It was so much less important than the story with Marina—all my mental strength went into dealing with that misfortune."

The expression on his face I remember to this day. It was not frightened, nor hunted, nor bewildered. His face, rather, expressed the perplexity of a civilized man present at a show staged by Neanderthals.

Actually, the testimony of some witnesses for the prosecution was so ludicrous that Iosif smiled a few times. For instance, when public prosecutor Sorokin stood up and said that Brodsky was being defended by parasites, bugs, and wood lice. (In fact the letters defending Brodsky were signed by the famous Russian writers Chukovsky, Marshak, Akhmatova, and the world-famous composer Shostakovich.) Or when the ready-for-anything redhead Romashova, faculty head of the department of Marxism-Leninism, began to bleat that she did not know Brodsky, had never seen him before in her life, had never read his poems, but that she had heard what young people said about him, and that his poems were "Horrible! Horrible!"

I don't remember if Joseph's favorite joke about a brothel existed then, but if it did, it was no doubt what he was remembering during comrade Romashova's speech.

[In a brothel the madam sends a girl in to a new client. In a minute the girl runs out of the room screaming, "Horrible! Horrible!" The madam sends in another beauty, but she also runs from the room screaming, "Horrible! Horrible!" Madam then goes to the client herself. In about ten minutes she comes out and calmly says, "Yes, it's horrible. But not 'Horrible! Horrible!'"]

As in the first trial, Judge Savel'eva implied that Brodsky was a parasite. This seemed to be a foregone conclusion so that the whole trial was not necessary. Still, they had to keep up the decorum of legality and respect for law. Here again are some segments from the transcript of the second trial made illegally by Vigdorova:

Savel'eva: Why did you not work while you were between jobs and why did you lead the life of a parasite?

Brodsky: I worked. I was busy with the same work that I do all the time: I was writing poetry.

Savel'eva: So, you were writing your so-called poems? . . . And what did you do of utility for the Motherland?

Brodsky: I was writing poetry. This is my work. I am convinced, I believe that what I wrote will be of service to humanity, and not only now but for future generations as well.

A voice from the public: Who would believe it? He thinks too highly of himself!

Savel'eva: So, you think that your so-called poems are of service to humanity?

Brodsky: And why do you call my poems "so-called" poems?

Savel'eva: We call your poems "so-called" poems because we do not have any other notion about your poems.

Defense Counsel: Were you connected with the translation section of the Union of Soviet Writers?

Brodsky: Yes, I participated in the collection *First Time In Russian*, and read my translations from Polish.

Savel'eva: (to defense counsel) You must ask him about the useful work he has done. Instead, you are asking about his public readings.

Defense Counsel: His translations are useful work.

Savel'eva: You, Brodsky, had better explain to this court why you did not work while between jobs.

Brodsky: I worked. I was writing poetry.

Savel'eva: But there are people who work in factories and write poetry. What prevented you from doing so?

Brodsky: People are different from each other. Even in the color of their hair or in facial expression.

Savel'eva: This is not your personal discovery. Everybody knows this. But you had better explain how we should evaluate your participation in our great progress building Communism.

Brodsky: Building Communism is not just standing at the lathe or plowing. It is also intellectual work which. . .

Savel'eva: Enough of this lofty speech! Did you arrive at any conclusions from your criticism in the media?

Brodsky: The article in "*Vecherka*" was all lies. This is the only conclusion I arrived at.

Defense Counsel: You said that the article "Drone from the Literary Fringes" published in the newspaper *Vecherny Leningrad* was incorrect. In what regards?

Brodsky: The only thing that was correct there was my first name and family name. Even my age was incorrect. Even the poems they quoted as mine were not written by me. There they name as my friends people whom I hardly know or do not know at all. How can I think that the article is correct and infer conclusions from it?

The witnesses for the defense were poet Natalya Grudinina who worked as an official mentor to beginning poets for eleven years, writer (and professor of foreign languages) Yefim Etkind who acted as an official tutor to young translators, and a professional translator, Admoni. They stated in no uncertain terms that they knew Brodsky's work well, that the amount of knowledge that he had accumulated from self-study was astonishing, that Brodsky was a talented poet and a hard-working translator who had already made a considerable contribution to literature and would no doubt make even more significant contributions. They spoke with passion and confidence, and I felt proud that at least some people had had the guts to stand up against the system and tell its representatives that they were wrong. At the end of the cross-examination of Professor Etkind, the judge asked him whether he had any trouble with his job. Etkind said. "No, I have not. However, I have not been to the office for two days. Maybe something has happened during this period."

Etkind was wrong, nothing happened in his office during those two days. But Judge Savel'eva had a point, and she made sure that Etkind and other defense witnesses started having problems very soon. She sent letters to their universities and to the Union of Soviet Writers stating that the defense witnesses "showed political shortsightedness, lack of political vigilance, ideological illiteracy." This was no small matter for them. Defending Brodsky or even treating him as part of literature became "radioactive": one could be punished, and punished seriously. In 1974, when Brodsky was already in America, writers Kheifets and Maramzin prepared a five-volume collection of Brodsky's works. Maramzin compiled the collection and resolved differences between different typewritten copies of the poems. Kheifets wrote an introduction to the collection, and Etkind wrote a review on the introduction. The KGB seized the manuscript, declared it "anti-Soviet" and accused all the participants of "the intent to distribute." Kheifets and Maramzin were arrested. Joseph Brodsky who was already in U.S. wrote in *The New York Review of Books* (Vol. 21, No. 14):

"In early August it was reported that the writer Vladimir Rafailovich Maramzin was arrested in Leningrad by KGB agents. Maramzin's name is certainly less known to the general public than Solzhenitsyn's. Perhaps this arrest will disclose to the reader that there is yet another writer in Russia. To put it in plain language, Russia is that country where the name of a writer appears not on the cover of his book, but on the door of his prison cell."

Kheifets served four years in a labor camp, two years in exile, and finally was allowed to emigrate to Israel.

Maramzin was sentenced to five years in a labor camp, but in July 1975 was allowed to emigrate from the Soviet Union—he wound up in France.

Etkind was expelled from the Union of Soviet Writers and from the university. Eventually, he had to emigrate, too. He moved to Paris, taught there, wrote several books, participated in conferences, was invited to speak on TV and radio.

Many years later, drinking vodka in our home in Boston, Etkind told me that he had felt sick to his stomach when the judge asked this question about the job trouble. But he decided that it was better to behave as a free person and suffer external persecution than to behave as a slave and suffer humiliation and pangs of conscience.

Witnesses for the prosecution were sticking to a simple line. They knew neither Brodsky nor his work. They knew about Brodsky from the newspaper, and they felt that a person without a high school diploma was an ignoramus who could not write poetry and that forced labor was an appropriate and just punishment for such a person.

One witness for the prosecution, member of the Writers' Union Voyevodin, served as a secretary for the committee for working with young writers. He submitted a letter to the court where he stated that Brodsky did not exist as a poet and his influence diverted young people from work, peace, and life. He presented this letter as expressing the opinion of the committee and the Writers' Union. It turned out, however, that this was a misrepresentation—Voyevodin had not discussed this letter with the committee. When asked whether he knew Brodsky personally he answered, "No. I've only been working at the Union for six months. I've never known him personally... I've read his diary and his epigrams. You would blush, comrade judges, if you were to read them. There's been some talk here about Brodsky's talent. Talent is measured only by acceptance by the people. And in this case there is (and can be) no such acceptance."

When judge Savel'eva asked whether Brodsky's talent had been discussed in the Union, Voyevodin answered in the negative. And here the name of the ill-starred Kuklin came up again. Voyevodin referred to him as to the highest authority: "My friend, the poet Kuklin, once—from the podium, in ringing tones—announced his indignation with Brodsky's poetry." When Brodsky asked how Voyevodin got hold of his diary and epigrams, Judge Savel'eva would not allow Voyevodin to answer this question. The sinister shadow of the KGB swept across the courtroom.

During the break, our friend Vika Belomlinskaya flew at Voyevodin, aiming for his face. But her husband Misha happened to be nearby and caught her hand. And although there was no resounding slap, Vika did manage to push Voyevodin and to punch him.

Later, I asked Vika why was it specifically Voyevodin who so infuriated her, since every single one of the witnesses for the prosecution had behaved like a complete pig. Vika related a story told her by her father, the journalist Israil' Markovich Antzelovich, who had been a friend of Iosif's father, Aleksandr Ivanovich Brodsky, a photojournalist at the Leningrad Front during the Second World War. They had gone through the entire war side by side.

Aleksandr Brodsky, on an assignment in the besieged Leningrad, stopped to visit his acquaintance Voyevodin (father of the witness for the prosecution) and found him semi-conscious, starving to death. Brodsky untied his kit-bag, pulled out a vial of glucose intended for his family and poured the glucose into Voyevodin's mouth. It saved him that day from a certain death. Voyevodin survived, and his son thanked Aleksandr Ivanovich by trying to destroy his son at the trial.

That Kafkaesque pageant took place against the background of a Greek chorus of workers herded into the court who understood nothing of what was happening, but who, nevertheless, were noisily indignant over a poet they had never seen, heard of, or read before, whose existence they had discerned for the first time in that courtroom. The defense council, Zoya Toporova, clearly showed that the prosecution had failed to demonstrate that Brodsky evaded "socially useful work," and furthermore that the witnesses for the prosecution had not produced any additional evidence of his guilt, and that the law about parasites could not be applied to Brodsky. All to no avail. The verdict: Joseph Brodsky would be exiled to a faraway region for five years—"*S primeneniem obiazatel'nogo truda*" [with forced manual labor.] He was sent to the village of Norenskaya, 20 miles from the nearest railroad station, in the Archangelsk region, near the Arctic Circle. [After a year and a half there he was freed thanks to the efforts of Russian and world intellectuals.]

When Anna Akhmatova learned the sentence, she exclaimed, "Oh God, what a biography they are shaping for our redhead!" [That is: "Great career move!"] It was clear that the trial and sentence would boost Brodsky's name recognition immensely. In one jump, his status had changed from little-known youth to that of a master whose name was known throughout the whole civilized world. Akhmatova was right, but Brodsky was always unhappy about this boost; he had wanted his talent as a poet to be accepted on its merits, not because he had been prosecuted by the Soviet government. Yet for everyone but Brodsky, perhaps, this trial was important principally because of the storm of protest it raised, both in Russia and abroad.

I am especially proud of what many young Leningrad writers, my friends, did in the wake of this trial. They wrote a letter to the Union of Soviet Writers stating that Voyevodin had perjured himself, lied to the court and obstructed justice. They expressed the hope that Brodsky's fate would be decided later within the framework of the law, and they stated that such an immoral and unscrupulous person as Voyevodin could not be trusted to work with young writers. Thirty-six people signed the letter! For an American, for example, signing such a letter is a normal exercise of civil liberty, mostly ineffectual, that rarely backfires. But for Russian citizens, this was a direct challenge to the KGB and the Party, and this was really the first. One of the Russian jokes of that time runs like this: "Do not even think about it. If you think, at least do not write it down. If you write, at least do not sign. And if you sign it, do not complain." I was not an official young writer at the time, so I did not have to go through the anguish of deciding whether I should sign or not. Several of the "signers" paid for their boldness, but the road to protest was open. Later, when writers Sinyavsky and Daniel were tried and imprisoned for publishing their fiction in the West, letters of protest gave the government much grief.

There was one important exception to the wave of support for Brodsky. When Etkind asked Solzhenitsyn to help Brodsky, he refused. Solzhenitsyn at that time was in favor with Khrushchev. He had just published *One Day in the Life of Ivan Denisovich*, and it was one of most important literary events in Russia. He had started working on *The Gulag Archipelago* but the KGB did not know about that yet. Solzhenitsyn explained to Etkind that no Russian writer was ever harmed by being prosecuted or persecuted in this way; indeed, that such persecution made one a better writer. Etkind told Solzhenitsyn that Brodsky was different: his health, both physical and emotional, was not robust, and humiliation and hardships could push Brodsky to suicide. Solzhenitsyn disagreed and told Etkind that this experience would make Brodsky more angry and fierce, and would be good for him.

In one of his first "Western" interviews, answering Michael Skammel's question "How did your trial and incarceration affect your work?" Brodsky said, "You know, I think it actually did me good, because those two years I spent in the village were, in my opinion, the best of my life. I worked then more than I ever have. During the day I had to do physical labor, but because it was agricultural work, and not something at the factory, there were many periods of rest when we had nothing to do."[3]

That evaluation of Brodsky's life in Norenskaya strangely coincides with Solzhenitsyn's opinion about the benefit of exile and hardship for the poet.

And although in our private talks I have never heard Iosif say that he was happy in Norenskaya, I have no reason to doubt the sincerity of his words.

Now let us jump eighteen years into the future, to the year 1982.

After receiving the Award of the MacArthur Foundation, Brodsky gave a television interview to journalist Dick Cavett. Cavett asked Joseph to talk about his time in the psychiatric prison and about the criminal methods of Soviet psychiatry.

We watched Brodsky's answers and could not believe our ears. (Unfortunately, I did not think to audiotape the interview, and so Brodsky's words, although placed in quotation marks, are not an exact quote, but convey his meaning very closely.)

"There's nothing terrible about the Soviet nuthouses, at least not about the one where I was," Brodsky said good-humoredly, sitting in a deep armchair, legs crossed, with a cigarette between his fingers. "The food was decent, much better than in jail. You could read books, listen to the radio. There were interesting people around, especially the psychos... But there were people who were quite normal, too, like me. The only bad thing was you did not know what your term was. In prison you know how long you have got to stay, but there it was complete uncertainty..."

We were dumbfounded, and I called him that very night: "Iosif, we are very upset about your interview." "Why, what's the problem?" "The entire Western world is freaking out because they put dissidents in psycho wards in the Soviet Union. There

151

are protest rallies in the universities, world-renowned psychiatrists sign letters and petitions, and you, a living witness, say 'Nothing terrible, the food is good, and the people are interesting!'"

Iosif was dismayed by my aggressiveness, but only for a second. He said that he had described only his experience, that he was a free man in a free country and had the right to say anything he pleased. I objected that as a "private person" he could show off on the air and chatter about anything he liked, but now that he had become a "public figure" he was heard by hundreds of thousands of people, and had to think before he...

Iosif did not listen to the rest, threw down the receiver, and for about two months I heard nothing from him.

Upon reflection, I could guess what brought out that nonchalant, even buffoonish tone of his. Brodsky categorically refused to be, or to be considered, a victim. The very thought that persecution, trials, psycho ward, exile—all these troubles at home—were what promoted his leap to the unattainable heights of international fame was intolerable to him. He wanted to be judged only by his literary achievements.

Once after "the Nobel" he asked me to let an organizational committee of some symposium (or congress) know that he would not participate. (I think it was in Paris, but I can't recall exactly.) It was a strange request, at the very least because Brodsky's professional contacts and business were normally taken care of by his secretary. Even though I served as his "personal emissary" on a few occasions, there was no good reason why I had to be involved in this case. Our conversation was so unexpected that I wrote it down.

"Ludessa, could you call N. N. and say that I won't be coming to the congress?"

"Why, what's the matter?"

"I don't want to..."

"Why? I have to explain it to them somehow."

"Explain it any way you like."

"But really, what's the matter?"

"Think about it. How can I come when Etkind will be there?"

???

I didn't have the slightest idea that there had been any conflict between him and Yefim Etkind, who was one of the three defenders at his trial, and someone who lost his job as a result and was forced to leave the country. So, I burst out with a "speech for the defense": "What's wrong with you? He defended you! He risked himself! He wrote about your trial in his books! He! He! He!"

"Well, can you call or not?"

"I'll call since you ask, but what did Etkind ever do to you?"

"One shouldn't skim cream off shit."

This conversation took place shortly after the publication of Etkind's book *The Trial of Iosif Brodsky* in 1988. Indeed, a significant portion of the book was reprinted from an earlier Etkind book, *The Notes of a Non-conspirator*, published in 1977. Still, this did not look like sufficient reason to avoid any contact.

I don't know if that was the real reason or just an excuse. Now I think there might have been more to this than met the eye. It's certainly true that Brodsky would grow irritated and flare up when asked about the trial. I was present in somebody's house when Iosif became quite rude to a very distinguished gentleman because he commiserated with him on "misfortunes he had known."

However, my reproach after his interview with Dick Cavett must have stayed with him. In *The Trial of Iosif Brodsky*, Etkind mentioned a certain interview that Brodsky had given to a *Nouvel Observateur* correspondent in 1987. In answer to the question "Which moment during the *épopée* of your trial was the *most painful?*" Iosif said, "The Leningrad jailhouse psychiatric clinic... They gave me terrible shots... Woke me up in the middle of the night, forced me to take baths in ice-cold water, then would wrap me up in a wet sheet and put me down next to the radiator. The heat dried the sheet and tore the skin off my body..."[4]

That interview was given after the Nobel Prize, when Brodsky had probably better understood the responsibility he bore for what he said while speaking in public. Or perhaps he felt that it would be OK at such a moment to express his true feelings.

Even more sincerely and frankly did he tell of his time in the psychiatric clinic in "The Dialogues" with Volkov, acknowledging that there people are subjected to "absolutely monstrous experiments... That is...they can be irrevocably crippled." And in the next sentence he gives an absolutely brilliant definition of prison: "A prison—what is it, after all? A lack of space, compensated by a surplus of time."[5]

---

[1]Gordin, Ya. "*Delo Brodskogo* (Brodsky's Case)." *Neva*, 1989, N. 2, 141-143
[2]Volkov, S. "*Dialogi s Iosifom Brodskim* (Dialogues with Iosif Brodsky)." *Izdatel'tsvo Nezavisimaya Gazeta*, 1998, 72
[3]Brodsky, I. "*Bol'shaya kniga interview* (*Big Book of Interviews*)." Zakharov, 2000, 8
[4]This interview was given by Brodsky to Giovanni Buttafava for "*Espresso.*" "*Nouvel Observateur*" published an abridged translation from the Italian. For the Russian translation see Brodsky, I. "*Bol'shaya kniga interview*".
[5]Volkov, S. "*Dialogi s Iosifom Brodskim*", 73

12

Departures

INSTEAD OF FIVE YEARS, Brodsky spent only eighteen months in exile. "Only" here means that his sentence was cut short, though the eighteen months did not seem short to him. His case was unusual in this regard, too. Unlike the American penitentiary system, the Soviet Union required prisoners to serve the full term of their sentences "from the first bell to the closing bell." Rehabilitation as such is never an issue—neither prisoners, nor jailers believe in it, and punishment as a deterrent to further crimes is the only goal of incarceration. This is why good behavior is no good reason for the early release of Soviet prisoners. However, an extension of their sentences is quite possible and can be easily triggered by almost anything, through a streamlined legal procedure referred to in prison slang as "hanging up another term." Prisons and labor camps are not in short supply, and there is no pressure to release prisoners because others have to take their place. And if prisoners have to be crowded into a small space, so what? Brodsky, for example, was transported to his place of exile in a prison car where sixteen prisoners were locked up in a space designed for four passengers. This was not meant as an additional punishment for Brodsky or for fifteen other inmates— it was done for the sake of efficiency. Nor was there any incentive to send a prisoner home to cut government expenses: prisoners work, and they earn their meager keep. (I remember my astonishment, almost envy, when I first saw an American prison on TV. It that the conditions were luxurious compared to the Soviet prison, but the very fact that a prison was shown on TV dumbfounded me. In the Soviet Union, any information about prisons is classified, and the producer could get arrested for divulging this kind of information.)

Why did the System relax its jaws and let the poet go home? There was only one reason: the indignation of European intellectuals after the Vigdorova transcripts were published in the West. Yakov Gordin told me that the last straw was a letter from Jean-Paul Sartre. Sartre, a staunch supporter of Stalinism, complained to Brezhnev that he would be bogged down by accusations about the harsh treatment of Brodsky during the upcoming literary congress in Paris. You can never know when a totalitarian regime will buckle under external pressure and when it will dig in its heels in denial. In this case, the Soviet government did both. Vigdorova was prosecuted for publishing her stories abroad without government permission. Ironically, it was her death that saved her from further harassment and humiliation. As for Brodsky, the screams from abroad did result in a reduced sentence. Still, the guilty verdict was never rescinded. In the Soviet Union Brodsky was a convicted criminal. He remained a convicted criminal even after he received the Nobel Prize. He was a convicted criminal even after the Soviet Union fell apart and the Communist Party disintegrated. Needless to say, a public apology to Brodsky would have been most appropriate and there certainly should have been many private expressions of remorse, but so far as I know he was denied these courtesies from the officials who were instrumental in hunting him down. To the very end a rapprochement of any kind seemed unthinkable to both sides.

His eighteen months in the tiny village Norenskaya in the Arkhangelsk region were hard and long for Iosif. Getting up at six o'clock in the morning...Hard manual labor in any weather— in rain or snow; in summer's heat or winter's freezing cold. No phone, no people to talk to, no women, horrible food. All letters to and from Iosif were opened and inspected, many were intercepted. Few visitors were allowed. The visitors did come, each visitor defying the System. They brought books, some food and booze. Iosif did not have a typewriter, and Vigdorova sent him her own with a visitor.

Again, Iosif did not complain about the hardships of his exile. He shrugged them off or even boasted at times that there were none. He was young and strong enough to endure the work. He often said that external circumstances of life were not important for what was most essential to him, his poetry. His internal processes were what mattered most—his life within the language. This is why he would shrug off the sympathy of friends. He always objected when people viewed him as a victim, or thought that his personality and his poetry were defined by his suffering. And he was always annoyed when somebody even hinted at the possibility that he became famous because of his unusual fate and not because of his talent and hard work, even his obsession with poetry. He felt that his hardships could be summarized as "a lack of mobility in space that was more than compensated by extra time available for writing poetry." Not a big deal.

I am not sure how much Brodsky was really shielded from external circumstances. To appear nonchalant about them might have been a pose. He was not ascetic at all. He loved good food, eating out. He loved drinking. He would drink wine if the situation demanded it, but he preferred vodka. He loved women. (One of his favorite statements was that adultery and promiscuity were the only forms of private enterprise that the Soviet System left to its citizens.) He loved "cool" clothes, meaning foreign clothes that were bought from a middleman who had bought them from foreign tourists. This form of private enterprise was called "*fartsovka*" and was relentlessly suppressed by the government. First, it was a form of private enterprise, period. Second, it involved socializing between Soviet citizens and foreigners. A foreigner, any foreigner was always suspected of being a spy. Even if the foreigner was not a spy, personal contacts would lead to the flow of "shameless blatant lies" to Soviet participants in the contact that the government would not tolerate.

Iosif was grateful to people who tried to defend him from the System, but his gratitude was, well, not exactly boundless. He was often skeptical about the dissidents and their defenders with their explicit opposition to the System. He felt that the scope of their activities was too narrow and too elitist. "All right," he would say, "I write poetry and this is why Sartre knows my name and my problems and writes about them to help me. But who would help countless Russians who live in poverty and ignorance? When they steal a bucket of grain from the government storehouse because their children have no food, and no food means no food, not bad food or little food, or unhealthy junk food, they are dragged into the labor camps and they kick the bucket there, and nobody, but nobody gives a damn, neither the BBC nor the Voice of America. The dissidents knew what they were doing, they had freedom of choice, but those poor Russians did not."

One side of human existence where Iosif felt that external circumstances could not be ignored was the relationship between a totalitarian state and its citizens. He did not recognize any compromise. Either you cooperated with the state and hence shared the guilt of this monstrous hydra that had killed 60 million of its subjects, turned the rest into slaves and robbed them all of human dignity—or you refused to cooperate, did not take anything from the state and accepted the consequences.

Of course, many intellectuals found the Soviet state morally repulsive. Many felt that it was shameful to be a Soviet citizen. Most of us tried to do our best, worked for the government and tried to build a fence around our private lives that would guard us from government intervention. We would analyze each situation as it evolved to decide what was moral and what was not. Iosif grew up as a staunch individualist who did not want to take orders (or hints) from the totalitarian society—or from any society. His teachers in school tried to teach him nonsense, so he walked out to protect himself from their influence (and from boredom). Soviet cultural and public service institutions were tentacles of the totalitarian state, and he did not participate in them, and did not cooperate with them, even if that meant that his poetry could not be published.

Iosif often made fun of my attempts (and others') to strike a compromise—for example, getting a Ph.D. in geology, working for research institutions and universities while avoiding Party membership and civic activities. "Listen, Kissa," he would say, "Your defenses are laughable. One movement of the state, and your life is in a shambles. But your participation legitimizes acts of theirs like the rape of Hungary in 1956 or Czechoslovakia in

1968." I tried to explain to him that Victor and I had chosen technical fields so that the content of our work was not related to Communist ideology. Our professional successes measured our real worth, and probably meant as much to us as his poetry meant to him. I am not sure I persuaded him. I am not sure I persuaded myself, but I did not see another life strategy that would lead to more meaning and stability.

For Brodsky, stability never meant much, but independence from the pressure of tyranny meant a lot. He did not hesitate to meet with foreign students, journalists, and intellectuals visiting the Soviet Union and to carry on wide-ranging discussions. Of course, he was not reckless—we all had to consider the possibility that our homes were bugged, and we would either cover the telephone with a pillow, or would turn the dial and put a pencil into one of its holes so that the dial could not rotate back (we thought that this would turn off eavesdropping devices) or better yet, we would go outside.

In addition he was not afraid to give his work to foreign publishers. His first book of poems (in Russian) was published in the United States in 1965, when he was still in the Arkhangelsk Region. His second book, "Elegy to John Donne and Other Poems" [in English] was published in England in 1967. His third book [again in Russian] was published in the United States in 1970. It was amazing that Iosif was able to get away with publishing abroad. In 1956, Pasternak was tormented to death for doing so. In 1965, Daniel and Sinyavsky were arrested, tried, and given long prison terms for publishing their novels abroad under pen names.

What was interesting, however, was that, unlike many authors (myself, for example), Iosif did not feel the need to see his name in print and did not feel an immense joy when he saw it. On the contrary, he was always complaining that his books were badly edited, that dedications were mixed up, that the dates were all wrong, and the order of the poems was ridiculous and did not represent the flow of his thoughts correctly. Such grumbling became quite typical for Iosif. Most of his books were put together without his participation. This was true about books published abroad while he still was in the Soviet Union. It was also true about books published in Russia while he was in the States. When he had an opportunity to put the book together, he felt he did not have time and asked somebody else to do it. "Why do you always accuse other people of doing sloppy work," I asked him. "Why won't you do better work yourself?" "Well," he said, "If I have time and inspiration, I would rather do what I do best, writing '*stishki*' [derogative word for poetry; as noted elsewhere, in talking about himself Brodsky carefully avoided the solemnity of the words "poem" and "poetry," preferring the more informal words "verses" or "rhymes"], and I actually like the process of writing most. In addition, I dislike many of my old poems. If I have no inspiration for writing something new, I am so depressed that I cannot do any other work. If I have no time, then this is the end of it—I have no time."

Meanwhile, a new phenomenon entered the life of Soviet citizens at that time—the possibility of emigrating from the Soviet Union legally. Before that, the borders of the country were, as Soviet propaganda proudly boasted, "locked." All eleven thousand miles (or whatever it was) of the land border were protected by a metal fence with barbed wire all over. During the day, the fence was guarded by patrols. During the night, searchlights from the guard towers lit the fence. The land around the fence ("the footprint strip") was raked every evening and inspected every morning—did anybody cross this strip of land during the night? Kids in school learned about spies who would sneak into the country wearing horseshoes turned backward, so that border guards would think that a horse had left the country— to no avail, because the brave border guards could not be fooled. (If a spy got through, according to the story being taught to our schoolchildren, the first village kids to spot him would report him to the authorities.) Every mile of the border beach was swept every evening, too.

Indeed, the border was locked, and one could leave the country only secretly, traveling through uninhabited lands and avoiding recognition by locals who were likely to report a fugitive. Once in a geological expedition in Karelia, near the border with Finland, our party of three was spotted by locals, and we were detained by the local branch of the KGB because we did not have the documents that would prove that we were indeed geologists. In a typical catch-22, we did not have the documents because the

on him and write to us...Only write the truth."

Such are the twists of fate: when Iosif was leaving he asked us to "keep an eye" on his parents, and now we were charged with the task of "keeping an eye" on him.

After we left Leningrad we kept in touch with Iosif's parents. I have kept several of their postcards and letters.

"Ludochka!

"We are taking this opportunity to also wish you a Happy New Year. Let us hope that all the noble wishes appropriate to the occasion will definitely come true.

"This letter is late in sending mainly because of Lev Tolstoy, whose anniversary had so absorbed your friend Iosif that he did not really have time to write us your address.

"But now he has written and said that you are living in a historically interesting place, and not in some hole in the wall. All the best to you.

December 1979, A. and M."

"Ludochka, how are you?

"Please don't think we've got swelled heads or anything like that. It's just that we did not know where to write to thank you for your interesting letter or, rather, your piece of eyewitness reporting. If you ever write anything like that again, and with a modern slant, it will be beyond praise. All in all we must say that a literary essay is definitely your next vocation, we believe in the endless talents that have yet to be developed. And so, we live in expectation.

"In the meantime we consult with the representatives of the science of medicine, who help with some things, and during the breaks we stop by cafeterias—naturally, health-food ones, and also allow ourselves some other pleasures—alas, very much of the intellectual kind.

"We trust that in your life everything is exactly the other way around, which makes us only happy for you. That's why you are never bored, and may you never be!

"Hugs and kisses.
Maria Moiseevna+Aleksandr Ivanovich
2. 20. 80"

"Luda, how are you!

"We wish you a happy Spring holiday and a happy March 8 'Lady Day.' We hope that there as here on this day the men show up with chocolates, flowers, *Chanel*, and vodka, which you now have in abundance, as we do Pepsi-Cola. Especially since vodka is Russian. As to what you'll have to eat, we'll leave it to you to tell. We are having special pancakes and Atlantic herring. There! On this festive day doctors cancel diets for women.

"Here is wishing you the same—that is, nothing but good times. Our best wishes to mother, daughter, and, of course, to the provider Vitya.

Maria M. and Al-dr Iv."

They always tried to be cheerful even though they struggled all their lives. Maria Moiseevna had never gone to college—her parents were merchants before the revolution, and this closed the doors of colleges and universities to their daughter. All her life she held different kinds of office or bookkeeping jobs. The bright side was that these low-profile jobs attracted less competition and scrutiny and were available even for a Jew of a less than proletarian origin. She said she never had trouble finding a job. In addition to her job, she ran the household—cooking (in a communal kitchen, alongside three neighbors), doing laundry (in the shared bathroom, without a washing machine or a dryer), shopping (this meant standing in several lines in several stores after work and carrying food home on foot), serving and cleaning (since her men were not particularly dexterous, and broke everything they touched, she preferred to do everything herself).

Aleksandr Ivanovich went to college, became an officer in the Soviet Navy, served tours of duty in several hot battles during the WWII, was decorated and promoted. It seemed that everything was going well for him, but in the Soviet Union success itself can be one's downfall. In 1948, Zhdanov signed a law that forbade officers of Jewish origin to hold high positions in the Soviet Navy. It was a secret law, you could not read about it in newspapers—but it was the law all right. Aleksandr Ivanovich was discharged from the Navy without a pension and for the rest of his life worked as a freelance photographer for small-circulation newspapers that belonged to different organizations and ministries. This was anything but a lucrative job, and the family relied on Maria Moiseevna's meager salary and on whatever Iosif would earn when he dropped out of high school at fifteen years of age.

It is a sad story, and I will end it on a sad note. It is about yet another interference in private lives. When Maria Moiseevna applied for a tourist visa to visit Iosif in 1979, her application was rejected. The OVIR did not have the effrontery to tell her that the degree of kinship was not sufficiently close. Instead, the official said: "We sent your son to Israel, but you are asking for permission to go to the United States. How did your son wind up there?" Fifty-three American congressmen signed a letter to Brezhnev asking him to let Brodsky's mother visit Iosif. Nothing helped. After all, the right to go abroad, even for a short visit, even to see a son, is not a Soviet citizen's. It is a privilege that the government grants. And if the government does not want to grant this privilege, there is no way a citizen can proceed.

Maria Moiseevna died in March of 1983. After her death Iosif's father, already very ill, applied for permission to go to his son, and twenty-three American and European intellectuals signed a petition to the Soviet government. Aleksandr Ivanovich was waiting for the response for almost six months. In April, 1984 the permission was denied, and that same month, on April 29, Aleksandr Ivanovich Brodsky died. It goes without saying that Iosif could not get a visa to attend his parents' funerals.

My blood boils when I think how cruel people can be to one another when they have power and lack morals. The storm of emotion Iosif experienced can readily be imagined. In his parting letter to Brezhnev he said, "I never felt offended by my country." Well, one might argue that a country cannot offend. But a country's officials can and do. From the time of his father's death until his own, Iosif did not want to come to Russia, even after the dissolution of the "Evil Empire." Until his own death he thought that cooperating with a totalitarian government offends intelligence, ruins integrity and profanes the soul.

13

In the New World

HOW TO DESCRIBE the feelings of a person who, having abandoned everything he had and knew, was crossing a border to face a new life for the first time, a life full of uncertainties? And what if this person was not just a regular down-to-earth type but a poet? And not just a poet, but Joseph Brodsky, for whom existential insecurity and loneliness were dominant feelings even in ordinary circumstances? Well, I will not tell you anything at all about it because Brodsky never told me how he felt, and you can imagine his feelings for yourself. Instead I will tell you that when Brodsky landed in Vienna, he did not have a chance to feel lonely. He was met by Carl Proffer, who flew in from the States expressly to make Brodsky's first steps in the new world easier.

Carl Proffer was the founder of the Ardis publishing house in Ann Arbor, Michigan, whose specialty was Russian literature. Carl and his wife Ellendea met Brodsky during their visits to the Soviet Union and befriended him. I met the couple at one of Iosif's birthday parties. They published (in Russian!) precisely those Russian authors who had been excluded from Soviet literature and were doomed to remain unknown to the Russian public—Nabokov, Babel, Akhmatova, Platonov, Tsvetayeva. Some books that were published in Russia many years ago and became forbidden for Russian readers had been reprinted by Ardis in facsimile—Mandelshtam, Bulgakov, Khodasevich, Zamyatin,

Pasternak. Later, they would publish modern Soviet authors suppressed by the System—Brodsky, Sokolov, Dovlatov, Yefimov, Limonov, Voynovich, Uflyand, Kopelev, Lipkin. They also published some Russian writing translated into English. Singlehandedly they have saved huge layers of Russian culture from oblivion.

Besides admiring Carl and Ellendea for their contribution to Russian literature I am personally grateful to them for ridding me of a common Russian stereotype about Americans (chasing money, pragmatic, unable to notice beauty and subtlety). When I first met them, however, I was not very impressed: they were just another American couple from the free world who were, I thought, somewhat naïve about life in the Soviet Union.

When Brodsky left Russia Carl did three important things for him. First, he met him at the airport and took care of a host of small (and not so small) details that had to be handled properly. Anyone who has come to an unfamiliar country where people speak an unfamiliar language, and the things expected of one are unfamiliar also, will immediately appreciate how Carl's presence quieted Brodsky's anxiety. Second, he negotiated a position for Brodsky as Poet in Residence at the University of Michigan, Ann Arbor. Anyone who has spent countless hours sending work inquiries around the country—getting nowhere, in despair—can readily appreciate how much easier this made life for Brodsky. Third, Carl introduced Brodsky to W. H. Auden, who was living in Austria at the time. Brodsky had discovered Auden's books accidentally while still in Russia, had been greatly impressed by him and thought that Auden was one of the greatest poets of all time. The opportunity to befriend Auden right after landing in Austria was viewed by Brodsky as an incredible stroke of luck.

Two weeks later Brodsky flew with his new friend Auden to London to speak at the International Festival of Poetry, where he met Isaiah Berlin and Stephen Spender. During the winter break after his first semester in Ann Arbor, in December 1972, Brodsky traveled to Italy. There was no need to ask anybody's permission or to explain to anybody what he was doing. In 1973, his selected poems were published in London by Penguin Books with a foreword written by W. H. Auden himself. [The foreword had been completed before Auden met Brodsky in Vienna in 1972, at the urging of Professor George L. Kline, the translator of the *Selected Poems*, who also wrote the Introduction.] As I saw it, Joseph's life in the new world had started in the most glamorous way.

Early in 1975 many curious things took place in our own life. We got a *vysov* and sent our application to OVIR [Department of Visas and Registrations]. When we started the process, we did not know how long it would last and whether we would be allowed to leave the country at all. But OVIR accepted our application and let us out with the speed of lightning—that is, eight months later. I am saying "with the speed of lightning" because others in our situation had waited much longer, and for some the struggle for emigration would last up to ten years.

Here I must digress and, for a couple of pages, delve into our family history.

As mentioned earlier, my maternal grandfather and grandmother led a comfortable and bourgeois life before the Communist revolution. Grandmother had eleven brothers and sisters who lived with their families—some in Petersburg, some in Moscow, some in Latvia and Lithuania. The Moscow and Petersburg branches of our clan disliked the revolution so much that they all emigrated by different routes and spread all over the world. The exception to the rule was my mother, who at age seventeen ran away from the family and back to Petersburg, so as to personally participate in the building of the new, better world.

Soon all communication between the family and my mother (a.k.a. the "black sheep") was to be severed, a state of affairs which would endure for nearly half a century. So it happened that for as long as I had lived I had never seen any of my numerous relatives, nor had I heard about them. My mother had had enough sense not to talk about relatives abroad.

But in the mid-sixties mother's only brother George had appeared in our lives. I mentioned him earlier, describing how I tried to visit him in France. He had become a successful American director of documentaries. He was working for NBC at the time and came to the Soviet Union to film a program about Soviet sports stars. He told us incredible things about the lives and fates of our relatives: many had perished in the Holocaust, but some survived. Among others, he told us about mother's favorite cousin, actress Zhenia Shtrom, who had lived in Lithuania before the war with her husband, son, and daughter. They had been sent to the Kaunas ghetto, then to a concentration camp.

The Germans had killed Zhenia's husband in a particularly cruel way: putting an automotive hose into his mouth and pumping water into him until he was literally torn in half. Zhenia had hung herself, leaving her seventeen-year-old daughter Margaret (Mara) and her seven-year-old son Alexander (Alik) alone in the camp. The story of their survival deserves an entire book, and someday I will write it. Here I will say only that a certain Englishman—Joseph Kagan, an engineer in the textile industry, who had come to Lithuania on business and was caught up in the war there—fell in love with Mara in the camp. He was a man of exceptional intelligence and courage. He arranged an escape and together with Mara, after wandering and hardships in Europe, managed to end up in England. There Joseph Kagan joined the RAF, shot down quite a few Messerschmitts, was decorated, and became friends with Harold Wilson, future Prime Minister of Great Britain.

After the war, Joseph Kagan's services in rebuilding the British textile industry induced the queen to knight him. And so my cousin Mara, of whose existence I had no inkling at the time, became Lady Margaret.

All of this was told us by my mother's brother. Then several years later, in 1973, Mara herself came to the Soviet Union. She turned out to be an enjoyable and lively woman, and what we in our arrogance called "one of us." She and I even looked a bit alike, except that Mara was about twice as thin.

In the mid-seventies the very air around us was filled with the "protons and electrons" of emigration. And we discussed that idea with our newfound relative. I remember Victor saying, "I am afraid we won't survive *there*," and Mara laughing as she replied, "Well, if you survived *here*..."

The procedure of emigration was as ridiculous as it was cruel. When one announced an intention to emigrate, OVIR required a reference letter from one's place of work. This reference letter looked exactly like any other: it described the applicant's responsibilities and way of handling them—that is, whether he or she was a conscientious contributor or a slacker, was respected by coworkers, had access to classified materials and so on. The only difference was at the end of the letter. Instead of saying "recommend without reservation" the letter would say "there are no objections to this person leaving the Soviet Union for Israel for family reunification" or... "at this time, it is not advisable to let this person leave the Soviet Union."

To receive the reference letter, one had to come to the director of the company and ask for one. The director pretended that the reference letter had to be written as the result of a department meeting. During this meeting at the workplace, colleagues had to publicly denounce the person who wanted to emigrate, curse his very name, and often physically spit in his face. Also, colleagues had to express contrition and remorse that they had not remarked this person's dangerous slide towards enemy ideology, had not stopped it or warned the KGB, depriving their wayward coworker of who knows how much enlightened guidance.

Of course the director did not need the meeting to write the reference letters. But if he failed to call one, he would be open to allegations that he had let the organization become a breeding ground for Zionists, that he was politically blind, that he had lost vigilance, and these political accusations were very dangerous for the director. Victor got all that and more. On their own initiative, his coworkers demanded that when Victor had found from bitter personal experience how bad life abroad was and asked for permission to come back, the government should not let him in. As in the popular Russian saying, "For this dog, a dog's death." The day following this procedure, Victor was sacked. His part-time faculty position at the Mining Institute was also terminated—a person with such a rotten state of mind should not be let alone with students in the classroom for fear that he would corrupt the students' minds. Living without a salary was hard, but thinking all the time about his reference letter and what would be written in it was even harder.

My bosses at the university behaved more cautiously: the devil only knows what unpredictable students will think of doing. Which is why, without any meeting, in the quiet of the dean's office I was told "Oh dear, oh dear" and given a recommendation letter full of ambiguous praise.

We carried all the pieces of paper to OVIR, and that was when Lady Margaret joined the battle. Literally in a day or so we began getting letters from her written on House of Lords letterhead, stamped, with coats of arms, watermarks, and other trimmings. The contents weren't too shabby, either. For instance, "Last night we had dinner with Henry K. He said to tell you not to worry, and that everything is under his personal supervision..."

Probably the KGB had no doubt that Henry K. was Kissinger. I imagined them thoughtfully scratching their heads: "What is to be done with the Shterns? They've got a security clearance and all... On the other hand, it is a low-grade clearance. Maybe we should let them get the fuck out, or there'll be an international stink..."

Our apartment helped also. All apartments in each town in the Soviet Union belonged to the town government. The town managed numerous waiting lists of people who needed living quarters, assigned priorities, and decided who would move to what apartment and with what other family. When one moved to another city or emigrated, the apartment returned to the stock controlled by the town government. Our family lived a block away from the City Hall at the St. Isaac Cathedral Square. So, our apartment became an ace in the hole for us—no doubt some KGB vampire or government official dreamt of living there. To make a long story short, they let us go eight months later...

And then, ten days before we had to leave, Vitya collapsed with a 103-degree fever "of unknown causes." It was impossible to take him anywhere in that condition, and I rushed to the OVIR office to ask for a postponement. The office was not receiving clients that day. I threw myself at the feet of the secretary and begged her to let me see our case manager, Comrade Kovaleva. In vain. But suddenly Kovaleva herself materialized at the door of her office. I started talking very fast, explaining our situation. She did not invite me into her office but behaved in no trivial manner. The moment a telephone rang and the secretary began barking into the receiver, Kovaleva, with a barely perceptible movement of her hand walked to the window and turned her back on the secretary. I went and stood next to her. Quietly, almost in a whisper, she said, "Stop hanging around and bugging everybody. Leave on time or earlier. You are being watched closely every day."

Three days later, I stopped by OVIR again to sign one last piece of paper. Kovaleva received me in her office.

"Why did you warn me?" I asked.

"Because twelve years ago I graduated from law school, and your father was my advisor."

The procedure of departure was heartbreaking. Many friends came to the airport to see us off, even though it was dangerous to be seen in the company of outcasts who were leaving the country. When our family— Victor, our daughter, my mother and myself—went downstairs to customs, disappearing from the sight of our friends, it felt like crossing the river Styx—it could be crossed only in one direction. We died for our friends, and we would never, never see each other again. But we still had to get on the other side of the river. As for Charon, who exacted a fee even from dead travelers, his role was played by the Soviet customs officers.

We did not have many possessions—our furniture, books, paintings and other stuff that people accumulate in life—all had to be left behind. The same was true of our bank accounts with our life's savings and other property. But what we were allowed to take with us was inspected with utter thoroughness. Everything that could pass as a work of art was taken away. Art was a state asset and had to stay behind. We all went through a body search to establish that we were not trying to smuggle out diamonds or other valuables. Our address books were photocopied. Our photo albums were inspected and all suspicious pictures like those of railroad terminals, bridges, ships were taken away. It was no use to argue: we could be fined for violating customs rules, arrested, or simply held back until the plane had departed.

The main fear, however, was not of fines, loss of valuables or mementos, or humiliation. The main fear was that the KGB would come calling and stop us just as we were boarding the plane. Or even when we were already aboard—things like this did happen. This is why even during the stopover in Budapest we did not feel completely safe—Hungary was a socialist country, and the KGB could get us there just as easily as in the Soviet Union. Only when we landed in Vienna and disembarked could we permit ourselves a sigh of relief. We had made it! We thought of the joke about a Rabinovits who was sending telegrams home from his trip abroad. First, "Greetings from free Warsaw. Rabinovits." Next, "Greetings from free Budapest. Rabinovits." And finally, "Greetings from Vienna. Free Rabinovits."

In those years most Soviet emigrants went to Israel. Only a thin little stream trickled into the United States. The choice of country could be announced only after you crossed the border—that is, in Vienna. According to the rules of the game, as I have already mentioned, one was allowed to leave the Soviet Union only to go to one's "historic motherland" [a new term invented by the Soviet bureaucracy] for a "reunification" [another invention] with one's relatives.

Those who wanted to go to America specified this only after arriving in Vienna. They applied for entry visas to the United States and then were sent to Italy to spend time in a kind of quarantine while they waited for American visas. We were checked for syphilis and TB, and for service in the KGB or membership in the Communist Party. The place in America where the immigrants were to start their new American life was chosen by them (or for them) also while waiting for the entry visa in Italy.

We spent four months in Italy. Looking back, I realize what a fairy-tale time it was. The Good Fairy of the Lilacs, Irina Alekseevna Ilovaiskaya—the future Editor-in-Chief of the Russian-language paper, *La Pensée Russe*, published in Paris—had us stay in her children's apartment in the center of Rome.

I've described our reunion with Fausto and Anna, who took care of us as if we were their favorite relatives. When they had lived in Leningrad and I had cooked them thick gray macaroni thinking it was pasta, they were very grateful and kept saying, "When you come to Italy, someday..." I had laughed off their comments, thinking that I would never be in Italy. And now we were in Italy, and they were showing us Ischia and Venice, and taking us to real Italian restaurants with real pasta, and everything was wonderful.

And yet we were never free from fear and anxiety: What awaited us in America? Where would we live? How would we find work? I suffered from bouts of depression.

Back home in Leningrad, stuffed to the gills with American novels, we assumed that we knew everything about America... It turned out that on the subject of real life in real America we were rather vague. On top of everything, my English was practically nonexistent.

I wrote panicky letters to friends in the States. The most intelligible and instructive answers came from Brodsky, an "old resident" with three years under his belt. At that time he had already returned to Ann Arbor after a teaching stint in New England, and again occupied the mysterious-sounding position of *Poet in Residence* at the University of Michigan.

One of his letters was typed on deckle-edged letterhead, looked imposing, and made a huge impression on us.

In answer to my questions—where to go in America, where would it be best to settle down and how to prepare for life there, Iosif wrote: [The following excerpts from the letter are full of English words—as well as one German and two French—that were, in the Russian original, written in English, German and French but in Cyrillic characters.]

"As far as '*advice*' goes, I'll tell you that it's too late to worry about New York, as everything there is already in place. If there is a chance to find '*Arbeit*,' then New York would suit your disposition, and your mom's and Vitya's, the best.

"On the other hand, if '*Arbeit*' is being offered somewhere in New England, then it would be best to take it, because NY is 3-4 hours away by '*car*' from everywhere around there. More than that, there is one thing you have to comprehend about the States: no situation (job, place to live) here is permanent. It's not just that you don't have to register with authorities—there is no such thing as internal registration either.

"On the average, once every three years (actually, it's oftener, but for you let it be once in three) an '*American*' loads his family into his '*car*' and hits the road. It's not just because there's milk and honey everywhere, but also because the job contracts in this country (be it in the sphere of academics or engineering) are entered into, as a rule, for about a two or three-year period. At that point it will be apparent whether or not the guys there want you and whether or not you want them. At any rate, every incoming offer should be considered as something temporary. Of course a Russian, even if a Jew, has a tendency to love something at first sight and for the rest of his life. That tendency has to be gotten rid of as quickly as possible—even if only speculatively—because otherwise it'll be too nerve-racking later—that is, in the realization process.

"As for quitting Italy, try to drag that out, because *'après'* you won't be able to go to Europe for about two years at the least. Altogether, the transition from the world of the gun to the world of *chistogun* (cash) is easier than movements across the latter: without citizenship you will need—even after two years—visas to all the promised lands, except Canada and Mexico.

"As for the States themselves, they and the Old World are, in a purely aesthetic sense, polarized, and the eyes—with the exception of NY and Boston—will feast but rarely. What there is, of course, in abundance here is Nature, but I don't think that's something you're desperate for.

"As far as finding work for you is concerned, that'll be a bit grim for a while—unless, of course, you go back to your old ways—that is, geology; because anything to do with the exact sciences makes things much easier here than does teaching literature, foreign gobbledygook, and so on. There are local personnel up the wazoo, and a "dude" with a Ph.D. behind the wheel of a taxicab is not a fabrication of Soviet propaganda, because that dude makes more behind the wheel and knows it. At any rate, the first two-three months you'll be up in the air, and since that is inevitable, it is better for you to spend those months in a big city like NY. And though I don't recommend splitting from Italy immediately, you—and especially Vit'ka—must realize that the distribution of loaves and fishes (at the educational institutions, at any rate) happens precisely in January-February-March. What I want to say is that everything will arrange itself in a civilized manner no matter what. If you get too anxiety-ridden, know that if worse comes to worst, there'll always be a job for you at a local publisher's [Ardis], working on a typesetting machine, typing Nabokov's novels in Russian. But that is for a rainy day, which, I think, will not come. But, in the meantime, that chance is here in *'Michigansk'*..."

Further on Iosif calmed my fears about English:

"As for '*English*,'" he wrote, "three months in front of a TV will do the job better than all the Berlitz courses—and, overall, remember that there is no such thing as a foreign language: there is only a different phonetic row of synonyms."

In that letter Iosif also wrote about his life. Avoiding the bombastic word "loneliness" he admitted that he was left completely on his own, that nobody cared about him, that he'd become nobody's business, and that, in a way, he even liked it. However, since there was no one to talk to, just a wall, and since he had been living without gossip for three years now, he asked me to write about how our friends were getting on—Rein, Naiman, and those who were with them.

"What is remarkable in this country," wrote Brodsky, "is the awareness that you are on your own, nobody fucks with your head, saying they'll help you, they'll die for you; that is, conditions are the same as those in a laboratory: without adulterants. In terms of personal contacts, Kitten, you'll definitely have problems, but I know that you will resolve them."

In the letter Iosif expressed his hope that we would soon see each other in Italy, because he planned to go there for Christmas, "of course, if the Jews don't send you West."

And, of course, at the end of the letter, he could not deny himself the pleasure of teasing me a little. He "regretted" that no longer would he and I stroll under the high walls of St. Isaac Cathedral discussing the private lives of our friends, no longer proudly would I wear some suede thing under the hungry eyes of the *fartzes* [speculators in foreign clothing and bric-a-brac] from the Café North on Nevsky Prospect in Leningrad, no longer would he "put Vivaldi's Concerto Grosso on the turntable to prevent those behind the wall from hearing the squeaking of mattress springs..."

The letter ends with "*ZHAMAYIS!!!*"[Our humorous word, a literal pronunciation of the French word "jamais"—"never."]

...We did not see each other in Italy. Brodsky was in Florence and came to Venice two days after we had left Venice for Milan. We stayed there for two weeks and came back to Rome on January 8th. When we got home there was a letter waiting for us, with the date of our departure for America—January 13th.

So it was that we flew to New York around the New Year Russian-style, the so-called Old New Year of 1976. Our housing luck held. An acquaintance of acquaintances by the name of Mrs. Harris was leaving to spend six months with her son in Italy and she sublet her apartment to us for what was even then the ridiculously low price of $300 a month. We settled in the heart of Manhattan, namely on 74th street between Columbus and Amsterdam avenues, a five-minute walk from Lincoln Center.

Brodsky still lived in Ann Arbor at the time, but visited New York fairly often and soon appeared on our horizon. He came with a bottle of wine and a bunch of carnations for Mother. After the initial oohs and aahs we sat down to dinner. He had changed in the three years we had not seen each other: either he had grown harder or simply grown up. His manner was free and unconstrained, without a shadow of the old, sometimes artificially enhanced shyness.

I even remember how he was dressed: brown pants and a tweed jacket in greenish-terra cotta tones, and under the jacket a blue Oxford shirt and a coffee-colored sweater. His tie was loosely tied and crooked. I remember thinking that no one takes care of Os'ka, and that a professor should be wearing a sober suit of one color.

Later I figured out the clothing subtleties. The style and manner of dress in America were meant to demonstrate the social status of the wearer. Brodsky dressed with deliberation, completely in accordance with a widely accepted image of a professor from a semi-liberal university.

We asked him numerous questions and he gave us wide-ranging advice about life. Possibly we looked slightly pathetic or our questions seemed to him silly and naive, for I noticed a certain haughty note that was unlike his old self. Or so it seemed with respect to our family, at least.

It was as if a successful Moscovite were teaching his poor relatives from a Kazakh *kishlak* (village) how to live in a metropolitan city. Of course in some ways, that's probably how it was.

Our requests for him to recite his poems were carelessly brushed aside: "Some other time." That was entirely unlike him. Usually you did not even have to ask him to read. It seemed to me that he had lost interest in us as listeners and connoisseurs. Probably, I thought, he circulates in "a whirlwind of balls and in exalted spheres." I shared my observations with Vitya, and he shrugged his shoulders. "Osya is all right," he said, "you've simply become paranoid because of an inferiority complex." And that was the truth.

Later I understood a lot of things. Brodsky did not begin to circulate in "a whirlwind of balls" for quite some time. He'd spent the first three years of his life in the West in almost total solitude. Except for short sorties into New York he had lived in Ann Arbor as if in a vacuum. If I were not so taken with my own problems at the time, I would have understood what stood behind the humorous line of his "Italian" letter: "I am very much on my own, and, all in all, I even like it—speaking only to the wall."

However, he never once complained that he was lonely when we saw him in New York. To understand what was what one has only to read "An autumn evening in a small town" (see Ch. 24, page 356) or "In the Lake District" below:

....

Whatever I wrote then was incomplete:
my lines expired in strings of dots. Collapsing,
I dropped, still fully dressed, upon my bed.
At night I stared up at the darkened ceiling
until I saw a shooting star, which then,
conforming to the laws of self-combustion,
would flash—before I'd even made a wish—
across my cheek and down onto my pillow.

(Translated by George L. Kline, first appeared in the Bryn Mawr *Alumnae Bulletin*, Fall 1974)

After Ann Arbor Brodsky was applying for a similar position at various universities, including Boston University. He did not get an offer from Boston University, and to my knowledge was not even granted an interview. Probably the administration was afraid that he would eclipse their professors. It reminded one of a certain Nabokov story that was circulating in the émigré community.

Nabokov had applied to Harvard for the post of professor of

comparative literature. Roman Jakobson, a fellow émigré who was then head of the department, objected, and Nabokov did not get the position. Many of Jakobson's colleagues were simply staggered by his decision: "Roman Osipovich, how could you? He is the greatest living writer!" Roman Osipovich replied, "So what? The elephant is the greatest of all animals now living, but we don't hire him to run the zoo."

Brodsky lectured at various universities, including Columbia University, until he received tenure as a Professor of Poetry in a conglomeration of five colleges: Mount Holyoke, Amherst, Hampshire, Smith, and University of Massachusetts. The "home base" was Mount Holyoke in Western Massachusetts.

After our first meeting Brodsky disappeared for about three weeks. But once, very late at night, he called and said he wanted to read me some poems... Right now, over the telephone. I felt relieved. There was the old impatience in his voice. Probably he missed the "near and dear ear" after all.

He read "December in Florence." It was an absolutely enchanting poem and I was terribly moved (perhaps because in December I had spent a few days there). I asked him to read it again. I was amazed by *what* he saw in Florence and *how* he described it:

> "The atmosphere of this city retains a bit
> of the dark forest. It
> is a beautiful city where at a certain age
> one simply raises the collar to disengage
> from passing humans and dulls the gaze
> of this city.
> ....
> Quais resemble stalled trains. The damp
> yellow palazzi in the earth waist-down.
> ....
> In a dusty café, in the shade of your cap,
> eyes pick up frescos, nymphs, cupids on their way up.
> ....

Like a great painter, Brodsky drew that city with broad, powerful strokes, called it "beautiful," and pronounced a death sentence upon it and himself. Listening to the last stanza I felt

my throat tightening.
　　There are cities one won't see again. The sun
　　throws its gold at their frozen windows. But all the same
　　there is no entry, no proper sum.
　　There are always six bridges spanning the sluggish river.
　　There are places where lips touched lips for the first time
ever,
　　Or pen pressed paper with real fervor.
　　There are arcades, colonnades, iron idols that blur your lens.
　　There the streetcar's multitudes, jostling, dense,
　　Speak in the tongue of a man who's departed thence.

　　Is this about Florence? Or Leningrad?
　　I could not speak for tears... And that's when, probably out of fear of being taken for a sniveling idiot instead of a judge of good poetry, I strayed from the straight and narrow.
　　"Remarkable poem, Osya," said I in an editorial voice, "except for the lines:
　　'On the Old Bridge - they have fixed it up now -
　　where Cellini is *busting* against the hills' blue background'
　　I don't like the word *busting,* in this case it is a show-off verb out of Andrei Voznesensky's vocabulary."
　　Brodsky hung up without responding.
　　What to do? Should I call and apologize? Write a letter? Ask our mutual friend Genna Smakov to be a go-between so we could make up? On the other hand, why couldn't I express my opinion? Wasn't this why he had read me the poem?
　　Finally I called, "fell down at his feet," and was forgiven.
　　In the English version of this poem, translated by Joseph himself, this line looks quite different:
　　...while the old Bridge (new after repair),
　　where Cellini is peering at the hills' blue glare,
　　buzzes with heavy trading in bric-a-brac.
　　(First appeared in *The New York Review of Books*, May 1, 1980)

　　...I'm reminded of an odd episode. Brodsky called and said he wanted me to hear his son Andrei's poems that somebody had brought him from Leningrad. He read these poems over the phone without the usual "Brodsky intonations," separating himself from the text, as if he were only a "poetic messenger."

In my humble opinion, poetry in the Russian language is more demanding than in English. Both the rhythm and the rhyme have to be exact. They are immediately obvious to the ear, and every deviation can be easily recognized as either a sign of mastery or as an error. But as far as those poems were concerned, not only do I not recall whether I liked them or not, I do not remember any of them at all. It left an unpleasant aftertaste of something technically weak and imitative. Brodsky asked, "Whose poems are better?" "Andrei's, of course," I said quickly. Why did I say that? I probably wanted to make my answer a pleasant one for Iosif, given that children always outstrip their parents and that is as it should be in the evolutionary process.

"So, aha. All right," mumbled Iosif.

Having thought it over I began to have doubts: were these really Andrei's poems? I had never heard—either before or after—that Andrei wrote poetry. Once Iosif had mentioned that his son wrote song lyrics. But there's one thing I am certain of—the author of those poems was not Iosif Brodsky. Could they have been Bobyshev's poems? In that case my "Machiavellian" answer couldn't have been more stupid...

When Brodsky moved to New York he often played the role of our family guru.

One episode was especially memorable.

LESSONS IN LIFE

Once, when he was already living on Morton Street, Brodsky invited me to his favorite café, the Reggio in Greenwich Village. We were drinking cappuccino, and Iosif was explaining how to survive in America. His favorite activities, after writing poetry, were mentoring and explaining... (We even paraphrased the old joke "The Communist Party teaches that gas expands when heated" to "Osya teaches that gas expands when heated.")

It was probably that quality which made him a first-class university professor. However, I suspect that humanity lost a remarkable Rabbi in him, and Vitya thinks a doctor.

Anyway, there we were in the Cafe Reggio, with Brodsky pontificating, while I gathered his pearls of wisdom. Many of his recommendations really did dispel our atavistic world-view. For instance, the painful question of prestige. I complained that NYANA (the Jewish organization that assisted Soviet immigrants in New York) dared to offer me, a Ph.D. in geology, a job at a factory that made jewelry. They thought that since I was a geologist, I should be successful in sorting semi-precious stones imported from South America by size and quality—that is, as a sort of quality control expert.

Iosif said that one should take any job offered, because paying rent was important and self-esteem and consciousness of social rank should not be based on the work one performed. He added that nothing in America was eternal but, on the contrary, everything was transient.

He also said that one should not worry about speaking English with an accent since the whole country is made up of immigrants, and the only important thing is to be understood. (However, I did notice that he himself was very sensitive about accents. He tried to sound British, and Russian accents annoyed him tremendously.)

One of his instructions, spoken rather loudly, sounded like this: "In general, Ludmila, look around to see if anyone's fucking you." In Russian these lines sounded like a rhyme:

"*Oglianis' vokrug sebya Ne eb...t li kto tebya.*"

At that moment a lady in a black hat stood up from the neighboring table and came up to us.

"Do please forgive me for interrupting your conversation. I am Russian, my parents brought me here when I was a child. I try not to forget the language, I read a lot, but still I am afraid that my Russian is old-fashioned and there are many new expressions that I don't know. For instance, you just used some sort of...proverb, I think...which I have never heard. Would you kindly repeat it for me, please?"

I burst into laughter, choked on my croissant, and cappuccino gushed out onto my dress. Iosif snorted and turned as red as a beet. "I don't remember what I said," he mumbled. Then he called the waiter, paid, and we quickly fled.

...We lived in New York, suspended, for ten months: studied the language, looked for work, and lived on NYANA's support.

It was enough to pay the rent and to eat frugally. We tried not to spend any money on transportation, since there was no need to go to Queens, or the Bronx, or Brooklyn. We walked whenever possible, as if we were living in a sort of a small village with skyscrapers. Everything was close by West 74th Street: the English classes which Vitya and I attended five times a week from 9 to 2, the supermarket, Central Park, Lincoln Center. Genna Smakov lived around the corner (having flown to New York three weeks ahead of us, he had become our guide).

The only person in our family who spoke English fluently was our daughter Katya, who had attended an English-language school in Leningrad. Vitya spoke clumsy broken English, using mostly technical terminology. Mama and I spoke no English at all—Mama knew German and French. I was considered to "half-know" French as well.

People tried to help. Friends living in America, mostly Slavic scholars we had known in Leningrad, gave us a lot of their time. They introduced us to their friends—college and university professors—in the hope that they might help us find jobs. We were invited to their houses and our resumes were passed around, but in my case all such efforts were hopeless.

In the fall Katya was accepted by Barnard College. Vitya got a programming job in Boston, and we moved to Brookline, Massachusetts. In reality, however, I was living in the Greyhound bus between Boston and NYC. In the first place, I missed Katya, and in the second, I was trying to find a niche in some "Russian sphere." Boston at that time had only a few Russian immigrant families, so any kind of "Russian sphere" there was out of the question. [For the record, as of 2004 there are about eighty thousand immigrants from the former Soviet Union living in Greater Boston, but I found a job outside the "Russian sphere" a long time ago.]

I remember the New York period with nostalgia. On the one hand, we were Sir and Lady Nobody—pathetic, confused, poverty-stricken immigrants. I could not put two words together, writhed with humiliation and self-disgust, and cried at night. Brodsky's predictions in his "Italian letter" about things being "too nerve-racking" were coming true.

On the other hand, we went several times a week to Lincoln

Center, which was a luxury that only very well-to-do people could afford. Baryshnikov was lord of ballet and he and Genna Smakov had been friends since their late teens. Genna had introduced me to Baryshnikov at the final exam performance of the ballet school in 1966. We had not seen much of each other in Leningrad, except at some big parties, but here in New York Misha was very helpful and even tried to help Vitya find a job in the computer science field. Unfortunately, his computer science connections were fewer than ours.

Genna had cultivated a huge circle of friends and acquaintances in New York in no time, and soon we too belonged to that circle. So we felt neither lonely nor abandoned.

But in our relationship with Brodsky certain changes became apparent over time. In Leningrad the elements of our situation were clearly understood. We adored Iosif, admired his poetry, and in the first years of our friendship took him very much under our wing. He was a young persecuted poet who could come to us at any time and count on a "sympathetic ear" and any help that our home could provide.

In New York our situation had changed. He had become a famous poet, a professor, and was surrounded by the cream of the American intellectual elite, with all doors open to him. And we were a family of lousy immigrants, awkward, inept, insecure, and poor—acquaintances from the maestro's past who nevertheless expected their pronouncements on art and life to be taken seriously. Probably we should have been wise to the new situation right away. We should have cut out all those *Os'ka*s and *Osyunya*s, we should not have critiqued his poetry, and, in general, should have known our place.

I think the same thing had happened to Brodsky (luckily, only temporarily) that had happened to other Russians who suddenly became very famous. He seemed embarrassed by his compatriots and, with a few exceptions, had begun to avoid them. (I am sure that those "few exceptions" would dispute this observation.) It seemed to me that Iosif did not wish to be reckoned part of the general stream of "third wave" Soviet emigration.

Distinctions between the "waves" of emigration were not clear-cut, but they existed, and every new arrival was trying to find his or her place in the overall picture. The first wave consisted of people who had run away from the Communist revolution and the Civil War that followed. By the time we came to the States, they had aged and were already not numerous. Still, most of them were highly cultured, remembered "the good old days," and a few of them belonged to the Russian nobility. The second wave came after World War II. It consisted of people who were swept from Russia to Germany by the war. They were either drafted by the Soviet Army and became prisoners of war or they were "displaced persons," mostly from rural areas occupied by the Germans. Those who were liberated by the Western armies could choose not to return to the Soviet Union. As awful as it sounds, to give up the chance to see family and friends again was the right choice, because those who returned (and also those who were liberated by the Soviet Army and hence had no choice) were accused by the Soviets of treason. Instead of reuniting with their families after surviving German concentration camps, they were sent to Russian concentration camps, where most of them perished.

I cannot help but mention here one of Brodsky's best political poems: "On the Death of Zhukov." Zhukov was the Soviet general who rose through the ranks and won Stalin's favor during WWII because of his ruthlessness and boldness. Even among the Soviet brass he was notorious for his cruelty and resolve, winning battles by shedding the blood of his soldiers without remorse. Brodsky could not sympathize with this faithful hound for the Empire, but he could not help feeling awe at the enormity of the man. When Zhukov died in 1974, Brodsky responded with these remarkable lines:

> How much dark blood, soldier's blood, did he spill then
> on alien fields? Did he weep for his men?
> As he lay dying, did he recall them—
> swathed in civilian white sheets at the end?
> He gives no answer. What will he tell them,
> meeting in hell? "We were fighting to win."
>
> Zhukov's right arm, which once was enlisted
> in a just cause, will battle no more.
> Sleep! Russian history holds, as is fitting,

Space for the exploits of those who, though bold,
marching triumphant through foreign cities,
trembled in terror when they came home.
 (translated by George L. Kline)

Actually, the literal meaning of the last two lines is: "These people were not afraid while storming somebody else's capitals but were returning in fear to their own capitals."

Among the second wave émigrés, then, were many "simple" people: soldiers, peasants, working-class people. Many of them spoke uneducated Russian, started their American life with manual jobs, and were looked down upon by those who had come with the first wave.

The third wave of emigration started in the seventies. It was predominantly Jewish because only Jews and members of their families could leave the Soviet Union legally at the time. This wave had a very high concentration of people with college and advanced degrees—it took education and international connections to cut through the Soviet propaganda and realize that the System could be challenged according to its own rules. People who had come earlier looked down on the third wave. They felt that its members spoke a Russian that had been polluted with Soviet bureaucratic inventions. They also felt that the newcomers had utterly unrealistic expectations about translating Soviet degrees and job experience into successful professional careers in the United States. There was probably an element of anti-Semitic feeling in this, as well. The members of the third wave of course felt that they spoke excellent modern Russian, that their skills and knowledge were highly valuable and that they understood the current situation in the Soviet Union much better than those who had left the country many years ago.

Brodsky tried to live among American intellectuals. He had a few friends from the first and second waves of emigration, but his "Russian" circle was mostly composed of stars—the dancer Baryshnikov, the cellist Rostropovich—and a few not-so-famous friends: art critic Genna Smakov, Lena Chernisheva, an ABT mistress, writers Yuz Aleshkovsky and Lev (Lesha) Loseff. Let those whom I have not mentioned forgive me. He clearly tried to limit his immersion into the third wave of emigration.

With us the situation was ambiguous. On the one hand, the

fact that our relationship was of long standing was a positive factor: we knew each other *extremely well*, we could be relied on, we belonged. On the other hand, our history was a negative factor: we *knew too much*, including things that one does not want to be remembered. It was not comfortable, in our presence, to spread a peacock's tail and set it rustling against the walls.

At first, I even had the impression that although Brodsky did not mind having us among his acquaintances, he wanted to keep us at a certain distance, unworthy even of hail-fellow-well-met treatment. Or perhaps this was merely an impression that my feelings of inferiority were churning up.

Victor Shtern, a person of great tact and delicacy, who is able to maintain a friendship without emotional and passionate coloration, felt no psychological discomfort whatsoever. But my temperament of a Spanish "passionaria" like Dolores Ibarruri (she was popular in the Soviet Union during the Spanish Civil War) rebelled against the new rules. Then, after one incident, I decided that I no longer wanted to be acquainted with Iosif Brodsky at all.

We already lived in Boston by then. Vitya was working for a software firm, and I for a geological sweatshop. One day we got a call from Iosif who said that he would be in Boston in three days to give a reading at the Public Library. The reading would start at 4 p.m.

We had only one car at the time and the companies we worked for were located far from each other, and far from the public library. We asked our bosses for permission to leave two hours early and Vitya picked me up. We were afraid to be late and so tore down the highway like crazy. But, thank God, we got there on time. It was impossible (as usual) to find a parking space in the center of Boston at 4 p.m. All nearby parking lots had a "Full" sign out. We wedged ourselves into a handicapped space three blocks from the library, risking the possibility that the police would tow the car and we'd have to pay about $100 to get it back.

Brodsky was standing at the library entrance. He was smoking and chatting with his friend and translator, poet Derek Walcott, also a future Nobel laureate in poetry. As we flew up, barely able to catch our breath, he saw us and nodded carelessly, "Hi...

Derek, here are some typical representatives of the third wave..."
Derek smiled and shook our hands.

I felt as if I had been slapped in the face. I froze for a second, then took Vitya's arm: "We are leaving." I pulled him around and we walked away.

Naturally, there is nothing offensive in being considered representatives of the third wave (typical or atypical). We are definitely part of the third wave and anyone could have introduced us in that fashion. But not Iosif Brodsky, not "our Osen'ka." Under no circumstances could we have been representatives of anything at all to Iosif Brodsky. For us he should have found other words.

Iosif called that very evening, "Ludka, why did you freak out over nothing?"

I am certain that he knew exactly what the problem was. Any explanation would be useless and humiliating. I said that we had guests, apologized, and hung up.

Several days later we received a package from him: no letter, only two books—*A Part of Speech* and *The End of the Beautiful Epoch*. On the fly-leaf of *A Part of Speech* was written:

Sentences made by this hand!
You will not be pressed to Ludmila's nightgown
like that bastard Vitya
who is playing with her titties.

Everybody, go to Ludmila's house.
When you enter, speak thus, "Are we not
from now on the new sacred tablets?
We want to be pressed to your breast."

Iosif.

And on *The End of the Beautiful Epoch* Brodsky wrote:
To the friend of days rather grim:
Accept this small object—
The fruit of unwholesome tendencies
"And the heart's sorrowful record."

The chain fell apart, but the links are alive.

The heart grows old, but not the breast!
Ludmila! In the arms of Shtern
Forget not the magical moment!

"The chain fell apart but the links are alive" is a symbolic sentence: it refers to our Leningrad circle that fell apart when certain of its "links" emigrated, and others became enemies.

I was deeply touched, and peace was reestablished, and from that time on Brodsky restrained himself in showing us his newly acquired greatness.

In January of 1993 Baryshnikov was dancing in Boston with the Mark Morris troupe and the tour coincided with his birthday on January 27th. We decided to throw him a surprise dinner. We called Brodsky in South Hadley and the Kaplans in New York. Iosif said he would "reshuffle" his schedule and definitely come. But Roman and Larisa could not make it together, one of them had to "mind the store," that is, their restaurant, the Russian Samovar. They tossed a coin. Larisa won and appeared on the day before the party.

We ordered a cake from the bakery and asked them to write "Happy Birthday Dear Misha" in frosting—and in Russian—on its chocolate surface, and left a sample of how it should be written. There were also to be candles around the inscription. We wanted candle holders in the shape of miniature ballerinas standing on tip-toe and carrying the candles in their upraised hands. The owner said, taking the order, "We'll do our utmost... I bet you anything this cake is for Baryshnikov." "How do you know?" "I've still got my wits about me," said the owner, rapping his bald head with his knuckles. "It's in all the news that Baryshnikov is dancing in Boston. And you want 'Misha' written on the cake in Russian, and with ballerinas, too."

While setting the table I said to my five-year-old granddaughter Vika, "Pay attention, Vikulya—today two men are coming to dinner. One of them writes the greatest poetry in the world, and the other one dances better than anyone under the sun."

"What, better than me?" asked Vika.

Everything went as though synchronized. Brodsky got into Boston during the day and he and Larisa were in time to see Misha's performance. (I had seen the ballet the day before.) After the show they all rode up together. On the book he brought for Baryshnikov Brodsky wrote:

> Though I'm a *Yid*, though you are a *Goy*,
> though you have a different profile,
> still I cannot perform with my hand
> what you can accomplish with your leg,
> but on the day of January 27th
> I want to be as drunk
> as on the day of May 24th,
> when you were also *très bien*!

[I realize that this is the vocabulary of racism to American ears, but to the Russian ear the word for Jew in Yiddish, *Yid*, along with *Goy*, the word for non-Jew, carries only a very mild derogatory connotation, if any, and both are often used by Russian-speaking Jews while making general statements. Incidentally, Brodsky spoke no Yiddish—the use of these words in the poem only shows how common they are.]

We started recalling different dedications Brodsky had written in books on Baryshnikov's birthdays. For instance, fifteen years before this evening, in 1978 to be exact, Iosif gave Misha *The End of the Beautiful Epoch* with the following dedication [here, Cyril and Methodius are Bulgarian preachers who designed the alphabet for the Russians]:

> On your day there was born an evil-doer
> nicknamed Wolfgang Amadeus.
> And on mine—Saint Cyril or Methodius,
> one of the literate people.
> Though the complicated fuckadiddle of symbols
> cannot be figured out either by us
> or by Cocteau himself,
> it pleases me when you are making *fouettés*..

> PS And will these stanzas be of *Barysh* [profit]
> to Mishel when he does read them?

And on January 27th, 1992, Baryshnikov received from

Brodsky his book "Watermark" published in English, with this dedication:

> A portrait of a winter Venice
> where birdies freeze in a recess,
> on the 27th day of January
> I present to dear Mouse.
>
> Forgive my English,
> but a hand—as well as a leg for dancing—
> is given so one could, at a distance,
> make oneself out a *Westerner*.

["Mouse" in Russian is pronounced as "mysh'". It sounds almost like Misha, and Brodsky often called Baryshnikov Mysh'.]

That same year Brodsky gave Baryshnikov the poems that were published in Russia for the first time:

> I am presenting my comrade-in-arms under the yoke
> with a book published by the Mongol.
> Evidently, the Mongols managed the burred word
> without screwing it up.

However, it's time to return to Boston of January 1993, to our family dinner in honor of Baryshnikov's birthday. We had not yet sat down when I remembered that I had Brodsky's collection *God Keeps Everything* without an autograph.

I slipped Iosif the book and asked him to sign.

"Let's have dinner first, I am starving," said Brodsky.

I began whining, "Come on, Iosif, you've already got a pen in your hands; later we'll forget or something will happen."

"What can happen?" He shrugged and wrote: *"Accept, oh Shterns, my creation; I'll later write the dedication."*

It was as if I had been gifted with second sight: this "later" never happened. At the end of the dinner Iosif was supposed to take some medication. He patted his pockets, could not find the pills, and went down to the street to rummage in his car. He came back gasping for breath and holding his chest: the car was gone.

Thank God we kept nitroglycerin in the house.

We called the police. They calmed us down—the car had been towed, not stolen. They gave us the address of the place where the car could be reclaimed. Evidently, Brodsky had blocked the exit from our parking area.

"Take a hundred bucks and let's go ransom your wheels," said I. But it was not so simple. They would not give us the car because they had found out that Brodsky's registration had expired. Actually, it had not expired yet but it would expire at 12 a.m. that night. However, we were allowed to take out the briefcase and other junk. The registration could not be renewed till tomorrow, and it could only be renewed in South Hadley where he lived and where the car was registered—two and a half hours away from Boston (in the car he did not have). Suppose he would take my car and then come back right away—that's another two and a half hours. And then he had to go to New York to take part in some important function—that was four hours more. The whole thing was patently not feasible...

We went home to finish drinking, eating, and go to sleep. The next morning we raced to the police station to talk the matter over. Our entreaty—to give us the car so Iosif could drive to South Hadley, renew the registration, and take off for New York from there—had no effect. That is to say, the poet was pinned down.

Every day the car stayed at that towing company would cost a hundred dollars. We needed to take it away immediately.

"It is against the law to keep an unregistered car in a public place, such as the street," said the police officer.

"What would you have me do—put it under my arm and carry it into a hotel?" barked Brodsky.

He was very worried. But surely no good could come of sarcasm or a raised voice in a police station. I stepped on his foot and put on one of my most "disarming smiles." My speech, though thick with its Russian accent, poured like honey.

"Mr. Brodsky is a laureate of the Nobel Prize and the American poet laureate. He writes poetry night and day... Which is why he is a little absent-minded. But this has been a good lesson for him and now he will be very careful with his registration dates...

Please make an exception for him, sir...We would be very, very grateful, sir."

The police officer frowned, his face became majestic. I realized that I had committed a gross, almost fatal tactical error. Now he would say something like, *"In our country all are equal before the law, the greatest and the lowest."* (The subtext being that if the "lowest" could, perhaps, be forgiven, the "greatest"—never! I immediately slid from the "greatest" to the "lowest.")

"We have a big problem, officer," said I, my eyes filling with tears. "It is very expensive to keep the car at that place. We simply can't afford it... Please, please, let us take it. We won't park it on the street. I'll put it in my garage (which, by the way, we did not have). Mr. Brodsky will drive *my* car to South Hadley, renew his registration, and come back to Boston for his."

"And I can take your word for it that Mr. Brodsky will not drive his unregistered vehicle?" The police officer drilled me with a gimlet eye. For some reason he did not address himself to Brodsky. Could he have been abashed in the presence of a Nobel Prize laureate?

"Do I look like someone who would break the law?" said I with a slight reproach in my voice. "I pay my taxes regularly and I value my reputation, sir."

The policeman called the towing company and told them to release the car. Bowing gratefully I walked out of the station. Mr. Laureate followed me, looking downcast.

"Well, Yablochkina-Gogoleva, you've got some nerve!" said Brodsky admiringly when the door closed behind us.

[Aleksandra Yablochkina and Elena Gogoleva: two famous Russian actresses.]

We raced to the towing company, paid the hundred, picked up the car, and Brodsky got ready to leave. In his car, of course...

"Only, for God's sake, don't drive like a madman," said Vitya. "If you get stopped for speeding and then the cops find out you have no registration, they'll take your license away, *capish?*"

"And how!" Iosif kissed us both and took off for South Hadley.

So the autograph *"Accept, oh Shterns, my creation; I'll later write the dedication"* on the book *God Keeps Everything* turned out to be the only one. We never got another.

And here is another story of the autograph on a slim volume *View from the Hill* (a collection of poems from the year 1992), published in Sweden, 25 copies in number, for Brodsky's birthday.

In 1993 we spent three months in Spain. Vitya was teaching the summer term in the university in Saragossa. We crossed the country...traveled through the Pyrenees; to Andorra and back; to France and back... And also went to the Ordesa national park, high in the mountains.

One gets there by taking a narrow mountain two-way road without the divider. On the left there's a sheer cliff wall, on the right—better not look—an abyss. There's no shoulder, only tiny white posts.

All my life my love of mountain views has coexisted peacefully with my fear of heights. But in the Pyrenees, crawling across a rickety bridge over a river with the promising name of Inferno, I felt the love dwindling and the fear growing. "They could've called that little river something else," grumbled Vitya.

At that moment a military truck with a trailer crawled slowly from around the corner, coming towards us. The truck load was covered with a tarpaulin, but judging by its size, it could have been cannons, tanks, or even rocket launchers.

The turn was so steep that, although the truck was driving on its side of the road, the trailer dragged along our lane. Vitya stopped the car to let the trailer straighten out. And at that moment another military vehicle—an amphibian—passing the truck, wedged itself between our fragile *Fiesta* and the truck. Apparently, the driver was demonstrating the art of passing on a mountain road.

The amphibian palpably smacked against the side of our car. There was a clang and a screech, and our little "soap-dish" seesawed and leaned to one side, firmly pressing against the tiny white posts. The crazed driver of the amphibian raced another fifty meters or so before hitting the brakes. The truck stopped, too. Behind the truck, the column of nine military vehicles stopped as well, and soldiers poured out. They were running to us, crossing themselves as they ran, while we sat there petrified, not daring to stir.

An officer yanked at the driver-side door and began to pull Vitya out of the car. The passenger-side door was smashed in and tightly jammed. A mud-brown bruise began spreading all across my right elbow and up the right arm to the shoulder. They pulled me out like a rag doll, also through the driver's door, and sat me down on the road.

The soldiers, clicking their tongues and calling on St. Mary, began pulling the car away from the edge. The Fiesta was a sorry sight—broken headlights, deeply bent bumper, stripped side, and a hopelessly smashed-in door.

I pulled myself together a little, walked to the little posts that had saved us, looked down, and, as a woman friend of mine once put it, "felt cold in my legs."

Perpendicular, jagged sides formed the "infernal" precipice, while far down, on the "bottom" I could see pointed crags and the tops of pine trees... A stunning view!

And what if the posts hadn't been there? Or if we had been hit just a bit harder?

...When we came back to New York a few months later, we went to see Brodsky. We told him about Spain, about the accident, and about the incredible view from the Pyrenees. "You know, Iosif, I often dream of that view—I have nightmares about it," I said.

When we were saying goodbye, he took a thin blue volume— the collection *View from the Hill*—from his desk drawer, autographed it and gave it to us:

"Accept, oh Shterns, the given 'View.'
I am afraid it won't surprise you.
But it's not easy to surprise
a pair of such well-traveled guys.

PS Unlike my pen, so smoothly wielded,
 this book is a shitload of typos yielded.
                                          Iosif."

---

[1]Joseph Brodsky, *Collected Works*.The Pushkin Fund, 1992, pp. 302-303
[2]*Ibid.*, pp. 383-385

1. *Young Joseph Brodsky. Leningrad, 1957. Photo by his father, A. Brodsky.*

2. *Nadezhda Philippovna Kramova, mother of Ludmila Shtern.*

3. *Yakov Ivanovich Davidovich, father of Ludmila Shtern.*

4. *Ludmila Shtern in the uniform of the Mining Institute in 1958, when she met Joseph Brodsky.*

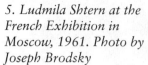

5. Ludmila Shtern at the French Exhibition in Moscow, 1961. Photo by Joseph Brodsky

6. Brodsky's famous American jeans, much admired, upon which he used to strike matches. Leningrad, 1959. Photo by Boris Shvartsman

7. Joseph in his "half-room" in Leningrad, 1960. Photo by his father, A. Brodsky.

8. *Ludmila and Victor Shtern on their wedding day.*

9. Pasik the cat, to whom much poetry was written. Early 1960s.
Photo by L. Shtern

10. Joseph with his namesake cat Osya, at home in Leningrad, 1960. Photo by Joseph's father, A. Brodsky

11. Joseph at the Yakutsk Airport. Geological expedition, summer 1961.

12. *From left to right: Anatoly Naiman, Joseph Brodsky, Gleb Gorbovsky. Komarovo, early 1960s. Photo by E. Korobova*

13. *Joseph Brodsky at home, Leningrad, early sixties. Photo by Boris Shvartsman*

14. *Boris Shvartsman's study*
of Brodsky in Leningrad.
Early sixties.

15. *Joseph Brodsky in*
Leningrad, early sixties.
Photo: Boris Shvartsman

16. *From left to right: E. Rein, M. Petrov, V. Shtern at Joseph's birthday party, Leningrad, 24 May, 1962. Photo by J. Brodsky*

17. *Evgeny Rein, Moscow, 1962.*

18. D. Bobyshev and E. Rein at Joseph's birthday party, Leningrad, 24 May, 1962. Photo by J. Brodsky

19. Evgeny Rein, Leningrad, 1962. Photo: B. Shvartsman

*20. Upper row, from left to right: A. Naiman, L. Shtern, G. Narinskaya.
Below, D. Bobyshev and E. Rein. At Brodsky's birthday party, Leningrad, 24
May, 1962. Photo by J. Brodsky*

21. *From left to right: E. Rein, A. Naiman, L. Shtern, D. Bobyshev, G. Narinskaya. At Brodsky's birthday party, Leningrad, 24 May, 1962. Photo by J. Brodsky*

22. *Boris Shvartsman and Joseph Brodsky, Leningrad, 1967. Photo by E. Sinyaver*

23. (above) Mirra Meilakh's birthday. Among those pictured, left to right, are V. Shtern, M. Petrov, Mirra Meilakh, L. Stern, E. Rein and D. Bobyshev.

24. From left to right: E. Rein, L. Shtern, D. Bobyshev at Mirra Meilakh's birthday party, Komarovo. Photo by V. Shtern

*25. Joseph Brodsky in exile
in the village of Norenskaya,
Arkhangelsk region. 1964.
Photo by Yakov Gordin*

*26. Joseph Brodsky
in exile.*

27. *Anna Akhmatova near the end of her life.*

28. *From the front, clockwise: A. Naiman, E. Rein, E. Korobova, D. Bobyshev, J. Brodsky and the casket containing the remains of Anna Akhmatova. March 10, 1967, Komarovo. Photo by Boris Shvartsman*

29. E. Rein and J. Brodsky, Leningrad, late 1960s. Photo by Joseph's father.

30. Joseph Brodsky and his father, Aleksandr Ivanovich, on the balcony of their apartment, Leningrad 1967. Photo by his mother, Maria Moiseevna.

31. Joseph Brodsky's parents at home, 1970. Photo by J. Brodsky

32. Brodsky at the Leningrad airport before leaving for exile, June 4, 1972. Yakov Vinkovetsky (right) with an unidentified person is seeing Brodsky off. Photo by M. Milchik

33. Fausto Malcovati.

*34. (below) Anna Doni and
Fausto Malcovati in Leningrad,
1965.*

35. E. Rein and A.
Naiman, 1962.
Photo by J.
Brodsky

36. Galina Narinskaya, 1968.

37. *Yuri Tzekhnovitzer.*

38. *Sergei Slonimsky.*

39. *Vladimir Maramzin.*

40. *Anatoly Naiman.*

41. *Mirra Meilakh.*

42. *Galina Dozmarova (Kharkevich) in 1960.*

43. *Igor Yefimov visits*
the exiled Brodsky in
Norenskaya (October
1964). Photo by Yakov
Gordin

44. *Igor Yefimov. (Pen*
name: Andrei Moscovit)

45. *Ischia. The large white villa on the right is Casa Malcovati.*

46. *The "dacha" in Komarovo where Marina Basmanova and Dmitri Bobyshev celebrated a notorious New Year's Eve (see Chapter 10). Photo by L. Shtern*

47. *Memorial plaque outside the building where Brodsky lived in St. Petersburg until his emigration.*

48. *Brodsky in Venice, early 1980s.*

49. *(left to right) R. Kaplan, J. Brodsky, A. Rabinovich, S. Dovlatov at Brodsky's birthday party on Morton Street, New York City, May 24, 1986.*

50. Brodsky visiting Igor Yefimov in Michigan, 1982. Photo by Marina Yefimov

51. Igor Yefimov and Joseph Brodsky, with Brodsky holding photograph of them taken 26 years before. Photo by Yakov Gordin

52. *Tatiana Liberman and Genna Smakov. Libermania (Liberman's House), Warren, Connecticut, 1978. Photo by Alex Liberman*

53. *Mikhail Baryshnikov and Ludmila Shtern in the Nakhamkin Gallery, New York City, 1980. Photo by P. Palej*

54. *Gennady Smakov and Mikhail Baryshnikov at the party the Libermans gave to honor the publication of Smakov's book,* Baryshnikov: From Russia to the West. *New York City, 1981.*

55. *Smakov and Baryshnikov in Libermania, 1983.*
Photo by Dominique Nabokov

56. *Alex Liberman in his studio. Warren, Connecticut, 1985. Photo by L. Shtern*

57. *(below) Joseph Brodsky in Libermania, 1983. Photo by Alex Liberman*

58. *Ludmila Shtern next to a Liberman sculpture in Jerusalem, 1987. Photo by Victor Shtern*

59. *(left to right) Alex Liberman, Ludmila Shtern, Genna Smakov and Tatiana Liberman in the Nakhamkin Art Gallery, New York, 1980. Photo: Pavel Palei*

60. *Victor Shtern with Alex Liberman at his "studio" in Warren, Connecticut. (On the grounds of "Libermania.") 1983.*

61. *Joseph Brodsky and Genna Smakov in Warren, Connecticut; mid 1980s. Photo by Alex Liberman*

62. *Yefim Slavinsky with Brodsky the day Joseph won the Nobel Prize.*

63. *Evgeny Rein, Joseph Brodsky and Sergei Dovlatov at a literary evening in New York City, 1988.*

64. *Joseph Brodsky and Misha Baryshnikov in Sweden, August 1992. Photo by Bengt Jangfeldt*

65. *Alex Liberman at home in New York City, 1996. Photo by Melinda Liberman*

66. *Alex Liberman and Melinda. New York City, 1995.*

67. *Victor Shtern at Alex Liberman's 80th birthday "luau," admiring the champagne fountain, 1992. Photo by L. Shtern*

68. Brodsky and Yakov Gordin visiting the Yefimovs in New Jersey, March 1990. Photo by Igor Yefimov

69. M. Meilakh and A. Naiman in the early nineties, when they were fast friends, before Naiman wrote the book B. B. and Others *about Meilakh. Photo by Boris Shvartsman*

70. *Yakov Gordin.*

71. *Roman Kaplan at the Russian Samovar, his restaurant in New York City.*

72. *Brodsky and wife Maria Sozzani visiting Professor Mikhail Petrov in Oxford, England, July 14, 1991. Photo M. Petrov*

73. *Brodsky with wife Maria visiting the Petrovs in Oxford, England, July 14, 1991. Photo M. Petrov*

74. *(above) Brodsky and Larisa Kaplan at the Shtern's home in 1993.*
75. *(below, left) Joseph Brodsky is singing "Lili Marlene" at the Russian Samovar restaurant in New York City on April 9, 1995.*
76. *(below, right) Brodsky relaxing at the Russian Samovar. Early 1990s.*

77. *Joseph Brodsky, Larisa Kaplan, Misha Baryshnikov. Misha's birthday at the Shtern's home in Brookline, Massachusetts, January 27, 1993. Photo by Victor Shtern*

78. *Victor Shtern, Ludmila Shtern and Joseph Brodsky at the Shtern's in 1993. Photo by Larisa Kaplan*

79. Baryshnikov smoking a cigar on the back landing during a break from birthday festivities at the Shtern's, a smoke-free facility, in January, 1993. Photo by V. Shtern

80. Brodsky at home with daughter Anna, 1993.

81. *Alex Izbitser, Helen Ostashevsky and Joseph Brodsky singing Russian kitsch at the Russian Samovar restaurant, April 9, 1995.*

82. *Alex Izbitser, Helen Ostashevsky, Joseph Brodsky and Ludmila Shtern singing Russian kitsch. April 9, 1995.*

83. *Joseph Brodsky and Ludmila Shtern outside Brodsky's house in South Hadley, Massachusetts. February 1995. Photo by Natan Slezinger*

84. *Brodsky at South Hadley, Massachusetts in February, 1995. Photo by Natan Slezinger*

85. *Joseph Brodsky and Nadezhda Kramova, Ludmila's mother, at the Cafe St. Petersburg, Boston, April 2, 1995.*

86. *Brodsky with S. Okshtein's painting in the background at the Cafe St. Petersburg in Boston, April 9, 1995. Photo by Natan Slezinger*

87. *Brodsky with Maria at his last birthday, May 24, 1995. Friend and translator George Kline had given him his WWII navigator's service cap, and he loved to wear it. Photo: M. Petrov*

88. *Joseph Brodsky. Photo by Mark Kopelev*

89. Ludmila Shtern in 1995. Photo by S. Rogozin

90. Anna Doni in Venice thirty-eight years later—April 2003.

91. Galina Dozmarova forty years later in Florence.

92. Roman Kaplan at Brodsky's wake. Russian Samovar restaurant, New York City, January 1996.

93. Roman Kaplan and Misha Baryshnikov at Brodsky's wake. Russian Samovar restaurant, New York City, January 1996.

94. Evgeny Rein and Ludmila Shtern at the Joseph Brodsky memorial evening at Boston, University. February 1996.

95. *Ludmila Shtern and Anna Doni tending Joseph Brodsky's grave in the San Michele cemetery, Venice, April 2003.*

96. *Ludmila Shtern reading chapters of her Brodsky memoir at the Akhmatova Museum in St. Petersburg, April 2003.*

97. The photo by which Joseph Brodsky is known to many of his countrymen today. The photographer was Boris Shvartsman.

14

The Section Five Problem

FOR A RUSSIAN READER, the title of this chapter requires no explanation. Everybody knows what "Section Five" is and why it's important: it is a reality of Soviet life that has to be lived to be understood. Brodsky claimed "Section Five" was one of the reasons that 20th century Russian prose is less known in the West than 19th century prose. According to him, Russian writers of the 19th century were describing conflicts that also worried Western people living under the same capitalistic system. Conflicts and relationships introduced by the Soviet state presented more than linguistic difficulties to Westerners accustomed to a regular life. They had no problems with Dostoyevsky, Tolstoy or Chekhov, but could hardly understand Zoshchenko or Platonov. I think Joseph was right: small wonder that when our "third wave" of emigration reached America, the "first wave" had difficulty understanding our neologism-filled Russian: *upravdom*, *zhilplotchad'*, *propiska*, *pyatyi punkt* (Section Five).

All Soviet applications and questionnaires—even driver's licenses and ID cards—are built on the same model. Actually, the ID card was not a card but a booklet, rather like an American passport, and they even called it a *passport* in Russian, but it had no pages for visas and customs records. One needed an *international passport* to go abroad. And I couldn't possibly exaggerate the fascination of Soviet citizens at the idea of going abroad. As an old joke has it, a Jew tells his friend: "This year I want to go to Paris again." The friend asks: "Did you go to Paris last year?" The punch line: "No, but last year I also wanted to go."

Anyway, Section One of a Soviet application asks for one's last name, Section Two—for the first name, Section Three—for the patronymic, and Section Four—for the date of birth. So far so good, and one would expect the Social Security Number to go next. However, there was no Social Security Administration in the Soviet Union (and forget about Social Security benefits). Instead, Section Five asked for *national'nost'*, the ethnic origin of the applicant (or the holder of the *passport*). The information in Section Five might affect your treatment by a policeman on the street, or what college would admit you, or what job you would be offered, or how far you would be promoted. Having "Russian" in Section Five would not provide you with specific advantages—after all, there were 150 million people with the same entry there—but would assure the absence of discrimination, at least, on this basis. Having "Ukranian" or "Armenian" or "Tadzhik" was mostly neutral; in a few situations, it might even be advantageous—the Soviets practiced some kind of an affirmative action directed towards creation of "national cadres," provided that these "cadres" worked diligently to strengthen the Soviet regime. At certain times some entries might be lethal: "Chechen" or "Crimean Tatar" or "German" or "Finn" during World War II. These ethnic groups were deported without exception—children, women, adults, the elderly. All were shipped to the East packed into cattle cars, and about half of them died in transit. The rest were abandoned in the middle of the steppe to fend for themselves. After having taken all their possession the state then took from them the right to leave the place of deportation.

Having "Jew" in Section Five was advantageous during the first years after the revolution because many (if not most) Jews embraced the revolution as the end of tsarist oppression. The Soviet government desperately needed new cadre because the old cadre could not be trusted. The government viewed literate, educated Jews (though not the strictly religious and bourgeois) as avid supporters of the regime. The designation became almost lethal toward the end of 1952, but the death of Stalin saved the Jews from deportation. Still, being a Jew usually meant being discriminated against. In one of my favorite jokes on the subject a physician is examining a patient and filling out the information sheet at the same time. The order of questions is already familiar to you.

Doctor: Please breathe. What is your last name?

Patient: Rabinovits. [The likelihood that a person with this name would be a non-Jew is zero. The appropriate doctor's reaction follows.]

Doctor: Do not breathe. First name?

Patient: Gennady. [This is a Russian rather than a Jewish name.]

Doctor: Breathe. Patronymic?

Patient: Moiseevich. [Well, even when the parents would give a child a Russian name, most parents still had typical Jewish names.]

Doctor: Do not breathe. Date of birth?

Patient: 1947.

Doctor: Breathe. [Section Five is coming.] Nationality?

Patient: Jew.

Doctor: Do not breathe.

Jews appeared in Russia about 200-250 years ago. They did not come to Russia—the Russian Empire came to them while expanding to the South and West and swallowing Ukrainian and Polish territory. The tsarist government first tried to convert them to Christianity. When it failed, the government enacted numerous laws restricting Jewish settlement and occupations. The "blood libel" trial of Beilis [he was accused of the ritual slaughter of a Christian boy], pogroms, and forced conscription into the Russian Army [where Jewish dietary laws and the Sabbath could not be observed] resulted in mass emigration at the end of the 19th and beginning of the 20th centuries. Despite the relatively small proportion of Jews in the Russian population, the "Jewish Question" featured prominently in the political and social life of the country.

The role of Jews in Russian history is discussed by Russians still, though most Jews have already left the country for Israel and the United States (and some for Germany). Solzhenitsyn found time to write a two-volume study called *Two Hundred Years Together*. He admits that the tsarist government was inept and insensitive in its dealing with Jews, but he cannot help but fault the Jews for clinging to the Talmud and their communal life and refusing to send their children to government schools. At the end of the 19th century, however, the Jews discovered that getting advanced secular education was the only way to circumvent laws tying them to the "pale of settlement" and barring them from living in metropolitan centers. Solzhenitsyn faults them again, this time for rushing into secular school and (despite percentage limits in school) crowding out the indigenous population in the areas of law, medicine, science, and even Russian journalism. He also noticed, and this is a fair claim, a disproportionate number of Jews among revolutionaries and in the top echelons of the first Soviet government and its punitive organizations. At the end, Solzhenitsyn called upon the Jews to repent and to acknowledge their role in crimes the Soviet government had committed.

Indeed, over the years, Soviet Jews led the same lives as Soviet Russians (or Ukranians, Lithuanians, Georgians, Tadzhiks, inter alia). They lived in the same neighborhoods, went to the same schools and universities, wore the same clothes, worked at the same jobs, were members of the same Communist Party and went to the same prisons and concentration camps. And they served in the same government and the same KGB. They were giving their children Russian names, they read Russian books, spoke only Russian at home and on the street, did not circumcise their boys, did not learn the Bible and did not keep its special laws. Still, they were constantly made aware of their Jewish identity. In Chapter 11, describing the Brodsky trials, I omitted several dialogues because I thought they would only confuse the reader without special explanations, and I already had enough to explain. For example, witness Etkind is called to the stand.

Judge Savel'eva: What is your name?

Witness: Etkind Yefim Grigorievich.

Judge Savel'eva: Show me your passport—your name did not sound clear. (Reads aloud) Etkind Efim *Girshevich.*

The judge knew well that the name of Etkind's father was Girsh—a Jewish name. For convenience in everyday use (but not in official documents) Etkind introduced himself as a son of Grigory, a more common Russian name. The judge demanded the passport not because the name was not clear. She wanted to humiliate Etkind and also to expose him to the audience as a Jew who was trying to pass as a Russian.

When a Russian Jew reached out to look for sources of spiritual knowledge, it was easier to find an Orthodox priest to talk to than a Jewish rabbi, to get a translation of Tillich than one of Maimonides. This is why all of my Jewish friends knew more of Christianity and its theology than they did of Judaism, and quite a few of them converted to Christianity when they felt the need of spiritual consolation.

Brodsky was an individualist who fiercely guarded his independence from the thinking or pressures of groups. He insisted on the difference between an egoist and individualist, and claimed that the Soviet system had made us even more individualist than the Americans. At least, this is what he discovered when he came to the States—special interest groups had more influence on the society and on the individual than he had expected. This is why he could not join any church or a synagogue. However, Christian references are frequent in his poetry, and he recognized the Judaeo-Christian roots of our modern civilization.

Brodsky's "Jewishness" and "Christianity" are the subject of many verbal and written speculations among Russian and Jewish writers. For instance, in his article "A Jew and a Hellene," Jewish journalist Shimon Markish analyzes these characteristics, not on a genetic or molecular, but on a spiritual-psychological level. A lengthy quote: "One must suppose...that such dazzling personalities, such individualities who are unlike anyone else, who submit to nothing and no one, can, in Russian poetry, be counted on the fingers of one hand. I dare suppose that this unique poetical personality had no Jewish facet at all.

"Poet Joseph Brodsky does not know the Jewish 'material,' the Jewish theme—that 'material' is alien to him. The youthful, almost childish 'The Jewish Cemetery near Leningrad...' does not count. By all the indicators this poem is not yet Brodsky, it is more representative of Boris Slutsky [an older Soviet poet], who cannot be omitted from Brodsky's poetical biography. Evidently,

Brodsky did not escape the charm of "Jewish Slutsky" either, but was caught only for a moment... 'Isaac and Abraham' (1963) is no more a Jewish work than Milton's 'Paradise Lost,' or Byron's 'Cain,' or Akhmatova's biblical themes..."[1]

Solzhenitsyn echoes Shimon Markish in his article "Iosif Brodsky—Selected Poems." Here is another quote:[2]

"His coming forward could have been invoked and demanded by the Jewish theme, so tense a subject in the USSR in those years. But even that did not happen. There was, still in his youth, 'The Jewish Cemetery Near Leningrad,' later, 'Isaac and Abraham,' but that was already on a level common to all mankind. And, yes, also a small chapter out of the 'Lithuanian Divertissement,' and that's all..." Both Markish and Solzhenitsyn feel it would be more natural had Brodsky been more Jewish.

The riddle of Brodsky's "Jewishness" (or non-Jewishness) excites the interest of "simple" readers as well. One is reminded of the Soviet classic "Twelve Chairs" by Il'f and Petrov, where the itinerant lecturer complained that, no matter what the topic of his lecture, the audience always asked the same two questions: "Why is sunflower oil no longer available in stores?" and "Do you happen to be Jewish?" As an individualist, Joseph strongly felt that this was nobody's business, and tried to be evasive. I do not think that he was particularly sensitive on the issue of religion. He was against any public discussion of his private life. He kept saying, mistakenly, I think, that the biography of the poet is in his poems, and the public does not need to know more than what can be surmised from them. He even asked his friends not to help researchers to research his biography. But for the Russians, a poet is a public figure, and his existential attitudes are as interesting to his readers as his romantic ups and downs.

I remember Brodsky's last public appearance before a Russian-language audience: April 9th, 1995, in Boston. Typical questions were: "Who do you consider yourself to be?" "Do you consider yourself a Jew?" "Are you Jewish or not?"

I tape-recorded his appearance, so I can quote Joseph's answers exactly. To "Who do you consider yourself to be?" Brodsky answered, "A Russian poet." Asked "Do you consider yourself a Jew?" he answered, "I consider myself a person." To "Are you Jewish?" he answered, "Jewish." To "Is it important to you that you are Jewish?" he gave a more extensive answer:

"For me the most important thing in a man is whether he is brave or a coward, whether he is honest or a liar, whether he is a decent person, which especially shows in how he treats a woman." This was a ringing phrase, of course, but again, it demonstrated Joseph's evasiveness more than his inner world. The terms "brave or a coward" and "honest or a liar" sound simple, but when one applies them to real-life situations, one finds many ways to justify one's choices that others would find spineless or dishonest. As far as how one "treats a woman," well, I remember what one poet whom Joseph admired (Auden) told Joseph about another poet whom Joseph admired (Lowell): "I do not like men who leave behind them a smoking trail of crying women." Auden had the right to say so, he was a homosexual. A year later, in February, Evgeny Rein and I were speaking in Boston at a public gathering dedicated to Brodsky's memory. We were showered with notes like these: "Is it true that Brodsky was baptized?" "Why did Brodsky have himself baptized?" "Where did Brodsky have himself baptized?" "Why did the Jew Brodsky become a Christian?" And a note to Rein: "You said that he was a Christian like any civilized human being. Are you sure that an atheist cannot be civilized?"

In private conversations—both serious and joking—Brodsky would "glide" over this topic like a speedboat over the waves, sending fairly contradictory signals, which, nevertheless, gave one cause to suppose that, although by birth Brodsky was undoubtedly Jewish, he was not a Jew either by faith or by world view. He would readily admit that "I am a bad Jew," but it was not clear what he meant by "bad."

I remember walking around the city one day when we were young, and we decided to go into a synagogue on the Lermontovsky Prospect (the only functioning synagogue in Leningrad in those years). There were five of us: Brodsky, Naiman with Era Korobova, then his wife, Vitya and I. As far as I know none of us had ever been to a synagogue before, and none of us knew any religious laws. We went up to the doors but they would not let us in. It turned out that the men had to have their heads covered—a skullcap was best, but if you didn't have one, then you needed a cap, a hat, a beret... something.

This was a time when gentlemen had already stopped wearing hats but were still carrying handkerchiefs. Amazingly, all three men in our company turned out to be gentlemen who had handkerchiefs. They tied knots in the corners and put them on.

Single file we proceeded into the main sanctuary of the synagogue, but were stopped again and told that in the synagogue men and women could not sit together; the men could stay downstairs but the girls had to go upstairs. Because our only references were secular, we felt that this was unjustifiable discrimination. Iosif and Tolya started to seethe and said they would go up with us.

At that time of day the synagogue was empty and dull. No services were being held, there was nothing to see or hear. In about ten minutes we left. Some of us left the synagogue forever.

But Vitya Shtern, a quarter of a century later, has become an Orthodox Jew. He keeps the Sabbath, and the holidays, and the rituals. Several times he invited Brodsky to attend the services with him (for instance, during Yom Kippur, to listen to Kol Nidre—the most melodious and sad of all Jewish prayers). Brodsky would shrug his shoulders and say that it was not interesting and he did not need it: "I, Vitya, with my sense of the divine, am closer to God than any Orthodox Jew." He had definite knowledge of his sense of divine, but it was not clear what he knew about Orthodox Jews.

Brodsky maintained, probably in truth, that he had not been in a synagogue since that time in Leningrad. Even when he died, the burial services were read for him both in an Episcopalian church and in a Russian Orthodox church, but no last rites were held in a synagogue. And he lay in his coffin with a Catholic cross in his hand. Whether it was his wish or Maria's is not known. However, I never heard him express interest in Catholic rites, concepts, or hierarchy.

Not only did Brodsky never enter a synagogue during services—he even refused to hold literary events in synagogue buildings. Many American synagogues rent out their prayer halls for secular community events. In terms of size and acoustics those places compare to first-class concert halls, but they are much cheaper to rent. Many renowned Russian singers, actors, and theatre groups perform in synagogue buildings when they come to this country on concert tours.

In the spring of 1995, when I talked Brodsky into a literary tour of America, producer Nathan Schlesinger rented some synagogue halls in several cities. I showed the list of places to Iosif and he said sharply, "No synagogues, please. I will not appear in synagogues."

Schlesinger did not expect that his choice of halls was of any importance and by that time he had already signed several contracts. He did not dare to justify the breach of contract with a synagogue by citing his client's aversion to them and consequently lost quite a bit of money.

Brodsky's attitude toward Israel was enigmatic, too. In 1985 Vitya Shtern was invited to read two lecture courses at Ben-Gurion University in Beersheba. We were going to spend the entire fall semester there. I called Brodsky to say goodbye, and also to invite him to visit—we were promised a big professorial apartment, a car, and other perks to which a "foreign" professor was entitled.

"You are going to spend four months in Beersheba?" asked Brodsky as if he could not believe his ears. "Vit'ka, I understand, will be busy from morning till night, but you...you'll die of boredom there."

I argued that we wouldn't have to sit in Beersheba, that everything in Israel is close to everything else; that Jerusalem is an hour away and so is Tel-Aviv, and the Dead Sea even closer; that we could take the car and drive around the whole country...but he refused the invitation: "You know, I am a bad Jew."

That sounded strange to me. For a Jew, and for a Christian, and for a Muslim, throughout the entire history of human civilization Israel has always been one of the most significant and moving places in the world.

I know that Brodsky—not once and not twice—had been invited to the University of Jerusalem to lecture or to read, but he would not even discuss it.

Once an American impresario asked for my assistance in talking Brodsky into holding literary events in six Israeli cities. The terms offered were magnificent.

I asked Joseph to grant me an "audience," and we met in the

Chinese restaurant on the corner of 80ᵗʰ Street and Second Avenue. (It was a nice restaurant; it's a pity it's not there any more.) For starters, I decided to break the Israeli ice, and told him about the warnings a mutual female acquaintance gave us before our first trip to the "historic motherland."

Warning number one: "Ludka, don't forget to take Tylenol for a headache. The heat is horrible there... and this hot wind, the *khamsin*... Now, Pontius Pilate had severe headaches—do you remember how it ended because of this?"

Warning number two: "Don't walk around Jerusalem alone, there's no point in getting blisters for nothing. Tour the old city with someone local, someone who knows where everything is... We did not do that, and we couldn't find the Holy Sepulcher to save our souls."

Joseph was very amused, and that is when I trotted out the "tempting" proposal.

"No, I won't go."

"But why?"

"Because the heat is horrible there—the *khamsin*," laughed Brodsky. "For me all that is contraindicated."

I said that in spring it was quite tolerable...He said he had other plans for spring...I said how about early fall, then...He said he'd be teaching the Fall semester...I said...He said...To make a long story short, he categorically refused even to consider the option.

...When Brodsky was 22 years old, he wrote a remarkable poem "Isaac and Abraham." This is how Brodsky describes the Negev Desert in this poem:

On the fourth day in the desert, alone
Isaac and Abraham walk toward the holy place
Over all the empty hills
Unsteady under them like dough.
But it's the sand, only thick sand.
<...>
Sand is all around. Hills of sand. Fields of it.
Hills of sand. They can't be counted or measured.
Actually, it is more like the sea.
Below, on the bottom, is the earth.

But that is hard to believe, it is hard to believe.
Hills of sand. Dunes, as they are called.[3]

Let us not quibble over historical inaccuracies. They were not walking alone (they had two companions) and they came to the holy place on the third day (Genesis, XXII).

But neither "the sand all around," nor hills of sand, nor dunes could have been there. (That's what the Sahara Desert looks like.) The road from Beersheba to Jerusalem lies across the stony Negev Desert. There are craggy, reddish hills and majestic mountains. The stones become weathered and crumble, turning into detritus and sharp splinters, but... not sand.

One could object: authenticity isn't needed—"what difference does it make?"—and that the poet sees the desert that way in his imagination. Had Brodsky seen it with his own eyes, however, I think he would have described it differently.

This is not a reproach. "Isaac and Abraham" was written in 1962, when Israel was further from us than another galaxy and never discussed. But Brodsky continued to be interested in biblical themes. Almost every year he tried to write a Christmas poem around Christmas time. More interesting, perhaps, is the fact that he never wrote anything about a grown-up Christ, or about the Crucifixion. And he would give his Christmas poems to his friends with charming dedications. For instance, the one to Baryshnikov in 1994:

For Mishel's bookshelf—a token;
and for his Christmas stocking.

And this is the poem he gave to Baryshnikov two months before he died:

To the dearly beloved Mouse
October 26, 1995

...And no one will recognize You
in the evening crowds of Bethlehem: either with a match
where someone has lit up the down on his lip,
or, where Herod raised his bloody hands,
the City struck a spark in a hurry

with an electric train
of the fear and tin;
or a halo began to glow, small in diameter,
from a doorway flashing by for all eternity.

Baryshnikov says that in the first version Brodsky wrote "in the reeking doorway." Then he changed it to "flashing by," and that's how it was printed. But when he gave Misha the poem Joseph scrawled "unsightly" to replace "flashing by."

Baryshnikov asked him which version was final—"flashing by" or "unsightly?"

Brodsky answered, "Any way you wish—you own it now."

This poem—one of his very last—offers earnest proof that to the end of his life Brodsky was interested in events that had taken place in the Land of Israel.

...But returning to our conversation with Joseph about going to Israel and to my futile efforts to talk him into it.

At the end of the dinner we got our crunchy fortune cookies. Joseph broke his and read: "Luck in a far journey."

"You see?" said I. "And you are displaying 'inappropriate stubbornness' (also an expression from our old lexicon)."

He was silent a bit, then suddenly said, very seriously, "You know, Kissa, I am afraid to...I am afraid I won't like it in today's Israel. I'd rather go to Syria."

Brodsky's attitude to his Jewishness was complicated from the time he was seven years old. He applied to the local children's library, and when the librarian reached Section Five on the application, Brodsky said he was not able to pronounce "a Jew." When he was in school, he suffered because during the breaks the teachers would leave the class registry, with Section Five filled for each student, open on the desk for everyone to see. He had clearly identifiable Jewish facial features. As with most Jews born and raised in Leningrad, his speech did not have even the trace of a Jewish accent, but he pronounced his r's in a French way, which in Russia was a giveaway that he was Jewish.

Once Vitya and I were spending the weekend with Alex and Tatiana Liberman at their estate in Connecticut (more of the Libermans later). Brodsky came down also. Every week Alex would bring a whole bale of videocassettes for Tatiana; among them, by the way, many Russian ones.

But that evening, after supper, we were watching a perfectly American movie, to wit, Woody Allen's *Annie Hall*. In case you do not remember, the story concerns two New York intellectuals. The main character, played by Woody Allen, is a high-strung Jewish neurotic from Brooklyn. He is constantly torn between megalomania and an inferiority complex. The heroine—played by Diane Keaton—is an Anglo-Saxon "blueblood," naive, trusting, even shy, but quite sure of her worth.

They have a torrid love affair. He is madly in love, madly jealous, and tortures her madly. That is, everything is done madly. They can't live together, and they can't live apart. Neither with you nor without you...

There is a funny scene in the movie: the main character comes to visit the heroine's relatives and holds forth at the dinner table, trying to get them to like him. He is talking about some "avant-garde" matters, considerably above their intellectual level or interest, and her mother and her aunt are unable to comprehend him. Nevertheless, looking at that refined Manhattan intellectual they "see" him with sidelocks, in a yarmulka, surrounded by Brooklyn relatives. That is, no matter how smart, talented, brilliant, modern and successful he is, in their minds he is and will always be a provincial, small-town Jew...

After the movie, as always, there was an exchange of opinions. Joseph swallowed some cognac, stretched, and said carelessly, "Well... nothing unusual about the combination—a dirty Jew and a white woman... That is my case absolutely..."

Everybody froze. Alex found what to say first. "Yes, mine too, isn't it, Bubee." He laughed and patted Tatiana's shoulder.

Since this conversation took place before he had met Maria, Joseph probably meant Marina Basmanova and the attitude of her family towards him, but this motif might easily have popped up to torture him in his other love affairs as well.

Maria came into his life later and was either a confirmation or a refutation of this self-disparaging theory.

It seems to me that Brodsky, having grown up in an anti-Semitic country, had an infantile fear of being identified with a prevalent Jewish stereotype which had formed over the course of history in the minds, eyes, and souls of the "white aristocracy."

...Only Jews know how comfortless it is to be a Jew in the Soviet Union. They seemed to react in two distinct ways to the anti-Semitism that saturated the air. Some were pushed by pride and national self-awareness into even broader "Jewishness." They began to study Hebrew and the Torah, to conduct—insofar as it was safe—religious rites. Others—and they were in the majority—tried to disown their Jewishness...For instance, to change their last name and to be put down as "Russian" in the *passport* (which was possible if one of your parents was Russian).

In tsarist Russia the passports, instead of a nationality section, had a section entitled "Confession." Therefore Jews were people who practiced Judaism. The moment they were baptized, they would become Russian Orthodox, Lutherans, Catholics, or whatever, according to their chosen religion. My father, for instance, was baptized in infancy in a Lutheran church, for which event we had appropriate supporting documents. My grandparents felt that this would open the way to better schools and greater social mobility. They were right. Even though my father's last name was unmistakably Jewish (Davidovich) he was admitted into one of the best gymnasia in town and was friendly with boys of the strictest aristocratic families.

In the USSR a Jew could be baptized under the auspices of any faith, but the "Section Five" in his passport forever announced him a Jew. He remained a Jew in the eyes of those around him, and in his own eyes.

Whenever Brodsky was asked directly if he was a Jew, he answered "Jew," sustaining the Soviet government's view of the matter, and, incidentally, official Judaism's as well. Anyone with Jewish parents remains a Jew in Jewish eyes no matter what confession of faith he or she might later choose.

In the Soviet Union "persons of Jewish persuasion," even without any religious orientation, often with a "benign" Section Five in their passports, were still recognized by other indications, to wit: first and last names and the patronymic, the burr in the speech—"The Jewish accent wanders..."; also by the color and curliness of the hair, and... the size and curvature of the nose. As in the sad Soviet joke about a Jew with "Russian" in his Section Five: "they beat you about the face, and not about the passport."

By the way, I once asked Brodsky a provocative linguistic

question: why was it customary for Russians who wished to insult Jews to say "his kike *snout*" but when they wished to insult Chinese to say "his Chinese *mug*," and never the other way around ("Chinese snout" and "kike mug")? The question took Iosif unawares.

And so, ethnically, Joseph Brodsky was a pureblooded Jew—as were many friends of his youth. In our circle in Leningrad the only absolute non-Jews were Dima Bobyshev and Misha Petrov. However, the best friends of the "grown-up" Joseph in the West were the Great Russians Baryshnikov and Smakov.

Once, about thirty years ago, during a certain heart-to-heart talk, one of our friends announced that every ethnic Russian carries the anti-Semitic gene. We took alarm and demanded a sincere confession from Misha Petrov—the only ethnic Russian present: was he or was he not a secret anti-Semite? Misha said firmly, "Yes, guys, I am. I am a confirmed anti-Semite in relation to men—*Jews and non-Jews*—but I am no anti-Semite towards women, Jewish and non-Jewish." Well, I can testify that out of Misha's three wives, two were indeed Jewish, and that's not counting a few romances "on the side, " including the one that produced a Jewish daughter of his.

In reality none of our Russian friends were anti-Semites, and the majority of Jews weren't real Jews. We were very much assimilated. Moreover, none of us would have felt Jewish, except that our motherland constantly, in one way or another, reminded us of it.

We grew up with the Russian language, Russian culture, Russian literature, and Russian traditions...We adored Russian nature, Russian forests and fields, Russian winter and Russian autumn, Russian vodka, Russian borsht, pickled herring with potatoes, and Russian "bread which goes in the oven for us" (Gumilyov). As Brodsky wrote in his letter to me while I was in Italy, "a Russian, even if a Jew, has a tendency to love something at first sight and for the rest of his life..."

First and foremost we loved all that concerned Russia, Russian language and Russian culture. One can only wonder why the most significant Russian poetry of the first half of the 20th century was written by Pasternak and Mandelshtam, and why Brodsky, Rein, and Kushner are numbered among the most significant

Russian poets of the second half. I think about this with emotion and pride—how much they contributed to the Russian culture! My husband Victor thinks about this with sadness—how much they could have contributed to Jewish culture had they chosen to stay Jewish!

Both Vitya Shtern and I are Jewish, but our attitudes towards our Jewishness were different from the beginning and have become more so.

My family represented a religious kaleidoscope. Mama was an atheist, Papa a believer, a Lutheran. Since the age of two I was raised by my nanny Nulya in the strict tenets of the Russian Orthodox religion. Every night I had to kneel and repeat "Our Father, who art in heaven," "King of Heaven" and "Hail, Mary" three times. I tried to cheat, would dive into bed when she left the room and pretend to be asleep when she came back. Nulya would mercilessly pull the covers off and shoo me out of bed with an adroit smack of her broom on my backside.

In the "Jewish" sense my life was lucky—I never heard anyone calling "Kike!" after me. I was accepted into the graduate school at the Leningrad University, and after I defended my Ph.D. was given a job in the department.

But in Vitya's life his Jewishness played a significant role. His father, a mathematics teacher, died from starvation in the siege of Leningrad at the age of thirty-five. The mother and two sons lived, as they now say, below the poverty level. The mother could not support them all, and after completing the seventh grade Vitya left to go to trade school. In two years he was working as a lathe operator at the Kirovsky Plant, making turbines for submarines.

Imagine a stooping Jewish four-eyes as a lathe operator. Where and by whom was he not beaten up! The Shterns lived in a rough worker district called Autovo. Once a group of neighborhood toughs surrounded him when he was coming home from the night shift. They beat him up and stabbed him with a knife. The scars on his back are to this day his "distinguishing marks."

Later he graduated from night school with straight A's in all subjects while still working at the Kirovsky plant. In the Soviet Union, the "gold medal" he had earned guaranteed admission to any university without the entrance examinations required of other applicants. Vitya wanted to become a mathematician, but in 1951 Leningrad University would not accept him. Next fall he gave up his mathematical ambitions and got accepted at the Mining Institute. Again he graduated with all A's, but no doctoral program would have him. He applied for a job in Leningrad, but was sent instead to Karaganda in Kazakhstan. All the positions in our home town went to C-students with friends in high places.

Many years later Vitya and his colleagues developed an automated system for aluminum production, for which their whole group was nominated for a State Prize. But they did not get it. The reason? There were too many Jewish names on the team. Especially crestfallen was Vitya's boss Forsblom. Despite a Jewish-sounding last name, he was an absolutely innocent Finn.

So Shtern was not allowed to forget for a minute that a Jew was a second-rate person...

Joseph Brodsky considered himself a Jew and called himself one. But did he *feel* Jewish? Did he feel the connection, or, rather, the belonging? I don't think so...Even when he was young he already saw himself as a "citizen of the world."

Brodsky existed in the medium of Russian and European cultures, admired English-language poetry, and was fascinated by ancient as well as modern Rome.

Not without reason did he earn one of the most absurd reproaches thrown at him by Solzhenitsyn—a reproach for insufficient "Jewishness": "There was <...> later Isaac and Abraham, but that was already on the level common to all mankind."[4]

Brodsky was deeply concerned with metaphysical issues of existence and what he considered the absurdity of our life. He accepted this absurdity but refused to do anything that would contribute to it. He thought that human beings were a pinnacle of creation because of the ability to communicate thoughts and emotions. He went even further. He thought that poetry, not just language, was the goal of creation.

Brodsky did believe in a Creator who not only created the Universe but also had certain expectations of human behavior. He often repeated that he hoped that the Creator liked what he, Brodsky, was doing. This Creator was inscrutable, but Brodsky did not like the word, it was too bland for him, and he called the

Creator cruel and unpredictable, and thought that it was pointless to expect justice in this world. Brodsky assumed that the Creator indeed judged human deeds, but he felt and often said that he, Brodsky, judged himself much, much more strictly than the Creator. I am sure that he judged himself harshly, but I am not sure why he thought that the Creator was not that harsh. Anyway, half-seriously and half-jokingly, he called himself a Calvinist— he said that he judged himself strictly and refused himself forgiveness. Even though he valued the Judeo-Christian tradition, he never came to recognize the spiritual power of repentance.

And here, I think, it is appropriate to recall Brodsky's famous poem "I have braved, for want of wild beasts, steel cages..." Its last lines are these: "Yet until brown clay has been crammed down my larynx, only gratitude will be gushing from it." [See Chapter 17] Victor says that these words call up the words of the Jewish prayer that is spoken each morning: "The soul that You, my God, gave me is pure. <...> While this soul is in my body, I will thank You, Lord, my God and God of my ancestors, Lord of all creation."

---

[1] Iosif Brodsky: *trudi i dni*. M.: Izdatel'stvo Nezavisimaya Gazeta, 1998, 209
[2] Solzhenitsyn, A. "*Iosif Brodsky - izbranniye stikhi*", Novii Mir, 1999, No. 12
[3] *Sochineniya Iosifa Brodskogo*. Pushkinsky Fond, 1992, 269
[4] Solzhenitsyn, "*Iosif Brodsky - izbranniye stikhi*."

15

His Alter Ego

GENNADY GRIGORIEVICH SMAKOV, as he was known to the official art establishment (or Genna, Genka, Gennasty, Gennusyk, as we called him) was one of Brodsky's closest friends. Iosif called him "almost my alter ego."

Smakov was remarkably well educated and had an exceptional memory; even at a relatively young age, he certainly was one of the most sophisticated and knowledgeable people of our generation. He knew eight languages, including Classic Latin and Greek, and spoke fluent English, German, French, Spanish, Italian, and contemporary Greek. He knew both Russian and world poetry as few others, and was a brilliant translator of many ancient and contemporary authors, among them Byron, Paul Verlaine, Jean Cocteau, the Portuguese Fernando Pessoa, and the famous Spaniards, Rafael Alberti and Federico Garcia Lorca. Brodsky considered his Greek-to-Russian translations of Cavafy unsurpassed. Smakov was a connoisseur of the arts: world cinema, the opera, and especially the ballet.

One romantic female fan called Smakov the "magical vessel, which contained a diamond mine of knowledge."

Brodsky used to say that Genna represented a "literal embodiment of culture" and was "his major university."

On the books given to Genna, Iosif always wrote funny and touching autographs. Here is an example:

224

A frequent reader of these lines,
Accept them, dear Gennalines,
Collected in a humble tome.
I also once built a home,
Dug earth, desired domestic blessings on my head,
Look: here twenty years lie, killed dead.

But Brodsky presented Smakov with more than autographs; "The Venice Stanzas"[2] are dedicated to him.

A mine of knowledge, Gennasty as a person was charming, merry, thoughtless, witty, carefree, kind, and generous. Envy never troubled him, the future never worried him.

He adored smart clothes, dinner gatherings, was an inimitable cook, and swore that he was a figure-skating veteran. However, for the quarter century that we were friends, he was on skates, so far as I could see, not even once. Did he exaggerate his achievements? I do not completely exclude this, but from my own experience I know that it is very hard to fake competence in cooking and in languages. Mere boasting is not enough.

And for me Genna Smakov became more than the brother I never had. He became my dearest and most loyal friend in the world.

We first met each other on the Neva embankment near the Leningrad University. I had just left the University courtyard in front of the famous Twelve Colleges building. The sidewalk was covered with ice-slicks—shiny black patches on the fresh white snow. I took a running start to slide jauntily along, and slid into the arms of two young men at once. One of them, in a gray coat with a raised collar and a cap pulled over his eyes was Osya Brodsky; the other, mustachioed, in a suede sheepskin coat (a rarity for those times, indicating that the owner was a person with both taste and connections) and a fur hat with long earflaps, was unknown to me.

"Hi. Can't you see where you are going?" said Iosif. "Come and be introduced... This is Genna Smakov."

We shook hands, stamped our feet, and I asked if anyone was going my way.

"I have to be somewhere," said Brodsky. "Walk me to the

bus stop."

We did and he rode away. Genna said he was not in a hurry and offered to walk me home.

We crossed the Palace Bridge over the Neva, and went into the deserted, snow-covered Alexandrovsky Gardens between the Admiralty and the Isaac Cathedral. Smakov brushed snow from a bench with a leather glove. We sat down and lit cigarettes. What followed was not exactly a *conversation*. Smakov never stopped talking. Cascades of famous names—poets, artists, dancers, opera divas—flashed before my eyes. It was a real frontal attack, marshaled to reduce me to dust, or tell me what a treasure I was so lucky to have met in the course of my life.

A quarter of a century later, three weeks before he died, Smakov asked me my first impression of him. I wanted to divert him somehow, to make him laugh, and the next day I sent him "an attempt at a psychological portrait." I suspect, however, that this portrait was formed not only by my first impression but also by countless conversations throughout out lives.

Here is the portrait:

He ran towards me with a bouquet of just-picked field cornflowers and clover, wearing Dior shorts and an Armani tank top, with a pair of field glasses hanging on his chest. His thick mustache gleamed in the sun, his soft contacts gave off a mild violet glow. Golden ears of wheat opened before him and then closed again above his head.

This is how I remembered the five-year-old Gennady, until fate, an eternity later, brought us together again in the vegetable section of the Leningrad Hay Market. The ears of his fur hat made of muskrat hung down to his knees, a chocolate-colored sheepskin coat made in the province of Korrinda in South Portugal fitted his well-proportioned body neatly. Genna was sniffing a bunch of radishes. I bowed timidly.

"You cannot make a soufflé out of rotten cabbage, even if you are Paul Bocuse, the chef of the three-star Michelin restaurant in Lyon," he muttered. "You must have at least two eggs or, to be more exact, two egg-whites, as the Larousse Gastronomique makes perfectly clear..."

I was so enchanted by the soft, deep timbre of his voice that

I dared to ask him what he was working on now.

"It's hard to say," he said thoughtfully in a language I did not know. "I am amused and touched by the lives of the leading actors of theater and cinema, opera and ballet, rock and pop music. Tragedies and vaudeville also do not leave me unmoved. And that is why I write books. About Gerarka for instance. (I was intimidated and didn't dare to ask who Gerarka was, and only many years later did I realize that he was talking about the French actor Gérard Philippe), about Marusya, Nurka, and Mishanya....A study of Natashka's work also lies within my field of inner vision... [After Gérard Philippe the diminutives refer to Maria Callas, Anna Pavlova, Mikhail Baryshnikov and Natalia Makarova (in that order).]

"As for jazz, *à vrai dire*, I would never bother myself..."

"Please, don't," I begged, afraid to look into the depths of his fragmented psychological world... But Smakov continued to speak of himself at length and with great affection... Actually, I am an expert at figure skating and the piano—everything before Bach-Busoni," he said bitterly, "but how can one express oneself in this vulgar world?" I became concerned that any system, whether totalitarian or democratic, would cripple this genius.

He was caring, sympathetic, delicate. But not deaf to the sounds of his own world, either. He was vulnerable but forceful; ascetic, but not averse to the joys of life; disinterested and artistic, widely and fundamentally educated. He could have written *Crime and Punishment* as well as *Lolita* if they hadn't, fortunately, been written before him by others.

He was a touch sentimental and childish, but how much charm and enchantment there was in his infantilism! Many loved him, but more were afraid of him. And all for no reason, because he was good and radiated kindness and affection.

I am proud to have lived in the same century with him. [End of portrait.]

Gibberish, perhaps, but this essay did express my awe when I first met Smakov: his erudition seemed to be inexhaustible. However, despite all his gleaming talents and qualities, Gennady was not ambitious or vain. All right, he was very vain, but... in a "homey" way. It was important for him to be the king of a dinner

227

table, to stun, trumpet, shine, glitter, and then fly away...

He really did have many talents. In the kitchen... Genna was a chef by the grace of God. He never went to any culinary school and he even scorned written recipes. Storing recipes in the computer horrified him. He was an improviser, a virtuoso, a culinary Paganini.

This is what Sasha Sumerkin, Genna's friend and one of Brodsky's friends and translators (from English into Russian), wrote of Genna's talent: "His culinary gifts were truly boundless... We need a Gogol to describe the feasts he organized for us. The suppers at Smakov's were an embodiment of the most incredible gastronomic fantasies, accompanied by the heavenly singing of his beloved prima donnas on his stereo." True in every detail, including the stereo.

In the book *Dialogues with Iosif Brodsky* by Solomon Volkov, Brodsky is quoted as also remembering Smakov's magical culinary gift: "...Smakov, as you know, was an absolutely phenomenal cook... I never knew another such magician in that field..."[1]

When we decided to seek ways to emigrate from the Soviet Union, we made all kinds of plans as to how we would survive in America. Opening a Russian restaurant together seemed to be a sure bet given Genna's (and my) prowess in the kitchen. Even though some of our émigré friends did open restaurants, we very quickly recognized that good and imaginative cooking is only part of the game, and is not worth much without management skills and financial backing.

Smakov was also far from realizing his true potential as a poet or writer, nor was he a great theater critic or a top-drawer translator... And he could have been. His book on Gérard Philippe, published in Russia, was the best book on the French cinema at the time. God blessed Smakov with many talents, but probably his greatest was the talent to live, and he lived like a Bengal light: brightly and transiently.

When I think of Genna, I remember Otar Ioseliani's movie *There Lived a Song-Thrush* about a young man who lived like a bird, smiling, singing, cheering up everyone he met and never worrying about the future. He did not know (and neither did the viewers) that there was indeed no reason to worry about the future—he was going to be killed in an accident before the movie's end. Just an accident, and it was waiting to happen. As far as his professional career was concerned, Genna did not trouble himself in the least. More accurately, he did a lot so as not to have one. In that sense, he was similar to Brodsky—he wouldn't bow before the system and he couldn't be bent. He went his own way.

He was born in the Urals, to a family of staunch supporters of the regime who knew little about world art and literature. It is remarkable that his parents were unable to straighten him out. They let him go to Leningrad to study, and there he learned languages, absorbed world culture and abandoned his parents' world view. His books and art reviews quickly made him a name that enabled him to survive outside the system. His flamboyant nature coupled with his knowledge of foreign languages allowed him to rub shoulders with foreigners. Of course friends were envious. Of course the KGB disapproved. So his behavior when we first met was not unusual for him; he had met and charmed Marlene Dietrich in the same way and in the same place on the Neva embankment. He struck up a conversation with her not because she was a star—initially, he did not recognize her. When he saw her on the street, he thought: this old lady must have an interesting personality and would be worth a conversation.

In America—as everywhere else—talent succeeds by connections. Thanks to the Libermans, of whom I will speak later, Smakov suddenly had connections beyond ordinary mortal's dreams. He was intimate with world celebrities—writers, publishers, critics, movie stars, theater directors, and politicians. I often witnessed how one or another of the "very useful" Liberman guests would, upon leaving, give Smakov his card along with an invitation to call, have lunch, and talk business. Genna's face in those moments wore an expression of "And what do I need that for?"

He preferred talking to his friends and even acquaintances to any useful meeting. He had no greater pleasure than getting together to have a drink, to read some poetry, and to chew the fat (he used a juicier expression) with Baryshnikov and Brodsky.

His unexpected trips to Boston were always a cause for celebration in our home. Putting his bag down in the foyer (and still wearing his sheepskin coat) Genna would say, "Let's go get some meat, we'll have *pel'meni* [Russian ravioli]... On the way we'll decide whom to invite..."

And we would race to the store of organic and exotic foods called "Bread and Circus." There Genna would demand that various pieces of meat be brought out for his inspection, look them over with a critical eye, be doubtful, shake his head, and then suddenly his face would light up with a heavenly light—he had found the one, the only...

Having decided whom to invite, and having made the necessary calls, we would sit down at the kitchen table and get to work.

First we would exchange the latest news and opinions of films and plays, then Genna, who was always in love with somebody, would lead me through the maze of his relationships. Later we would gossip, divulging our own secrets and other people's, and still later we would read poetry.

In the end we would have about four hundred melt-in-your-mouth, heavenly *pel'meni*, consuming which you could distinctly hear the music of the spheres.

Smakov came to the West by way of marriage to an American woman that his friends had sent over from New York. Not having a single drop of Jewish blood in his veins, he could not leave with an Israeli visa. To marry a Jewish woman and emigrate with her was another option open to Smakov, but at the time he could not find a safe partner for this way of escape.

His fiancée, a twenty-five-year-old journalist, was promised generous reimbursement. She was also warned that the marriage would be strictly fictitious, as the bridegroom was not interested in ladies (even though he was previously married and had a son).

At that time Genna was already divorced and lived at various friends' places, including ours. He asked our permission to bring the bride to us straight from the airport, for a supper and intellectual conversation, after which he would take her to the Hotel Astoria.

His bride, Sally, turned out to be charming, plump and pleasant-looking. Unfortunately, problems began just two days later. She fell head over heels in love with Genna, and announced that she did not want any presents or reimbursements: only for the marriage to be a real one. She would cry on my shoulder, and then, being an optimistic Yankee, would recite her cherished hope that one fine day... I did not discourage her.

According to the Soviet laws of that liberal time, marriages with foreigners were already allowed. However, the prospective newlyweds had to apply for a marriage license first and then examine their feelings for two months. Sally's visa was only good for two weeks, so she had to fly away over the ocean, ask for another guest visa and then come back again. We worried that she would change her mind, or that *they* [the KGB, always "they" to us] would not let her reenter the country—with the Soviets, anything could happen. But she came and the marriage took place. Sally robed herself in a lace-trimmed white dress, and Genna bought her a ring. Witnesses to the marriage were: a ballerina of the Maryinsky Theater, Kaleria Fedicheva; an old friend, Yakov Gordin [introduced in Chapter Two], and yours truly. Smakov, in a green velvet jacket, snow-white shirt, and a claret-colored bow-tie, was dazzling. After the ceremony we went to Fedicheva's grand apartment and had an improvised supper with three bottles of "Soviet Champagne" amidst her antique Karelian-birch furniture. At midnight, Genna said that he would take his wife to the Astoria and then come back to us for the night. And that's when Mrs. Smakov began to rage. A day later she had to leave the country.

The OVIR shuffled Smakov from post to pillar for quite a while, so he got his permission to reunite with his wife only after we had already left the country. On the way to New York he caught up with us in Rome. We met him at the airport. He emerged from Customs, sheepskin unbuttoned, talking to everybody in fluent Italian as if he were used to crossing international borders, and it was his first trip abroad! He spent about ten days in Rome with us, but got to the States three weeks before we did. On the 14th of January, 1976, he met us at the Kennedy Airport and he said "All right, you greenhorns, I will show you the ropes. After all, I have been here fully three weeks, and I already know everything."

In New York, Sally finally realized the futility of her efforts, and they became good friends. We all spent a lot of time together until she got a job with the *Rutland Herald* and went to live in Vermont. We read her political editorials, with interest, to this day.

While in America, Smakov wrote many articles and books: "Baryshnikov: from Russia to the West" (Farrar Straus & Giroux; 1981), "Great Russian Dancers" (Knopf, 1984) and edited (or, more accurately, wrote) a book about Natalia Makarova, yet another émigré dancer (Knopf, 1979).

To write a book about the great Baryshnikov would be a dream come true for any ballet critic, no matter how famous. But Western critics did not know the work that Misha did before defecting to the West. Russian critics knew Misha's work, but no Russian critic in his or her right mind would dare to write a book about Misha: after he defected, Misha's name disappeared from all art books published in the Soviet Union, as if Misha had never been the pride of Soviet art or even existed. Genna had known Baryshnikov from the first stages of his professional career, and had followed it closely. Misha agreed to the book being written by Smakov, who was at that time unknown in the West. This was done with best intentions, to give Genna a chance to reveal his ability and possibly make some money.

In his turn, Smakov, who had known Baryshnikov long and intimately, could have written a bestseller filled with gossip and "juicy bits," and become rich and famous. Best friends, lovers, and even relatives of the stars in the West do it all the time. But Genna loved Misha very much, valued their friendship, and did not make use of Misha's name for his own benefit. This is confirmed by Brodsky in his interviews with Volkov:

"...Baryshnikov's biography is, in my opinion, a highly deserving work, the merits of which were, up to a certain point, the reasons for this biography not being financially successful. For it had no gossip, it did not wash the star's dirty laundry in public, and so on."[2]

So the *New York Times Book Review* published an article entitled "The Magnificent Misha" by Laura Shapiro, which was rapturous about Baryshnikov, and which criticized Genna's book for lacking sufficient analytical depth and, at the same time, for being on the dry and dull side and thus not likely to be a commercial success. Some people who belonged to that world maintained that such a sour review of a book by an unknown Russian author is only natural, because the New York journalistic mafia does not want to let a newcomer near their feeding-trough.

Small wonder that this review did not help sales of the book.

The *New York Times Magazine* of April 11, 1982, ran an article by Deborah Trastman about Baryshnikov's life and work, as well as an interview with Baryshnikov and Brodsky. In that interview Joseph found no kind words for Genna's book as he had later in the interview with Volkov. This was most unfortunate because a defense would have been timely and carried a lot of weight.

An amusing thing about this interview was Joseph Brodsky's explanation of what is important to Baryshnikov in ballet. "It is important for him to have a plot, that is, to tell a 'story.' According to Brodsky, continued Trastman, he once advised Misha to dance Mozart's bassoon concerto. Misha asked, "And what, Joseph, will I dance?" To which that "connoisseur of ballet and prominent choreographer" Joseph Brodsky answered, "Just dance to the music, that's all." [Tantamount to Baryshnikov asking Joseph to compose a poem by suggesting that he "put a clean sheet of paper into the typewriter and just type."]

Misha shook his head, "No, you write me a libretto."

Further in the interview with Trastman Brodsky justly observed that "Misha helps a great many people. He finances immigrant publications and supports newly-arrived acquaintances..."

Which is nothing less than the absolute truth. Misha tried to keep many of his acquaintances "afloat." With one, he paid his rent for months, with another, who lived in a "bad" area, he paid for a child to go to a private school, fed the third, simply gave money to the fourth. When our family came to the States, Baryshnikov was very kind to us, too. He not only gave us passes to performances, but he also tried to help Victor get a job at IBM.

But during this ill-starred interview, when the journalist asked Misha why, exactly, was it Smakov whom he allowed to write the book, Baryshnikov answered, "Since it was a chance for him... Why not?" Not a word about Genna's experience in writing books, his familiarity with ballet in general and with Misha's work in particular, nothing about Genna's broad and deep erudition.

That is, neither Brodsky nor Baryshnikov tried to protect

Genna from the overt ill will of the New York ballet critics. This episode took place many years ago and the reader might question my reasons for resurrecting it now. At the time I took the story quite close to my heart, and I am still in anguish over it. Had events played out differently at this critical time, Genna's professional life might have taken a different shape. I am not saying that Brodsky and Baryshnikov gave up on Genna. After this episode, they had an ample opportunity to demonstrate their support and friendship, but at this critical juncture they failed him.

Several days after the article came out Brodsky called me in Boston, "You know, Kissa, Genka's been terribly depressed lately. Maybe you can come visit, be with him for a while?"

"And who pushed him into his depressive state?" I snapped.

In spite of the lukewarm reception of the hardcover edition, a paperback edition of the Baryshnikov book was published in 1982 [Noonday Press]. After all, Smakov was not that much of a butterfly [the Russian symbol for a playful hedonist who enjoys life and avoids hard work]. In 1984, Knopf published Smakov's major work, a truly fundamental history of Russian ballet, *Great Russian Dancers*. The subtitle promised coverage "from the days of Petipa and Pavlova to the era of Baryshnikov, Makarova, and Nureyev." With its 343 photographs, the book describes the magical world of 33 legendary Russian ballerinas and dancers in word and in picture. The book contained both deep analysis of the character and technique of the artists and amusing stories of their lives and fates. Today, it is a collectors' item. Despite all this, Smakov had no permanent income and earned money only sporadically. Thanks to the Libermans' financial support, he seemed to be living a carefree life, never setting a penny aside or worrying about the morrow. However, from time to time, the thought of a "poverty-stricken old age" made him shudder for about fifteen minutes. And really, with all the thought he had given it, Genna's old age could have been squalid and sad... if he had lived to see it.

...Spring and summer of 1987 Vitya and I spent in Belgium. And that is why, when Smakov was diagnosed with AIDS, we were not at his side. He wrote to us often in Brussels—ironical letters, even more full of buffoonery than usual. However, that did not make us suspect anything—another bout of the blues…That had happened before, how many times? A devil-may-care tone had been known to accompany those splenetic fits of his. But that spring of 1987 he had received a death sentence…

"May 20, 87, Libermania-City.

Dear old lady Krisonogova (*Ratfoot*). I am glad you have discovered that your spreading bloated body bears a striking resemblance to Rubens's Bacchus and Hog—this indicates the eye of a true artist which you are in the depth of your soul. And I am glad that you are running from museum to museum like a madwoman as if somebody had tied a burning rocket to your tail. It is much better than running from hospitals to the columbarium. I have no such potent joys. I am but a peasant, and life flows, partially pouring itself out of one empty vessel into another empty vessel [a Russian saying for wasting time], partially as a chain of grotesques and almost-tragedies.

Tatiana [Liberman, see next chapter] fell down and broke her hip. She was operated on, despite her howling and yelling for them to let her die in peace. The operation went well—really, the local sawbones are something special again. This is no Sklifosovsky Clinic [the Moscow hospital] where they still, I think, saw limbs off without anesthesia as they did during the Russo-Japanese War of 1904-1905, no doubt vividly remembered by you as your very personal experience.

The heat here is Egyptian, I am black as any Ethiopian, am writing about *The Sleeping Beauty*, and, in general, have climbed into the "Epoch of Masterpieces," the last chapter about the great master who will soon—I can't wait!—kick the old bucket.

All this is somehow chaotic and complicated by bad thoughts and insomnia. I am out of sleeping pills, and in the rare moments of oblivion I see Rudick Nureyev upon the mast in the arms of Callas who wears a Moorish costume from the Napoleonic era.

But I am still svelte, intolerant, and slightly angry, although the polished poem does not shine brighter than new-minted copper. On May 24th I am going to Mikhail Barysh [Baryshnikov] to gnaw a knish on the occasion of the grand birthday festivities of your friend and confidant Jozephius [Brodsky] whom I haven't seen since the fall of Troy...

This morning it is foggy and practically damp. I am reading—to my great surprise—Solzhenitsyn's "February-March 1917." I must say that the work is first-class, and stunning prose, if it was not for multiple "*udurchivye and ugnels'a*" [new words invented by Solzhenitsyn that almost no Russian understands]. It's on a simply grandiose scale, almost Tolstoy-like. All the strata are grasped, and what characters!—Nicholas II, and Protopopov, and Tzarina Alex, and Rodzyanko, and Guchkov, and Kerensky—and that whole churned-up picture of how Russia was collectively pissed away.

I am simply ecstatic, have already read 400 pages of the tiniest print (you know those eye-killing YMCA Press editions), with 800 still ahead. And I am not bored even for a second. No, it's not for nothing he was sitting in his Vermont. [Solzhenitsyn bought a huge estate in Vermont in 1974 and lived there almost twenty years in virtual isolation until he returned to Russia in 1994.] My dear old lady, keep writing about various colorful events and remember me, the prisoner of creativity and miracle-working. How doth Viktor, shaking the foundations of the Universe?

There, it started raining, curse it, kisses to you both. Keep writing to me constantly, write every minute. Your G."

Smakov was already almost completely bedridden when, at the end of March 1988 Boston hosted a Soviet-American musical festival, "Making Music Together," organized by Sarah Caldwell. More than four hundred people came from the Soviet Union—the best representatives of all musical genres. Baryshnikov also came to take part in the festival.

The best concert halls in Boston were rented for the event, guest participants stayed in the best hotels, and receptions followed one after another. The whole undertaking cost mountains of money. And though the festival turned out to be an outstanding event in the cultural life of Boston, in financial terms it was a disaster that cost Sarah her career.

Smakov could not, of course, miss such an event—especially the evening when his friend Maya Plisetskaya was to dance "*La Rose Malade*."

Despite doctors' warnings—and ours—that the trip might prove to be too much for him, Genna came.

His birthday was the day before this gala-concert, and we decided to throw him a surprise party. Our apartment was not large enough for a big gathering and our friend Lena Zaretzky hosted the party at her place. There were about fifty people, including Baryshnikov, composer Shnitke with his wife Irina, conductor Gennady Rozhdestvensky with his wife Victoria Postniklova, poet and old friend Andrei Voznesensky (without his wife, writer Zoya Boguslavsky, who stayed in Russia)... A few of Genna's friends came from New York.

Smakov, emaciated, with a drawn face, was a trouper all evening and looked almost happy.

But in the morning he could not get up. When we took his temperature it was 103 F. I gave him some aspirin, but he said he needed to take the medicines his doctor had prescribed, and he had felt so good before the trip that he left them at home. In a panic, I called Liberman, and Alex told us to fly him to New York immediately—there would be a limousine with a doctor and a nurse waiting at LaGuardia.

Somehow or other we got him dressed and Vitya drove us to the airport. But the plane had left ten minutes ago, and there was an hour's wait for the next. Genna was semi-conscious. I held him in my arms like a child with long—"two-chairs-long"—legs. Thank God, an attendant brought us a wheelchair—he did not have the strength to board by himself.

I will not forget that hour-long journey to the end of my days. Genna was burning up and breathing hoarsely and with difficulty. I held his head and prayed for him to get there alive...

Smakov lived another five months. Alex Liberman did not want to put him into a hospital—there was no cure for AIDS anyway. He organized excellent care for Genna: there was a nurse on duty by his bed day and night. That is, three nurses, on duty eight hours each. Very little was known about AIDS at that time, and people were frightened: what if Genna were infectious, like a plague victim? Consequently, nurses who agreed to take care of AIDS patients charged very high fees. Liberman and Baryshnikov paid all the expenses, and Brodsky also helped, as far as he was financially able.

But more than money was provided. Misha and Joseph both visited Genna often and at his bedside reminisced, joked, told funny stories, read poetry. I am sure that the presence of dear close friends prolonged Genna's life.

At that time Baryshnikov had an apartment three blocks from Genna's. Misha let me stay there during my visits to New York, saving me the trouble of traveling to the friends who usually gave me "political asylum" in New York. Having spent four to five hours with Genna in the morning I would need a moral and physical break before being with him again in the evening.

One day, after sitting with Genna, Brodsky stopped by Baryshnikov's apartment as well. Everybody needed to relax. We had a drink and...started to sing. We were singing "The Officers' Waltz": "The night is short, the clouds are asleep... *And your unfamiliar hand lies on my epaulette.*" "Stop, stop," said Joseph. He sang "*na pogone*" (on my epaulette), and Misha and I—"*na ladoni*" (on my palm). A discussion ensued as to where the hand was supposed to lie, and led to a phone call to Vitya Shtern in Boston who was reputed to know the exact words to all the songs. "Who the fuck knows?" said the expert.

The last two months of his life Smakov, lying there with his eyes closed, muttered poetry to himself for hours, or would ask me to read to him. Mostly Tsvetayeva, Mandelshtam, and of course Brodsky. It seemed that Genna's memory was as reliable as ever, though his strength was failing.

Shortly before his death he said that he "had said goodbye to Joseph" and now wanted to read and listen only to Alexander Kushner's poems. He asked me to tell Kushner of his resolve.

A few days before he died, being fully conscious, Genna said, "I don't regret anything... I had a marvelous life."

Smakov died August 21st, 1988 at the age of 48. In his will he asked to be cremated, and wished his ashes to be scattered over the Aegean Sea: Genna wanted to be near his goddess Maria Callas after he died. During the memorial service her voice sounded in the Campbell funeral home—Maria Callas singing an aria from Bellini's opera *La Sonnambula*.

His will was fulfilled three years later. In 1991, Genna's friends Leonid Serebryakov and Yuri Vider were going to Greece. They took the urn with Genna's ashes, and Tatiana Liberman gave them a white silk kerchief, asking them to throw it after Genna. In the Aegean Sea, on the way between the islands Mykonos and Paros, Leonid scattered Genna's ashes from the stern of the ship and sent the white kerchief floating after them—Tatiana's goodbye...

   After the farewell ceremony at the Campbell funeral home Brodsky and I went to a nearby café to have a cup of coffee. We were remembering sad and funny episodes from Genna's life. I read Joseph some of Genna's poems—Genna was always too shy to show them to Brodsky.

> How can I overcome this delirium of the soul,
> My madness, my caprice, forbidden glamour?
> I'm getting gray, and you are so young...
> Wait only, don't hurry.

> Oh, if you knew how bitter is our union,
> How irksome the tatters of the heart!
> Oh, Lord! I am ashamed for the first time
> Of my obstinate, irrepressible flesh.

> But still I am drawn to you like a beast to water,
> To drink my fill but once by drinking in your gaze.
> You are far, but the passion is with me
> Thus misfortune will come of this.
> *1973*

APRIL IN DECEMBER

> Again you overtook me, love,
> Stunned me, threw me on my back,
> Not for the first time; I am ready for anything,
> And I don't intend to play at hide-and-seek with you.

> The winter crawls in, ice and silver,
> Like a candle-stub, the night can't warm one.
> Close to New Year's in the magical December
> You are simply a Christmas gift for me.

Which magi must I thank that once again
I drink the forbidden bliss,
Chew anguish with a grinning mouth,
Tortured by my imperfection?

Where did I have a presentiment of you? Was it
Again in Shakespeare, or in the tale of Tadzho...
My eyes are blinded by the blizzard of my love.
You stirred it up, boy of Caravaggio!
1973

And here are some fragments of his last long poem "A Summer Ghost," written in July of 1987, a year before he died:

Without reason, without call or fear,
Like words of a poem rising up,
You appeared before me out of the dust
Of young hope and nonsense.
<...>
How can I keep the bittersweet taste
Of happiness become grief...
Remember me inwardly, love,
Remember me at least once a year...
<...>
Keep something—these words, these sounds of parting,
The tension of greedy eyes, a slip of the tongue, a trifle...
Keep something... Our parting is before us,
Our parting for years, for centuries... Forever, for eternity.

Then Joseph read me some of Smakov's translations of Cavafy. The poem "Walls" sounded like Genna's epitaph:

Without pity, without compassion, with no consideration or shame
Did they build walls around me, blind and mute.

I am walled up. How did I get here?
My mind cannot grasp this change that has happened.

I could have still done so much: my blood is still hot.
But I overlooked the building. Apparently, my sight was
clouded,

And I did not notice the growing layers of bricks.
By degrees but irrevocably am I closed off from the world.[3]

We walked around Madison Avenue for a while, and then
Brodsky took me to the Kaplans', where I was staying. We
embraced on the doorstep and Joseph said, very sincerely and
warmly, "I don't know, Kissa, if I'll be able to, if I'll manage, but
I'll try to become Genka to you..." We both knew that this was
impossible, that Joseph's character, explosive and unstable, would
prevent it, but I was moved.

After Smakov's death I very much wanted to tell Baryshnikov
how endlessly grateful we were to him for his concern and care
for Genna. But Misha cannot stand sentimental outpourings, so
I waited until his birthday and wrote a congratulatory letter.

"January 27, 1989.

Our dear Mishanya!
Vitya and I have been trying to wish you a happy birthday
verbally, but you flew away on a silver wing in the direction of
Miami. More than that, I composed a congratulatory poem "*alla
cantata*," but became afraid that you will show it to our
"Nobeler" and make me an object of his brilliant wit. And thus
destroyed the poem in the crater of a fireplace. Don't I make a
good Gogol? [The 19th century Russian writer who in a bout of
madness burned the second volume of his classic *Dead Souls*.]
We congratulate you and wish you healthy legs and joy in
your heart. We will never forget what you did for Genka.
However tragic his fate, it was a great happiness that Alex
[Liberman] and you were near. You saved him from loneliness
and humiliation. He was not rejected and abandoned. I often
talk to him in my mind and tell him about you both, because in
the last months he, of course, did not think straight enough to
understand to whom he owed his comfort, and so could not
thank you.

I don't want to fall into playing the Symphony *Pathétique*, but in times so harsh in human terms, what you did is very rare. May God bless you!

Hugs and kisses, and we'll do everything possible to see you in "Metamorphosis," although they say that it is easier for a camel to pass... than to get tickets to your performance.

Always yours, L. and V. Sh."

...On the first anniversary of Smakov's death, August 21st, 1989, Brodsky wrote a remarkable poem:

TO THE MEMORY OF GENNADY SMAKOV

Sorry about the silence. Now
it is precisely a year since, in kilowatts,
you accorded us the status of blind bats
Or in decibels, deaf posts...

A great drought has come to my eye,
and a cuckoo clock blocks my hearing:
having died, you—like a traveler to a settler—
seem now to be omnipresent.

It is possible, cricket,
black-mustachioed moralizer and braggart,
who felt even a country to be
address-less, that this is to your taste?

If so, hedonist, Latinist,
Hellene, freezing in a northern wilderness,
who threw his life, like a scribbled sheet
into the flames—be boundless,

universal, almost detectable
by thinking aloud, like another celestial being.
Not to say "cherubim, seraphim,"
But—a trespasser in the three-dimensional spaces.

15: His Alter Ego

Evidently now, unreachable by gravity's
rein, by the twirling of plates
and of heads, you are really everywhere,
gastronome, critic, egoist.

That means that every mouthful of air,
a torn cloud, a sparse copse of firs,
is you, schoolfellow, of the same crop,
suckled by the same wet-nurse, confidante, artisan.

It may be that you are really more secure
in a dance of atoms, in a scuffle of the molecules
of hydrogen, crystals, salts,
than when your passions crowed.

Maybe it is true, as your blood-brother sang,
that sentiments are stronger without vessels
and postscripts are a hundred times more showy
than the flowers of theater schools.

< >

Table-companion, of the same age, double,
generous scatterer of thunderbolts and pearls,
guide of the best lines, conductor
of enlightenment, best reader!

Pauper-lord, progeny of backstage,
scourge of drawing-rooms, Pasha of the couch,
cypress-tree of the enduring groves,
drunk on the singing of the great Grecian

—there is no point in calling after you. You,
having yourself squeezed out everything you could from loss,
are indifferent to the accent of futility,
and when you are looked for in the orchestra seats,
you are shuffling along, like that rain, elsewhere,
you are rising up in streamers over coffee,
ruffling the trees in the park, running on the sand

243

as a wave, somewhere in Peterghof.

Not for the first time! this is how you make circles
in the empyrean as in the depths of a well.
Having become nothing, a person—despite
the song of the chorus—remains in everything.

You are now a master-of-all-trades—
a rebellion of leaves, the fall of a junta—
part of everything, an ordinary tick-tock;
to put it more simply—fuel for the seconds.

< >

[We are] a long way from a Urals ridge
with the catchphrase "freedom for the free"
to the discharged outer sphere
of the magnetic field!

That means that nothing, clanking its chain
like links of cause and effect,
can threaten you there, except
oblivion, famous for us.[4]

   These frank, strong lines written by Brodsky to his "double, suckled by the same wet-nurse," became a great memorial to Gennady Smakov. The void that Brodsky felt with the loss of Genna Smakov never left him.

---

[1] Volkov, C. Dialogues with Iosif Brodsky. *Izdatel'stvo Nezavisimaya Gazeta,* 1988, pp. 301-302
[2] Ibid., p. 302
[3] Brodsky, I. God Keeps Everything. Mif, 1992, p. 176
[4] Iosif Brodsky, *Selected Works.* Vol. III, Pushkinsky Fond, 1994, pp.179-181

16

The Libermans and Libermania

IN THE PREVIOUS CHAPTER I have mentioned Alex and Tatiana Liberman, close friends of Brodsky's and Smakov's who played a very important part in their lives. Russian by birth, Alexander and Tatiana Liberman belonged to the disappearing class of the old Russian intelligentsia, "the last of the Mohicans," as we Russians say of the precious vanishing remnant of a group of *confrères*.

Thanks to the Russian revolution, the civil war that followed, and the final establishment of Soviet rule in Russia, their destiny, having taken the most fantastic twists and turns, brought Tatiana and Alex to the top of *Everest* [in Russian we say "*Mont Blanc*"] in New York society—in the life of which they both played a significant role.

For many years Alex Liberman was an art director and then the Chairman and Editorial Director of one of the largest magazine empires, Condé Nast Publications, which publishes such popular magazines as *Vogue, Vanity Fair, Allure, Traveler, House and Garden, Mademoiselle*, and others, selling millions of copies in America alone. Besides, Liberman was a first-class photographer, a gifted painter and one of the best public sculptors in the United States.

His wife, born Tatiana Alekseevna Yakovleva, a niece of the well-known émigré painter Alexander Yakovlev, became famous in the Russian literary world as the Paris love of the Soviet poet Vladimir Mayakovsky.

Brodsky met the Libermans in New York in 1974 and they introduced him to everybody who was anybody in the art world, and brought him into New York literary circles. Alex was the first to publish Joseph in English, in mainstream American publications. When Tatiana, in 1974, first heard his poems, she stated categorically, "Mark my words, this boy will get a Nobel Prize."

When Smakov came to New York, Brodsky brought him to meet Alex and Tatiana, and soon after our arrival in the U.S., Joseph and Genna introduced us to the Libermans as well.

It happened in the New York Metropolitan Museum, where there was a showing of the documentary, "Lifetime Burning," dedicated to Alex Liberman's sixty-fifth birthday.

The film covered various aspects of his creative work—as painter, sculptor, journalist, photographer—and made a big impression on us.

At the reception Brodsky and Smakov brought us over to the Libermans...

Alex was very good-looking—gray-haired, slim, green-eyed, with a closely trimmed moustache. His impeccable manners and flawless pronunciation of Russian, English, and French made him irresistible. After we were introduced, he asked questions that were obligatory in such a situation, but he listened to our answers with such attention that we might have been alone in the museum, with no admiring fans crowding around to congratulate him and shake his hand. This quality—an ability to give the person with whom one is speaking one's full attention— is very rarely met in people of his rank.

Tatiana—a tall slim woman with short blond hair, in a red silk pantsuit—seemed strict and unsmiling. She wore no jewelry except a huge spherical garnet ring on her left hand. She did not look younger than her 70 years, but it was obvious that she was once a stunning beauty. We were amazed that evening by her likeness to Marlene Dietrich. We later learned that Tatiana and Marlene had been close friends, and because of their likeness had often been taken for sisters. Back in Russia, I knew another Mayakovsky muse, Lilya Brik, quite a remarkable grande dame.

Her sister Lisa married the French writer Aragon and went on to become herself a popular French author as Elsa Triolet. Lilya Brik also resembled Tatiana in appearance, but Lilya was much more self-absorbed in her role as a grande dame of the literary world.

Tatiana looked us over with a searching eye and apparently approved because, turning to Brodsky, she said in a very low voice, "Bring them to us for a weekend in the country."

This is how we became acquainted. Later we became friends and our friendship lasted to the end of their days.

The Libermans were extremely influential in New York. The gulf between our social positions seemed unbridgeable to me, but they must have remembered that three and a half decades ago they themselves had come to New York as immigrants who had to start all over again—they understood our problems very well. The warmth of their kindness and its delicacy helped us believe in ourselves.

Providence had been very good to Alexander Liberman. He had enjoyed the satisfaction, rare for an artist, of world recognition while he was still alive. Today his paintings hang in the best museums in the US and he has been the subject of hundreds of articles, a few dissertations, and monographs. His monumental, scarlet sculptures tower over the squares of world capitals, including Tokyo, Seoul and Jerusalem, and in the largest cities in America, from the Atlantic to the Pacific. Breaking up the monotony of the urban landscape, they highlight the rhythm and pulse of the modern city.

But Liberman was also a legendary figure in the fashion world. The employees of the magazine empire that he headed, Condé Nast Publications, called him the Silver Fox. Many feared him and trembled when he criticized their work, many more admired him and learned from him, but everyone listened to his every word. In magazine design, he was ahead of his time—he developed layered layout methods that became widespread only with the advent of computers and their visual applications.

Alex was raised to the summit of fashion journalism by a combination of many talents. He was a superb administrator, a remarkable editor, and he had excellent taste. It is curious, however, that Alex viewed both his journalistic and administrative activities with some irony. Chuckling into his silver moustache, he would shock his colleagues with the statement that he did not consider fashion journalism a serious undertaking, and that he himself was in the business only to make money. (Loads of it, as a matter of fact, at least by my standards.) However, he took the art of magazine design seriously, and his suggestions influenced many generations of art designers. He would say, "From the beginning of time artists in France used to sit for days in a café, so as to spend time with each other. That's what Condé Nast is—my café." He loved to say "True art needs privacy and solitude," and "An artist's workshop is a place for pangs of creation."

Alex Lieberman was a remarkable photographer as well. Every summer for twelve years, starting in 1947, he went on a "pilgrimage" to Europe, to the studios of European artists. Video cameras did not exist then. With only a 35-millimeter *Leika* and some notepads in his possession, he spent long hours in studios and workshops, taking thousands of photographs and notes.

Artists at work, their portraits, paintings and sculptures, the implements they used, their homes and their things, objects that provided their inspiration, spouses that provided support or a challenge—everything was documented scrupulously. Alex was trying to demonstrate the visual impressions that gave birth to the creative images of one or another of the masters.

Liberman became friends with many of the artists of the Paris school of painting. Among them, with the "fathers" of European modernism, who were still actively working at the time. Matisse, from whom Liberman learned the most, was seventy-eight, Rouault seventy-six, Brancusi seventy-two, Frantisek Kupka seventy-eight. Braque, Léger, and Picasso represented the middle generation, being all sixty-five years old. Giacometti, Salvador Dalí, and Balthus were still considered the young ones.

Drawing on his experience, Liberman published a unique book—*The Artist in his Studio*—in which he figured both as photographer and writer. In an unusual format of essays and photographs he gave us close-ups of the greatest modern artists.

...Five days a week Alexander Liberman set the standard for elegance—navy blue or dark gray suit, a snow-white starched shirt, and an austere tie. But on Friday nights, on the road to his country house, Alex would transform himself completely. Instead of an impeccable suit one would find him in a pair of paint-smeared khaki pants. In the summer, he would wear a sports jacket, and in the winter a real Russian *vatnik* [a thick quilted jacket worn by prisoners in labor camps and low-level manual workers working outside in cold weather] and a hat with ear-flaps: one flap pointing up, the other down.

This is how [in his hat with ear-flaps] Victor and I saw Liberman for the second time, in his studio in Connecticut, a hundred miles from New York, where Brodsky and Smakov brought us for the weekend.

Actually, there were two studios. The "painting studio" was a large room with floor-to-ceiling windows built onto the second floor of the house. Most of the floor was covered by a white cloth (with blots of different colors) with a large number of paint cans of different sizes. The "sculpting studio" was a huge snowy field two and a half miles away from the estate. Mighty constructions, like dinosaurs—the framework of future sculptures—stood frozen all over that field. Their models—five to six per sculpture—stood in rows on shelves in the workshop on the edge of the field.

Asked which of the models was to be the final version, Alex shrugged: "I haven't decided yet... This one is too static, and this one is too heavy. This one I think I like, although it repeats what went before. As soon as I decide on one, I'll destroy the others."

"Won't you be sorry?" I asked.

"Not a bit. You see, in my time I had occasion to witness not only the destruction of sculptures and paintings, but the collapse of great civilizations."

...Alexander Liberman was born in Kiev on September 4th, 1912. His father Simon Liberman managed some of Russia's largest forested estates, including the lands of the Earl of Oldenburg, uncle of Nicholas II; he also advised the government on the export of Russian timber.

His mother, Henriette Pascar, was an actress. Her claim to fame was that she had an opportunity to found the Moscow's first State Children's Theater.

249

After the revolution Simon Liberman was summoned to the Kremlin. Lenin considered him one of the most prominent specialists in the area of international economy and finance. During one of their conversations the leader of the world proletariat advised Liberman-senior to join the Bolshevik Party. It was dangerous to refuse such an offer, whereas its acceptance would open all doors for a former "servant of capitalism." Not only did Simon Liberman refuse, he lectured Lenin on the nature of his flock: "Like singers, Bolsheviks, Vladimir Il'ich, are born, not made."

Before the Bolshevik coup the Libermans lived in Saint Petersburg, but in 1918 they moved to Moscow. In 1919, by the directive of the Commissar of Culture, Lunacharsky, Henriette Pascar was allowed to open the Children's Theater. They performed dramatic renderings of Kipling's stories, Stevenson's *Treasure Island*, Mark Twain's *Tom Sawyer*, Daniel Defoe's *Robinson Crusoe*. Actors, dramatists, artists, and designers gathered not only at the theater but also in the Libermans' communal apartment. Henriette Pascar encouraged her son to make sketches and drawings for the sets. Sets ten meters high were made by Russian scenery shops and towered over seven-year-old Alex. It was those sets, as well as the Tsar Cannon at the Kremlin and the St. Basil Cathedral, which were, according to him, the most powerful visual impressions of his childhood. The Tsar Cannon was the pride of Russia's nascent defense industry. It was manufactured in 1586 with the goal of making it larger than any other cannon of the time. It was so large—35 inches—that it could not be effectively discharged, but the Russians proudly put it in Red Square as a memorial of their superiority for everybody to see. It stands there even now, through all the wars, revolutions, and other changes, and the sign next to it is still proudly telling its story, including the fact that the cannon had never been fired.

According to Alex, he was a nervous and uncontrollable child, got terrible grades, and by the age of eight had been kicked out of every decent Moscow school. His parents worried what could become of him.

In 1921 Simon Liberman was sent by Lenin to London, to negotiate trade contracts, and took his son with him. He came back with signed contracts but without Alex. As though he had a premonition of the tragic events about to take place in Russia, he left the boy in England with his friend Leonid Krassin, the Commissar for Foreign Trade, and Alex lived with this family for the next three years. He learned to speak English with a British accent and acquired good manners there.

In the early 1920s Henriette Pascar's Children's Theater was closed down—because she did not produce revolutionary plays, pleasing to the Bolsheviks. Friends warned them that storm clouds were gathering. Every day Simon Liberman was summoned by the Cheka (as the KGB was then called) for questioning. Every night, with a razor blade under his pillow, he waited to be arrested. He was most likely saved by his international reputation. Henriette Pascar left for England, but Simon Liberman stayed in Moscow until Lenin's death in December, 1924. He was allowed to leave the Soviet Union in 1925 along with other intellectuals whose presence within the country was viewed as detrimental at the time, but who were spared imprisonment and execution because of their international status. The Libermans eventually moved to Paris, and Alex spent six years in an exclusive private school. Then he was accepted at the Academy of Fine Arts where he studied art history, painting, philosophy and architecture.

Henriette Pascar began performing on Paris stages as a dancer. Her choreographer was Bronislawa Nijinska, sister of dancer and choreographer Vaslav Nijinsky. Costumes were designed by Lanvin, sets by Marc Chagall. Alex drew the posters.

After a year and a half in the Academy, Alex started working for the illustrated magazine "*Vu*," and was soon given the post of art director. In 1937 the twenty-five-year-old Liberman won the gold medal at the International Exhibition in Paris for the best illustrated magazine project...

In Paris, Henriette Pascar got involved with Tatiana's uncle, artist Alexander Yakovlev. That's how Alex met Tatiana. However, their romance was yet a long way off. The great revolutionary poet Vladimir Mayakovsky was in Paris at that time, and fell in love with the young Russian beauty. In one of the poems dedicated to her he wrote: "Come to the crossroads of my big and clumsy arms." He showered her with roses, pursued her doggedly, proposed several times, and begged her on his knees

251

to come back to Russia with him. Eventually Tatiana refused the poet, who went back to Russia. Tatiana married a French diplomat, Vicomte Bertrand du Plessix and became Madame la Vicomtesse du Plessix.They had a daughter, Francine, now the well-known American writer Francine du Plessix Gray. In the family she was called simple-heartedly and tenderly by the Russian nickname "Frossinka."

In 1940 Germany occupied France. Vicomte du Plessix was killed in a plane crash while on his way to England to meet with De Gaulle and join the Resistance.

Alex Liberman took it upon himself to take care of Tatiana and ten-year-old Francine.

Escaping from the Germans, Alex fled to the South of France with his mother. From there Henriette went to the U.S. while Alex was waiting for Tatiana and Francine, who joined him three months later. In December, after stopping in Lisbon and Madrid, they crossed the Atlantic and arrived in New York on January 8, 1941. Starting from scratch, in a few days Tatiana, who had impeccable taste, was designing hats for Henry Bendel. Alex began working for *Vogue*. Soon Tatiana had organized a millinery design studio for Saks Fifth Avenue. Their American life began thus...

In 1960 the first one-man exhibition of Liberman's abstract works took place, and by the end of the decade he began to gain the reputation of a talented artist. In New York the Libermans occupied a four-story brownstone on 70th Street, between Lexington and Third Avenue. In the end of 1960s they could already afford to live on a large scale, with a butler and a cook. In 1968 they also bought a house in Warren, Connecticut, two hours drive from New York City. The house was down the road from the estate of Francine and Cleve Gray, so that Alex and Tatiana could be close to the family and enjoy their grandchildren Thaddeus and Luke.

Until 1980 they organized grand parties and receptions that were written up in the gossip column in the *Daily News*. We happened to be present at one of the last of those parties—in honor of the publication of Genna Smakov's book *Baryshnikov: From Russia to the West*.

Alex and Tatiana were a truly loving pair and despite (or

252

perhaps because of) diametrically opposed personalities, lived in harmony. Alex was restrained, courteous, imperturbable, ironical. In today's slang he could be approvingly described as "a very cool guy." We never heard him speak a harsh word, or raise his voice, or be irritable, and we saw him in all kinds of difficult domestic situations. As for Tatiana, her feelings were written on her face. If she did not like someone, if she found that "someone" unpleasant, the object of her scorn knew of it right away.

And she never changed her opinion—that is, the verdict could not be appealed.

When the Libermans met Brodsky, they immediately sensed how extraordinary he was, and appreciated his poetic gift. They treated him with tremendous respect or, as Genna Smakov would rudely say, "fussed over him like a fool over a new toy." Being sensitive people, they understood very well what he had lost by coming to an alien country, and did everything to make him feel at ease in their home. But Joseph kept some distance from them, asserting his independence, as he did in all his relationships. Also, Joseph had a teaching job, and a demanding one, that kept him away from New York and from the Libermans for long stretches of time.

But it was Genna Smakov that Tatiana loved like a son. (Genna, despite his flamboyance and braggadocio, was quite vulnerable when he came to this country.) I think that it was primarily because of what Genna had to say about us (along with Joseph) that Vitya and I also found ourselves in favor.

In 1981 Tatiana was seriously ill in the aftermath of gallbladder surgery, and the doctors forbade long trips to Europe. Their crowded city receptions were also forbidden.

Every Friday afternoon the Libermans would drive to their estate, which we called "Libermania." And we were often invited to spend a weekend there. It was usually Alex who would call us a few days in advance. For us, it was a three-hour drive from Boston, but we rarely declined the invitation. Both of them had us under their spell. We admired the warm atmosphere of their family life, and were touched by our welcome there.

The white, two-story house looked fairly modest from the outside. The only architectural excess was Alex's painting studio, which had been added on. Alex painted there in the first half of the day, while loud music issued from the studio. It could be Bach's Brandenburg Concertos or Haydn, but more often it was rock 'n' roll. He used to assure us that abstract expressionism harmonized best with Madonna, Michael Jackson, and Tina Turner.

Sometimes he allowed us to visit the studio and would ask what we thought about this or that painting he was working on. It's not easy to say something intelligible or meaningful about canvases that are strictly abstract. Alex listened to our stammering seriously, with mocking imps dancing only in his eyes. It would be simplest just to say "I like it," or "I don't like it," but I don't remember anyone saying "I don't like it" to Liberman's face. Once I dared to squeak that a black-and-white painting that Alex was working on at the time looked too gloomy, and I suggested that he put a scarlet spot in the left corner of the painting. Alex started giggling and called me a great American art critic all day long. He teased me about this ill-fated scarlet spot for a long time. However, when Vitya made some remarks about interactions between black and white spots in different parts of the composition, Alex found them interesting, and as a prize, gave us one of his paintings.

The heart of the house was a spacious living room with a fireplace. In the corner by the window there was a round glass table which seated no more than eight. So the large receptions were organized *à la fourchette*.

The house was simply decorated. Inside everything was white—white walls, white furniture, white carpets, white mirrors. Even the television set was white. The only colorful spots in the living room were roses in the floor vases and paintings—Alex's pictures, Larionov's originals, some of them damaged by direct sunlight. Two of the house walls were glass and they made the room one with the grounds. The view from one side was of the English park, which displayed the Liberman's sculptures, and from the other, of the garden where two hundred and fifty rose bushes had been planted. Next to the house there was a pool with heated water which Tatiana called, after the Italian manner, the *piscina*. And from there, as far as the eye could see—blue hills and promenading deer. In the evenings the most curious of them would come up to the house and look in the windows.

Except for the deer, the Libermans, and their guests, there wasn't a soul in sight.

The stream of guests, however, never stopped flowing into Libermania. Their *"dacha"* became a sort of artistic salon, to which international celebrities were invited—gallery owners, writers, poets, and well-known fashion designers, some of whom were neighbors. Among designers I met Yves St. Laurent and Oscar de la Renta...The Greek billionaire Goulandris and his family paid a visit (in the past, friends of Onassis and Maria Callas). Sometimes Henry Kissinger was there with his wife Nancy. He looked like a sluggish and gloomy owl.

The socialite fashion designer baroness Diane von Furstenberg made frequent appearances. She loved the Libermans so much that she even called her children Tatiana and Alex. Having met Brodsky in Libermania, the baroness lost her head. She admired him openly, talked with him on "clever" subjects, even went so far as to read several of his poems. Joseph radiated icy arrogance.

Brodsky (just like Tatiana Liberman) did not deign to hide his feelings. In the very first minutes of meeting people it became clear whether they had a chance to "be acquainted with our genius" in the future or whether they were "doomed."

Thanks to Genna Smakov's cooking, Libermania hosted royal feasts. On weekends while Genna was cooking he would turn on Maria Callas full blast. The combination of his Italian opera and the American rock streaming from the Liberman's studio was...indescribable.

Right before the guests were due to arrive, Smakov, tired from all his cooking, would sprawl on the white couch in the living room to rest—in a sweaty T-shirt, shorts, and unlaced sneakers. When Tatiana begged him to change before the party she would meet with furious resistance: "I am wearing pants, aren't I? But if my appearance shocks you, I can stay in my room and not come out at all." (With Tatiana, Genna used the familiar "ty." He and Alex used the more polite plural "vy.") With these words our *enfant terrible* would stalk to his room, slam the door and lock it.

Tatiana would send me to talk him into shaving and putting on decent slacks. "Only, please, do it delicately, so as not to hurt his feelings."

I would go to his room and "talk to him delicately" from behind the closed door: "Genka, what is this shit? Who the fuck do you think you are? Why are you fucking over the old folks this way? Give a pig an inch..." The door would open, and the slacks would be put on.

Smakov behaved in this infantile manner because of the complexes which tormented him—his feeling that he was a poor Russian immigrant, taken out of pity into a rich house, cooking for the master and mistress...He wanted to let everyone know that he did not give a damn about all the "star" guests. That particular quality—"not giving a damn about the star guests"— was noted by Yakov Gordin as far back as 1965, in a poem dedicated to Genna Smakov:

> Those who have rubbed up lightly against power,
> Do not, of course, understand,
> That our subtle rebellion [*Fronde*]
> Is a lump of killed pride.
> <...>
> Why a plume on the three-cornered hat?
> Ripple, you thinking reed.
> It is so intoxicating and bitter
> To tease the great ones of this world.[1]

Alex and Tatiana admired Genna's encyclopedic knowledge, valued his sense of humor and his impeccable literary taste. For them, his talent for making excellent coquilles St. Jacques and bouillabaisse was simply a pleasant addition to his "diamond mine of knowledge."

Alex was indifferent to poetry, but Tatiana loved the Russian poets of a famous period at the start of the 20th century called the Silver Age and knew them well. Smakov, an expert in Russian poetry, had a phenomenal memory. So those two found each other. Together they made a notable picture—lying in deck chairs, among rose bushes, before immense American vistas, tirelessly reciting Blok, Annensky, Gumilyov, Akhmatova, Mandelshtam and Tsvetaeva by heart. Mayakovsky was not forgotten either. And whenever they were joined by Brodsky, Tatiana's happiness knew no bounds.

With the appearance of Brodsky, Baryshnikov, Smakov, ballet mistress Lena Chernysheva, and us, an enduring "Russian circle" was forming in Libermania. Tatiana never liked speaking English; at home she and Alex spoke either Russian or French. Their friends used to joke, not without a touch of jealousy, that Libermania had been "Russified" and was beginning to look like a Russian *dacha* from one of Chekhov's plays, with long hours of sitting at the dinner table, vodka from the freezer (though freezers didn't appear in Chekhov plays), *pirozhki, borsht, pel'meni*, tea with berry preserves, arguments about literature, and conversations on "life in general." However, the state of Connecticut suffered from a shortage of black bread, proper sauerkraut, and pickled Russian herring. Delivering these necessities to Libermania from Boston was our pleasant duty.

The elegant, hospitable house standing among the great American open spaces, the blue pool and pink garden, the latest books in the "divan-room," the refined cookery—all this made Libermania a true paradise. The poems and songs we dedicated to it and its landlords would make a good-sized book. Here's one of mine:

> If the sky seems to constrict about your head,
> If you are tortured by fears and manias,
> Throw some fish and bread into a bag
> And direct your steps toward Libermania.
>
> Race ahead over roads and fields,
> Flying through towns and endless forests,
> Race without fear across mountain peaks,
> Put grief and sorrow behind you.
>
> Art awaits you, paintings and sculpture,
> Drowning in a pink paradisiacal garden.
> Blue salty *piscine*, summit of culture,
> Heavenly pleasures await in your ardent waters.
>
> Wine is pouring from deep crystal vessels,
> Heartfelt songs are sung sweetly;
> Feather beds promise dreamless sleep...

"O what is this name in my ears ringing?"
Don't look on the map; no, it's not Pennsylvania.
A secret oasis is our Libermania!

A luxurious way of life plus staff—a gardener, a maid, a chauffeur, a nurse, engineers for calculating the stability of the giant Liberman sculptures, and workers for cutting, hoisting, and welding metal—demanded considerable financial capacity. I believe that at least part of these expenses were paid by Condé Nast.

"It is terrifying to imagine," Brodsky used to say, "what will happen to Tatiana, Genka, and Libermania itself if anything were to happen to Alex." (It was assumed that Alex, who had already had an ulcer surgery, diabetes and developed cardiac symptoms, would depart before the rest of us.)

However, providence arranged otherwise. The first to die, on the 21st of August, 1988, at the age of forty-eight, was Genna Smakov. He was followed three years later, on April 28th, 1991, by Tatiana Liberman.

The death of Tatiana, to whom Alex had been linked by fifty years of love and happy marriage, was a horrible blow for him that led to a second, very bad heart attack. The only chance to save him lay in an operation, but the doctors doubted that he could survive it. Alex insisted, and the surgery was successful. He was nursed to health by Melinda, the nurse who took care of Tatiana during the last ten years of her life.

Half-Spanish, half-Chinese, Melinda was born and raised in the Philippines. She was loyal and delicate, had a quick and lively mind, and a great sense of humor. Her nursing and her care of Alex not only saved his life, but enabled him to fully return to his creative work.

However, he could no longer live by himself, and asked Melinda to move in with him. But not in Libermania—Alex did not want to stay there. Without Tatiana, the house and the rose garden and even the studios were lifeless and empty. Alex sold the place and never went there again. Jumping ahead, I will say that two years later he married Melinda Pechangco and lived with her for eight happy years.

In the summer of 1992 Alex rented a huge house on the beach

in Long Island. At the end of August we got a letter from him, inviting us to come to a "luau" on September 4th. We had no idea what a "luau" was until we realized that on September 4th Alex would turn eighty.

Alex gave Melinda *carte blanche* to organize the festivities according to her desire and taste, and her taste amazed everyone, including the person whose birthday was being celebrated, by its extravagance. This celebration even had an entire chapter dedicated to it in the biography of Liberman.[2]

It turned out that a "luau" is a "Philippine gala." There were about a hundred and fifty guests—relatives, colleagues, publishers, and all of New York's "journalistic aristocracy." The "Russian delegation" was represented by Brodsky, Baryshnikov with Lisa and their two children—six-year-old Peter and baby Anna—and also by Victor and me.

A plane circled the sky, flying a banner that read "Happy Birthday, dear Alex!" A wooden stage was built on the shore right in front of the house, where the Philippine National Ballet, then on a New York tour, performed exotic dances. Melinda hired the group to entertain the guests. Even Tatiana had not allowed herself such grand gestures.

In a new denim outfit, his hair white as snow, Alex was, it seemed, for the first time since Tatiana's death, glad to be alive, and simple-heartedly wondered at Melinda's imagination.

I don't know who was in charge of the food, but the menu was eclectic. First of all, mysterious Philippine dishes with unpronounceable names. It was difficult to say what they were made of, but one sensed the presence of various sea creatures. Among the recognizable foodstuffs were roasted suckling pigs, ducks, partridge, sea bass—a fish the size of a shark, baked, if I remember correctly, in black caviar... In the center of the deck, on a table, was a three-tiered mini-fountain gushing champagne. For a base this fountain had a giant chocolate cake on which, in gold (but edible) letters, were written good wishes—for health, for peace of mind, for creative inspiration.

Among the guests was Dr. Rosenfeld, Liberman's doctor. Alex believed in him as if he were God. He owed the doctor his successful surgery and miraculous recovery. At one time Brodsky consulted Rosenfeld as well, but not for long. Joseph used to say that Rosenfeld "knew fuck-all about cardiology." Joseph hated Rosenfeld with a passion and would never call him anything but "that illiterate idiot." Our poet, as we know, was not shy about expressing himself, whether his assessment was fair or not.

And here, at the "luau," Brodsky ran into him face to face. "You still smoke?" asked Rosenfeld, shaking his hand.

Joseph, one of the few smokers in this society gathering, would go and smoke out of sight, behind the parking lot. So as not to be bored, he asked me to go with him. A certain "telepathic" moment has stayed in my mind: we are leaning against the hood of somebody's Mercedes, I am lighting a cigarette to keep him company. The ocean is perfectly motionless; overhead there is a scattering of too-large and too-bright stars. Joseph: "Are they mutants or something?"

I thought about the incredible twists and turns of fate. Our beloved Leningrad, Moika (my address), Pestel Street (his address), Yusupovsky Garden, Komarovo, the House of Writers on the Neva Embarkment, the Marsovo Pole, Pavlovsk...Another continent, another universe, another life... Where had we been going? How and why did we get here, to Long Island, to a "luau" with a fountain of Dom Perignon?

"It's incredible, Ludessa, where we have gotten to, how we got here," Brodsky is saying, as if reading my thoughts, "Long Island, a champagne fountain, a 'luau'... it's crazy."

The guests left late in the evening, but Alex and Melinda put Joseph and us up for the night, along with Misha and his family, so that in the morning we could finish up eating and drinking and wag our tongues in gossip to our hearts' content. Rosenfeld and his pearl-bedizened spouse stayed also. When Brodsky found that out, he grew sulky and said that he was "an idiot to agree to stay, and now it's too rude to split."

Luckily, the Rosenfelds drove off at sunrise, before breakfast. Misha's wife Lisa and the children and Vitya were still asleep, but the three of us went for a walk on the endless, empty beach and I remember that quiet sunless morning perfectly: pale pearl-gray ocean, and Baryshnikov telling us about Japan from which he had returned two days ago...

On the previous day, in the midst of the celebrations, standing by the "champagne fountain," Alex was telling Brodsky about the idea for his new book.

Every year for twenty years Alex went to Rome and spent a great deal of time on the Capitol Hill. The trapezoid plaza, surrounded by three palaces, with the equestrian statue of Marcus Aurelius in the center—this epicenter of Roman Empire—was probably one of the first attempts in history to organize architectural and sculptural components as a harmonized whole. It astonished and fascinated Alex by its aesthetic perfection. He had photographed the statue of Marcus Aurelius and surrounding palaces in different seasons and times and from different angles. There was quite a collection of unique photographs, and Liberman had decided that it was time they were published.

Knowing how much Brodsky loved Ancient Rome, Alex asked Joseph if he would agree to write the essays about the Roman Empire and Marcus Aurelius for the book. [Once again I was amazed by his delicacy—the request was accompanied by words "I am sorry to bother you, I understand how busy you are, but if you can find the time..." and so on.]

Joseph agreed readily, and, in few days, Alex sent him a box of photographs.

Two years later, in 1994, they published *Campidoglio*, a book of photographs by Alexander Liberman, with a brilliant essay by Joseph Brodsky.

If Liberman was fascinated by the sculpture and the architectural masterpiece created by Michelangelo around the statue, Brodsky was an admirer and a worshipper of Marcus Aurelius.

"He was loved by the historians, he was loved by the philosophers," wrote Brodsky in his essay. "He was a model of an emperor-philosopher, and today we remember him primarily for his famous *Meditations*. If this book did not make civilized people of us, what will?"

A funny detail to be mentioned: Alex and Joseph gave a copy of *Campidoglio* to Baryshnikov with this inscription by Brodsky:

Man and his horse
couldn't do worse
than putting to use
two Russian Jews.

A year after Tatiana's death, on May 8th, 1992, Marlene Dietrich, linked to the Libermans by thirty years of close friendship, also passed away.

Tatiana and Marlene had met in the South of France, in Antibes, but had not became friends until 1948. They had a great deal in common besides their looks. Tatiana used to tell us that in Marlene—one of the greatest stars of show business—two absolutely opposite personalities coexisted. One, a seductive femme fatale, the other—a nice, homebody-ish, modest woman, a wonderful cook, a loyal friend who was always prepared to go across town to bring some chicken broth to a friend who happened to be sick. It was that sunny side of her that was turned to Tatiana and Alex.

Alex made and kept hundreds of photographs of Marlene: Marlene in her film roles and on various stages; Marlene the legend, who won the hearts of the hundreds of thousands across all the continents; Marlene at home with friends, in the kitchen, or in the garden with her grandchildren.

In 1994 Alex published a collection of photographs of Marlene Dietrich from his archive in a book: *Marlene: An Intimate Photographic Memoir*. With the book came an enclosed CD of her most popular songs, among them the famous "Lili Marlene," which Brodsky loved so much and used to perform in Russian without fail after two or three shots of vodka.

Alex lived a long, amazingly varied life. He was surrounded by fascinating and picturesque people. And, since photography was not just his hobby, but one of his professions, he collected a tremendous archive of photographic portraits. In 1995 he decided to publish a sort of photo-diary. That is how still another book by Liberman appeared under the intriguing title *Then*. Here were photographs of the women he loved, of friends, family, colleagues—sculptors and painters, famous European fashion designers, writers, actors, Nobel Prize winners. Among them, two photographs of Joseph Brodsky in our beloved Libermania.

All the friends captured on film by Liberman's camera cannot be listed, but here are some names: Leonid Krassin's daughter Lyuba, with whom Alex had a passionate but short-lived love-affair, Coco Chanel, Christian Dior, Alberto and Annette

Giacometti, Salvador Dalí with his wife, Picasso, Braque, Matisse, Chagall, Osip Tzadkin, Le Corbusier, Max Ernst, Stravinsky, Mark Rothko, Truman Capote, Vladimir Horowitz, Misha Baryshnikov with his family, members of European aristocracy, the Abbess Sister Alexandra—formerly the Romanian princess Ileana… A stunning kaleidoscope of people to be found on one man's path in life.

In September 1997 Alex celebrated his eighty-fifth birthday. This time the reception took place in his Manhattan studio with a view of all New York. For a present I brought Alex a copy of the Moscow magazine *Prestige* with my essay about his life and work.

"Before I read it myself, would you tell me immediately how my life ends?" asked Alex, accepting the gift and going "tsk, tsk" at the sight of his portrait.

"That I, of course, do not know, but I think that the last book will be the one you just published: *Then*. I was under the impression that it was a sort of summing up. Am I right?"

"Absolutely not. I just finished a book about Greek, French, and Italian places of worship. It will be called *Prayers in Stone*. I hope to see it out in about two months."

Prayers in Stone turned out to be his last book, published in 1997.

In 1993 Alex and Melinda bought a penthouse in Miami and each year spent an increasing amount of time there. New York temperature changes, winds, and high humidity were difficult for Alex to tolerate. He dreamed of going to the Philippines with Melinda, but she did not dare risk such a long journey.

Alexander Liberman passed away in Miami, with Melinda at his side, on November 17th, 1999, in his eighty-seventh year, having missed the new millennium by a bare month and a half. The fortieth day after his death was marked with great pomp by a gathering in the New York Metropolitan Museum of Art. Friends and colleagues came from all over America and from Europe. There were many speeches honoring this truly remarkable man.

Si Newhouse, the owner of Condé Nast Publications, spoke of Alex with tenderness and kindly humor.

Among other things, he said "Every morning in the course of

fifty years Alex put on an ordinary gray or navy blue suit, an ordinary white shirt and a tie. Those were the only ordinary things he did in the course of the day. Everything else was extra-ordinary."

---

[1]Gordin, Ya. *To the Memory of a Bird*. Pushkinsky Fond, 1999, p. 46.
[2]Dodie Kazanjian and Calvin Tomkins. *Alex*. New York: Alfred Knopf, 1993.

17

Fortieth Birthday and the Almanac

ON MAY 24TH, 1980 Joseph Brodsky turned forty. Grisha Polyak, a Russian émigré publisher, called me several months before and asked me if I'd like to be on the editorial board of an almanac he wanted to publish by that date as a birthday gift to Brodsky. Of course I felt honored to participate.

The "Part of Speech" almanac, whose first issue was dedicated to Brodsky, was supposed to become, in the future, a periodical that would reflect literary and artistic developments in the current century. In the Soviet Union, we were cut off from Russian literature written outside the Soviet Union. By definition, it was subversive and had to be prohibited because a Soviet citizen could not resist its corrupting influence. Hence the Government felt that the best policy was to treat this literature as anti-Soviet propaganda and punish those who read it and even more severely those who gave it to others to read. This is why Third Wave émigrés from the Soviet Union who were pouring into the United States were so eager to learn as much as they could about the writing of Nabokov, Bunin, Berdyaev, Frank, and other luminaries whose works were forbidden in Russia. The almanac would publish their works and critical essays about them. Contemporary literature would be represented also (meaning that I too could be published). I enthusiastically embraced this ambitious goal.

There were six people on the editorial board: Peter Vail,

Alexander Genis, Sergei Dovlatov, Lev Loseff, Gennady Smakov, and I. Except for the Riga-born Vail and Genis—journalists half a generation our juniors, who had met Brodsky already in New York—all the other board members were people from Leningrad who had known Joseph and each other for many years.

Lev Loseff, a poet himself and a professor of Russian literature at Dartmouth College was, as well as Genna Smakov, one of Brodsky's closest friends. Sergei Dovlatov, a brilliant writer with a long history of futile attempts to dodge government persecution in Russia, had become Russia's best-loved writer after his emigration and subsequent death in 1990. He had also known and admired Brodsky back in our "Russian years."

Holding this issue of the almanac in my hands today, I feel something like a painful jab in the heart. Several people very dear to me are gathered on these pages—who are no longer alive.

Gone is Brodsky. Gone is the publisher Grisha Polyak, a golden heart, who was not a writer himself but who loved literature so much that he selflessly dedicated all his efforts to publishing the works of others, even though it meant a life of poverty for himself. Gone is my dear friend Sergei Dovlatov, one of the tallest people I knew, a cross between a heavyweight boxing champ and a toreador in appearance, for whom writing prose was the most important thing on earth. Like Brodsky, he could hardly think about anything but writing. Like Brodsky, his writings did not fit into the framework of "socialist realism" expected from a Soviet writer. He almost published his first book while in Russia, but the KGB ordered the publisher to stop publication and destroy the galleys. Like Brodsky, he was able to publish and achieve fame only after he had emigrated from the Soviet Union. Like Brodsky, he never came back to Russia. Like Brodsky, his writings became extremely popular in modern Russia after the Empire fell apart.

Gone is Genna Smakov, with whom the best quarter century of my life is associated. Gone is Tatiana Yakovleva-Liberman, who appeared in the "Part of Speech" with her reminiscences. Vail and Genis are not gone, but they do not write brilliant and humorous books and essays together anymore, each having gone his own way. Only Lev Loseff is doing exactly what he was doing at the time, teaching literature at Dartmouth, writing poetry, and translating.

Grisha Polyak asked me to participate in the almanac wearing, as it were, three hats: those of an author, a member of the editorial board, and a "go-getter"—that is, I was delegated to go and get rare materials for the almanac from émigré classics. I came up with the idea to publish an early short story by Nabokov, as well as a little-known interview with him, which we planned to translate into Russian.

I offered the short story "Do You Believe in Miracles?" as my contribution.

Genna Smakov had served as a prototype for that story, and I dedicated it to him.

To get a Nabokov short story was no easy task. We needed the permission of his widow Vera Nabokov, a hard and intractable person. She was known to give permission to publish Nabokov only to proven publications with an excellent reputation. Our as yet nonexistent almanac did not qualify. Grisha Polyak was afraid, and with good reason, that she would not allow an unknown publisher of an unknown almanac to publish (moreover, without payment, as the almanac had no budget, only our time and enthusiasm) a short story from her husband's legacy. Only personal contacts could help here. Which is precisely why Grisha delegated the "getting" of the Nabokov story to me.

It so happened that our family had been, for a long time, well acquainted with Nabokov's younger sister, Elena Vladimirovna Sikorsky. Unlike her brother, who refused to visit the Soviet Union, Elena Sikorsky used to come to Leningrad often and would visit us. When we emigrated, she came to see us in Rome, and we were several times her guests in Geneva. She took us first to Nabokov's place in Montreux and then to Clarence, to visit Nabokov's grave.

I called Elena Vladimirovna and asked her how I should best approach Vera Yevseevna so that she would look favorably upon our request. Elena Vladimirovna promised to put in a word for us.

She called two days later and said that I should write Vera Nabokov a letter describing the goals and quoting the mission statement of our almanac, along with a list of its authors (whose names, naturally, would tell her little). Soon I received a reply.

Montreux-Palace Hotel
1820 Montreux, Switzerland
February 19, 1980

Dear Ms. Shtern,

Thank you for your letter of February 11.

I have no objections to your reprinting in the first issue of your magazine "Part of Speech" my husband's story "Sluchaynost'."

As for the translation of an interview, I could only tell you if I agree to its publication in Russian after I know which interview you have in mind, and send me the translation for approval.

My best regards.

Sincerely yours,

Vera Nabokov

I was profuse in my expression of thanks. Unfortunately, as we pottered around getting the almanac together it became clear that we could not translate the interview, offer it for her judgment, and receive her consent (or refusal) on time. So we decided to drop the interview and publish the short story.

I am relating all these details to explain how I got "burned" and found myself in an awkward situation after our brainchild saw the light of day. It is rather a common occurrence with volunteer efforts, perhaps: you act with the best intentions, but since you cannot control all the factors, the results blow up in your face. Or, as former Russian prime minister Chernomyrdin put it after a typical fiasco, "We intended this for the better, but it came out as always."

Grisha Polyak's idea was that the members of the editorial board would revise all the materials, including each other's writings. Thus began what Brodsky disparagingly called *"Russian doings."*

The authors sent or brought their texts at the last minute, and so it was out of the question for all the members of the editorial board to read through them.

Polyak showed Smakov and me the "Part of Speech" for the first time already in a finished form on the evening of May 23rd, that is, on the day before Brodsky's birthday.

The almanac opened with a poem by Brodsky, dedicated to Marina Basmanova: "You, a guitar-like thing, with the tangled web of strings..." It is followed by his essay "Leningrad," originally written in English and brilliantly translated into Russian by Lev Loseff. And after that, an interview with Brodsky by Solomon Volkov under the title "New York: a Poet's Landscape."

Allow me to quote a small excerpt:

"*Volkov:* The first issue of the highbrow *Canyon Review* which just resumed publication featured your translation of a poem by Nabokov—from Russian into English...What did you feel while translating Nabokov's poem?

Brodsky: I had rather a lot of various feelings. First of all, complete disgust for what I was doing. Because that poem by Nabokov is of a very poor quality. Overall, he is, I think, a failed poet. But it is exactly because he is a failed poet that makes him such a remarkable writer. It's always like this. As a rule, a writer without a poetic element tends to be wordy and bombastic. And so, disgust. When the publishers of *Canyon Review* chose me to translate Nabokov's poem, I said, "Have you gone berserk, or something?" I was against the idea. But they kept insisting—I don't know what their reasons were (it would be interesting to investigate the roots of their insistence). Well, then I decided—if this is how it is, I'll do what I can. It was a sort of mischievousness on my part... And I think, by the way, that now—that is, in English—Nabokov's poem sounds just a bit better than in Russian. Just a touch less banal. And, maybe, it is, in general, better to translate the second-class poets, the second-class poetry, like this poem by Nabokov, for instance. Because you feel—how should I put it?—a higher degree of irresponsibility. Yes? Or, at least, your degree of responsibility becomes just a little bit less. It is *easier to deal* with this sort of person!" (!)

Very sharp, indeed, but not exactly what the new immigrants from Russia would like to know about Nabokov after so many years of knowing nothing about his work. And you can imagine what *I* felt after reading this passage and thinking what Vera Nabokov would say when she saw it.

Yes, Nabokov was not a poet of the highest order. He himself knew it, and did not have any particular illusions about his poetic gift. But he kept writing poetry, gave public readings of his poetry (I have tape-recordings of his reading—it is different from Brodsky's, but is very moving nonetheless.) And "it is *easier to deal* with this sort of person" sets a vulgar, insulting tone...

The one excuse could be the fact that the almanac was being prepared as a surprise (or a semi-surprise), and Brodsky had no idea that I had asked Vera's permission (and that she had gracefully granted it) to include the Nabokov short story. Possibly, had he known about it, he would have behaved with more delicacy, and would have chosen a more propitious occasion to take a swipe at Vladimir Vladimirovich. But who knows? Brodsky was not the sort to abstain from sharp comments just out of politeness, or political expedience, or to keep from hurting someone's feelings.

If I had gotten a copy of the interview in advance, I would have asked Joseph to take that passage out (especially since the deletion would not have hurt the interview one bit). Or I could simply have resigned from the editorial board so as not to look an ungrateful swine and a manipulator in the eyes of Nabokov's family.

But that was not all. The second "anti-Nabokov" blow was struck by the young critics Vail and Genis. The almanac featured their article "Literary Daydreams." This essay, provided with graphs and arrows, jauntily, with youthful fervor, analyzes contemporary Russian prose and its worthiest representatives: Solzhenitsyn, Iskander, Voinovich, Aksyonov, Yerofeev, Popov, Bitov, Dovlatov. The authors of the essay also found it within themselves to speak warmly of quite mediocre writers, for instance, of Mamleev or Limonov. And so, after an in-depth analysis of the talented contemporary confessional prose, "our" Dobrolyubov and Belinsky [two famous and influential 19th century literary critics] end their article with this grand finale:

"...When literature believes itself to be the main spiritual treasure of the world—to be such in and of itself, and not as a textbook on life—then a new, not so sensational but, possibly, brilliant phase will have began. And its banner will be the empty-dazzling Nabokov!"[2]

Empty-dazzling was the only definition bestowed on Nabokov's prose...

Freedom of speech being a blessing (had we not all longed for it?), I found myself nevertheless in a truly idiotic position. After all, I had promised to send copies of the almanac both to Elena Vladimirovna and to Vera Evseevna. After sobbing on Smakov's shoulder for half a day, I called Polyak and expressed my opinion eloquently. Apparently, too eloquently, because in the consequent advertising blurbs about this issue of the almanac Ludmila Shtern is not mentioned, but appears under the pseudonym "and others."

Maybe it's still worth mentioning that our almanac got a warm reception later on. Polyak received many flattering letters. Harrison Salisbury wrote to him: "Dear Mr. Polyak, Thank you so much for letting me see a copy of the first issue of *Chast' Rechi* (Part of Speech). The quality of the contributions by Etkind, Rannit, Shtern, Smakov and Tatiana Liberman I found especially impressive. You have launched an important and impressive venture in the best tradition of Russian culture."

However, my relationship with the publisher of this venture never got warmer.

Even without the misfortunes of the "Part of Speech" almanac, Brodsky's fortieth birthday—that is, the celebration of that birthday—left a scar on my soul. Smakov and I even came up with a name for that day: "D. U. I."—the Day of Undeserved Insults.

That spring I circulated between Boston and New York, doing some sporadic public relations work for Eduard Nakhamkin's art gallery on Madison Ave. Nakhamkin exhibited the works of Russian immigrant artists, among them Chemyakin, Tselkov, Neizvestny, Okshtein, and Tulpanov. As had most Soviet intellectuals, these artists had experienced tremendous difficulties in the Soviet Union because of their work. When in 1963 the government permitted an exhibition of young artists at Moscow's *Manege*, the largest exhibition hall in the Soviet Union at the time (burned to ashes in February 2004), Khrushchev visited the exhibition and became enraged. With his usual directness, he said that this kind of art could only be created by people with a perverse nature. He publicly called the artists homosexuals, using foul language—the Russian equivalents of fags, queers and other concepts with which the English language has not yet come to terms (or so I think).

Neizvestny's claim to fame is that he was not afraid to argue with Khrushchev. He denied accusations of homosexuality and publicly bared his chest, showing Krushchev the wounds left from WWII. This did not help, and the exhibition was closed. In early 1975, a group of young artists exhibited their work in the *Izmaylovo* public park. The government ordered them to disband. They did not. Well, the government sent bulldozers to level the exhibition and the bulldozers leveled the exhibition. When I was emigrating from the Soviet Union in late 1975, I went to the Ministry of Culture to ask permission to take with me a few heirlooms that Customs thought should not be taken from the country without a special permission from the Ministry. In the hall of the Ministry I bumped into my old friend, artist Edik Zelenin. "And what are you doing here? You are not Jewish and hence cannot emigrate." (I was wrong. In a couple of years Edik was pushed out of the country even though he was not Jewish.) "Well," said Edik laughing, "I came here to order some bulldozers." It turned out that he came for a permission for yet another exhibition of young nonconformist artists.

Nakhamkin gave these artists an opportunity to show their work to the American public. My responsibilities at the Nakhamkin gallery included talking the artists up, inviting people to openings and private viewings, talking to the press and bringing the "rich and famous" into the gallery.

Having no place of my own in New York, I used to stay at Genna's.

About a week and a half before Brodsky's birthday we started thinking about a present. Genna the intellectual said he would look for something interesting in the second-hand bookshops. Either that, or he would give Iosif some records by Haydn and Purcell. My earthbound quest was leaning towards "something for the house"—dishes, a cooking-pot, some bed linen. Iosif was uncommonly undemanding and indifferent to creature comforts. It is doubtful that he would ever go shopping for something useful. And the guests would probably be embarrassed to give the poet houseware.

I decided on wineglasses and liqueur glasses—after all, people came to visit him and those people drank. My glasses were already all packed and tied with a bow, and Smakov still had not found a worthy present. But about three days before the event Genna announced that he and Lena Chernysheva, another friend of Brodsky and a coach of Baryshnikov, found a table lamp in an antique shop, and were going to buy it together: "The lamp is a beauty, Joseph will like it..."

"How do you know he needs a lamp?" I wondered.

"Well, he called last night, to invite me... I asked him what he wanted for a present, and he said a table lamp would be good."

"Listen, he never called *me*."

"How would he know you are in New York? He probably called you at home, ask Vit'ka."

But it turned out that Brodsky had not called Boston either.

"Don't get silly," said Smakov. "Os'ka will find and invite you, what else is he going to do?"

The day of the birthday came. Iosif had not manifested himself after all. There is an old English saying: "A real gentlemen will never offend unintentionally." So the non-invitation to his birthday meant something, most likely some kind of punishment. But for what?

I thought over various scenarios. Either I had blundered by saying something or, on the contrary, by not admiring something. Or, possibly, some "compromising material" (*compromat* in KGB parlance) about me had been delivered to him by a third party.

Let us not forget that the scandal with the "Part of Speech" almanac had taken place the day before, so that on Osya's birthday I went to work at Nakhamkin's Gallery in the gloomiest mood possible. Two hours were spent senselessly shuffling papers. But my heart could not take it, and I dialed his number. Brodsky was at home.

"Hi, Joseph! How should I congratulate you? Should I do it personally or send a telegram?" "You should just tell me to go fuck myself," replied the poet.

I felt as if I had been scalded by boiling water. I was so stunned, I just put the telephone receiver on the desk. I couldn't stay another minute in the gallery and left. Crossed Central Park in tears to Smakov's place on Central Park West and 82nd Street.

Smakov was not at home. I kicked the box with the glasses,

hoping to break them all, took a shower, and collapsed on the couch to wallow in my misery. And then the phone rang.

"Kissa, forgive me... I am a complete idiot and a cretin..."

Hearing Joseph's voice, I began choking on my tears in earnest.

"Kissa, miau...don't cry...come and spit in my face."

"Osya, what happened? Why did you do this to me?"

"Consider me a psychopath. Don't pay any attention... Please..."

"Tell me, what happened?"

"Ludka, we'll hash it out later, come on over, do you hear?"

"But still, what is the matter?"

"Well, you know... You see Bobyshev... And all that..."

"What is this nonsense! What does Bobyshev have to do with it?"

"All right... Nothing. Please, come over in the evening..."

I was bewildered. I had no idea what had gotten into him. It had been four years since we left Leningrad, but even when at home we had not seen Bobyshev for a long time. A week before we emigrated we had talked on the telephone, and he had sent me a nice farewell card.

Smakov appeared in an hour, bearing the antique lamp. "How come you are sitting around with a swollen mug?" he asked tenderly. I stated the situation. "Should I go or not?"

"Of course you should go," Genna said, "because otherwise Joseph will be racked by Jewish guilt."

"And think hard, by the way, when did you see Bobyshev last?" he asked.

All of a sudden I realized what had happened. Some time ago Brodsky had called me in Boston and said that Bobyshev was in America. He had married an American woman, settled in Illinois and had come to New York for a few days. Brodsky had asked me if I knew about it. I had no idea.

"I have a favor to ask of you," he said. "Find Bobyshev and ask him about Andrei. How is he doing in school, what does he go in for, what does he read...and, in general, what's he like?"

I was just going to New York. I don't remember who gave me Bobyshev's coordinates. We met in a bar not far from the Rockefeller Center. Had one cocktail and talked about everything under the sun, including Andrei.

I was glad to see Dima Bobyshev after all that time: we were connected by having been young together and by years of friendship. Once I had even "published" his early poems myself. The small, orange chintz-bound volume of poetry written between 1955 and 1962 was called "Partita." There were, as in the case of a collection by Rein, five copies printed. Unfortunately, I have not a single copy left. It turned out that Bobyshev also had nothing left of that "publication" except for a few bedraggled pages.

Whatever Bobyshev thought about me after all those years, he was eager to tell me everything I wanted to hear—going through the travails of settling in another country makes one meek and solicitous, because help could come unexpectedly, and being arrogant could chase it away. The New York meeting with Bobyshev had no sequel. We did not even exchange telephone numbers. Dima left for Illinois, and we again lost sight of each other for a long time. But I did what Brodsky asked and questioned Bobyshev about Andrei. I remember that Iosif listened to my report in silence, did not ask a single question, and glumly snorted "*merci.*" I felt that he was irritated with me. But then I forgot all about it.

I went to the birthday party, of course, but sat in the corner all evening gloomy as an old owl. The events of the last two days—the "Part of Speech" fiasco and Brodsky's outburst—precluded any jollity. I don't even remember who was there and what went on. But I decided that I would not leave until I knew what was in the air and asked Genna to bear with me. We outstayed all the guests. I can recall our conversation word for word:

"So, Osya, what am I guilty of?"

"You are friends with Bobyshev behind my back."

"But it was you who asked me to meet with him!"

"And you jumped at the chance! You could have refused! You know very well how I feel about it!"

So much for tolerance and forgiveness.

"So why did you ask me to do it? What were you, setting me up?"

Genna broke into our wrangle. "You are both abnormal and deeply insane. Stop this and let's have a drink!"

But I was on a roll.

"Have I the right to know what I am being accused of?"

"Never mind. Forget it," grumbled Iosif in English.

He went to the bookshelf, took down a yellowed copy of *Stopping in the Desert*, wrote an autograph, and handed it to me with the words: "I hope, Kissa, you appreciate the fact that I am giving you the last copy I have."

The inscription was as follows: "To Ludmila Shtern from a less bright star." Over the word Ludmila he drew a heart with two arrows. One arrow pierced the heart and the other was flying over it.

I was both touched and upset. Touched, because I had once, long ago, complained that I did not have *Stopping*, and he remembered. And upset because, as if it was not enough that the inscription was sarcastic, it also had a double meaning.

"Thank you, Osya, from a brighter star," I said. "Still making fun?"

"Kitten, but you are 'Shtern's star,' and I really mean it..."

Looking back, the events of that day were a tempest in a teacup. When Genna and I got ready to leave and were already at the door, Brodsky started up: "Wait, I'll read you a poem...wrote it today." He went into his study and came out with a typewritten sheet of paper. It was one of the most powerful and piercing of his poems:

I have braved, for want of wild beasts, steel cages,
carved my term and nickname on bunks and rafters,
lived by the sea, flashed aces in the oasis,
dined with the-devil-knows-whom, in tails, on truffles.
From the height of a glacier I beheld half a world, the earthly
    width. Twice have drowned, thrice let knives rake my nitty-
gritty.
Quit the country that bore and nursed me.
Those who forgot me would make a city.
I have waded the steppes that saw yelling Huns in saddles,
worn the clothes nowadays back in fashion in every quarter,
planted rye, tarred the roofs of pigsties and stables,
guzzled everything save dry water.
I've admitted the sentries' third eye into my wet and foul
    dreams. Munched the bread of exile: it's stale and warty.

276

Granted my lungs all sounds except the howl:
switched to a whisper. Now I am forty.

What should I say about life? That's it's long and abhors transparence.

Broken eggs make me grieve; the omelette, though, makes me vomit.

Yet until brown clay has been crammed down my larynx
only gratitude will be gushing from it.
(translated by Brodsky)[3]

I thought then about the difference in the scale of feelings and thoughts that visited us on the very same day, and felt awkward and penitent. What were my fleeting and transient hurt feelings and grudges against him in comparison to his meditation on life, in which he "felt solidarity only with grief."

I should probably end this chapter on that high and tragic note, but I cannot resist the temptation to relieve the tension of the moment and to bring a smile to the reader's lips.

About three years ago a certain Russian magazine came into my hands wherein that poem was published. [I am not naming the magazine on purpose, so as not to place its editor in an awkward position.]

Brodsky wrote: "guzzled everything save *dry* water."

The magazine printed: "guzzled everything save *unboiled* water." [In Russian, *sukhuyu* versus *syruyu*.]

The editor, apparently, decided that despite his hard, sorrowful life, Brodsky took good care of himself and drank only boiled water. I am certain that Iosif would have appreciated this bit of editing.

---

[1] "Part of Speech" Almanac. New York, 1980, No.1, pp. 30-31
[2] Ibid, p. 233
[3] Joseph Brodsky. *Collected Poems in English*, FSG, New York, 2000

18

Russian Samovar

FOR CENTURIES it has been a European tradition for poets, writers and artists to hold regular informal gatherings in clubs or cafes. From 1910 to the mid-1920s, for example, French and American writers and artists in Paris congregated at La Coupole, La Rotonde, and Le Dôme, the legendary cafes on Montparnasse immortalized by Hemingway.

Russian émigré poets, writers, artists, and musicians in Paris after World War II patronized the restaurant Dominique on rue Brea. Intellectual Russian immigrants turned the Dominique into a kind of artistic club. Its owner, an emigrant from St. Petersburg, Lev Adolfovich Dominique, was an educated man, an art historian and a drama critic, who wrote reviews of Paris plays from time to time and even established a "Dominique prize" for the best dramatic production of the year.

His apartment above the restaurant was a real museum, with an extremely valuable collection of Russian paintings: Kandinsky, Chagall, Larionov, Goncharova, Lubov' Popova...

Dominique also collected Russian porcelain and silver and, when I visited him, showed me a silver hatchet with which Peter the Great was supposed to have taken several symbolic swipes on the day the foundations of the future St. Petersburg were laid. (I, of course, cannot vouch for the authenticity of that hatchet, but I also have no reason to doubt what Dominique was saying.)

The most famous bohemian hangout in St. Petersburg was the Stray Dog, which acquired its cachet just before the revolution, during Anna Akhmatova's reign. Her subjects were mostly avant-garde poets, though she had many friends and supporters among the artists of the time. It was the Stray Dog she described in her beautiful poem:

We are all drunkards and sluts here,
And are not in a cheerful mood.
On the walls, flowers and birds
Long for the clouds.
You are smoking a long pipe,
How sweet the little smoke over it,
I put on my tight black skirt
To make myself look even more slender.

Brodsky and Smakov, knowing how much I liked to recite this poem, used to tease me with allusions like the following: "Luda, put on your tight black skirt so as not to look so fat."

The Stray Dog café was opened on New Year's Eve in 1911. It had a small stage where for four years musicians, actors and even famous dancers, such as Tamara Karsavina, performed, and poets like Mayakovsky, Gumilyov and Mandelshtam read their verses. The Stray Dog was closed by police in 1915, even before the revolution. Censorship was not invented by the Bolsheviks.

But it was not closed for good. Eighty-six years later, in 2001, the Stray Dog café has opened again at the same location. We will soon see if young St. Petersburg poets will again choose it for their base of operations (when I visited this new incarnation of the cafe I was impressed by the artwork and photographs on the walls, but thought the prices a little steep for young poets).

The Russian Samovar restaurant in New York, on 52nd Street between Broadway and 8th Avenue, became in our time a kind of combination of The Stray Dog, La Coupole and Dominique. It was presided over by Brodsky and by my friend, Roman Kaplan.

In his "previous life" Roman was an art historian. He was well-suited for that profession by a happy combination of qualities—erudition, artistic sensibility, and impeccable taste. But his true calling turned out to be the restaurant. What makes Roman a born restaurateur is his charm, his sociability, and his boundless hospitality. If he were rich and lived in Russia a century and a half ago, he would have been some kind of magnanimous country squire, a landlord from a Gogol or Turgenev novel who lived in a grand way, with a crowd around his table of family, friends, neighbors, guests, orphan nieces and dependent aunties. And with a whole bunch of house-serf children running around, half of them the squire's.

Brodsky and Kaplan had one feature in common—their morphology. In the early 60s the Soviet press classified both of them as insects. As I related earlier Iosif was a "Near-literary Drone." Roman was styled a "Dung Fly." That was the title of the newspaper article about Kaplan published by that very same "*Vecherka*" (*Evening Leningrad*). Unlike Brodsky, however, quick-thinking and practical Kaplan, who had a rich imagination, had previsions of the "black Maria" that would transport him to the notorious Kresty ["The Crosses"] prison in Leningrad, and managed to do what Brodsky could not: vanish from the sights of the Leningrad KGB at just the right moment and arrange to have himself swallowed up by Moscow.

The fury of the KGB had been roused by the way Roman was hanging out with foreigners, using his fluent English and French. The last straw was the fact that he had spent time with the American composer and conductor Leonard Bernstein when the latter came to Leningrad on a tour. The article "Dung Fly" colorfully described Roman's crime: Bernstein, leaving for his home across the ocean, gave Kaplan a farewell present, a silver dollar with a hole in the middle as a memento. Roman was touched and later wrote him a thank you note, saying that he would put a string through the hole and wear it as an amulet, which would protect him against trouble and the evil eye... However, the amulet was no protection against one source of trouble and the evil eye: the letter was intercepted...

"Kaplan was licking American boots for a lousy dollar with a hole in the middle," according to the article. So Roman Kaplan "dissolved" himself in Moscow. In the eyes of the KGB, Kaplan was not such a big catch that they would start an all-out manhunt for him. But he also was not so insignificant that his disappearance would be considered sufficient reason to drop the case. By twisted KGB logic, somebody had to be punished. The person who suffered as a result was Roman's absolutely innocent twin brother (and my college friend) Tolya Kaplan, who had never seen Bernstein in his life. Tolya Kaplan, my fellow geologist, was kicked out of his postgraduate program for nothing, just because his brother was a target of KGB prosecution. This kind of "guilt by association" was quite common in those days.

I first met Roman in 1961. The British Royal Ballet was on tour in Leningrad with its then prima ballerina, Margot Fonteyn, in a performance of *Undina*. I got two tickets, but three days before the show Vitya was sent on a business trip and I could not decide with whom to share the rare treat.

I promised one, promised another, hinted to the third, keeping the first two in my sights. As a result, an hour before the show I had nobody to go with. The Maryinsky Theater was ten minutes away on foot. So I wasn't in the best of moods as I was walking along Dekabristov Street and a pigeon on a rooftop dribbled on my shoulder.

I dragged myself to the theater, anyway. There was an excited, buzzing crowd in front, everybody asking if anybody had an extra ticket to sell. Scalping was not practiced in those days, it was not socially acceptable among theatregoers. But dumping an extra ticket for the nominal price was all right. I was looking around for someone to grace with my ticket and my company, and at that moment an imposing-looking young man with a short beard, dressed entirely in suede, appeared before me.

"What is it, miss, you don't have a ticket? Would you like me to get you in?"

"No, I have a ticket—I have mine, and I have an extra."

"Then YOU get ME in."

That is how I met Roman Kaplan.

The ballet *Undina* turned out to be boring and green—the action took place "in water." We left after the first act, and walked along the banks of the Neva for a few hours, our words a contest to see who had the best credentials to be considered a member of the intelligentsia. The next day Roman invited me to the Zoo.

To make a long story short, we recently celebrated forty years of friendship in the Russian Samovar.

I knew Kaplan's three or four wives, each better than the one before, but none could bear comparison with the present one—Larisa.

My language is too poor to describe Larisa in prose, so I will yield to Joseph Brodsky.

On October 20th, 1985, the *New Yorker* published an essay by Brodsky called "Flight from Byzantium." Brodsky presented a copy of that edition to Larisa Kaplan with the following inscription:

Presented on October 26, 1985,
To Larisa on her birthday.

To Larisa—the best pair of eyes,
of hands, of legs, and of everything hidden,
this face's broken mug
screaming "Hooray!" Whispering "Alas."
When I stand before the Angel, I'll growl, "Sorry.
You, Angel, look like a church rat!"
Yes, Angels' looks don't compare to yours,
And you are dressed much better, Larisa!

Nine years later Brodsky congratulated Larisa with the following lines:

To Larisa from Iosif on her
fiftieth birthday, with tenderness.
October 27, 1994.

Normally, I like blondes,
being, apparently, a brunet in my heart
or a shined shoe,
without a spot of light on it.

Which explains my lifelong praise
of golden curls, gray eyes.
Yet I consider You, Larisa,
an exceptional case.

Black hair like yours, brown eyes
and your skin's dusky silk
say to me, Joseph, you are a proletarian
and a big bad wolf.

Your eyelashes, Your eyebrows,
the trembling of Your eyelids,
make this tainted Jewish blood
course faster in its veins.

There are faces like a sketch of Paradise.
Like an outline of happiness. But
they are given us to behold
only on canvas, while we grow faint.

But You, Larisa K., with our own eyes,
we see in full daylight,
and Romka sees You even at night,
which tortures not only me.

After seeing you once,
forget the glittering Pleiades,
All nations must follow Russia
and wait in line for centuries.

After seeing You, one looks for You everywhere,
abandoning nightly dreams.
Like a waiter his dishes,
You break hearts.

An actor goes into the wings,
and a poet is forgotten.
But the face of Larisa cannot be,
especially at night...

To hit fifty is no joke.
Fifty makes for wonders:
everywhere a doghouse,
with no dog in it.

We experienced it all: the world of guns,
the world of money and the beggar's bowl.
This shit is everywhere,
but, sitting at Roman's, we,

who were born in socialism,
who are fooling around in the States,
will justify our lives by saying:
we have seen Larisa K.

So Roman Kaplan is a man in his rightful place on earth, and
the Russian Samovar is a celebration for body and soul. The
food is tasty, the decor is elegant (there is a white grand piano in
the middle of the restaurant: a gift from Misha Baryshnikov),
the music caters to every taste, and the pianists are first-class.
One can listen to Mozart, to Chopin, to the old romantic songs,
to gypsy music, and even to old love songs about Stalin.

But the main thing in the Samovar is the atmosphere. It is
precisely that atmosphere, which is neither strait-laced nor wild,
but informal and easy, that makes the Samovar a Russian oasis
in the English-language world.

Its location is wonderful, right in the heart of the theater
district. Some people eat there before a show, some after, some
instead of. Amazing and unusual people go there: a list of visiting
stars could make a phone book. Some are internationally famous:
Gérard Depardieu, Robert De Niro, Milosz Forman, Avedon,
Susan Sontag, Ann Leibovitz, Philip Roth, Michel Legrand. One
day Liza Minnelli stopped by, drank a glass of Coca-Cola, took
the mike and sang for twenty minutes.

For visitors from Russia the Samovar is a dream come to life,
where they can breathe in the spirit of people they had always
wanted to meet: the Russian figure-skating world's champions,
famous hockey players, writers, musicians and ballet dancers.
And those who come there often become regulars: conductor
Yuri Temirkanov, singer Dmitry Khvorostovsky, poet Bella
Akhmadulina, actor and writer Mikhail Kozakov.... Director
Nikita Mikhalkov celebrated his Oscar at the Russian Samovar.
These are not emigrants who live near by. These are people who

live in Russia and come to the Samovar whenever they visit New York City.

Roman has an album in which the guests draw pictures and cartoons, write poems and "love notes" to the hosts. For instance: "Forget the blues—we're in the Samovar! Let's think of love. Mstislav Rostropovich"

Once, a group of about eight people stopped by the Samovar after a performance in the Metropolitan Opera. Among them were Vladimir Atlantov, Sergei Leiferkus, and the world famous opera diva Cecilia Bartoli.

It was one o'clock in the morning and the Samovar was almost empty: there were only two tables occupied. The "songbirds" were eating and drinking, and seemed to be humming something. Suddenly Cecilia Bartoli and Leiferkus' accompanist, Semen Skikin, went up to the piano, and the diva sang for half an hour for the people at those two tables.

One of those people, greatly shaken, came up to Roman: "Not long ago, in London, in Covent Garden, there was a Bartoli concert, and the tickets were unbelievably expensive: two hundred pounds. I was ready to pay, but could not get any tickets at all...And tonight Cecilia Bartoli sings for me and my friends for free. I will not forget this night for as long as I live."

In 1992, the Virginia Theater across from the restaurant was playing the successful musical *Jelly's Last Jam*.

The main character, Jelly Roll Morton, a real-life mulatto musician from New Orleans at the turn of the last century, got it into his head that he was the father of jazz. The show was about his life, his relationships with colleagues and family, his star years, and his sad and lonely end.

Jelly was played by the incomparable Gregory Hines. The production was exciting, colorful, dynamic, the actors were excellent, the music first-class. The theater critics were incoherent with delight. It was directed by a talented black director (George Wolfe) and the entire cast was African-American as well.

After the show the worked-up actors did not feel like going home at once, and the cast, often in its entirety, would cross the street and burst into the Samovar. They would have supper, drink a glass or two, discuss the show, and sing.

And this is what happened at the last performance of *Jelly's*

285

Last Jam. The director George Wolfe asked Roman to come and watch it. Roman had seen the musical twice already, but did not want to hurt Wolfe's feelings.

So, to the finale: the curtain fell, the theater exploded in an ovation. Wolfe came out on the stage, thanked the actors for doing a marvelous job, the New Yorkers for a warm reception, and then said, "Ladies and gentlemen, I would also like to express our gratitude to the owner of the Russian Samovar restaurant for his care and warmth. During the run that place became our home. We felt there that we were among friends... Thanks, buddy!"

Spotlights were trained on Roman, he had to stand up, and George asked him to come up on stage. The entire audience got to its feet and applauded Roman, whose eyes were wet.

Accidental meetings were also possible in the Samovar. One day Roman said that he had a ticket for me for *Jelly's*. I walked into the restaurant twenty minutes before curtain and saw the lonely and forsaken Soviet poet Yevtushenko at the bar. He was facing a mirror and thus could see what was happening behind his back. There Brodsky stood in cap and coat, with bags stuffed with Samovar take-out food, talking animatedly to Roman— that is, telling him jokes. Instead of joy, however, Kaplan's face expressed suffering. Brodsky's *pel'meni* were in danger of defrosting, his meat-jelly/aspic was in danger of liquefying, but the poet stood his ground to prolong Kaplan's torment. Roman couldn't leave him to pay attention to "Yevtukh" in the presence of Brodsky. Putting the two poets together was also out of the question. Brodsky hated Yevtushenko with a passion. This should not be understood as professional jealousy. Brodsky looked with disdain upon anyone who was part of the System. Yevtushenko was not simply a prosperous Soviet poet who had no problem publishing in the Soviet press. He was one of "the cultural ambassadors," one of those artists sent abroad to testify that there was indeed freedom of speech and artistic freedom in the Soviet Union. And Yevtushenko would so testify. I remember visiting Edinburgh, Scotland, during the theatre festival there and reading an interview with Yevtushenko who had published a poem about Babi Yar, the place near Kiev where the Nazis killed all Kiev Jews and where the Soviet government did not want to put a sign acknowledging the tragedy. "And you see," said Yevtushenko in the interview, "I was not punished." Words that were certain to make Brodsky's blood boil! In addition, he thought that Yevtushenko served as an expert advisor to the government in reaching its decision to throw Brodsky out of the country. Naturally Yevtushenko denied this, but he did indeed rub shoulders with the highest echelons of the Communist hierarchy.

Watching this scene in the Russian Samovar, I wanted to sing: "*Should you not laugh before your hands are bloodied, should you not part in amity?*" (Evgeny Onegin, the opera), or recite Shakespeare: "*Rebellious subjects, enemies to peace, / Profaners of this neighbor-stained steel, / Will they not hear*" (Romeo and Juliet, Act I, Scene 1), but I was afraid I'd get in trouble.

Brodsky observed the humiliation of his brother-poet, repeated for the third time that he was double-parked and would probably get a hell of a fine, or maybe even get his wheels towed, but... continued to stand there as if someone had glued him to the floor. Poor Roman was on the verge of a heart attack. Yevtushenko's back regarded him in dumb reproach.

Finally, Iosif took pity on him: "Bye, Ludka, bye, Romka"—and took himself off.

The show would start in a few minutes, it was time to run across the street. "Give me my ticket," said I to Roman.

"Zhenya (Yevtushenko) has the tickets, you are both going."

Gloomy Yevtushenko and I went out, and there by the entrance stood...Who do you think? Brodsky's car (a "Skorpio") with Joseph inside, waiting to see who was going to the theater with whom. Saw my embarrassment, waved at me, and took off.

Yevtushenko and I were nodding acquaintances. That is, we had seen each other at various gatherings without ever having a personal conversation. Somehow he worked it out that since I knew Brodsky I must be from the same herd as Brodsky and Rein.

"So, how's Rein doing over there?" he asked. I said that I had not seen him in a long time because Rein is "over there" and I am "over here." "He is an unreliable person," said Yevtushenko. "What's wrong with you?" I snapped back, "Zhenya Rein and I have been friends since childhood..."

"This is precisely why I am warning you that he is a very unreliable person."

He went on with this gibberish, though he too knew Rein very well—they were friends and he had tried to get Rein's book published.

What did this nonsense mean? Was it an awkward joke? Or did he feel an overwhelming need to be avenged for his humiliation by saying something nasty about somebody, but did not dare take a swipe at Brodsky?

"Yevgeny Alexandrovich, I repeated. Evgeny Rein is an old friend of mine..."

I did not want to watch the show next to Yevtushenko anymore, and using a tall person sitting in front of me as an excuse, I found another seat.

...Yevtushenko wanted very much to establish a civil relationship with Brodsky and asked Roman to mediate. Once, recalling the humiliating episode with Brodsky in the Samovar, he said to Roman, "Even the Jews and Arabs are talking to each other. Why can't Iosif and I meet at your place, have a drink and talk?" Roman passed this on to Brodsky and received the following courteous reply: "The messenger gets killed first." But characteristically Brodsky succumbed to pressure and did what he did not want to do. He did meet with Yevtushenko. And Yevtushenko said that he had heard Brodsky was trying to invite his parents for a visit (how could a poet hear about an application to a government office?), and that he, Yevtushenko, would try to help (how could a poet help in such a political matter?). Brodsky said thanks, please do it, and then in Moscow later Yevtushenko boasted that Brodsky had sought a meeting with him and begged him to help with his parents' permission for a visit (why would Brodsky have thought that Yevtushenko was so influential?), but he, Yevtushenko, would not help this traitor and dreg of society. And Joseph's parents were not allowed to visit their son.

Iosif liked the Samovar. He loved Roman and Larisa and was always (or almost always) present at the Kaplans' "jubilees." For Roman's fiftieth birthday he greeted him with the following poem:

I take out of my pocket

a poem for Roman,
and in it is written: "Old man!
Having changed continents,
it is easy to change diets,
friends, girlfriends.
Such doings are celebrated
In romance novels."

But there are no romances about Roman,
the old-order gourmand.
Roman is rigorously opposed to change;
Except for different courses at table.

But since these changing courses
always feature *pel'meni,*
when I relocate to the Moon
I will direct my steps to Kaplan's.

Another gift to Roman that day was a copy of the collection
"New Stanzas to Augusta" with the following dedication:

Look with compassion, Roman,
upon the wool gathered here,
upon these hoofprints of Pegasus
that have trampled twenty years.

But Brodsky did not come to Roman's fifty-fifth birthday on
time. He showed up the next morning with a headache and
needing a shave, swallowed two aspirins and handed Roman an
"explanatory note":

Forgive me, Roman, I'm a bastard!
Punch me in the eye!
It so happened that the poet
got soused last night,

and that is why only Yuz howled
in your drawing room yesterday.
Roman! I have always been a swine

and a swine I shall remain.

There's no forgiveness for such a creature!
(And a Jew, no less!)
And there's no place for it in the Samovar
among the blessed!
This degenerate will no longer be invited
into decent homes.
Where Lorka and Ludka sparkle
I cannot come!

Now doubtless I'll be given
Only matzo to eat.
No more shish-kebab, no more *pel'meni*,
no more jellied meats...

From now on, no free drinks!
With a moribund soul
I'll walk like Moses in the desert,
To the nearest watering-hole

and whisper, pressing my dry lips
to the glass:
"Hooray! Roman is fifty-five.
And I'm an ass."

[Yuz: Yuz Aleshkovsky, a writer and Joseph's close friend;
Lorka: diminutive-familiar of Larisa; Ludka: diminutive-familiar
of Ludmila]

...Roman Kaplan became the owner of the Samovar in 1986.
It was once an Italian restaurant, Jilly's, which Frank Sinatra
had bought for a friend of his (Jilly Rizzo). When Sinatra was in
New York, he used to stay in the apartment on the second floor
of the building. Jilly's flourished—the possibility of glimpsing
the legendary Sinatra attracted people. In the late 70s Sinatra
left, the place changed hands, and in 1978 Jilly's turned into
Johnny, a modest little restaurant patronized by actors. It lasted
for seven years before closing in its turn. In 1986 it was an empty

space full of archaic restaurant equipment.

Roman found some partners and started the Russian Samovar.

Everything in that building was old and run down—roof, floors, heating system, electric wiring. Everything needed to be replaced or repaired, but where would the money come from? The partners, including Roman, were not exactly rich. Besides, none of them was a real professional, none knew the ins and outs of the restaurant business yet.

For a new place to flourish in the heart of the Manhattan theater district, millions have to be plowed into it. The competition is unbelievable—there are restaurants and cafés in every building along 52nd Street. For two years the Samovar barely flickered, now disrupted by a flood, now by a fire, now by burst pipes, now by a rotten ventilation system. Pennies earned by the heart's blood had to be spent to plug the holes that were appearing hourly.

The situation became critical. The partners were beginning to grumble and demand their investments back. The restaurant urgently needed to be "ransomed."

Although Brodsky was friendly with Roman and Larisa, he had no idea what storm clouds were gathering over the Samovar. And it never occurred to the over-scrupulous Kaplans to ask Joseph for help. In general it is harder to ask for something for oneself than for others. What the delicate Roman and Larisa did not dare to do, I, being of coarser stuff, did for them. Even so, despite my lack of scruples, asking Joseph to help ME would have been a lot more difficult.

Brodsky had recently got the "Nobelevka," and there was hope that he had not spent all the money yet. I reported the Samovar situation to the poet and appealed to him for help.

"You think the bucks won't be wasted?" That was his only question. Not only did he invest his own money, but he talked the financially mightier Baryshnikov into joining in as well. The shares of the grumbling partners were "ransomed" and the flickering flame of the Samovar began to burn brighter.

Brodsky went to the Samovar often. Not counting fashionable invitations into the rarefied atmosphere of restaurants like La Grenouille and Lutèce, his "restaurant life" was limited to various Chinese establishments, Café Reggio, and the Samovar.

His favorite menu included pickled herring with potatoes, *studen'* (meat jelly), *satzivi* (spicy chicken pieces under a nut sauce), and *pel'meni*. Roman had invented about a dozen vodka recipes and Brodsky's favorites were horseradish vodka and coriander vodka.

After two or three drinks, Brodsky would take the microphone, lean on the white "Baryshnikov piano" and sing. People would immediately gather round. From his early years Iosif, as our mutual friend once said, "had a Mike for his brother." In his twenties, at our Leningrad home, he sang leaning against our Becker piano. Young Osya loved American songs and skillfully, in a hoarse bass voice, imitated Louis Armstrong. But in the States the Nobel Prize laureate's repertoire consisted, besides "Lili Marlene" and the Polish "Red Poppies," exclusively of Russian songs: "Why do you stand there swaying..." "Black Eyes," "My Fire," "Where ships ride at anchor at night..." and so on. Probably this repertoire expressed a tangle of conflicting emotions: nostalgia, arrogant irony, love, contempt, and anguish.

In the Samovar he relaxed and would often say how warm, cozy, and tasty it was for him to be there. These words have documentary proof. In the restaurant visitors' book there is the following inscription:

It's winter. What can we do in New York
—it's colder than the moon.
Let's get a little caviar,
a little vodka on a savory crust...
We'll warm ourselves at Kaplan's.
Iosif Brodsky

And now—a short digression from the story of the Russian Samovar.

...In 1991 Brodsky was offered the position of American Poet Laureate in the Library of Congress—the first time this position was offered to a foreigner. It is prestigious but fairly burdensome and poorly paid work. It is supposed to last two years, but Brodsky resigned after one—citing administrative aspects of the position that were too hard for him.

He explained to his friends that he accepted the position in order to organize mass publication of poetry collections and make them available to everybody. Brodsky dreamed of spiritually and intellectually transforming Americans by getting the masterpieces of world poetry into their pragmatic heads. Standing in every supermarket, next to the tabloids promising every week either the end of the world or the arrival of aliens, would be pocket-size volumes of Auden, Frost, and even, perhaps, Dante. "The Russian romantic," as one middling American poet called Brodsky, "hoped that human baseness, vulgarity, boorishness, cowardice, and greed could be cured by the 'immortal poems.'"

Unfortunately, poetry still has not become an integral part of American pop culture. But his dreams about the popularization of the Russian classics are beginning to come to life.

Once I took the train from Boston to New York. As I walked into the car I saw that on every seat there lay a small book—a mass market edition of Nikolai Gogol's "The Overcoat" and "The Nose." I took a few copies and gave one of them to Brodsky with the inscription: "Hooray! The time has come when a peasant carries home from the market—not Blucher[1] or the silly milord—but Gogol and Belinsky!" (this is a line from a famous poem by the nineteenth century Russian poet Nikolai Nekrasov).

But to return to the Russian Samovar... In 1997 the Kaplans decided to expand and turn the upper empty floor of the Samovar into a "cigar room." It was supposed that, after (or instead of) dinner, the guests would sit there and stretch their legs like the lords in British clubs, enjoying cigars and cognac. Layout and design were done by remarkable émigré artists Yuri Cooper and Lev Zbarsky. Layout of the floors, furniture, lamps, the bar, the color design—everything was done according to their sketches and in impeccable taste. The space ended up looking elegant and "noble."

But the idea itself was not successful. Russians—be they immigrants, or tourists, or a new breed of businessmen (called "New Russians," but really *nouveau riche*)—prefer a shot of vodka and the tail-end of a pickled herring to the best cigars and cognac in the world.

The Cigar Room, which cost a huge amount of money, the nervous systems of six people, and a year and a half of their lives, turned out to be non-functional. People would come there as to a museum, to admire the decor.

And then Roman, remembering how Brodsky dreamed of popularizing poetry, decided to turn the Cigar Room into a literary club.

Iosif would be glad to know that now, every Thursday, the second floor of his beloved Samovar hosts literary evenings. And not only Russian poets and writers appear there, but American intellectuals as well... So literature is finding its way even in pragmatic America.

---

[1]Gebhard von Blucher—Prussian field marshal, a military opponent of Napoleon.

19

"...for the Base Life There Were Numbers"

[*"Slovo"* - Nikolai Gumilyov]

To say about Brodsky that he was not "practical" is to say nothing. And really, could you expect a practical approach to life from a poet who was never interested in material possessions, who all his life tried to evade the coercion of a totalitarian government, and the pressure of any group in general—who felt that generating words, sounds, rhythms and rhymes was the highest possible intellectual achievement, and probably the highest spiritual attainment? When his principles clashed with the demands of "normal" life such as the need for stable income, security, approval, and the like, his principles won most of the time. Not only was he not practical about present exigencies, he was even less so about those of the future. Many people bypass needs of the moment to ensure some positive result in the future. Sometimes they cannot enjoy living in the present because they are so busy preparing for contingencies that could arise later. Brodsky did not live for the future, he did not save for the future, and he was not even sure that his future was real. His lines

What can I say about life?
That it happened to be longer than expected, and abhors transparence.
(from Urania, in *The Times Literary Supplement*, May 29, 1987)

295

were written when he turned forty, and this was typical Brodsky—
he did not expect to live too long. He was generous, paid for
others in restaurants, let people stay in his place, did all kinds of
expensive favors to others and gave lavish gifts—not necessarily
because he was a kind person (often, he was not kind at all), but
because he didn't have it in him to calculate: "Well, should I do
this favor now, or should I wait until a better moment or for a
better recipient?"

Even when no principles were involved, even when no person
was to be helped, Joseph's allocation of expenditures or, rather,
his way of spending was sometimes inexplicable from the
common sense point of view and left us lesser mortals
dumbfounded. As for his financial papers, despite the efforts of
professional financial managers they remained in an artistic
disarray.

Under "senseless spending" we can list the hefty sum that
Brodsky put into his apartment (that is, *not his own*, but one he
rented) on Morton Street. He had been renting it for many years
from a New York University professor with whom he was
friendly. Brodsky loved Greenwich Village, was comfortable on
Morton Street and had never thought of moving.

The apartment was a bit run down. It had, as American real
estate brokers say, a "tired look," and needed "some attention."
But it was still quite "viable," that is, in decent shape—and an
easygoing tenant like Brodsky might well live there happily ever
after.

So it was here on Morton Street, in his second floor apartment,
after he became a Nobel Prize laureate and got the prize money,
that Brodsky was gripped by a paroxysm of what he called
"housekeepery." He began a renovation that would cost
eventually tens of thousands of dollars.

At that time I worked in a real estate office, and friends often
sought my advice. I was no guru; I hadn't made a killing in real
estate, and owned only the apartment where I lived, but I knew
more about the real estate market than most Russian intellectuals
who had brought to these shores a totally irrelevant set of
experiences and wanted only to continue their lofty pursuits.

When Joseph announced his plans for the renovation, I was
horrified. I tried to explain to him that most people of sound

mind *do not repair* somebody else's apartment. One has to be a kamikaze to do that—a lamentable result was assured. Either the landlord would raise the rent steeply, or out of the blue, get married—or his nephew would appear (or his auntie, or Grandma, or an ex-wife's brother) and the tenant would be sent packing.

Joseph did not heed my warnings: the renovation was done, and done very well. The apartment was transformed and looked much better. But it was as if I had second sight. A few years after the repairs were finished, Brodsky's landlord suddenly married a Finnish doctor. Obviously, he needed the apartment for himself, and Brodsky had to look for another place to live.

But Joseph was still living on Morton Street when Maria entered his life. She was expecting a baby—that is, three would be living where once there was one. The solitude and quiet Brodsky needed for his work, was about to be compromised, and he decided, in addition to the Morton Street apartment, to rent a studio not far from home.

He studied the Real Estate section of *The New York Times*, liked one ad and decided to take a look.

The apartment was also located in Greenwich Village, on Barrow Street, number 34, not far from his house. It was a studio of about four hundred square feet in size on the third floor of a brownstone. At one time the brownstone had belonged to a single family but had been turned into a three-apartment condominium. The studio apartment in the ad was, in its previous life, simply an attic, with a lovely view of Greenwich Village.

The owner of the studio, a young man named David Salovitz, had been living in the studio with his friend Stephen. They were a pleasant, young gay couple, both musical and artistic. David was handsome, and his deep, velvety baritone was right for grand opera, but such a career was out of reach because he lacked the requisite height. David was sometimes invited to sing at concerts, but not often. Unable to make a living that way, David was working part time as a second cook or sometimes as a waiter at a catering agency that specialized in dinners and receptions in the homes of the wealthy.

Stephen, a middling rock musician, played guitar in various bars in the evenings, and during the day worked as a doorman in a luxury building on Fifth Avenue.

One fine day a third member was added to the family—a boxer named Lucy, taken from the local SPCA.

Already crowded and noisy, the studio became impossible with Lucy's howling while David practiced opera arias and Stephen strummed his guitar. The owners of the two other apartments lost patience and gave David an ultimatum.

The young people could neither abandon their music nor part with Lucy. They would have to move out.

David found a suitable rental place in Brooklyn for the three of them. As for the studio, he decided to rent it out and pay rent for the new apartment out of the proceeds. They placed the ad that caught Brodsky's eye...

Joseph called and said who he was, but the name Joseph Brodsky meant nothing to David. Still, he was relieved to hear the name. At any rate, a man named Brodsky was unlikely to belong to an unwanted minority, so further awkward probing was unnecessary.

Joseph expressed his desire to look at the apartment and David, before making an appointment, decided to ask his potential tenant a few "permissible" questions.

"Do you work?"—"Yes."—"May I ask where?"—"Mainly at home."—"Are you a professional?" (Literature was far from David's mind.)—"I think so," patiently answered Joseph.—"How many of you will be here?"—"Just me."—"Do you have a dog?"—"I have a cat, but it won't be living here..."—"Forgive me, but do you play any musical instruments, by any chance?"— "No... However, I clatter on the typewriter." [Brodsky never learned to use a computer]—"At night?"—"Well, that may be, but in general I am not planning to spend nights there."

Brodsky came to look at the apartment with Maria. Maria was pregnant and still stunned David with her beauty. "Like someone from a painting in a gold frame," he told me. But her husband did not impress David much. "A guy, not young, balding, in a pair of rumpled pants and a rusty-looking jacket, and all his clothes were sort of mottled."

Brodsky looked over the peeling walls from the threshold, looked into the bathroom with the yellowed toilet and a sink full of cracks, and, without asking a single question, went to the window.

He stood at the window for a bit, admiring the wet roofs of Greenwich Village, and smoked two cigarettes, muttering that he liked it very much here because it reminded him of a Parisian garret. He would be moving in a week, with a writing desk, an armchair, and a typewriter.

The fact of his smoking two cigarettes in ten minutes upset David terribly. By mutual agreement the apartment owners had designated the building non-smoking. But it was too late to bring it up now. Still, he might induce the prospective tenant to refuse the apartment if he jacked up the price.

David asked 1,500 dollars a month for the apartment. Normally, landlords ask for triple the rent—first and last month's, and also a security deposit which the tenant gets back when he moves out (if the place is left in decent condition).

Tenants, in their turn, usually ask that one month's rent be knocked off, but Brodsky wrote a check for 4,500 dollars without a murmur.

David was immediately seized by typically Jewish guilt. He started blaming himself for asking so much. The new tenant had obviously overpaid. Before Mr. Brodsky moved in, the conscientious David painted the walls, whitewashed the ceiling, polished the floor, and washed the windows. David also blamed himself for taking a security deposit, as if he were afraid that when he got the apartment back from this quiet gentleman it would look like crap. However, two years later, when Brodsky got his deposit back and moved out, David blamed himself even more for not keeping the deposit. "The place was smoked in so much that the walls turned yellow and the ceiling started to peel," he complained.

You never know what others will think of your actions. When Brodsky came to pick up the key, he glanced over the rejuvenated studio, and sighed, "What did you do all these renovations for? I liked how it was before, there was the spirit of an old European place here."

The agency where David worked did catering for Broadway actors and literary celebrities. Among the clients of this agency were journalism's most famous and influential players, like Tina Brown and her husband Harold Evans. [At the time, Evans had already been the director of Random House while Tina had been editor of two important magazines—first *Vanity Fair*, then *The New Yorker.*]

Usually, guests on the parties David catered for, were the *crème de la crème* of literary society. And so, a month after the new tenant moved into David's studio, one of the agency's clients held a dinner at Sutton Place in honor of the birthday of some famous writer. [David asked me not to reveal the names of participants, but they are not important for the story anyway.] David was one of the waiters and I will give him the floor:

"The dinner was a black-tie affair. The ladies were mostly in evening gowns, the men in dinner jackets and bow-ties. And all the service people, except the cooks, were also in dinner jackets.

"They had not gone to the table yet, all the guests were crowded in the drawing room, and I was carrying the aperitifs around. Suddenly the door opened and in walked my tenant—in the very same jacket and pants that he wore when he came to look at my place. My mouth fell open, I almost dropped the tray with wineglasses on the Persian rug.

"All the guests surrounded him in a bunch, everybody looked as thrilled as if Bill Gates or Mario Lanza or Leo Nucci had showed up. The room was buzzing: 'Joseph, how wonderful that you found the time... Joseph, thank you for coming... Joseph, we've held dinner for you... Joseph, Joseph, Joseph...'

"Of course, he did not notice me or, if he noticed, gave no sign of recognition. That is, it could not occur to him that I would be there.

"I slipped into the kitchen and said to the chef, 'Give me a job in the kitchen, I am not going to work the rooms, because I cannot and I will not, *morally and ethically*, serve my tenant. I am his landlord, after all... And anyway, where did he come from?'

"The chef said that Brodsky was more important than anybody there. He was a Nobel Prize laureate, and the American Poet Laureate, making him the number *one* poet in America, anyway..."

The news left David flabbergasted. That night, he never did go back into the "rooms," but hung out around the doorway, studying his tenant, while the other waiters scurried back and forth. So doing, he made some interesting observations. He said that Brodsky immediately became the center of attention. All the guests, open-mouthed, were taking in his every word. When asked whether it just seemed that way to him because of his shock, David confidently said "No." In his catering career, he had had a chance to see many stars, including three Nobel laureates in literature—Czeslaw Milosz, Tony Morrison, and Nadine Gordimer from South Africa. But no one created an energy field the way Brodsky did. Everybody sat there, hanging on his every word.

For the two years or so that Brodsky rented the studio from David he did not spend time there regularly: five or six hours a day sometimes, but then he did not show up for weeks. He did not pay his rent in a regular way either—sometimes on time, sometimes ahead of time, and sometimes there would be no check for two months. "I was too shy to call and remind him," said David, "but it was only with those checks we could pay for our Brooklyn apartment."

David had trouble with his former neighbors as well. They used to call him to complain that Brodsky made duplicate keys, gave them to various acquaintances, so that Russians of all sorts were spending the night in the studio fairly regularly. They smoked not only in the apartment, but on the stairs, and didn't lock the front doors either by day or by night... Professor R.S. on the ground floor told him: "We feel as if we live in a volcano." For the honor of being in the same building with a Nobel Prize laureate they were prepared to put up with it. Still, everybody was relieved when Brodsky moved out, taking the volcano with him.

When the landlord of his apartment on Morton Street announced that he needed Brodsky's place for himself, Joseph made a historic decision to buy his own place for the first time in his life. His first choice was a condo in Manhattan's West Side, Broadway and Sixty-something, almost across the street from Lincoln Center. He made an offer and it was accepted.

A few days later he called me: "Ludessa, can I jump from the trolley without breaking my leg?" "It depends. If something is wrong with an inspection, you can." "No. Unfortunately, the inspection is fine." "What's wrong then?" "Location. The place is too close to everything and anybody. A beetle and a toad will stop by without even as much as a warning phone call. I won't be able to work there." "You have to come up with a different reason, Joseph, otherwise, I am afraid, you'll lose your deposit."

As far as I know, he did not come up with a better reason, and he did lose the deposit. Eventually, he bought an apartment in Brooklyn, far from the Russian beaten path. It was nice and spacious, but it was on two levels, and it was clear that climbing the stairs was not good for Brodsky. But this "practical" consideration was not important enough for him.

Another financial story: Every Russian who comes to this country lives through the shock of discovery that in America there is a crime punished more heavily than murder: non-payment of taxes. In Russia, we thought that Al Capone had been jailed for his horrifying crimes. It was only in America that we found out that he had not been punished for all the murders he had committed or ordered, but for tax evasion. So I was not just a little worried when, on July 7th, 1991, I saw a Boston Globe article with the following intriguing title:

IRS PENS a FEW LINES to US POET LAUREATE

"Poets toil in obscurity, at least in America," wrote The Boston Globe, *"How was the IRS to know that the Joseph Brodsky it was trying to reach for weeks was this nation's poet laureate and a former Soviet dissident?"*

Then the author of the article explained that for Internal Revenue Service *"it's all the same – Brodsky, Trotsky or Tchaikovsky."*

Marti Melecio, the spokeswoman for the IRS said in a phone interview: *"We treat everybody the same way,"* but refused to explain why the IRS has been looking for the poet. Their search for Brodsky went so far that the IRS had sent letters to his South Hadley neighbors asking whether they knew where he was. The neighbors knew nothing about his whereabouts.

But I was pleased that the neighbors at least knew who he was. *"That's that Russian-whatever-poet,"* said one neighbor who refused to give her name. *"I've read his poetry."*

In the meantime Brodsky was in London giving a poetry reading. His secretary Ann Kjellberg was surprised to learn that the IRS was trying to find Brodsky. She said that Brodsky also didn't know anything about it. When she was asked whether it was possible that he forgot to pay his taxes, Ms. Kjellberg said: "I really don't know. He is a very disorganized, creative type of guy, so it is conceivable... He just doesn't keep good records."

Brodsky had an accountant who was supposed to take care of his finances. It looked rather mysterious that the IRS contacted neither him, nor Ms. Kjellberg, nor Brodsky himself before sending letters to his neighbors.

Thank God, eventually the problem was taken care of. I still do not know precisely what it was. I was not comfortable asking Joseph about it and he did not volunteer any information to us. No one was hurt, there was no damage to his reputation—nor was there any sign that he had become or would ever become a more "practical" man.

20

Perfidy and Love

IN OUR OLD HOMELAND young Brodsky was the spiritual master of many minds and souls. However, he had no authority in other realms—he could not recommend anybody for publication, or help with obtaining a teaching position, or publish a positive review, or write a flattering foreword to one's book. On the contrary, he needed help every step of the way in navigating the Soviet system, and many friends extended him a helping hand to protect him from that harsh reality or make his life more bearable. In America, for the last ten or eleven years of his life, Brodsky became a fortune-maker for certain friends. He was a professor, on a first-name basis with the heads of publishing houses; he knew everybody who was anybody in American literary life. Many Russian intellectuals, both in Russia and in the States, thought that his influence in American literary circles was boundless. It was assumed that, at a word from him, doors would open to American publishing houses and university lecture halls. His acquaintances truly thought that one phone call from him would get them a grant or a book contract. Those who were hitting their heads against a wall trying to "break in" felt that a grant or a publication might assure "at least some kind of career" in the West and, possibly, even a literary destiny. Small wonder that Brodsky's phone was ringing off the hook with all kinds of requests. In the end, he had to get an unlisted phone number that he would give only to those friends who could be trusted to keep it secret.

Unfortunately, this confidence in his clout was naïve. Like any powerful and influential person, Brodsky had many enemies in literary and academic circles, and there were many people who envied him. His attempts to get somebody a grant, to help somebody get a university post, or to influence their chances of being published in American magazines did not always succeed. But he was open to newcomers, and he was trying to help them. Actually, he tried to help so many people that in the last years his recommendation no longer meant a great deal.

I will not name names. He helped many people, that's all. Those he could help know this very well, as do those he could not—or would not help.

Every action of his in this area (if it became known) provoked much gossip and many rumors and conflicting opinions—from whole-hearted approbation to severe condemnation.

One of the best-known episodes of this kind is the one concerning Vassily Aksyonov's novel *The Burn.*

The bare facts of this story are as follows.

Aksyonov was an immensely popular Soviet writer. His books and short stories did not praise the Soviet system—at least, not explicitly. His characters lived their lives within the System, but they tried to be as independent as possible within that framework. These characters, robust, brave and ruthless, had an appeal that was in sync with young professionals of 1960-1970. While Brodsky's name was known to connoisseurs of high art only, Aksyonov's was known to every college-educated Russian. Successful as he was, Aksyonov still felt that what he really wanted to say was hard to say in the Soviet Union, and he emigrated to the USA on the peak of the "third wave." Here, he wrote *The Burn.* Joseph read the manuscript for the publishing house of Farrar, Straus & Giroux, and his comments were so disparaging that the publishers turned down the novel. This generated a storm in the Russian intellectual community. After all, we are supposed to help each other no matter what, aren't we?

Now for the details, gleaned by different people from different sources. Brodsky's motives were also subject to varying interpretations, by the way.

Brodsky's version as told to me personally went as follows: "I was at Farrar, Straus, saw *The Burn* and asked if I could read it. The novel turned out to be a piece of shit, which is what I told Roger." (Roger Straus, the editor, was a close friend of Brodsky's.)

In answer to my question as to why he had sunk Aksyonov, his colleague who had recently emigrated and could have used the help—in my opinion, an "unkosher" thing to do—Joseph said that the novel was badly written, and that he had expressed his honest opinion on the subject, as it was his right to do. Recent arrival or old hand, it was all the same to him.

To Lev Loseff, Brodsky said that Roger asked him to read the manuscript and give his opinion. And since he disliked the novel very strongly, that was what he honestly said. Brodsky said to Loseff (as he did not say to me) that he was not very worried about Aksyonov's fate in the new country because he was sure that Vasya would get published elsewhere and thus *The Burn* would find its readers. It was not clear who he thought would publish such a bad novel, but Brodsky turned out to be right. This episode did not close other publishers' doors to Aksyonov. He published *The Burn* (it was not such a bad novel after all), and after that he has been published successfully in America for years.

But, as they say in Russian, "everybody understood as they could." Yet another opinion was being expressed on the fringes of literary circles. To wit, that Brodsky did not want to promote those who were published in the Soviet Union in "mass quantities" and who were successful and famous there. That is, he did not want to help those who chose a path different from his own and "cooperated" with the System. The names of poets Yevtushenko and Voznesensky were given as a pair of persuasive examples.

However, as may be ascertained from various interviews with Brodsky, and from what I described in Chapter 18, his dislike of Yevtushenko stemmed not only from his literary success but also from personal motives and was, from my point of view, understandable and justified. In reality, nobody knows for sure what part Yevtushenko played in what the Soviet government did to Brodsky, both in the matter of his exile from Russia and that of the official refusal to allow his parents to visit him in the States. It is very likely that Yevtushenko was consulted by the authorities in both cases. It is significant, however, that in 1989 Brodsky resigned from the American Academy of Arts in protest when Yevgeny Yevtushenko was accepted as a member. Joseph's true motive for this gesture remains unknown.

Brodsky's strongly negative attitude toward Andrei Voznesensky is less intelligible to me. Apparently, Brodsky did not like his poetry, but he had no personal reasons to dislike Andrei. Only, perhaps, a general irritation with Voznesensky for being "officially left wing"—his poetry often contained lines that could be understood as criticism of official Soviet policies—but who, nevertheless, loudly proclaimed his allegiance to the values of the Soviet system and was very successful in publishing everything he wrote. His fame among college-educated Russians was similar to Yevtushenko's (after all, sophisticated poets like Brodsky did not have a chance for broad name recognition). Voznesensky, like Yevtushenko, was often sent to the West to demonstrate the existence of freedom of speech and artistic freedom in the Soviet Union, and he participated in that willingly and successfully.

Smakov and I were friends with Voznesensky from time immemorial, and Iosif often made biting remarks to us on the subject of this friendship. And I, in my turn, tried to explain to him how decently Andrei had behaved in several far from simple situations, how many people he had helped, and what a loyal friend he had turned out to be.

I will never forget our meetings with Voznesensky in Italy. We had been living in Rome waiting for a visa to the U.S. In the mid seventies, Soviet émigrés were considered "untouchable" by the Soviet government and any contact between them and Soviet citizens while on business trips abroad could destroy a citizen's career. Moreover, such contacts could be considered grounds for a ban on all future trips. (And permission to travel to the West was one of the greatest perks for a Soviet citizen.) When people were getting their permissions to go abroad, they were always warned by the KGB about avoiding contacts with émigrés in no uncertain terms, and they took these warnings seriously.

For example, one of my very close friends came to New York for a business visit soon after our arrival there. He was such a close and dear friend, that he could not miss a chance to see me. But he also was such an experienced Soviet administrator that he understood what seeing me could do to his successful career. So our meeting had all the features of a spy movie, with him leaving the hotel alone, giving false pretences to his Russian colleagues, changing trains in the subway, and hiding behind a parked car to wait for me at the place appointed for our meeting. And I found all that natural because every group of Soviet citizens sent abroad had at least one member (often there were more) whose task was to report on the behavior of other group members, and nobody knew for sure who these special members were.

Here is a joke about the Soviet delegation at a musical competition abroad. One member of the delegation gets the second prize and is desperate that he did not get the first, because the first prize was a violin made by Stradivarius. Another member of the delegation who took the last place tries to console him and says "Big deal, Stradivarius." The first musician says: "You do not understand. For me to play on the Stradivarius violin is the same as for you, let us say, to shoot from a gun that used to belong to Comrade Dzerzhinsky." [KGB founder.]

Voznesensky, the famous Soviet poet, arrived in Rome with a high literary mission. His schedule included meetings with Italian celebrities, gala dinners with Pierre Cardin and Fellini, and maybe even a breakfast with the Pope. Andrei found out that his Italian translator, Silvana, happened to be our friend. He asked her for our phone number and address, called us and said that he would cut short his "dinner with Pierre" and spend the rest of the evening with us. At that time quite a few Soviet celebrities, on state-permitted trips, had asked for political asylum, while in Europe or in the States, and the Soviet embassies were so nervous that they were sending KGB agents to follow Soviet guests everywhere. Voznesensky knew it very well. He left his gala dinner, got a taxi and asked the driver to stop at the Termini, a few blocks from via Gaeta where we lived. He wandered around the station for some time "covering his tracks," then walked to our house. Halfway to via Gaeta, a motorcycle with a wild driver flew by, and the passenger tore the *sumka* from Andrei's shoulder, the purse with all his money and documents, including his passport, a visa and a plane ticket. Later he had to give a detailed explanation at the Soviet embassy. The report of his behavior that they would send on to Moscow was something he could live without. Despite all these troubles he spent the evening with us, read his poetry, and even offered to take some letters and clothing back to our friends in Moscow. We went to the flea market and bought enough used clothes to fill a whole suitcase. To each piece I attached a note saying who was supposed to get what. The suitcase came with a broken zipper, and when Andrei took it from a luggage claim in Moscow, it opened and all these dresses, blouses and shirts fell on the floor. Andrei was crawling on the floor picking it up under the malignant cameras of journalists and reporters. The next day one of the Moscow papers ran a big picture of this scene with the following caption: "The poor famous Soviet poet bought half of Italy."

Being an "officially left-wing" poet, Voznesensky visited the States often, and he was not afraid to meet with me and other émigrés. The negative attitude of Brodsky to him bothered Voznesensky because this attitude labeled Voznesensky as too official, too closely aligned with the police state. Being accepted by Brodsky would mean that Brodsky saw Voznesensky as an independent poet, not as a Soviet functionary. This was not important for Voznesensky's success among Americans— Voznesensky entertained many American intellectuals when they visited the Soviet Union and they reciprocated by arranging his visits to the States, public readings, and publications. However, this was important for Voznesensky's reputation among Soviet émigrés in America and, to some extent, for his reputation among free thinking people back in Russia. Voznesensky was just as eager as Yevtushenko to make up with Brodsky and asked me to be an intermediary a few times. I wanted them to have a normal talk together sometime, at least once, and I tried to bring Joseph around, but, alas, without much success.

Eventually, the meeting took place: Voznesensky talked Brodsky into allowing him to visit him on Morton Street. Iosif told me about it personally, and Andrei described the visit in his book *In the Virtual Wind*.

As the episode was related by both participants, it reminded me of Kurosawa's immortal film *Rashomon*. In this movie four characters—a samurai, his wife, a bandit, and a woodcutter—tell a story of rape and murder as witnesses or as participants. Each of them speaks the exact truth, but all four versions are drastically different.

1. The story told by Brodsky that I wrote down that very day:
"Listen, Kissa, your dream came true. I met with Voznesensky. I was at the reception at the Swedish embassy. Oodles of unfamiliar visages all around. I haven't a clue as to whom I am saying "How do you do." Suddenly somebody stretches out his hand. I shake it without looking, and then I see... it's *your* Voznesensky. So I think—this is it, I am stuck, I can't get out of it. He asked could he come see me, and that's where I got slack. Next day he showed up, we had a cup of coffee. There was absolutely nothing to talk about. Thank God, there was Mississippi stretched out on the couch, so we chewed the fat about cats... In half an hour he split."

2. The story told by Voznesensky in his book *In the Virtual Wind*:
"...Brodsky and I were not closely acquainted. Once he invited me to the snow-white burrow of his little apartment in Greenwich Village. There was not a shadow of his famous arrogance. He was open, cordially hospitable, not without ironic correctness of behavior.

He made the Turkish coffee for me himself. Flashing the graying bronze, poured vodka into narrow liqueur glasses. Though he had a bad heart, he smoked greedily. What did we talk about? But, of course, about Mandelshtam, about how Akhmatova loved a joke. About irony and the ideal. About the fall of the Empire. 'Too bad about the Empire,' he gave a small grin. A cat with a collar bumped against my side on the couch. A dark cat with a white chest.

'What's his name?' I asked the host.

'Mississippi,' he said. "I think that a cat's name has to have the sound "s" in it.'

'And why not USSR?'

'The letter "r-r-r" gets in the way,' he laughed. 'Do you have a cat? What's her name?'

'Couscous,' I confessed.

The poet's eye lit up: 'Oh, this is amazing. Truly there is something Arabic about a cat. Night. The crescent moon. Egypt. Mystique.'"

The discrepancies in these stories remind me of a joke about a rabbi who says to two arguing men, "You, Shapiro, are right, and you, Rabinovich, are right also." And when his wife, who hears the conversation, confronts the rabbi and says that it is impossible that both men with opposing views are right, he pauses, puzzled, and then says, "And you are right too, dear."

I already mentioned several cases when Brodsky did what he thought he had to avoid doing, and he did that succumbing to pressures he could easily resist (like meeting with Yevtushenko). He called these incidents "I done (or gone) bad," or "I got slack," or "I slipped up." As to why he felt an urge to tell about those things even when he was contrite about them, I have no clue. Either so that the "slip-ups" might be recorded by the "Pimen" for all eternity, or because he wanted to hear that they weren't slip-ups at all.

For instance, I remember this confession:

"Ludka, it looks like I done bad yesterday."

"In what way?"

"I am walking home through Washington Square. Some dude pops up beside me from somewhere and almost throws himself into my arms. 'Iosif Aleksandrovich! What luck meeting you! Because it's impossible to get you on the phone! I want to give you greetings from...and, in general, tell you how they cherish and honor you at home! Blah-blah-blah. Could you possibly spare me half an hour?' 'Not now I couldn't.' 'Maybe tomorrow morning?' and he shoves his card at me. I look at it—it's Mellor Sturua. And that's where I done bad and gave him my telephone number."

Mellor Sturua used to be a speechwriter for Khrushchev (he might have been the one who scripted the shoe-banging at the United Nations). Later, he was a U.S.-based correspondent for *Izvestia*. During Soviet times, he thrived writing articles about America. In his articles, nothing good ever happened in this country. Exploitation of workers was merciless, blacks were discriminated against in the worst way with impunity, crime was everywhere. The American government was totally corrupt, every act of the government had an ulterior motive. The Hollywood movie companies were enmeshed in a tight web of interests with big Wall Street banks and the U.S. military-industrial complex.

From Mellor Sturua articles, Soviet readers were getting a clear impression that Americans were a wretched lot, while the Soviet people were the happiest people on earth, thanks to the ceaseless care of the Soviet government and the Communist party. In brief, Mellor Sturua was a faithful and skillful servant of the Soviet regime, and he was not a person with whom Brodsky would like to shake hands. I do not know how Sturua reported this experience. For me, it is just another example of how meek Joseph could be sometimes to people he wanted nothing to do with.

The hypothesis that Brodsky was jealous of poets who were widely published in the USSR is strengthened by a conversation cited by poet Alexander Kushner in his article "Here on Earth...." Kushner was an old acquaintance. His poetic voice could be compared with Brodsky's in the way that a chamber orchestra compares to a "full size" symphony orchestra—that is, a voice much softer and less philosophical. (I do not mean to denigrate Kushner, I just want to say that he was different.) Since Kushner's topics were more personal than Brodsky's, censorship did not oppress him much, and Kushner was allowed to publish and to develop as a poet. Indeed, today Kushner is one of the best known and most widely published Russian poets. Kushner and Brodsky were talking about a book by Brodsky that was being prepared for publication in Russia. Here is a quote from Kushner: "They sent him a contract which cited a print run of fifty thousand copies. The first thing he asked me was, 'And what kind of print run does Yevtushenko have?' This competition with Yevtushenko seemed to me very characteristic. Yevtushenko remained for him the model of a poet who was successful in Russia—and, however strange it may be, he continued his argument with him, which had stopped making sense a long time ago."

In the very same article Kushner tells about his poetry reading in Boston. Brodsky made the introduction, and he had come to

Boston from South Hadley for that purpose. Kushner writes that Brodsky's introduction showed a very high appreciation of his poetry and that he spoke "excitedly, warmly, unselfconsciously, just as he read his poems in public...." Kushner took Brodsky's panegyric at face value—he was used to praise and felt he deserved it. Little did he know how Brodsky really felt.

I was present at that reading and can confirm that Iosif's introduction was not just rapturous. I have never heard such a cascade of praise from him on behalf of any living author. But he pronounced that panegyric very fast, almost speed-talking. After the reading I said to him, "Joseph, you spoke beautifully, but you rattled like a machine gun." "To get it over with. It was an unpleasant job," said Brodsky. "Hey, then why did you agree to come here to speak? You could easily say that you had a scheduling conflict or something." And Brodsky gave me his usual line: "Well, he was so anxious that I do this introduction for him, he said it was so important to him, and I gave in."

In 1993 Kushner and his wife Lena Nevzglyadova were again in Boston. Every time we saw each other, it was our custom, along with the poetry and intellectual conversation, to pick our mutual acquaintances to pieces. Of course, we spoke of Brodsky. It was like a law for us. Whenever literary people who knew Brodsky got together (be they writers or readers), his name was always first on their lips. Everybody felt an insatiable interest not only in what he last wrote, but also in what he had recently said and done. During one of the "picking" sessions I told the Kushners just who our "Nobel-man" had been deprecating "during the last quarter of the current year." Kushner shook his head sympathetically: "Really? Poor guys. Well, he never said anything bad about us.... I am sure that he loves us, right, Lena?"

Of course I did not have the heart to tell them about Brodsky's poem "A Letter to an Oasis" which had already been making the rounds. "A.K." here means Alexander Kushner.

A LETTER TO AN OASIS
—A.K.

Don't talk about me. Don't talk of anyone.
Take care of yourself, of her who rides the mattress.

I was not another mouth to feed,
a rodent secretly gnawing the vocabulary.

Now in your eyes of a farmhouse cat,
Guarding the granary from spoilage and loss,
a sadness can be read, which slumbered when
the Pharaoh was after me with his poleaxe.

Why the sudden sadness? A silvered temple?
A sour taste in the mouth from sweets of the East?
An otherworldly sound? But that's the rustling of sand,
talisman of the desert, in my hourglass.

It is cruelly ground, its grains are heavy,
and the bones in it are whiter than those picked over.
But it is better to gnaw than lick your lips in the heat
in the shadow of a crumbling pyramid.

When Kushner learned about this poem (thank God not from me) he was in tears. He phoned Brodsky. I don't know the content of their conversation, but Joseph took pity on poor Kushner, "got slack" and took out the dedication, the initials "A.K." Still, he could not help telling Kushner: "But the poem is good, isn't it?"

Generally speaking, the sacramental question of Brodsky's favor was a subject of frequent discussions both in private and during crowded Russian literary get-togethers. I even listed Brodsky's good friends and acquaintances and divided them into four categories:

1. Those he loves.
2. Those he thinks well of.
3. Those he tolerates.
4. Those he can't stand the sight of.

One day we were having drinks and goofing around in the Samovar, and I slipped that list to Joseph, asking him to make changes and corrections, and sign it. Which is what he did. But since everything in the world, including the way Joseph Brodsky felt about his acquaintances, was changeable and inconstant, it was decided that the list was valid only for the date, day, month, and year of its creation.

The "He loves them—he loves them not" list is kept in my archives under seventy locks and keys. I have no plans to make it public in the foreseeable future. It will be declassified a hundred years after my death.

To the reader curious about my place on the list I am ashamed to admit that I found myself assigned to category 3—"*Tolerates.*" I thought that he would put me higher, if not sincerely, then out of politeness, as in the case of Kushner, but Brodsky did not feel he had to get slack with me. Come to think of it, I should have felt lucky to escape category 4.

In the final years of his life Brodsky complained that he was deathly tired of being asked to write or call somebody, to exert his influence for somebody, to assist in something, to give money or to allow somebody to stay at his place.

Once he said that he was leaving for Europe for two weeks, and asked me if I could find the poet N. N., little known to me, a place to stay in New York.

I asked him why N. N. could not stay on Morton Street, since Joseph was leaving anyway. "I am afraid he'll pinch the Nobel medal," replied the laureate. I was upset: "And what about the people I would place N.N. with? How could you ask for such a favor if you know that he would steal from them?" It seemed, however, that Brodsky knew everything there was to know about human nature in general and the kleptomaniac habits of N.N. in particular: "Since they would be sharing the place, he would not dare to steal in their presence." I was not convinced and said that I did not know of any possibilities at that time.

Talking about the Nobel medal reminded me of an amusing episode. Brodsky always said that being awarded the Nobel Prize came as a complete surprise to him. That was not exactly so.

In the middle of November of 1986, on the day before the Nobel Prize laureates were announced, he called us in Boston, very excited and agitated, and said, "I have got 24 hours of normal life left.... Tomorrow things will start up...."

The next day it turned out that he did not get "the Nobel." And, snake that I am, I was tempted to call him up and congratulate him upon the continuation of "normal life" for at least another year. But I did not give in.

Brodsky's reaction (and that of his friends) to getting "the Nobel" the next year has been the subject of various oral and written accounts. Remembering *Rashomon*, I would like to quote several people. First, an excerpt from the letter written to me by our mutual friend Slavinsky, who worked for the BBC in London at the time.

"...When the Prize was announced I called '*La Pensée Russe*' and dictated my response to them, something like 'Hooray, we're breaking through, the Swedes are wavering....' [A line from Pushkin's poem 'Poltava' describing the battle that Peter the Great fought against Swedish King Carl XII.] I hope that my joy in this event is shared by those who were directly responsible for tutoring B. in poetry: Rein, Naiman, and Bobyshev..."

Slavinsky continues: "I found out about the Prize while sitting in my office at the BBC. This producer rushes in. 'Slavinsky, congratulations, you were right!' she says. 'About what?' 'Remember, you asked me to keep all the Brodsky recordings, because any day now he is going to get "the Nobel?" Well...'

"And soon after, John Le Carré took me to that same restaurant in Hampstead where he and Joseph were sitting on the very day... They were having hors d'oeuvres, and in ran the old lady Brendel with whom Brodsky was then staying, 'My boy, come home quick, they just called from Stockholm...' Le Carré said that he immediately slipped Iosif a book for an autograph. And he also said that Brodsky became dreadfully embarrassed and began mumbling, 'Why me? What about Borges, Graham Greene?' He was almost apologizing. Le Carré answered him, 'It's all about winning.'"

Many Russians responded as Slavinsky had: one of our own has been recognized, this is great! For many intellectuals, emigrants and non-emigrants alike, there was an additional poignancy in this event. It decidedly proved the Soviet government wrong: they prosecuted Brodsky saying he was no poet, they pushed him out of the country saying his influence was harmful, they suppressed any mention of his name as if he did not exist, and now the world recognized him.

But not everybody was excited. As for Brodsky's friend Naiman, one of Akhmatova's four orphans, "the Nobella" was a blow to the solar plexus. I remember how, when he first came to America in 1988, he told us, irritably, about the episode that made him angry. About how, on the day Brodsky got "the Nobella," Rein called Naiman "in a state of euphoria" and with congratulations on "our mutual success and our mutual victory." And how Naiman adroitly cut him off: "This has nothing to do with us."

In the book *The Glorious End of the Inglorious Generations*, in the chapter "Lies, for lies, with lies (*or 'Lying, etc.'*)" this episode is also described—except that the call came not from Rein, but from a fictional M. M. and he talked not with Naiman, but with his wife. The essence, however is the same. I quote:

"When they announced the Nobel Prize, M. M. went berserk. That day I was out of town, came back late, and by my wife's face realized that something was very wrong. She told me about the Prize, I answered with a tried and true joke that this was no reason to get upset, and she added that M. M. had called in a maniacal state, choking, 'Congratulate Tol'ka! It's our mutual victory, our mutual prize!' Then she said that no, it was his, Brodsky's, and he growled, 'God damn you both!' and slammed down the receiver."[2]

The really touching line in this excerpt is "realized that something was very wrong"—as if Naiman's apartment had been robbed, or his wife had smashed up their car.

Bobyshev also felt envy and irritation. In his memoir *I Am Here* he stubbornly maintained that he was a better poet than Brodsky and Brodsky did not deserve the Prize.

As for myself, I have never asked Brodsky to help me get my writing published... out of delicacy, maybe—or because I was afraid he would refuse.

It was enough for me that he, on his own initiative, gave me a recommendation to the MacDowell Colony. Thanks to his recommendation, I lived in the middle of pine woods, in a log cabin on "chicken legs," with all my needs taken care of for two months. Unfortunately, I was in the middle of depression then and did not create a single work of high art. However, staying in the Colony healed me, and I am grateful to Joseph for opening that door for me.

From time to time I dared to give Brodsky my short stories and novellas to read. Vitya would say, "You, Zin, are asking for it." [A quotation from a popular song by famous actor Vysotsky, whose songs were never published in the official way or performed from an official stage in the former Soviet Union but were circulating in a kind of musical *samizdat*]. Mama would respond with a German saying which translated approximately thus: "He will slam you against the wall so hard that we won't be able to pry you out with a knife."

Why did I fearlessly climb into the lion's mouth? Because I had nothing to lose. My manuscripts were not lying around Farrar, Straus & Giroux, so Joseph's response could not influence a decision as to whether they were published or refused. It was just important for me to hear his opinion. What if he were to praise my work? So I would send my manuscripts to Iosif accompanied by this note: "If you should like it, call me at any hour of day or night. If you don't like it, don't call me ever."

However, I rarely had the patience to wait for a call or a "no-call." In a few days I would dial his number myself.

The question would be asked in various forms, depending on the level of my embarrassment and foreboding:

1) Quotidian: Joseph, did you read it?

2) Panicky: Iosif, please forgive me, am I calling too early?

3) Buffoonish, writhing with embarrassment: What is your verdict, sir?

Brodsky verdicts were also divided into several categories:

1) Well, Kissa, how can I put it... (Things are lousy.)

2) Not bad, not bad... (I don't have to shoot myself and may continue scribbling.)

3) You know, it's quite... (highest praise, practically worth opening champagne for).

"You know, it's quite" was said, for instance, about the novella *The Russian Blues*. And sometimes he praised separate sentences. For instance, "Frankel cried, clutched at his heart, at the bedposts and then again at the heart" ("The Prematurely Gray Wolf-Puppy"), or "A yellow balloon was crossing the gray sky, and Chris was soothed by this quiet combination" ("Ten Minutes about Love").

In general, talking to writers about their work is tricky. Many, many years ago I wrote Dovlatov a letter that criticized one of his early short stories. His response, which was a lesson to me, was: "I agree with your observations, but if I were you I would not be ironic in such a case. In situations like these it is desirable to be as delicate as if you were discussing the looks of somebody else's child."

To give Brodsky his due I must say that in his role of critic he was, with me, quite delicate. More than that, I have heard that Iosif cited me as an example to other émigré writers because I began writing in English instead of staying with the Russian-language media exclusively.

Unfortunately, writers who desired Brodsky's opinion were not always pleased to have it. This is what Brodsky's friend and translator Sasha Sumerkin wrote in his essay "Sorrow and Reason" about the time when publishing abroad stopped being a political crime for Soviet writers, and became as in all the civilized world, a sign of honor:

"With *glasnost'* the amount of Russian poetry and letters received by Brodsky began to grow in geometric proportion. A couple of times he asked my secretarial help with the answering. He would honorably look through yards of poetic sentences, trying to find in them something that was, from his point of view, alive, and to dictate a few encouraging words to the author. Often it was not that easy. Once he received some hand-written poems by a young man who had moved to Israel from Russia not long before. The poems were nothing. In such cases a standard phrase thanking the author in Brodsky's name was written and, changing only the address, the letter would be signed by me. A month or so later, when next I came "to do letters," Iosif, with a sly grin, said "Well, there's a little letter for you, too." The envelope bore my name, the address was Brodsky's. In the same hand, but with larger letters the angry poet wrote, STICK IT UP YOUR ASS! <...> I think we both thought the same thing: this was the poet's best line."[3]

---

[1] Kushner, A. "A Thousand-leaved." Russo-Baltic Information Center "Blitz," 1998, p. 255.

[2] Naiman, A. "*The Glorious End of the Inglorious Generations.*" Vagrius, 1998, p. 208.

[3] "*La Pensée Russe*" 1996. May 16-22, No. 4126. Special supplement "Iosif Brodsky (May 24, 1940 - January 28, 1996)," p. IV

21

Other Anniversaries

IN AMERICA as in his Leningrad youth, Brodsky loved his birthdays. He celebrated them on a grand scale—sometimes at Baryshnikov's house, but more often at home, where "*tout New York*" would gather.

As I remember it, the most crowded and magnificent celebration was his fiftieth birthday. (The most significant and unusual one was his fifty-fifth as celebrated in St. Petersburg. However, Joseph was not present at that birthday because he did not want to come back to Russia.)

Brodsky celebrated his 50th at Morton Street. The place was piled with presents: baskets of roses, boxes, packages, books and disks, cashmere sweaters, as well as scarves and gloves (which Brodsky never wore). Alex Liberman sent two cases of wine. Larisa Kaplan and I presented the poet with a set of bed sheets and pillowcases, and with bath towels in "dramatic colors."

His many guests represented the different aspects of his life.

The everyday: his landlord, his neighbor-friend Margot, his physician, his ladies: "the past one" and "the present one"—the designer Alina in a green velvet dress.

The intellectual: among the "American intellectuals" I recall Derek Walcott, Mark Strand, and Brodsky publisher Roger Straus. Susan Sontag did not come, instead she called, and I remember hearing Joseph say: "Susan, why are you just calling instead of being here and sitting on my lap?"

"Our" people: among them I recall Lena Chernysheva, an old friend of the late Genna Smakov and the ballet mistress, with whom Brodsky was flirting for years; Sasha Sumerkin, his friend and translator, the Dovlatovs, the Aleshkovskys, the Loseffs, the Yefimovs, the Belomlinskys...

In other words, "everybody" was there: it is easier to say who wasn't. Let me say who wasn't. Misha Baryshnikov wasn't. He was touring at the other end of the earth. His family was represented by Lisa and their little son Peter.

A huge yellow tent was set up in the garden in case of rain. I can't remember if it rained or not. My memory is of a warm, stuffy, almost "subtropical" evening, a black, starry sky, the songs of cicadas. However, the sky with stars and cicadas might have been supplied by my romantic imagination.

Two chairs stood on a platform in the middle of the tent. One, decorated with paper streamers, resembled a throne and was intended for the man of the hour. But Joseph kept jumping off it to greet the next guest, and most of the time the birthday chair was vacant. However, when we arrived it was occupied by the already tipsy Ira Aleshkovskaya. Derek Walcott, in exotic headgear—either a fez, or a gold-stitched skull-cap—was settled in the second chair, in leisurely conversation with the guests who were approaching him one after the other. It was he, important-looking and handsome, who most behaved like the honoree.

Larisa Kaplan and I showed up late, because on that day Roman wanted, without fail, to indulge Brodsky with his favorite dish: roast partridge. The birds were ordered from Tanya Hutchinson, a well-known New York culinary specialist of Russian extraction. Larisa and I were responsible for bringing them to the birthday boy, and we stopped at Tanya's on our way to the ball to pick them up. The partridges were still in the process of being roasted, and we waited for them to achieve the necessary brownness, tenderness, and crunchiness.

However, the intended surprise did not come off well. The host did not think it would be appropriate for him to hide in the bathroom or in a closet to revel in the delicious partridges all by himself. And to make them public would mean that "the winner" might not take anything at all. But the guests would not enjoy them either: partridges are tiny birdies, and there was not exactly a flock of them on hand. Joseph thanked us and asked us to place them in the refrigerator for better times—that is, for tomorrow. Whether they kept their heavenly crunchiness till the next day, I know not.

However, even without the partridges the table groaned under the delicacies: pickles, smoked meats and fish, salads, *kulebyakas*, pies, meat jelly (*aspic*), pastrami and shish kebabs... Everything had been prepared by the Russian Samovar, and prepared beautifully.

Iosif, with a glass of coriander vodka in hand, basked in the rays of adoration and glory. The almost Georgian toasts followed one after another. The proper Georgian toasts are famous for their length (up to 15 minutes), shameless panegyrics, bold exaggerations, and an absurd sense of humor. We had all been in Georgia many times and had Georgian friends, so we enjoyed this kind of toasting tremendously.

One of the speakers wished Iosif to get married and become a father as soon as possible, to which Brodsky retorted "It is my fate to live and die a bachelor."

But... man proposes... In a few months, he met Maria Sozzani, and a year later married her. I even remember my congratulatory postcard: "From Iosif and Maria—waiting for the messiah." (In Russian pronunciation, messiah rhymes with Maria). In 1993 their daughter Anna-Alexandra was born. She bore an amazing likeness to Iosif's mother Maria Moiseevna—the same wide-set eyes and cheekbones. To everybody's surprise, Joseph turned out to be a remarkably good father. Once, I visited him when Maria wasn't home. Nyusha (the little girl's happy nickname) was about six months old. She was sleeping in the other room. I wanted to look at her, but Joseph said I would have to wait till she woke up. When we heard her crying, I offered to change her. "I will do it better," said he with his usual self-assuredness and disappeared. From her room, I heard his babbling and her lisping, it sounded like a love dialogue. I am not sure whether he indeed managed better than I would, but he managed. In a few minutes, he appeared holding Nyusha high as a Soviet banner. I never saw such a proud and exultant expression on his face.

Five years later, in the spring of 1995, the Petersburg magazine *Zvezda* organized the first international conference dedicated to the work of Iosif Brodsky—in connection with his fifty-fifth birthday. An official celebration of Brodsky's birthday in Petersburg appeared to me to be both symbolic and historically significant. I decided to go, and told Iosif over the telephone. Also, I wanted to probe whether he would go there himself. He often toyed with the idea of going back for a visit but never acted on it. Despite all his experience as a famous poet who created a stir wherever he went, he had always felt ill at ease being the center of public attention and a participant in official proceedings. The unavoidable prospect of rubbing shoulders with people who were part of the system that he felt was dishonest and mean was also repellent to him. With Baryshnikov, he was discussing a ship cruise from Helsinki to St. Petersburg, whence they would go ashore disguised with false beards and mustaches. But the idea of going to Russia as a tourist did not sit well with Joseph. He explained that he would rather go to a poor place like Mexico. There, too, he would also suffer from the sight of people he could not help, but less than he would in Russia.

I remember our conversation about going to Russia:

"Joseph, let's go. What kind of birthday celebration can there be without the person whose birthday is being celebrated?"

"Maybe I'll go," said Brodsky, "some other time."

"If you will eventually then why not now?"

"Can't stand public admiration."

"Then, if you don't mind, I'll take you to Peter on a videocassette."

[A month and a half earlier there had been a Brodsky poetry reading, and I had a video recording of it. I'll describe this event in the last chapter.]

"I don't care," said Joseph.

His voice was unusually dull and sluggish.

"You feel unwell?" I asked.

"As always... lately."

I wanted to cheer him up, but it came out vigorous, clumsy, something like: "Don't you worry about a thing, sir. You will be all right. As for the birthday celebration, I'll report when I get back, and act out everybody's part for you."

"If I'm still around."

I flew out alarmed, with a heavy heart, and, while in Petersburg, was sorry every day that he could not witness his very real triumph in his homeland.

The whole city was hung with huge posters advertising a concert. The combination of names was shocking. I'd never seen them together in print even though Joseph often listened to Haydn:

From the series "The Past and Some Broodings"
A musical-literary evening
IOSIF BRODSKY
JOSEPH HAYDN

Yes indeed, Joseph has returned to Russia. Not as person, a human being, but as a poet. And to see these posters in the city where Joseph was hunted down as a runaway slave by the slave owners was almost as strange as it would have been to see Joseph walking the streets of Leningrad in person. Getting ahead, I will say that this concert, which concluded the conference, took place in the Anichkov Palace. In our Soviet past, it used to be the Palace of Young Pioneers, and as children it had looked to us like a paragon of luxury. Before Soviet times the Anichkov Palace belonged to the Emperor's family. I don't know how the Palace looked before the Revolution, but that night it was spectacular. Marble columns shone, crystal chandeliers glittered, floodlights flashed, reporters and journalists with video and movie cameras scurried everywhere.

The auditorium was filled to overflowing. A string orchestra played a Haydn concerto, Brodsky's poems were read aloud; those poems which had been set to music by Sergei Slonimsky were sung, and the audience chanted in unison: "More! More! More!" The Petersburg mayor of that time, Anatoly Sobchak, issued a decree that Iosif Brodsky was to be awarded the title of "honorary citizen of St. Petersburg." When Brodsky's old friend Yakov Gordin read the decree, the whole audience stood as one and exploded in an ovation. [By the way, honorary citizenship did not restore the rights of citizenship that were stripped from Brodsky when he emigrated.]

Had this been predicted by Nostradamus or by a gypsy fortuneteller in the Alexandrovsky Garden where we hung out almost forty years ago we would have answered in unison: "This cannot be, because this can never happen." At any rate, not in our lifetime.

Everything during those days seemed symbolic to me. The conference took place in the *Zvezda* editorial office on Mokhovaya Street. When Brodsky went to his #196 school, he used to come to this street every day. The late Ilya Averbach, our mutual friend, who was trained as a physician but later became a famous movie director, used to live on this street, and we often got together at his place. Brodsky's photo portraits, all taken at different times in his life, hang on the walls of the conference auditorium. On one wall he was shown as a small boy with his mother, and next as a young man, standing in the doorway of his book-stuffed "cupboard," his favorite black cat Osya in his arms. Here he is with his father on the balcony of their house, and there in exile in Norenskaya, with a stern, almost tragic face, in a convict's padded jacket...

On the other wall, another era. Stockholm. Brodsky in tails, at the Nobel Prize ceremony... Brodsky giving an interview at the Library of Congress... Brodsky in Venice, after the poetry reading in the Doge Palace. On the next photograph Brodsky is being presented with the *Légion d'honneur*...

Those presiding at the conference are seated at the table— Yakov Gordin, Andrei Bitov, and Evgeny Rein—all had had their problems with the Soviet system. Today, in the minds of many, Rein is the best living Russian poet, Bitov is the best living Russian novelist, and Gordin, Editor–in–Chief of the best Russian literary magazine, *Zvezda*, and the author of many books. Above them there is a most expressive photograph of Brodsky at his jubilee, in a cap pulled over his eyes, which are slightly screwed up, while his lips are lightly touched by a smile... No former Soviet citizen could fail to see the resemblance to a famous photo of Vladimir Il'ich Lenin that used to decorate office walls all over the Soviet Union. This portrait of Brodsky became very popular and I have been seeing it these days in many editorial offices of St. Petersburg and Moscow newspapers and magazines.

Once Marx and Engels hung over the heads of editors, along

with the portraits of Lenin and Stalin, Malenkov and Bulganin, Khrushchev, Brezhnev, Gorbachev. And now, if you please, a new icon. A slightly absurd one, perhaps, but how wonderful that we have lived to see these times! [This reminds me of an old Soviet joke: a Pole brings a hard-earned $30 to a bank to open an account, but worries about what will happen if the bank goes under. The clerk reassures him: "Our bank is backed by all the assets of the Polish Socialist Republic, and if Poland itself goes under, by all the economic might of the Soviet Union." "And what if the Soviet Union disappears?" The clerk is astonished: "And to live to see these times, you would not part with $30?"]

I think that not a single television channel, not a single radio station, not a single newspaper or magazine failed to cover the poet's jubilee.

I came back from Petersburg loaded with gifts for Brodsky. The "tribes of the young and unknown" [the quote is from a Pushkin poem] had contributed their poetry collections; composer Sergei Slonimsky, a cassette of the Brodsky poems he had set to music; Elena Chukovskaya, the granddaughter of Korney Chukovsky, sent his "Diaries," and film director Roman Tzurtzumia sent *A Course in the History of Russian Literature*, published in 1866, which he had dug up in an old book store, with the inscription: "To Iosif Brodsky, an aristocrat of the spirit. With love."

Brodsky was cheered by a souvenir that was sent to him by photographer Boris Shvartsman—an old copy of the "Koster" (*Campfire*) youth magazine (No. 12, circa 1966) with a charming and sly poem by Iosif. In the past thirty years it had not been published again, and Brodsky said he had completely forgotten it. He liked the poem and even wanted to know if I had read it to my grandchildren Daniel and Vicki... But my grandchildren are Americans, and the breadth of their knowledge of world history is, how shall I put it, not spectacular. They did not laugh.

THIRTEEN POINTS, or a poem about
WHO DISCOVERED AMERICA

- Shakespeare discovered America.
A long time ago - during the time of - Caesar!

He guided his ship to shore,
Then his throat was cut.

- What are you saying? Shakespeare and America?
He died before they set sail.
It is Copernicus who
had the honor of that discovery.

- Oh, no. Under the pen of Copernicus,
a French poet,
the tragedy, "Romeo
and Juliet" was born.

- No! you are simply crazy!
Really, what's the matter with you?
America, my friends,
was discovered by Torricelli!

- No, no, you are all confused.
Understand this thoroughly:
it was Newton and not Torricelli,
who... - Wait a minute,

it was not Newton, but... - But must we
insist on a name?
Since it was discovered
by the Romans, in something B.C.!

- Without a name
I feel completely depressed.
What's wrong with you? What Romans?
It was discovered by Darwin!

- Not by Darwin, by Byron!
- The bald and browbeaten one?
- No, a well-known lord.
- It wasn't Byron, it was Schiller!

- Stop being silly and trust

a well-founded opinion:
America was put on the map
by Beethoven!

- Beethoven's exemplary
service to science
is well known, but America
was discovered by Leeuwenhoek.

- No, something is wrong here.
It was discovered by... - Lies!
- Bonaparte, I think.
- Exactly, Buonarroti!

- No, no, His Majesty
Charles V... - A delusion!
- ...in the epoch of electricity!
- ...yes, before the Ice Age...

- Shakespeare gave us a detailed...
- Shakespeare? He is from Italy...

Well, and so on
And so forth and so to speak...

The students disputed
Sitting on a windowsill.
I closed the door.

I ask you, urgently,
tell them who it was, really,
that discovered America!

Each correct answer will earn a point!
Tell us, what were those people
here mentioned
famous for?
We're awfully busy,
but the truth is needed.

We hope that you will manage,
though it may not be easy.
There are thirteen people,
historically famous, every one.
FOR EACH CORRECT ANSWER YOU GET A POINT.

[The poem was written for young children to probe their knowledge, and written so that it could be published in the Soviet Union. Yet even here—and this is typical of Brodsky—all the names are the names of Westerners! And this was written at a time when the official position was that Russians are and always were the leaders of world culture.]

I brought Brodsky, as my personal present, an album filled with newspaper and magazine cuttings concerning his jubilee. Iosif (as one would expect) snorted and rolled his eyes to underscore the needlessness and vanity of my efforts. But I could tell that he was pleased, and not indifferent to what was being said and written about him, and how he was being honored, in Petersburg. For instance, he was very touched by Samuel Lurie's congratulatory "Something Like a Toast," and also by Tatiana Vol'tskaya's poem "On the Possible Visit of Brodsky," printed in the newspaper *The Neva Times*.

Now, after his death, Lurie's article seems to me prophetic. Here is a small excerpt from it:

"...Brodsky is so brave that he believes in the existence of the Universe without him... Actually, what he constantly does, is the testing of the given by somebody's absence—most often, his own—showing an incredible presence of mind:

"Only the ashes know what it means to be burnt to the ground.
But I also will say, having nearsightedly glanced ahead:
that not everything is carried off by the wind, not everything picked up by the broom,
When with wide strokes it sweeps the courtyard...

"Brodsky is the most attractive hero of our time and space. The metaphysics of his puns shames death and entropy and inspires the reader with something like respect for the human lot..."

And the poem by Vol'tskaya begins like this:

Do not come back. You will find no one here, Orpheus.
You cannot summon us, like Eurydice.
We are only shadows thrown by the lines of your poem.
The snow is falling and our faces are wild.
<...>
This land, guilty of a crime against you,
Does not want you back and is tired of us,
Since the shadows in shabby coats
Are unworthy of greeting or parting.
And are known to Heaven only because,
Their hands were too weak to hold you...

Five years before the jubilee, in 1990, having come to Russia for the first time after a fifteen-year absence, I photographed Brodsky's house, the balcony, and the windows of his apartment. On the wall next to the building entrance the following message had been scratched with a knife: "In this house, from 1940 to 1972 lived the great Russian poet Iosif Brodsky." "Russian poet" was painted over with green paint, and below it somebody had scratched: "Kike."

"And you are surprised that I don't want to go there?" said Brodsky, putting the picture in his desk drawer.

Unfortunately, he didn't live to see another picture. The year after his death a bronze plaque appeared on the wall of his building with his profile *in relievo* and the following words engraved beneath: "In this house from 1940 to 1972 lived the great Russian poet Iosif Aleksandrovich Brodsky."

So far, nobody has defaced the plaque.

22

After a Long Separation

IN 1988, THE LITERARY WORLD celebrated Anna Akhmatova's 100th birthday. Festivities were not limited to her own country. Harvard hosted an international conference dedicated to her life and work, and there were literary events in New York.

The two "orphans" who were still living in Russia came to the U.S. for the festivities. The arrival of Anatoly Naiman and Evgeny Rein was an important event for Brodsky. After all, when these close friends parted in 1972, all three were sure it was for good. Permission to travel abroad was a special perk which the Soviet government awarded only to a select few. Naiman and Rein had never extolled the virtues of the Soviet system and there was no chance whatever that they would receive such a perk from their "grateful" government. As for Brodsky, the government had washed its hands of him when he emigrated, and didn't want him back. A reunion with his old friends seemed absolutely out of the question until the start of perestroika in 1988. Already the old friends hadn't seen each other for sixteen years, which looked and felt like an eternity.

In America, Brodsky was surrounded by "Western intellectuals" and a swarm of new émigré acquaintances and admirers. Yet I doubt he had any truly close friends besides Baryshnikov and the Loseffs.

Still, his whole youth in Russia had been intertwined with

"Akhmatova's orphans." No one else understood him and his poems so acutely and subtly... Iosif used to say about Rein: "Zhenya has perfect pitch."

I knew that Brodsky was very generous towards his friends—generous not only in the sense of being gracious, helpful, making suggestions for contacts, volunteering references and recommendations and so on, but also generous in the most trivial sense, with his own money. Even when the Soviet system graciously allowed its citizens to go abroad, it was careful not to let them take out enough money to live on. This is why the visitors from the world of forgotten shadows depended on their American hosts for everything, from living accommodations to hot dogs from street vendors.

Being generous is one thing, however, and feeling empathy and excitement quite another. This is why I made a point of asking Joseph what he thought of his old friends after their long estrangement. Had they lived up to his expectations, or was he disillusioned? It turned out that he was not disappointed in Rein after sixteen years of absence. He said, "Everything is fine with Zhenya, it's like we haven't seen each other for a week. He is the same, only wiser and more subdued." When I asked about the way he looked, Brodsky said, "Older, of course... But that was over after five minutes."

Half a year later, Rein came again, this time with his new wife Nadia, twenty something years younger. We knew that Rein had got married, but none of us had seen her. Nadia told me how they first visited Brodsky on Morton Street. Naturally, she was nervous, this first visit was something like a test. Brodsky, according to her, seemed tense; he didn't expect her to be so young (she had just turned thirty) and didn't know what tone to take with her.

Joseph offered a drink right away, but there was only whiskey in the house and Nadia said that she didn't drink anything stronger than wine. This didn't help matters. Joseph seemed to wall her off in his mind. He and Rein had a drink and Brodsky said, "Zhenya, look around the room and choose a present."

"Zhenya, don't miss out! Take something big and valuable," Nadia said. Brodsky snorted; the wall separating them cracked and fell apart.

Then he showed them Greenwich Village and Nadia took many pictures of them during their walk. "That's for Eternity," she said to Brodsky when he asked her to "take it easy."

"You look better than both of us, so give me better a picture of you," Brodsky said to Nadia when they were leaving.

"I don't have one. In our family, I am the photographer," Nadia said.

Later, Brodsky recollected this episode in his conversations with Volkov. When Volkov asked him why he never saw a photograph of Brodsky and Anna Akhmatova together, Brodsky said: "That's right, there is no such photograph. It's funny. Yesterday I was talking to a friend, the wife of a very remarkable poet. And I said to her, 'Give me your picture.' And she said, 'I don't have one. In this marriage, I am the one who takes pictures.'"

Brodsky liked and accepted Nadia. When I asked his impression of her, he answered (as it often happened) in English. "I like her snap, she is a great find for him."

Brodsky thought very highly of the poems of Rein that he hadn't heard before and repeatedly (and publicly) said that he considered Rein his most important mentor. For Rein, who was just starting to establish professional connections in this country, these assertions were of great consequence. They also helped his reputation in Russia.

Rein started writing poetry in the mid-fifties, but by the late eighties, he was still virtually unpublished. All those years he was making his living by writing scripts for documentary movies and other literary moonlighting, and he disdained these sidelines. On several occasions, collections of his poetry were accepted by state publishing houses only to be killed by political forces, sometimes when the book was already in production, two or three weeks before it was due to be shipped to the bookstores. For years, Rein had been fighting deep depressions with intermittent success. Who knows what turn his life would have taken if the Soviet Empire hadn't crumbled.

Rein and Brodsky remained friends for the rest of Brodsky's life. I am sure that Joseph would have been happy to know that Rein, now widely published in Russia and abroad, was awarded the State prize several years ago, and the very prestigious Pushkin

Prize this year.

The reunion with Naiman was not a success, however.

"Well, it was embarrassing," Joseph said to my question, but didn't elaborate.

Naiman and Brodsky had been very close when they were young. In 1961, Brodsky dedicated to Naiman several parts of his poem "The Petersburg Romance." The late friend of Brodsky, Andrei Sergeev, in his book *Omnibus* recalls Brodsky's words: "When I was becoming somebody, I dreamed of learning to write like Naiman. Then I read Frost and realized I could never write like him."

But as early as 1968, Brodsky dedicated "Elegy" to Naiman, indicating a definite crack in their friendship.

> ...Once in this southern town, this
> Backwater, my friend and I chose to meet.
> We were both young, and met on a mall
> built in antiquity. From books
> we'd known of its existence.
> A lot of waves have broken since that time.
> My friend on dry land choked on small
> lies; and I went traveling.
> And now I am standing here
> once again. No one
> met me. And I have no one
> to tell: Meet me someplace, sometime.
> Screams of seagulls.
> Splash of breaking waves.
> A lighthouse, whose tower
> attracts the photographer's gaze, not the sailor's.
> I stand alone on ancient stone,
> my sadness does not defile antiquity,
> but deepens it. The earth, apparently,
> is truly round, since you come
> to a place where there is nothing
> except memories.

Perhaps when we were all young, certain character traits were hidden and when they showed themselves, we would explain them away or brush them off. Wittiness and mastery in playing with words overshadowed self-centeredness and callousness. Young Naiman was fun to be around. This is, for example, how one morning I invited Naiman for dinner that same day: "And please bring a little cheese and a lemon. I hope my request will not burden you too much." His answer: "Oh no, you do not need to worry at all about your request burdening me because I will bring neither cheese nor lemon." I am not sure what you would make of it, but I thought it was witty and I laughed it off.

Young poets didn't need anything from each other except a sensitive ear. They were all equally powerless and oppressed by the system, and in a practical sense could be of little help to each other.

Years later, when it became clear how famous the exiled poet had become, traits like envy, pushiness, and tactlessness became visible in some people, like rust spots. Naiman provides a good example. For years, we corresponded with each other, and I kept him posted about mutual friends. When I wrote him something about Brodsky's plans for the summer, he wrote me back: "Please do not keep me current about the adventures of this *loathsome gentleman.*"

I had no idea why he was characterizing his old friend this way, and was not interested enough to asked Naiman further questions because I thought it must be a trifle rather than real duplicity or enmity. I laughed it off.

Two years later Naiman arrived to the US to celebrate Akhmatova's 100th birthday.

Naiman realized right away how lucky he was to be able to come to the West as a friend of Brodsky's youth, and he cashed in on these opportunities with a vengeance. Because of Joseph, doors opened to him at the universities, and a New York publisher bought out his book *Stories about Anna Akhmatova*. In his essay "The Great Soul" Naiman even quotes Brodsky as saying about this book: "Leave me your manuscript and we'll push it for publication here immediately." [Indeed, Brodsky did so even though he told me he didn't like the book.]

Anyway, Joseph undertook to help publish the *Stories about Anna Akhmatova* and even wrote a foreword to it. Whether he did this of his own free will or got slack "under the gun" as

Naiman later admitted, is not important. I believe that he wouldn't have written it if he didn't want to. But he did write this foreword and put a drop of tar into it. Instead of just praising the book, he compared Naiman's *Stories* to the famous memoirs of Lidya Chukovskaya, an intimate friend of Anna Akhmatova ["*Notes about Anna Akhmatova*"] and he called Naiman's book "second to the best," that is second in quality after the *Notes*.

It doesn't seem right to me to denigrate a book in the foreword by comparing it unfavorably to another book. Newspaper articles and critical reviews do make such comparisons, and that's where they belong. One review would praise the book, another tear it apart, a third would say that not *Stories*, but *Notes* by Chukovskaya is "second to the best." Reviews will be read and forgotten (or remembered), but the foreword is forever linked to the book under the same cover, like a hump on its back.

Why Joseph acted so illogically, was so magnanimous and unfriendly at the same time, remains a mystery.

Nevertheless, Naiman owed to Brodsky both his publications and his academic jobs in America. In "The Great Soul" Naiman confirmed in passing that Brodsky was of help and support to him. "He never refused when something was asked of him."

Without hesitation, Naiman had asked Brodsky (and others) for many favors. Later, Joseph remarked with irritation (and quite justly) that making a career out of friendships with "names" must have been Naiman's preordained role in life. His literary recognition in Russia was due to Akhmatova, his publications and visiting academic positions in the States were due to Brodsky, and his teaching at Oxford was due to Isaiah Berlin...

"A.G. [Naiman] is always demanding something, he is such a perfect user," Joseph once said in English. By the way, Brodsky often switched to English to describe his negative opinions of people, as if the foreign language helped him conceal or "neutrally" express a particular range of feelings. Sometimes it even seemed as if he found speaking English more comfortable and even pleasant. In any case, in English he didn't stammer as much as he did in Russian, didn't pretend to be tongue-tied, didn't repeat and rephrase his thoughts over and over, while his listener waited tensely for the end of the sentence.

Joseph even spoke English with Maria, though she was fluent

in Russian. The fact that the First Russian poet and a Russian-Italian aristocrat communicated with each other in a language foreign to both seemed so unnatural and absurd to me, that I even asked would their daughter ever learn how to speak Russian. Would she be able to read her father's poetry in the original?

"She will if she wants," Brodsky muttered.... So far, Nyusha doesn't speak Russian.

But let us return to Anatoly Genrikhovich Naiman, whom Brodsky called A. G. and addressed formally in the plural and with the patronymic—after so many years, they were still not on a first name basis.

A.G. Naiman was very good-looking in his youth. More than good-looking, he was dazzling. I have a 40-year old picture of A. G. in profile, in a heavy sweater. My female coworkers used to take it on business trips to show to the local supervisor there. Let him see how handsome her husband was and not bother her with the "indecent proposals" so frequent in Russian offices.

A.G., a witty and sparkling chatterbox, was the gem in every gathering. Like a fencing genius, stinging his opponent in a split-second with the sharp point of his rapier, A. G. had a lightning-fast reaction to any remark, elegantly getting the best of his conversational partners.

And he had tons of charm. He could offer compliments, sincerity, irony and sarcasm in such a precise measure, that the resulting mixture was irresistible. In repartee and verbal duels he kept a masterful balance between light flattery and light insult. A.G.'s "charm switch" turned on automatically when meeting a new person or even a domestic animal. If he boarded a streetcar and the woman conductor was not immediately charmed, his day was ruined. He needed everybody's adoration like oxygen.

But time takes its toll. Once when Brodsky ran into a lady of his acquaintance he hadn't seen in many years, he "gallantly" greeted her by saying "Years spare no one." I am not sure whether that lady deserved this greeting, but Naiman definitely did.

And so years did not spare A.G., and not only in terms of good looks. He lost his unique ability to balance on a knife edge. He either leaned too much on the side of insults or too much on the side of flattery. As Joseph said, "A.G. doesn't catch mice any more."

I came in for some of Naiman's light insults, but without a hint of flattery.

I remember the first time A. G. came to visit us in Boston in 1988. Again, it was the first time after so many years of separation during which we did not think that we would ever see each other again, and I was stirred by all kinds of emotions at the thought of this meeting with one who had "risen from the dead." He greeted me by saying: "Ludmila! You know, I cannot help but love you, despite all your shortcomings!" The first, second and third sets of hugs and kisses were followed by smoothly polished tales of mutual friends. We were a grateful audience, starved for news and gossip after thirteen years of absence. Even though we corresponded through letters, we expected the letters to be examined by the censor and could not put too many details on paper. So here in Boston, A.G. was in his element, the center of attention. As expected, his stories about mutual friends were finely crafted, wickedly funny and sometimes malicious.

"Tolya, it seems to me that your mantle of Christian all-forgiveness is fraying," I said. [A few years earlier Naiman had converted to Christianity and became Russian Orthodox.]

"You can't imagine what a shit I'd be without Christianity," replied A.G., who must have known himself better than anyone.

During A.G.'s visit we gave a party to honor him. When I opened our china cabinet and he saw the shelves full of dishes, he exclaimed, "Why, you are so rich!" The nasal voice and folksy intonation signified condescension, something that a real intellectual steeped in spiritual thoughts could feel towards people who devoted all their energies to making money. I began to make excuses—most of the china was bought at yard sales and cost pennies—but A.G. interrupted my feeble apologies with irritation, "Just don't start, 'We came to this country penniless, we achieved everything with hard work...' I can't stand this emigrant nonsense."

After breakfast, A.G. lay on the couch with a phone in his lap and called various countries and states. He would call a friend in England and talk to him in great detail, and then would call a friend in France and describe the previous conversation in the same great detail. A.G.'s telephone escapades would not be worth mentioning if they didn't characterize his general tone and style.

He felt that his old friends, who were so glad to see him and wine and dine him, had become so affluent that he had an innate right to fleece them. And he used this right freely.

On one of A.G.'s visits, he was invited to a party by a mutual friend. One of the guests asked A.G. if he saw the poet K.K. in New York.

A.G. sneered. "That slime, K.K.? Didn't see him and hope I never will."

The guest crawled into a corner as if drenched in camel saliva. (By the way, K.K., an exotic but very amiable person, had never done any harm to A.G. or to anyone else.)

After the party, probably the devil made me do it, I lectured A.G. "Why have you insulted a stranger? What if he is a relative or a friend of K.K.? Otherwise he would not have asked you about K.K. You were not asked what you *thought* of K.K. In the civilized world, when asked whether or not you've seen someone, you answer whether you've seen him or not..."

This provoked an avalanche of accusations accompanied by the already familiar refrain, "What have you all turned into here?"

...After the Nobel Prize, Brodsky's generosity and willingness to help others became legendary in the Russian literary community both in Russia and in the West. [The "West" here is understood as being not only the U.S., but also England, France, Italy and of course all the former Soviet republics that had become independent]. On top of requests for monetary assistance, Brodsky was always buried in pleas for help—arrange a grant, write a letter of recommendation or a foreword/afterword to a book, introduce a literary reading, secure a semester's teaching job at a university. He bought a car for one, a suit or a coat for another, for a third, whose daughter was not recognized as a Russian citizen anymore (the girl was born in Estonia to Russian parents, was not recognized as an Estonian citizen and wasn't admitted to an Estonian university), he paid for her education at a private Moscow university. Many people stayed gratis at his apartment or at his studio, sometimes people who were not particularly close to him.

But Joseph's endless help and attention did not prevent A.G. from complaining about the lack of sensitivity and tact on the part of his benefactor. For instance, Brodsky invited A.G. to a restaurant and on the way they picked up Baryshnikov. Or maybe Baryshnikov picked them up, it doesn't matter. Brodsky and Baryshnikov were sitting in front and A.G. in back. His vanity was wounded. "You see," A.G. said to me indignantly, "they are chattering between themselves, not including me, as if I am not even in the car. And I couldn't take part in their conversation, anyway. They were talking about some Caribbean islands and exotic food I'd never heard of. Why were they showing off in front of me?"

"Sorry, Tolya, but they were not showing off. Just discussing their everyday life. And please notice (I couldn't restrain myself) that they have built this life with their own hands... and legs."

And Brodsky was irritated with A.G.'s meddling in his family and personal business (in particular, his advice for Brodsky to be baptized.) In "The Great Soul," Naiman complains that in response to his suggestion that Brodsky had been stylistically influenced by Henry Miller, Brodsky "began to deny the very premise with the vehemence similar to the rage he had unleashed at me for the *quite innocent* mention of a resemblance to him of an infant born to one of our mutual female friends..."

In other words, Brodsky was annoyed by Naiman's tactless hint even though Naiman called it "a quite innocent mention."

And as much as Brodsky continued to treat Naiman's wife Galya with affection, his attitude towards A.G. became cooler with each visit.

In his essay, Naiman wrote that differing attitudes towards God and Christianity were the cause of their conflict. He mentioned in passing a postcard that Brodsky sent him from London in 1978. I was told of the contents and history of the postcard by our mutual friend Slavinsky. Here is his letter.

"One rainy evening [several days after the death of Elvis Presley] Brodsky and I met in London. Joseph was going to a party, I was on my way to work the night shift at the BBC.

"We both had half an hour to kill which we whiled away with coffee, gossip and literary chatter.

"The conversation touched on the Naimans, with whom I was then in constant and friendly contact. I reported that they were friends with the priest Krasovitsky, that they had a Russian Orthodox idyll going between them... etc.

"'So who is in charge there?' Joseph asked. Perhaps I didn't like something about his tone, or I did not know what he meant and I blurted out at random, 'Seraphim Sarovsky.'

[Seraphim Sarovsky, the Russian Orthodox ascetic, canonized for Sainthood 100 years ago.]

"'Seraphim Sarovsky, Seraphim Sarovsky...' Joseph muttered, and the moment passed. We talked about something else.

"A couple of days later, our mutual friend, Masha Slonim, brought me a postcard written by Brodsky, which he asked to be sent to Naiman. Iosif didn't have his address with him in England. Since the postcard contained a new Joseph poem rather than a private letter, I felt that I could make a copy of it.

"The face side had Elvis at his best—black tie, pomaded hair, very young, leaning on a piano. On the reverse side there was text that Joseph had composed sitting in a pub with Masha and a British friend of hers.

Masha sealed the card in an envelope, wrote the address that I gave her and ... the letter was evidently lost. Naiman says he never received it. But I had a copy and I wrote the text of the poem in a letter to Naiman, which he did receive. [Note: Masha is Russian for Mary and Seraphim is the Russian word for an archangel. Verses in italics are originally in English.]

"Dear Anatoly Genrikhovich,
Look who has died!
Elvis Presley has been taken by the Almighty,
And Seraphim Sarovsky has someone new to talk to.
And Elvis said to Seraphim,
You ain't nothing but a hound dog
Cryin' all the time.
Joseph and Mary and their British buddy sit in a pub,
Seraphim has a halo and Elvis has an aura,
And Joseph has a bald spot and it's all life's fault,
He's cryin' all the time.
Whiskey for a man is like iodine for a cut.
Joseph had a heart attack but now he is all right.
Elvis doesn't drink and Seraphim doesn't drink,
Just a-rockin' and a-rollin'.
Mary hasn't remarried and Joseph, alas, could not,

Seraphim was a bachelor and Elvis was an eagle.
You ain't nothing but a hound dog
Cryin' all the time,
Cryin' all the time,
Cryin' all the time,
You ain't nothing but a hound dog, so bark like the rest.
Elvis tells Seraphim, "I am going,
The next station is Dimitrovsky Highway."
[Dimitrovsky Highway was the street where Naiman lived]
Votre strongly SkuCharlie."

... And now a few more comments about Naiman's literary work. As was the case with Rein, Naiman had been unable to publish his poems under the Soviet regime and he made ends meet by literary moonlighting, mostly translations from foreign languages and from languages of small and large Soviet nations. The Communist Party thought it fitting that culture in the republics should flourish under its guidance. Even mediocre poets and writers in local languages could easily publish their work (as long as it was politically correct), and their books were immediately republished in Russian to demonstrate the cultural achievements of smaller nations. Sometimes Russian translations appeared even before the local original. In some extreme cases, the local "original" did not even exist. This is why the government needed translators into Russian, and accepted the work of people who had not been allowed to publish their own. Unfortunately, unlike Rein, Naiman has not become a significant poet. In my opinion, his poems are lacking depth and passion and sound like pale replicas of certain poems written in the Silver Age.

Maybe he realized this at some point. In the last ten years he has turned himself into a belletrist. I read Naiman's prose with great interest. The author wrote about many people I knew well, a number of whom are good friends.

For example, in the book *The Glorious End of Inglorious Generations*, one of the characters, Naiman's closest friend in the past, Evgeny Rein, was camouflaged by the initials M.M., and this poor M.M. was covered by a thick pile of dirt. In the novel *B.B. and Others*, another close friend, Misha Meilakh, was depicted as a spawn of hell under the initials B.B.

22: After a Long Separation

Those readers who are not familiar with the real-life models would not care if B.B. is really M.B, and M.M. is E.B. But friends of these real-life models got an insight into the charitable Christian heart of the author. This literary exercise had an interesting real-life continuation. In 2003, Naiman took part in a round table at the Russian Book Fair in Frankfurt, Germany, justifying his approach to describing real prototypes. When he finished speaking, Misha Meilakh went to the mike (as a professor of literature at the University of Strasbourg). He said that Naiman had abused his trust in the way he had used the archive that Misha had entrusted to him, and that Naiman would meet his deserts now. Then he turned back and gave A.G. a good slap in the face. The audience had a good time.

The essay about Brodsky, "The Great Soul," made a particularly painful impression on me.

This title is taken from a poem that Brodsky had dedicated to Akhmatova.

Just one quote: "A quarter century later Brodsky's biographer Valentina Polukhina was interviewing me on the way from Nottingham to Stratford on Avon. We were on a bus, I was sitting next to a window in the hot sun. There was no escape, so I regarded the question 'When did you realize that he is a great poetic genius' as part of the general unpleasantness of that trip and snapped that I haven't realized it yet."

It sounds bizarre. One would think that Naiman, a poet and a knowledgeable connoisseur of Russian poetry should be competent to judge who is a genius and who isn't. Yet, amazingly, Naiman considered this question simply unpleasant, as part of "the general unpleasantness of this trip." Yes, it is easy to believe that a genius has friends. But it is much harder to admit that your friend is a genius. Especially if you started together, and at the beginning you played the role of a senior friend to the one who went on to become a genius.

There are quite a few examples of this mean-spiritedness in the text. It seems that Brodsky's worldwide fame and renown irritated Naiman like an itchy boil on his neck. Poison is dripping from his tongue even when he sings Brodsky's praises.

Speaking of Brodsky's independence, Naiman "good-naturedly" described its physical manifestations. "His constant and merciless demonstration of his independence created an awkward, fraught atmosphere that often resulted in angry scenes. It was a trial for a stranger to be in the same room with him for more than five minutes: He wore people out with his 'no,' 'stop-stop,' 'the end of the world,' or even a roar, something between Tarzan and a bull (if bulls roared), with eyes fixed as if in idiotic elation."

I wonder if Naiman would have dared to write this when Brodsky was alive and capable of bestowing further favors?

Elsewhere in the essay Brodsky was depicted as authoritarian, needing to attack, enslave, dominate, an aggressive boor.

"Reciting poetry, the roar of reciting, concerned above all the domination of listeners, bending them to his will and only then conveying to them his meaning. He simply swept people away."

However, Naiman's essay still has glimmers of love for Brodsky. The author allowed himself such a "weakness" after describing an episode humiliating for Brodsky. "It was going on two in the morning, we [Brodsky and Naiman] were walking past the Kuibyshev Hospital where the railing makes a semicircle and inside it there are benches, and someone tripped him from the bench. He lost his footing and began falling, didn't fall all the way, but had to run several steps leaning forward and grabbing the pavement, and there was laughter from the bench. We turned around and the laughter immediately became a threatening growl: some toughs were sitting there, drunk, on drugs, everything you'd expect. He turned away, I did too, we walked on with an air of something between "nothing happened" and "it's one of those things." His hand was scraped, I gave him a handkerchief, or maybe he took out his own, who can remember now? *And I felt such pity for him and such love and did not think of this, and when I remembered, again felt such pity and loved him so much, I wish it were I who got tripped!* " [My italics.]

Was there nothing else to love Brodsky for?

23

Encounters with Mayor Sobchak

BEFORE I FINISH THIS BOOK, I want to write about a man who tried to reconcile Brodsky with his native country. This man, the Petersburg mayor Anatoly Sobchak, did all he could. I have already mentioned that he made Brodsky an honorary citizen of Petersburg and held a large-scale celebration of Brodsky's fifty-fifth birthday.

I first heard of the Petersburg mayor in the fall of 1991 when a friend brought me an amateur videotape of Anatoly Sobchak, speaking at the Palace Square before the Winter Palace on the second day of the putsch—the 20th of August, 1991. The situation was very dangerous, on the verge of a real explosion. The putschists, the old Soviet party and military guard, had arrested Gorbachev and were ruling as an Emergency Committee. They counted on the usual passivity of unorganized people. Indeed, most of the country was passive. Afraid of the outcome for themselves personally, it was hard for individuals to leave their chairs in front of the TV screen, take to the streets and make themselves heard. The putschists' expectations were based on previous events. When the Soviet Union invaded Hungary in 1956, absolutely no one took to the streets. When the Soviet Union invaded Czechoslovakia in August of 1968, only seven people came to Red Square to register their protest and get themselves sentenced to a long prison term.

At the time we did not think about them as "only" seven. We were amazed that even seven cared enough to confront the system. The rest of the country remained quiet. Even though we felt shame at being part of this oppressive regime, none of us openly demonstrated against the invasion in Czechoslovakia. A few poets wrote admonitory poems, but they did not take to the streets.

The putschists expected the same reaction in August of 1991, but to be on the safe side, they sent tanks and troops to Petersburg (it was still Leningrad at the time)—a city that Moscow's rulers had always viewed with suspicion.

Justifiably! The Petersburg mayor Anatoly Sobchak publicly called the putschists criminals that had to be punished. City streets were blocked with barricades to make the movement of troops difficult. Sobchak persuaded the commanders of the Leningrad Military Region to prevent movements of any troops in the city. For the second day of the putsch, August 20, he announced a city-wide strike, and urged the city people to demonstrate against the putsch. More that 300,000 came. Caught by the camera at random, these were not the typical tired and grim Soviet faces to be seen in any context, but energetic faces full of joy and enthusiasm. Pride in their city and their mayor could be seen in their eyes. And Sobchak himself, inspired and courageous, looked like a real people's hero.

Again and again, with a lump in my throat, I reviewed this tape, envying those who were then and there in Leningrad and for the first time regretting that I had left my country sixteen years ago and had not waited for this.

I wanted to know more about Anatoly Sobchak. I found his book, *Going for Power*, in the Harvard library, and from an information agency ordered everything that had been written about him by the American, Russian, and French press.

Having read a pile of articles, essays, interviews, letters written to him, poems of various length, and limericks, I was puzzled by the contradictory—sometimes mutually exclusive—feelings that Anatoly Aleksandrovich inspired in his contemporaries.

He had been compared to Robespierre and de Gaulle, he had received confessions of love and hate. If he was admired by some, he was also hated and threatened by others. He was clearly viewed as one of the top politicians in the country and a possible contender for the Presidency.

One poem (by G. Grigoriev) turned out to be prophetic:

> Arrogant, in an admiral's uniform,
> Kolchak walked proudly toward his fate, born in the city of Peter,
> To become a ruler in Chita.
> Events echo one another,
> And there, probably, is a secret sign
> In that today Peter (sburg) is ruled
> By the born-in-Chita Sobchak.
> How like us, how Russian it all is...
> Comrades from the Cheka
> Put Kolchak before a firing squad in Irkutsk.
> What awaits Sobchak?

[Kolchak was the Russian general who during the Russian revolution remained faithful to the Tsar and was trying to lead troops to Petrograd, but didn't succeed: Communist propagandists got to the troops and demoralized them so that they stopped listening to orders. Chita and Irkutsk are cities in East Siberia.]

The figure of the Petersburg mayor Sobchak seemed so intriguing, so unlike the familiar stereotypes of the Soviet leaders, that I sent a proposal to *Vanity Fair*, offering to write an article about him.

The proposal featured, among other things, this paragraph: "Sobchak indirectly owes his swift rise to power to the American human rights advocate Martin Luther King. As in Martin Luther King's historic speech, where each paragraph began with the words 'I have a dream.' Sobchak began his election campaign for the Supreme Soviet of the USSR in January 1989 with the words 'I also have a dream' in his speech...."

The comparison of a Soviet politician to a black human rights advocate seemed significant to the editors, and Tina Brown, then editor-in-chief of *Vanity Fair*, asked me to come in for an interview. I had already published a few articles for glossy magazines in English, but it was my first experience with *Vanity Fair,* and I was very, very nervous.

"It looks like your mayor is a fascinating character," said Tina Brown. "We've decided to have you do the article. Your task is to do a close-up of Sobchak, get under his skin. And for that you need to talk to his present and former colleagues, political opponents, friends, enemies, wives and mistresses. And, of course, you have to get an interview with Sobchak himself. Do you think you can do it?"

"No problem," said I, bravely.

I was told that Sobchak wasn't well disposed toward journalists, especially those who were also emigrants. In 1992, all emigrants still looked suspicious to the government. No longer viewed as traitors and turncoats, perhaps, still they served as uncontrollable sources of uncensored information for the Soviet people. It was also hard to control what they would say or write after they returned from a visit, and this also annoyed the image-conscious government.

Getting ready to go to Petersburg, I was racking my brains trying to figure out how to get through to Sobchak and overcome the caution which would be inevitable in an interview with an emigrant.

It was clear from his book *Going for Power* that Sobchak was not your run-of-the-mill Soviet leader. In the first place, Soviet leaders did not write books. Why would they? They did not need to work on their image—anything positive that needed to be said about them could be said by official propaganda. There were two exceptions. Nikita Khrushchev wrote his memoir after he was forced out of the office—an illiterate and grumbling piece of work, written to settle scores. It was a transitional time in Soviet history. Khrushchev was the first Soviet leader sent into peaceful, however obscure retirement. However, this did not mean that he could talk directly to the people—publishing was still in the hands of the government, and TV and newspaper journalists were in no hurry to ask Khrushchev for an interview. It was funny to see the former supreme leader resort to *samizdat* to vent his irritation, the same *samizdat* that he was trying to choke while in power. Another memoir was written for Brezhnev to glorify his accomplishments during World War II. It was published during Brezhnev's reign, and Brezhnev clearly had no difficulty finding a publisher (and a ghost-writer as well). The book was written in the official Soviet style, unmistakably pompous, so that it was clear that everything in it was a lie. Even the truth sounded like a lie.

The Sobchak book was different: it was well written and looked as honest and sincere as possible under the circumstances.

Sobchak was born in a rural area far from metropolitan centers, to uneducated parents, but he was bright, ambitious, and hard-working. He was able to enroll in Leningrad University, where he received an excellent education. Eventually he became a law professor at Leningrad University. When the old Soviet election rule—one slot, one candidate—was replaced with a more competitive system, he got into politics. An accomplished speaker, he was heads and shoulders above other candidates in articulating problems and offering ways to solve them, and he became the first freely elected Leningrad mayor. The mayor was no stranger to the fine arts, especially poetry. Sobchak's favorite poet, according to his book, was Marina Tsvetayeva. Here and there glimmered the names of Akhmatova, Mayakovsky, Mandelshtam, Samoilov, Brodsky—the poets that suffered under Soviet power.

It also became clear that Sobchak valued personal relationships with people in the arts and liked to rub shoulders with performers and literary celebrities. Witness to that was his meeting with Yevgeny Yevtushenko, described in the last chapter of his book. A quote:

"And then, till morning—no, not a reception, but rather a get-together. And it turned out that friendships could begin instantly. Yevgeny Yevtushenko and I hid in a corner, and although we had met for the first time that day, couldn't stop talking for a long time."

I couldn't help thinking, cynically, that it was usually the ladies who hid in corners with Yevtushenko, but later I realized that Sobchak's weakness for poets would be my trump card. I decided to bring a very special present for Sobchak: an autographed book from a Nobel Prize laureate.

I called Iosif and the following dialogue took place:

"Hi, Joseph, I am calling to say goodbye. I am flying to Petersburg in a week."

"*Warum?*"

"Tina Brown wants me to write an article about Sobchak."

"Congratulations. You are flying high."

"I will fly even higher, if you do me a *huge* favor: inscribe a book for Sobchak."

"Like hell! What the devil for?"

I had to explain that the mayor was a poetry-lover, and that in one interview he said that during a visit to America he had read six volumes of Brodsky that were still unavailable in Russia. "He called you an astonishing poet by the Grace of God."

"I am so-o flattered."

"Don't get a swelled head—in that same interview he called Gena Khazanov a man with an astonishing mind." [An actor and a satirist.]

"It seems I am in good company," laughed Brodsky. "So what do you, or rather what does he, need my autograph for?"

"It is important for the Petersburg mayor to receive as a gift a book autographed by an exiled Leningrad poet. It is striking and symbolic."

"And what do *you* need all those symbols for?"

I had to confess that it was to help me. A book from the Nobel Prize laureate Iosif Brodsky would be an "Open, Sesame"—extremely vital for my assignment.

"Well, old fox, if it's so important, come over," grumbled Iosif.

And that is how I got a present for Sobchak: the collection *The End of a Beautiful Era* with a great inscription:

To the town Head from the town Lunatic.
                              Iosif Brodsky

During our very first meeting in the Smol'ny Palace I handed Sobchak the blue volume, published by Ardis. Anatoly Aleksandrovich was sincerely touched.

He asked me quite a few questions about Brodsky: about his health, his family, his work as poet laureate. And then he said: "We'd like very much to invite him to visit Petersburg. Do you think he would come?"

I did not have a good answer for him. Brodsky was in no hurry to join the stream of former exiles who were coming back to show off before old friends, as good as telling them: "You see,

they did not want me here, but look what became of me there."
Brodsky knew that during any party, reception, presentation or
even on the street, he would hear friendly words from people
who in the past had cooperated with the System, and he did not
want to smile back and say small, nice things. Neither did he
want to be blunt and tell them what he thought of them.

Afterwards it turned out that all my fears about the unfriendly
mayor were groundless. Both Sobchak and his press secretary,
Vasilevskaya, turned out to be former students of my father who
remembered him very well.

I wrote an article for *Vanity Fair*. Unfortunately for me, by
that time Tina Brown had moved on to *The New Yorker*, and the
new editor of *Vanity Fair*, Graydon Carter, couldn't have cared
less about the St. Petersburg mayor. So my article in English was
killed. For the Russian-language readers, I wrote a larger piece
that was printed in installments in the New York Russian-
language newspaper *Novoye Russkoye Slovo*, but no magazine
in Russia dared to publish it—it was quite irreverent, and Sobchak
was at that time a serious contender to become Yeltsin's heir.

Two years went by. In 1994, the rumors that Sobchak "had
made personal contact" with Brodsky had been persistently
circulating for some time. He invited Joseph to come to Petersburg
and promised that he would be treated like royalty: he would
stay in a mansion on Kamenny Island [usually reserved for
political dignitaries], he would have a personal cardiologist on
call around the clock, parties and receptions on the highest level
would be given in his honor. Sobchak loved "the flash and crackle
of balls" [to quote Pushkin's *Evgeny Onegin*] and wanted to
make the visit of the Nobel Prize laureate the social and cultural
event of the year. However, that was exactly what Brodsky wanted
to avoid. Iosif did not find the prospect of mass jubilation
tempting. Not that he didn't want to "come home" on principle.
He and Baryshnikov often discussed a possible visit to Petersburg,
but only in a "private capacity"—without welcoming committees,
without pomp, without floodlights. One of the ideas was to come
on a boat with a tour group from Helsinki. The tourists would
spend three days in the city and sleep on board the ship. Such an
arrangement did not even require a visa. Iosif joked that to be
completely incognito he would wear a wig and Misha would

wear a false moustache and a beard. Or the other way around—
Iosif would wear a beard and Misha a wig.

In March of 1995 Sobchak came to New York. The itinerary
of his visit was very intense, but included a meeting with Brodsky.

Sobchak stayed at the Waldorf-Astoria. He called Joseph and
invited him to breakfast with him at 9 in the morning. Joseph
did not want to go—for Brodsky, Sobchak was not a former law
professor but an active high-level Russian official. Also, he did
not like the Waldorf-Astoria. However, as he had before and
would again, Iosif gave in and accepted the invitation. And, as
he had before and would again, he regretted it. Not the meeting
itself—he liked Sobchak. It seemed, however, that Joseph's pride
was hurt that all the St. Petersburg mayor's lunches and dinners
were given over to other meetings, so that he could find only the
early morning for Brodsky. "I don't understand," Iosif groused
afterward, "why did I drag myself over there so early?...."

He was very displeased with himself and did not hide it. As to
whether Sobchak had talked him into going to Russia, Joseph
said that he had made no decision yet. But it seems that during
their meeting, Brodsky had not been able to say "no" and had
told Sobchak that he would come, even though he did not want
to admit it to me.

Why do I think so? On the sixth of April, 1995, Iosif called
me from South Hadley and asked whether I had Sobchak's
coordinates. I gave him his home phone number and the fax
numbers of the Petersburg city hall and of his office in the
Maryinsky Palace.

Coming to Boston two days later, Brodsky gave me a letter to
Sobchak, suggesting that I read it and send it to Petersburg as
soon as possible. I asked his permission to make a copy for myself.

Among other things, Brodsky wrote:

"...It is with regret that I wish to let you know that my plans
for the summer have changed drastically, and it looks like I will
be unable to visit my home town at this time. I apologize for the
inconvenience and the trouble; I hope, however, that they are
minor.

"Aside from the purely concrete circumstances that interfere
with the visit taking place at the proposed time, I am also held
back from it by a number of purely subjective considerations. In

particular, the prospect of finding myself the object of a positive experience on a mass scale grates on me; such things are difficult enough on a personal level.

"Do not misunderstand me: I am extremely grateful to you for taking the initiative. This gratitude is sincere and is directed to you personally; it was precisely this that made me accept your invitation in the first place. But I am afraid that the realization of this project demands certain inner, as well as purely physical resources, which I do not possess at the moment.

"God willing, I will come to my home town; apparently, it is inevitable. I think it would be best to do it privately, without making too much noise. If this happens, be assured that you will be among the first to learn of it: I will let you know by appearing on your threshold..."

Brodsky never appeared on Sobchak's threshold. And the very same year that Brodsky passed away, Sobchak's star had waned. Yeltsin had come to fear his influential rival and made sure that Sobchak was not reelected as Petersburg mayor. Then the legal prosecution of the former leader began, and Sobchak was forced to emigrate to France. He says that he went there, first and foremost, for medical treatment. However, true to his nature, he used his time there to write several books discussing the past and future of Russia. Then, as it very often happens in politics, the tables were turned, and the careers of several of Sobchak's former protégés took off: one of them was Putin. Sobchak returned to Russia at the end of 1999. Nevertheless, his political resurrection was not complete. A force more powerful than electoral returns interfered with the fate of Russia, and Sobchak died from a heart attack on February 20, 2000. He was buried in the Nikolsky cemetery of Aleksandro-Nevsky Lavra. He was only 62 years old...

...By a strange coincidence his grave is next to the grave of Galina Starovoitova, a Russian politician with whom Joseph Brodsky became friends in 1994, when she was a visiting professor at Brown University. Starovoitova was a rising star of the democratic faction in the Russian parliament (the "Duma"). At one time she was a Yeltsin adviser on ethnic and national issues. She was a fearless human rights advocate and one of the earliest and most vocal opponents of the Chechen war. Brodsky and Starovoitova met in 1994, in Sweden, and liked each other very much. Iosif loved talking politics and, although he usually had inflexible opinions about everything, he listened to Starovoitova's judgments with great interest and trusted them. He fully appreciated her erudition and her logical mind. Knowing that Galina Starovoitova is a good friend of mine and stayed with us when she came to Boston, Brodsky sent us a book for her with a very warm inscription, and always asked us to give her his greetings. He used to say that if the Russian government was made up of people like Starovoitova, he would not be ashamed of his country.

And Galina Vasil'yevna admired Iosif Brodsky, knew a great many of his poems by heart and loved to read them out loud.

Once, talking about the nostalgia which haunts many immigrants, I confessed to her that all my nostalgia was focused on Leningrad. (I left the country before Sobchak renamed it St. Petersburg.) Starovoitova said that she understood that very well, and that she herself, not from across the ocean but only in Moscow, often felt a piercing, almost painful love for Petersburg.

"Iosif expressed these feelings best," she said once, with his poem "Stanzas to the City" in mind.

In November 1998, at the age of 54, Galina Starovoitova was gunned down in the stairwell of her home in St. Petersburg. Yeltsin swore that the killers and those who ordered the murder would be found and punished. So far, the oath has not been fulfilled. In Russia, not only are poets an endangered species; democratic politicians should be on their guard as well.

When Sobchak came back to Russia from his exile in France, he visited Starovoitova's grave. In one of his interviews he said that he had liked the place and would like to be buried there some day. He did not know how close that day was. But his desire was fulfilled.

It is remarkable that the only two Russian politicians that Brodsky personally knew and accepted survived him for a very short time only. If the mortality rate among selfless politicians was lower, a serious blot on Russia's reputation in the family of nations would be removed.

24

The Final Chapter

WHEN I WAS A TALK SHOW HOST on the Russian language radio station WMNB, listeners often asked me "Why does Brodsky never read to a Russian audience?"

The "never" was an emotional exaggeration of course, but in truth Joseph addressed his compatriots rarely. He was lecturing and reading poetry on university campuses, and these events catered to Americans. When faculty and students from Slavic departments were in the audience, Brodsky would read some poems in Russian, but most poems he read in English, in his own or in somebody else's translation, and questions and answers were in English, too. This is why few Russians attended these readings. In general, Russians love poetry and adore poets as much as Americans love rock music and adore pop stars. In the last ten years of his life Brodsky became a living legend among Russian émigrés, and Russians were eager to meet him and hear him read, but only when he was reading in Russian.

Most Soviet émigrés are "big city" people. In America, most of them had settled, by preference, in large metropolitan centers. Jobs were a big factor in this, of course. There were more white-collar jobs in urban centers, and potential employers were less likely to be put off by a foreign accent or broken English. Another factor was the proximity of other Russians. For newcomers, the Russian community was a source of friends, job leads, and professional references. Previous arrivals who had already earned a good reputation among employers for their skills, education, and work ethic made it much easier for the newcomers to find a job. Finally, Russians are avid museum-goers and eager to attend exhibitions, concerts of classical music, classical plays. In many cases Russian intellectuals who had settled in places where there were few other Russians, even a nice university town, felt that they were living in a cultural desert, a place where there was nobody to talk to. Often such Russians would hie themselves to New York City, Los Angeles, Boston, or another center of the Russian diaspora. Joseph's poem about his life in Ann Arbor, written in 1972, soon after his arrival in the US, gives a vivid description of the desperate loneliness some Russians were feeling.

* * *

An autumn evening in the modest square
of a small town proud to have made the atlas
(some frenzy drove that poor mapmaker witless,
or else he had the daughter of the mayor).

Here Space appears unnerved by its own feats
and glad to drop the burden of its greatness—
to shrink to the dimensions of Main Street;
and Time, chilled to its bone, stares at the clockface
above the general store, whose crowded shelves
hold every item that this world produces,
from fancy amateur stargazers' tel-
escopes to common pins for common uses.

A movie theater, a few saloons,
around the bend a café with drawn shutters,
a red-brick bank topped with spread-eagle plumes,
a church, whose net—to fish for men—now flutters
unfilled, and which would be paid little heed,
except that it stands next to the post office.
and if parishioners should cease to breed,
the pastor would start christening their autos.

Grasshoppers, in the silence, run amok.

By 6 p.m. the city streets are empty,
unpeopled as if by a nuclear strike.
Just surfacing, the moon swims to the center
of this black window square, like some Eccles-
iastes, glowering; while on the lonely
highway, from time to time, a Buick beams
its blinding headlights at the Unknown Soldier.

The dreams you dream are not of girls half nude
but of your name on an arriving letter.
A morning milkman, seeing milk that's soured,
Will be the first to guess that you have died here.
Here you can live, ignoring calendars,
gulp Bromo, never leave the house; just settle
and stare at your reflection in the glass,
as streetlamps stare at theirs in shrinking puddles.

(Translated by George L. Kline, first appeared in *Confrontation 8*, Spring 1974)

So...I thought it was a good idea for Brodsky to go on a Russian literary tour across America, giving public readings in the centers where Russians lived in large numbers. In February 1995, I visited Iosif in South Hadley, brought him a few pounds of exotic coffee beans as a bribe, and painted a tragic picture of the Russian communities in the US, starved for poetry. Though I had tried to persuade him to give poetry readings before, this time I really pressed him hard. Why was I so persistent? Did I feel that he would not be around for a long time? I do not know.

Fortunately, this time Iosif was in a mellow mood and, to my surprise, quite agreeable. Moreover, he looked enthusiastic. We decided that he would read in New York and Boston in April 1996, and then would continue the tour in November, since he was not teaching the Fall semester. Natan Slezinger and I worked out his itinerary, and Iosif asked us to coordinate the schedule with his secretary Ann Kjellberg. I have kept a copy of my letter about the upcoming "tour."

"Joseph, dearest!
I called Ann several times, left messages, but she, *hélas*, did

not respond. Perhaps she is not in town? Natan has to reserve the halls, so we need a confirmation of your fall readings ASAP. The Russian masses, having heard of your coming, are full of literary enthusiasm.

This is the proposed itinerary:
October 28, Saturday - Detroit
November 12, Sunday - Chicago
November 15, Wednesday - San Jose
November 16, Thursday - San Francisco
November 17, Friday - REST
November 18, Saturday - Los Angeles

There is no decision made about Toronto as of yet. It could be combined with Detroit - then the reading there would take place on October 29, or with Chicago - in which case it would be on the same weekend, that is, Friday, November 10.

I coordinated these dates with Ann previously. She said that on the weekend of November 4-5 you are busy in Texas, but the weekend of November 10-12 got conveniently freed up due to some NYC events being canceled.

Please, call me or ask Ann to call right away. I'll be in town till August 19, after which you can reach me in Hyannis.

Hugs and kisses to you and your ladies.

Your L."

A few days later Brodsky called me, approved the schedule and we started working on the details.

His first appearance took place on April 2 in New York, in the Home of the Society for Ethical Culture on the corner of Central Park West and 64th Street, and his second one on April 9, at Boston University. This reading turned out to be the last one.

The Morse Auditorium at BU is a large hall with an eight-hundred-seat capacity... but over a thousand people came to the Brodsky reading. People sat in folding chairs and on the floor in the aisles, they stood against the walls all along the auditorium. Even so, a large part of the crowd remained "overboard."

In both these events I had the honor of introducing Brodsky

to the audience. After the reading in Boston, somebody asked him: "What finally induced you to read before an immigrant audience?" Brodsky said, "Shtern. Ludmila Shtern induced me..."—and offered no other explanation. The memory of these words is dear to me.

Before the reading Brodsky surprised me by asking: "Any suggestions, Ludessa? What poems do you think I have to recite?"

I said that we expected a very mixed audience. Some people would be literary by education, some would know only his early romantic verses, and others, especially youngsters, might not know his poems at all, and would come because he was so famous. Therefore, I suggested that he should choose poems of "medium length" that were not terribly sophisticated or philosophical. Joseph nodded as if he agreed with me... and read, among others, some of his long and difficult poems, such as "Portrait of Tragedy," "Cappadocia" and "Triton."

It turned out that I underestimated the Russian audience. Also, that there was some sheer magic in the way Brodsky read his poetry. The tone of his voice, its loudness, the movement of his hands and torso—everything was beautiful and raised deep emotions. The manner of the presentation was almost as important as its content. For that matter, Brodsky disliked the way professional artists read his poetry, and professional artists, my friends among them, spoke of the way Brodsky recited with obvious condescension. That night in Boston his audience received even his most difficult poems ecstatically, with genuine admiration. I was happy to see that Joseph was moved...

Very moved and very tired. The written questions formed a pile of white notes.

Here are some of them:

Q. *You have been living in the U.S. for 23 years, but you will always remain a Russian poet in history. Your mass readership will always be in Russia. Would you like to follow the footsteps of Tsvetayeva and Solzhenitsyn?*

[Marina Tsvetayeva had returned to the Soviet Union from France in 1939 and committed suicide in the town of Yelabuga in 1941. Alexander Solzhenitsyn returned to Russia in 1994 and tried to help his country by playing the role of a prophet who knew in what direction it should move, but found a deaf ear, and the ratings of his TV show and sales of his books declined.]

A. I certainly don't want to follow in Tsvetayeva's footsteps. I don't want to follow the Solzhenitsyn example either. My life is my life, but not a life of literature, or the literary tradition.

Q. *How have you managed, without even graduating from high school, to think and write the way you do. A genius? But one needs a great erudition, a knowledge of the laws and rules of versification and prosody. Who helped you to develop into a serious poet so fast: a person or the books?*

A. The books.

Q. *What is happening with the Russian language of Russian emigrants in the U.S.?*

A. I can speak only for myself. At the beginning, I was in a state of real panic and trepidation. For instance, on the third or fourth day after I landed in Vienna, I was trying to find a rhyme to some word. I didn't succeed and was really shocked. That had never happened before. I could get a rhyme to any Russian word, or so I thought. I got scared that something horrible was happening. I started forgetting Russian. The next day I found that damned rhyme. But, generally speaking, some conservation of a living language by people who live outside their native country is inevitable. But in 1995, it is not as frightening as it was 20-30 years ago.

Q. *Do you love beautiful women and what exactly do you love?*

A. Yes, I do. But I am not Karl Marx to formulate.

Some of the questions, concerning his ethnic origin and "relationship" with religion were too bold and somewhat tactless. Joseph was trying to answer them good-naturedly, without a trace of his traditional sarcasm. The years of teaching in American universities, obviously, had schooled him in patience and tolerance.

After the reading we went to the St. Petersburg Café in Brookline. Natan Slezinger and his wife Lusya, the owners of this small, elegant place, fixed a delicious dinner with all of Brodsky's favorite dishes: *studen', lobio, vinagrette, herring with dill, and pel'meni.*

Joseph looked relaxed, praised the food and the ambience of

the café and asked to get himself photographed with Simon Okshtein's painting (a picture of a half-naked lady) in the background.

I congratulated myself on the success of the "Brodsky enterprise" and anticipated his triumph in the fall.

In June of 1995, Baryshnikov and his troupe performed at the Jacob's Pillow Dance Festival in the Berkshires (in western Massachusetts). At the entrance to the Art Center stood a man, holding a full-grown bear by the collar. I asked if the bear was going to the show. The man nodded: "Mishka is a fan of Misha." [Mishka in Russian is a nickname for a bear.]

The show would begin in twenty minutes. I walked into a café under a tent and saw Brodsky. He sat alone at a table, looking somehow lonely and estranged. I thought that a ballet performance was not at all where he wanted to be at the moment.

"You are the last person I expected to meet here," I said, coming up.

"I can't refuse Misha'..."

"Your presence is God's gift to him," I said, "but I didn't come to the show with empty hands. Look what I've got"

Just two weeks earlier I had attended a celebration of Brodsky's 55th birthday in St. Petersburg and had picked up a few copies of his new collection *V Okrestnostyakh Atlantidy* (*In the Environs of Atlantis*) which had been published in Russia. I handed Joseph a book and asked him to write an inscription for Misha.

"What should I write?" he asked. He really looked exhausted.

"Tell him that he even won the heart of a wild bear." I told him how I had met the bear at the entrance, and that he might even come to the show. He nodded, took a book and wrote a two-line dedication that rhymed a "mishka bear, prancing" with "Mishka dancing."

"If I knew you were going to be here," I said, "I would have brought my copy of the *Atlantis* to be signed, too..."

"There'll be time... If I am still around."

He looked very tired that evening. I asked him about his health and he replied "Now every day is a gift or... a miracle."

I said something trite, something to the effect that the "miracle" could last many years if he would change his habits and start taking care of himself.

Joseph shrugged. He did not want to change anything: did not agree to any diet, drank whiskey and very strong coffee, and smoked, smoked, smoked, breaking the filters off his cigarettes.

For about a year and a half I had been trying to drag him to see a famous Boston physician who was successfully treating smokers using hypnosis. Two of our chain-smoker friends, who used to smoke from one-and-a-half to two packs a day, were broken of the habit for good after one session with him.

Brodsky either laughed it off or waved the whole subject away. But on that ballet night in the summer theater I just would not let go. He said, "Maybe, we'll see." I asked when exactly he was going to see this doctor. He said that he was planning to be in Boston in the next few days, and I suggested that I would make the appointment and go to the doctor with him. Joseph asked if I had the doctor's phone number. I did. He wrote the doctor's number down and said, "If I decide to undergo it, I'll manage the appointment myself."

He called me several days later: "Ludessa, you owe me 100 bucks."

It turned out that the good doctor had a special policy of no money back. The first thing his receptionist had demanded was a check.

The doctor invited him into the office, told him of his methods, and proceeded with the hypnosis. Joseph started giggling at the very first "passes," and in three minutes "lost it completely," as he put it when he described the experience to me later. The doctor grew wrathful, stopped the hypnosis, and said that he wouldn't waste his valuable time on such a patient, since Brodsky, supposedly, did not respond to hypnosis. "You have a willpower of steel," said he. "What good is my willpower of steel, if I can't quit smoking?" Iosif objected. "Not can't—won't," said the doctor, who then went to the door, indicating that the session was over.

"What about the money?" asked Iosif. "My time is expensive," said the famous hypnotist in an icy voice.

In late April Brodsky left for Italy. He had a literary reading in Florence, in the Palazzo Vecchio.

The *Sale Cinquecento* (The Hall of Five Hundred) was packed. Brodsky was awarded an ancient Florentine coin—a *fiorino d'oro*.

Before Brodsky this honor had been given to only two Russians: academician Andrei Sakharov and Mikhail Gorbachev. Joseph seemed amused to find himself in the company of Gorbachev. After the reading he was signing a lot of autographs and answered questions in English, until our mutual friend Galina Dozmarova yelled: "Could you please speak Russian? You've been simultaneously translated into Italian." So Joseph switched to Russian.

I called him in July, he was in Lucca that time. We discussed his upcoming fall tour, but deep inside I felt a foreboding. With reason, as it turned out. Those literary evenings, so anticipated by lovers of Russian poetry, had to be canceled. In October Brodsky fell very ill, complaining that he could not walk a hundred yards without nitroglycerin. He said he was unable to read or fly, and apologized for letting everybody down.

I saw Iosif for the last time at the *Russian Samovar* toward the end of December 1995. He said that the doctors were insisting that he have yet another surgery, and that it had to be done before the start of the spring semester. That is, the surgery had to be done right away or postponed for several months. I tried to encourage him to go through with the surgery—not to postpone it. "Look, everybody is undergoing all kinds of surgeries these days, with all these cancers, heart attacks and strokes around us. Why should you be different? Take my husband, for example. A healthy person, quit smoking twenty years ago, keeps to his diet, runs and walks for exercise—he is scheduled for surgery in early January of next year. Cancer. It is not a good idea to wait."

The medical luminary who performed the surgery on Vitya screwed it up: there were complications and Vitya was suffering dreadful postoperative pain. January 15th Brodsky called us and asked a dozen questions about the surgery and Vitya's condition. They weren't formal questions that people often ask out of politeness. He really moved us by going into all the details and showing a genuine concern. As far back as I could remember, Brodsky had been reading medical books and was familiar with the treatments for all sorts of diseases. He was not stingy with medical advice and, I was sure, had he not discovered his poetic gift from God so early in life, he would have become a physician.

On that day he discussed Vitya's problems in a professional way. And we, in our turn, were asking him what he was waiting for and why he did not go for the "procedure" immediately.

Iosif said simply, "I know that it's my only chance. But, I am afraid. If I manage to make it to the end of the spring semester I'll go... But I am so scared."

It was the nineteenth of January and that was the last talk we had with him.

...Sasha Sumerkin, Brodsky's friend and a translator of his English language essays into Russian, told us how Elena Chernysheva, who lived in Philadelphia at that time, came on January 22 to New York and met Iosif for a cup of coffee. Iosif was then on his way to the doctor, to discuss the results of yet another cardiological test (results that were no comfort, as it turned out). They did not talk much about health issues—mostly about friends and what each was doing. Iosif could not have been feeling very cheerful. The inscription he wrote on "*Atlantis*" was as follows:

> *To Elena Chernyshova* [sic][A.S.]
> with a great many kisses.
>
> Let this small volume remind you
> that the author was no lout, no pansy,
> no coward, no snob, no liberal,
> but a general of sad thoughts.
> Joseph
> New York, January 22, 1996

Handing her the book, he said, "And the next one you will get from Sumerkin." Dumbstruck, she did not ask him why.[1]

And on the day before, on January 21, Iosif gave yet another book to Baryshnikov with a very similar inscription:

> To Michel', with tenderness.
> This small volume will, perchance, remind you
> that the author was no lout, no pansy,
> no coward, no snob, no liberal,
> but a general of sad thoughts.

On Friday, January 26, Sumerkin visited Brodsky along with

their mutual friend, the pianist Elisaveta Leonskaya. This is how Sumerkin described that evening:

"Maria prepared a wonderful supper, which was crowned by a homemade and absolutely heavenly *tiramisu*, and Iosif, with his usual hospitality, bought various Chinese delicacies for the rare guest. To our joy, he was in fine fettle: he looked well, his talk was, as always, inspired, he ate with appetite and drank some extremely powerful Swedish herbal vodka—I got dizzy just from smelling it. It was an idyllic picture, helped along not a little by Anna, blue-eyed and bright, who got angry at me whenever I did not understand her English sentences right away.

After the supper we went up to his "ship's-cabin-attic" on the second floor (one could smoke there). On the table lay proofs of the big, half-a-column's worth, poem "The Emperor" from the *Times Literary Supplement,* and out of the typewriter stuck the latest children's poems in English (so that Anna could have something to read when she knew how). The usual piles of books, magazines, letters lay around. Iosif, as was his habit, broke a filter off his Kent, rolled the cigarette lovingly in his fingers for a while, then lit it. All the business we had together was, for the moment, concluded: the final additions to "The Landscape" went to Ardis; the texts for "The Briefcase" were proofread; we talked a little about making a collection of his occasional verse—he clearly liked that idea. He gave Lisa a copy of *"Atlantis"* with an inscription:

> I am giving poems to Elisaveta,
> She will forgive me them
> As I, growling in my heart,
> Forgave her Petr Il'yich.

January 26, 1996. Iosif.

These were, possibly, the last lines Brodsky wrote in Russian. [He could not stand Petr Il'ich Tchaikovsky, whose concertos Leonskaya was playing on her New York tour.] A day later, on Sunday, he was going to go to his college in South Hadley—the Spring semester was beginning, and he hoped to repeat his last year's trick: to hide from the doctors and from illness in quiet

Massachusetts.[2]

January 27 is Baryshnikov's birthday. Unlike Brodsky, who loved birthdays and always had crowds to celebrate them with him, Misha usually did not celebrate his at all. Nevertheless, on that day he and Iosif always tried to get together. But on the 27th of January, 1996, Baryshnikov was in Miami and Brodsky congratulated him over the phone. Misha remembers that they spoke for about forty-five minutes. Nothing important was discussed. Iosif said that if he could, he would fly to Miami for the evening, but he did not feel very well. He asked Misha about his health and "ordered" him to drink lots of vodka that night. Baryshnikov answered that he could not drink "as he should" because he would have a headache the next morning.

"You have a headache the morning after?" Brodsky sounded alarmed. "Isn't that horrible? It means that something is definitely very wrong. Please, talk to your doctor as soon as possible."

This joking advice, given a few hours before Iosif's death, became branded on Misha's mind forever.

Brodsky was speaking to Baryshnikov from his study on the second floor. He said that some friends had just dropped in, and he had to go down to them to say goodbye...

After the guests left, he again went upstairs to his study...

On the following night, at two in the morning, I received a telephone call from Moscow. The person calling was Galina Starovoitova. I heard, from the tone of her voice, that she already knew about the death of Iosif Brodsky. I felt that she was in tears.

"I cannot help repeating these lines again and again," she said and began reading to me over the telephone from Brodsky's poem "Stanzas to the City:"

Let it not be my fate
to die far from you,
in the dovish mountains,
echoing the bowlegged boy.

[Poet Mikhail Lermontov was killed in a duel in the Caucasus Mountains in 1841 during a war against the Chechens.]

Let it not be my fate,

either, hurrying the clouds,
to see in the dark
my tears and my pitiful grief.

Let my burial service be sung
by the choir of water and sky, let the granite
embrace me,
let it swallow me,
remembering this step;
let my burial service be sung,
and let me, a fugitive, blaze
with your eternal earthly glory
on a white night.

Everything will fall silent around.
Only a black tug will scream
in the middle of the river,
frenziedly fighting the dark,
and the flying night
will betroth this poor life
to your beauty, and to
the truth that will survive.[3]

The telephone receiver crackled, the voice from across the ocean was muffled. How could we know that these lines would turn out to be prophetic for Galina Starovoitova also...?

Starovoitova called not only as a friend and a lover of poetry, but also as a Russian government official. She was asking if there was a hope that the family would agree to bury Brodsky in St. Petersburg, in Aleksandro-Nevsky Lavra, the last resting place of Russian cultural icons, or in Komarovo, next to Anna Akhmatova.

She said that the Russian government would pay all the expenses. I gave Starovoitova Maria Brodsky's phone number and the next day she approached her with her request.

There were many speculations at that time about Brodsky's final resting place. Some people thought, and rightly, that he had to return to his homeland. Everybody in Russia knew by heart

Pushkin's famous poem, "The Monument."

> I erected the monument to myself, not made by human hands,
> The people's path to it will not be overgrown...

Well, even though Pushkin did not think about his fame in terms of physical monuments, the Russian love for poetry decided otherwise. Monuments to Pushkin made by the greatest Russian sculptors decorate public squares in Moscow, Petersburg and other cities. Romantic couples, when meeting for a date, wait for each other at the Pushkin monument. Pushkin died more than 150 years ago, but people still bring flowers to his monuments. He is buried far from Moscow and Petersburg, but his grave is a popular tourist attraction. Granted, not all the visitors understand poetry; some come just because it is a "must" to see the great Russian poet's grave. But for many lovers of poetry, visiting a poet's place of final rest is an uplifting spiritual experience. And Pushkin is not the only poet whose grave draws visitors. Akhmatova and Pasternak died relatively recently, and no monuments to them have yet been erected. But their graves in Komarovo near Petersburg and in Peredelkino near Moscow draw a lot of visitors. So, Brodsky's admirers in Russia hoped to be able to beat "the people's path" to his grave for years to come. Obviously, more people would visit his grave if it were in Petersburg than if it were located abroad, no matter how important the city or situation.

There were some indications that Brodsky himself thought about being in his homeland after death. In 1962, when he was only twenty-two years old and still lived in Leningrad, he wrote one of his most famous early poems, which starts with beautiful lines about Vasilievsky Island, one of the districts of Leningrad:

> I don't want to choose the country, or the grave,
> I will come to Vasilievsky Island to die.

These lines are often interpreted as the poet's "last will" to be buried in Leningrad. However, Brodsky was not in the mood to give instructions about his funerals at that time. There are no cemeteries in Vasilievsky Island: it is all residential except for a few colleges and a harbor. The poem just speaks of the poet's love for a woman who lived on Vasilievsky Island.

The first line of his "Stanzas to the City" that Starovoitova read to me over the phone from Moscow are also interpreted as Brodsky's desire to be buried in Leningrad:

Let it not be my fate
to die far from you...

But this poem was written in the same 1962, and also tells about the poet's desire to die close to the object of his love, and not about his desire to be buried there.

As far as I know, Brodsky didn't leave any written request about his final resting place. One of our mutual friends said that Joseph had told him that if he died in Mount Holyoke he wanted to be buried there just to spare his family trouble and expense...

We said goodbye to Brodsky in his beloved Greenwich Village, not far from his former home on Morton Street.

The coffin was open and half of it was covered by a green silk cloak with a yellow ribbon in the middle. There was a Catholic cross in his hands. Whether it was his will or Maria's decision, I do not know. A grieving crowd surrounded the funeral home for two days. On the second day a pompous cortege arrived. The Russian Prime Minister Chernomyrdin with his retinue and reporters showed up bringing an ugly official-looking wreath, just like the ones they were using for the funerals of the highest Soviet officials and military brass. Maybe his feelings were sincere, but I cannot help but think that government officials had only dared to approach Brodsky now that he was not able to reject their overtures. They hadn't expressed any repentance or paid him any particular respect when he was alive, despite many opportunities to do so. We Russians were startled to learn that American officials like Clinton felt the need to apologize to African-Americans for the slavery that had been abolished a hundred and fifty years ago, at the same time as serfdom was abolished in Tsarist Russia. Why had Gorbachev and Yeltsin not apologized to Brodsky for what their predecessors had done to him and to his family? (Or, for that matter, to all the people who had been forced into exile, forced to give up their earthly goods, their pension rights, and the right to see their friends and relatives.)

To say goodbye to Joseph, two of "Akhmatova's orphans," Rein and Naiman, arrived from Moscow. The third one, Dmitri Bobyshev, didn't come. Evgeny Rein wrote of this farewell as follows:

A small crush of people on Bleecker Street in Greenwich Village,
  greet each other quietly, a cigarette is being offered.
  Good Lord, what won't you see here for the occasion -
  the limousine of a Prime-Minister, a superstar of ballet!
  <...>
  They are coming back, getting something to eat during a break,
  they present some argument, who knows why.
  But the one I've been waiting for, three days now,
  does not come, oh my God, does not come.[4]

Brodsky's body was being kept at Grace Church, Brooklyn Heights. During the service it was announced that he would eventually be buried in Venice.

A year later Brodsky was buried in San Michele cemetery in Venice. Was it his will? I do not know. But in 1974, 22 years before his death he wrote a letter to his good friend, poet and translator Andrei Sergeev. This friendly, humorous letter, written in verse, of course, had a prophetical quality. To fully appreciate it one ought to remember a famous poem written by Alexander Pushkin in 1829, eight years before his fatal duel. A few lines:

Though the senseless body
is indifferent to the place where it decays,
Still, I would prefer to rest
Closer to my native place.

Here is an excerpt from Brodsky's letter:

Although to an insensible body
it is all the same... but, more to the point:
I am again in Venice – You bastard! –
Here you will exclaim, Andrei.
And rightly so: I am that Jew

who's been to Venice twice,
which in this century,
even the Slavs could not manage.
....
....

Now gondolas are before me.
The water reminds one of a dollar
By its liquidity and bottle-green
Color. A palace's façade
Is more pleasing than a women's face.
All told, you needn't be a poet
For stone to become an embrace
Pleasanter than the thing under a dress.
....
....
Although to an insensible body
it is all the same where to decay,
deprived of its dear native clay,
it won't object to decomposing
in the alluvium of the Lombard valley; since
the continent is the same and so are the worms.
Stravinsky sleeps on in San Michele
Having doffed his traditional beret.
But here! Be it far or near,
I am warmed through by your remembrance.
Sensing its imperial sweep,
I put my candle out in Venice
And go to sleep....
(translated by L. Yefimova)

To visit San Michele, one has to take a boat. The cemetery
has a small section allocated for Russian exiles. Stravinsky,
Diaghilev and Nijinsky are all buried there. But the Brodsky
family was not able to get permission to bury Joseph in this
place because, for the authorities, he was not a Russian, he was
an unbaptized Jew. What an irony! The Brodsky grave is in
another section of the cemetery, the one where Ezra Pound (whom

Brodsky could not stand) is buried. To make matters worse, the plan initially was to bury him next to Pound. But Fate decreed otherwise: there was already another grave in the initial plot, and Brodsky was buried far from Pound.

As for "the people's path," it did not grow over, but some poetry lovers do take the boat and come to San Michele. Last April, I saw little pebbles left on the grave according to Jewish custom, little crosses left according to Russian Orthodox custom, photographs, two miniature cat figurines and little notebooks dedicated to Brodsky with poems, left according to no custom I know of.

All his life, Joseph had struggled with the consequences of his identification with a group: as a political dissident, as an émigré, as a Jew, as a Russian, as a male, as a cardiac patient, and so on. He fiercely defended his right to be what he was, unlike the other members of all the groups to which he was thought to belong. He defended his right to be himself against those who expected conformity and were often hostile to outsiders ("I was accused of everything but bad weather..."). He succeeded, but this struggle accompanied him literally to the grave.

---

[1] *La Pensée Russe*, No. 4126, May 16-20, 1996. The special supplement "Iosif Brodsky (May 24, 1940 - January 28, 1996)," p. IV
[2] Ibid.
[3] Iosif Brodsky, *Collected Works*, Pushkinsky Fond, 1992, p. 184
[4] "Iosif Brodsky: His Work, His Personality, and His Life." The Summary of Three Conferences. *Zvezda* magazine, 1998, p. 306

INDEX